The
SEARCH
for
STABLE
MONEY

Copublished by the
Cato Institute

The
SEARCH
for
STABLE
MONEY

Essays
on
Monetary Reform

Edited by
James A. Dorn
and
Anna J. Schwartz

University of Chicago Press
Chicago & London

The University of Chicago Press, Chicago 60637
The University of Chicago Press, Ltd., London

Library of Congress Cataloging-in-Publication Data

The Search for stable money.

  Includes index.
  1. Monetary policy—United States.   2. Monetary
policy.   I. Dorn, James A.   II. Schwartz, Anna Jacobson.
HG540.S38   1987   332.4'973   86-25654
ISBN 0-226-15829-2
ISBN 0-226-15830-6 (pbk.)

Cover design: *Susan Gould-Martin*

To Fritz Machlup
and
Robert E. Weintraub

CONTENTS

EDITORS' PREFACE

The importance of stable money has long been recognized, but insufficient attention has been paid to the problems of implementing and maintaining a sound monetary constitution. Without changes in the present discretionary regime, it is unlikely that lasting price-level and economic stability can be achieved. Thus, it is useful to go beyond a mere appraisal of the tactics of monetary policy and consider fundamental monetary reform. Examining the properties of a sound monetary regime, as Milton Friedman notes in his essay, will help determine if changes in the current regime are likely to be beneficial and pave the way for meaningful reform if a monetary crisis does occur.

Improving the tactics of monetary policy, of course, may help avoid future monetary instability, but the public choice aspects of monetary policymaking warn against optimism on this count. Thus, in considering monetary reform, James Buchanan, like Friedman, emphasizes the need for moving to a "strategy of constitutional reform." More attention, says Buchanan, must be paid to developing "a positive theory of constitutional choice" so that political forces can be harnessed to foster predictability rather than uncertainty in the monetary regime. By considering the choice among alternative monetary regimes from a constitutional, public choice perspective, the essays in this volume offer a fresh approach to the rules versus discretion debate.

The volume begins with a historical overview of the search for stable money and proceeds, in turn, to examine The Erratic Nature of Federal Reserve Policy (Part I), Constitutional Monetary Reform (Part II), Monetarism and the Search for Stable Money (Part III), Monetary Policy and Gold: The Central Issues (Part IV), The Denationalization of Money (Part V), and The Future of Monetary Policy (Part VI). A brief summary of each part follows.

Variability of money growth and inflationary bias are inherent characteristics of a discretionary paper money regime. The papers by *William Poole, Lawrence K. Roos,* and *Michael D. Bordo* and *Anna J. Schwartz,* in Part I, all point to the interconnection between the absence of any effective constraint on the government's monopoly of base money and the erratic nature of Federal Reserve policy. Under the present monetary regime, the political process drives the monetary policymaking process, giving the Fed an incentive to adopt multiple policy goals and dodge accountability for maintaining stable money and prices. The central bank's success in maintaining respectability, even in light of its dismal performance, attests to the Fed's ability to create uncertainty and engage in scapegoating.

By focusing on what Poole calls the "number one policy syndrome," the Fed can trade off less politically viable goals for other goals that have an immediate effect on vote-getting. Thus, price-level stability may be sacrificed in the short run for a temporary reduction in unemployment and lower interest rates. However, in the long run such political tradeoffs are inconsistent; excessive money growth will reveal itself in terms of higher inflation, higher nominal interest rates, and no lasting impact on employment.

In contrast to the present discretionary regime, an *effective* rules-based regime—with price-level stability as the chief aim of monetary policy—would eliminate the stop-go nature of monetary policy and depoliticize the money supply process. Within a constitutional monetary regime, where money growth was limited to a noninflationary path, the inherent conflicts of monetary policy discussed by Roos would disappear. And, as Bordo and Schwartz note, both theory and evidence indicate that the increased certainty stemming from stable money and prices would be conducive to economic stability and improved resource allocation.

In Part II, the papers by *Peter Bernholz, Axel Leijonhufvud,* and *Thomas D. Willett* emphasize the importance of constraining the monetary powers of government by means of a sound monetary constitution. Unless the incentive structure is changed so that government is prevented from tampering with the money supply process to further the goals of bureaucrats and politicians, admonishing monetary authorities to behave more efficiently will be of little avail.

The extensive historical evidence presented in Bernholz's paper supports the feasibility of implementing and maintaining a sound monetary constitution. Moreover, his analysis suggests that even in a period of moderate inflation it may be possible to gain public support for constitutional monetary reform. Leijonhufvud, like Bernholz, favors providing a "constitutional anchor" for the current "random walk monetary standard." The Reagan administration has reduced inflation but has done nothing to change the discretionary monetary regime. To remedy this, Leijonhufvud recommends establishing a National Monetary Commission to consider basic institutional change, including amending the Federal Reserve Act to make price-level stability the key objective of monetary policy. Such an objective could be achieved by incorporating into monetary law either the quantity principle of monetary control or the convertibility principle.

Willett accepts the need for constitutional monetary reform but thinks that political constraints on monetary reform may necessitate a compromise scheme. A monetary rule, therefore, may have to allow for some discretion on the part of monetary authorities. Yet discretion should be limited by the overall objective of achieving long-run price stability. Under his two-part rule, the monetary authorities would select a target variable (say, the price level), and if the actual price level moved outside the target range, the Fed would adjust the growth of the monetary base until the target range was achieved.

The papers by *Karl Brunner, Allan H. Meltzer,* and *Robert P. Black,* in Part III, reinforce the fact that the uncertainty of the present monetary regime stems from the lack of any constraint on the monetary powers of government or the central bank. The monetarist doctrine, which calls for limiting the quantity of money by a legislated rule aimed at achieving stable money and prices, has never been implemented, argues Brunner. Thus, monetarism can hardly be called a failure from a cognitive viewpoint. Nevertheless, from the viewpoint of political acceptability, monetarism has been a dismal failure compared to the Keynesian activist policy prescription. The political economy of monetary reform, therefore, needs to be addressed.

In the choice among alternative monetary regimes efficiency is achieved by minimizing costs, including those associated with risk and uncertainty. A monopoly central bank is a relatively efficient arrangement, says Meltzer, only if it is limited by a rule that fixes the growth rate of inconvertible paper money and is accompanied by a fiscal rule constraining the taxing and spending powers of government. President Black of the Richmond Fed also thinks uncertainty can be reduced by a rules-based regime in which price-level stability is the sole aim of Federal Reserve policy. In accepting the mandate of price stability, Black observes, the Fed would be acting in accordance with Article I, section 8 of the Constitution and therefore would increase its credibility and independence.

The papers by *Joseph T. Salerno* and *Phillip Cagan,* in Part IV, consider the importance of depoliticizing money by incorporating the convertibility principle into the monetary system. Salerno advocates a 100 percent gold standard to provide an anchor for the monetary unit and restore sound money. Market forces would then determine the demand for and supply of money and hence its value. Unlike a pseudo gold standard, the pure gold standard would remove government from the monetary regime.

Cagan argues that monetarists and advocates of the gold standard have a common aim, namely, to achieve sound money by moving to a rules-based regime. However, Cagan thinks the gold standard can be improved upon by combining the convertibility principle with a monetary rule. He therefore advocates fixing the growth rate of the monetary base and allowing the government to issue "compensated federal dollars" convertible into base money. By adjusting the conversion rate between federal dollars and base money, their value would be stabilized. Some discretion could still be exercised over the supply of federal dollars but only subject to the convertibility requirement and the goal of long-run price stability. Cagan argues that if "compensated private dollars" ("Roe bucks") were allowed to compete against government base money and proved unstable, government might then have an incentive to introduce compensated federal dollars.

Since the publication of Friedrich A. Hayek's *Denationalisation of Money* in 1976, there has been an increasing interest in free banking and private currency competition. The papers by *Roland Vaubel, Leland B. Yeager, Gerald P. O'Driscoll, Jr.,* and *Lawrence H. White,* in Part V, consider the case for deregulating banking and ending the government's monopoly of base money. Vaubel sees free currency competition among central banks as a way to lower the expected rate of inflation. Furthermore, he finds no conclusive arguments against *private* currency competition and questions the traditional arguments used to justify the government's monopoly of base money. The public goods argument for government provision of base money is redundant, notes Vaubel, and the natural monopoly argument is meaningless in the absence of free entry. Vaubel therefore advocates private currency competition as a mechanism for discovering the most efficient monetary arrangement.

Yeager views the present discretionary fiat money regime as "preposterous." There is no well-defined unit of account with stable purchasing power, and changes in the value of money disrupt economic calculation and coordination. In particular, since money has no market or price of its own, monetary disequilibrium can be prolonged and generate significant macroeconomic disturbances. To rid the system of these problems, Yeager proposes establishing a unit of account with stable purchasing power and separating it from the medium (or media) of exchange. Government would initially define and adopt the new unit of account but would no longer issue money, which would be supplied by private issuers. In what Yeager calls the

"BFH system" (a payments system he and Robert Greenfield formulated based on the work of Fischer Black, Eugene Fama, and Robert Hall), there would be no outside money (i.e., base money). Thus, instability due to fractional reserve banking and pyramiding would be eliminated. Introducing the BFH system would also be conducive to financial innovation, says Yeager.

O'Driscoll reminds us of the essential properties of money—its perfect liquidity and nonpecuniary yield—and that the unit of account and medium of exchange functions of money are typically combined to reduce transactions costs. He therefore sees no reason to accept the claim of legal restrictions theorists that in a laissez-faire payments system money would disappear as a unique financial asset because consumers no longer would be willing to hold non-interest-bearing money. Nor does he accept the idea that economic fluctuations would necessarily disappear in a fully deregulated financial system.

White makes a strong case for deregulating inside money and denationalizing outside money. He points to the success of Scottish free banking before 1846 to reinforce his argument that banking deregulation would not be inherently unstable. And, like Vaubel, he dismisses the public goods argument and natural monopoly argument for government control of base money. White also finds the lender-of-last-resort rationale for a monopoly central bank unconvincing. What should be done, says White, is to open the provision of both inside and outside money to competitive forces. Consumers' preferences would then determine the preferred money and banking regime, and there is no reason to assume they would opt for the present regime.

The papers by *Milton Friedman, Friedrich A. Hayek,* and *Fritz Machlup,* in Part VI, emphasize the need for focusing on the strategy of monetary policy rather than simply discussing policy tactics within a discretionary regime. The problem is to restructure monetary institutions to achieve stable money and prices. In this regard, Friedman points to the perverse incentives facing Fed officials and suggests freezing the monetary base as a simple and effective strategy for depoliticizing the money supply process. A zero growth rate for the monetary base would help create a more certain monetary regime and pave the way for financial deregulation, notes Friedman.

According to Hayek, the only sure way of achieving stable money and prices is to abolish the money-creating powers of government. Competition among private money producers would then provide the discipline necessary for securing sound money. Unlike government, private entrepreneurs would have an incentive to control the quantity of money even if there were no link to gold, says Hayek.

This is so because in a free-market monetary system only those producers who supply stable currencies will survive. Hayek therefore urges private entrepreneurs to immediately begin experimenting with private currencies.

In the final paper, Machlup considers the inflationary bias of the discretionary fiat money regime as it operates within the modern democratic state. The political process continues to dominate the money supply process, and unless there is a consensus that any inflationary episode must be stopped immediately rather than gradually, says Machlup, inflation is likely to remain a persistent problem. That inflation can be quickly halted is borne out by the experience of Austria during the hyperinflation of the early 1920s and during the post–World War II inflation. When the decision was made to abandon gradualism and end the inflation at once, unemployment initially rose, but the basis for long-run prosperity was established by stabilizing money and prices. What concerns Machlup about present-day politics is the dominating influence of special interest groups and their adverse impact on wage and price flexibility. In the absence of such flexibility, the costs of monetary correction will increase and there will be greater resistance to achieving lasting price stability. Thus, Machlup believes that "the back of inflation has at most been scratched," not broken.

Whether the present discretionary monetary regime continues or whether we switch to an alternative monetary regime in the search for stable money will ultimately depend on the public's understanding of the inherent conflicts of monetary policymaking and on the likelihood of continued monetary instability in the absence of a sound monetary constitution. Although the inflationary waters are somewhat calm at the moment, the inflationary bias of the current political-monetary regime is likely to reappear as the high and variable rates of money growth once again exert their influence. Indeed, in the absence of fundamental monetary reform, there is little likelihood of future price-level stability. The essays in this volume are therefore timely and essential reading for anyone interested in understanding the problems of monetary policymaking in the existing discretionary fiat money regime as well as for anyone interested in the problems of implementing and maintaining a sound monetary constitution.

Many of the essays in this volume first appeared in the Spring 1983 issue of the *Cato Journal*, which was based on the Cato Institute's first annual monetary conference, The Search for Stable Money. The Winter 1986 and Fall 1986 issues of the *Cato Journal*, which were based on subsequent monetary conferences sponsored by the Cato Institute, also contained essays included in this volume. Thus, in compiling this volume, our greatest debt is to the Cato Institute—especially to Ed Crane for his enthusiastic and ongoing support of basic monetary research aimed at investigating alternatives to the present fiat money regime. The assistance of Susan Earle, Marianne Keddington, Holly Klaine, David Lampo, and Janet Rumbarger is also appreciated.

Permission to reprint articles from sources other than the *Cato Journal* is acknowledged on the title pages of the relevant articles and extends to the American Enterprise Institute, D. C. Heath and Co., the Hoover Institution Press, the *Journal of Libertarian Studies*, and North-Holland Publishing Co. Finally, Jim Dorn gratefully acknowledges research support from the Earhart Foundation and the Towson State University Faculty Research Committee that helped facilitate the completion of this volume.

1

INTRODUCTION

THE SEARCH FOR STABLE MONEY: A HISTORICAL PERSPECTIVE*

James A. Dorn

> Whether a writer or a speaker undertakes to unfold principles, to
> set them in a novel and more striking light, or to recommend their
> application, he should know what has been already undertaken,
> what has been accomplished, and what remains for discovery and
> elucidation.
>
> —John Ramsay McCulloch[1]

The double-digit inflation experienced in the 1970s and early 80s
has subsided, but money growth remains erratic. There is still no
anchor for the paper money regime; the Fed still has broad discretionary powers; and there is still great uncertainty about future monetary policy. Within this regime, the money supply process can easily
become politicized—especially in the face of mounting budget deficits, historically high trade deficits, and large pockets of unemployment in declining industries. The erratic nature of Federal Reserve
policy, along with the Fed's proclivity for fine-tuning the economy
and targeting interest rates rather than the money supply, continues
to plague the discretionary fiat money regime. In such an environment there is no guarantee of long-run price stability, and variability
in nominal GNP is likely to be greater than under a rules-based

---

*Partially extracted from Dorn (1983, 1986a, 1986b).

The author is Editor of the *Cato Journal* and Associate Professor of Economics at
Towson State University. He is also a Research Fellow of the Institute for Humane
Studies at George Mason University. The research embodied in this paper was sup-
ported in part by grants from the Earhart Foundation and the Towson State University
Faculty Research Committee.

[1]From McCulloch's *Literature of Political Economy* (1845, pp. vi–vii); quoted in Marget (1938, p. vi).

regime.[2] The lack of certainty with respect to the future course of money and prices is an inherent feature of the current discretionary regime and provides a strong rationale for refocusing attention on the importance of stable money and the need for a sound monetary constitution.[3]

The essays in this volume examine the erratic nature of Federal Reserve policy and point to the need for a credible monetary regime that maintains long-run price stability. Replacing the current discretionary fiat money regime with a constitutional money regime—that is, with a rules-based regime in which the monetary powers of government are narrowly limited by law, whether by a constant money growth rule, a commodity standard, or a competitive currency regime—requires a sound understanding of the importance of stable money. Such an understanding can be enhanced by an examination of the doctrinal history of the search for stable money.

Economists have long recognized the linkage between erratic money and business fluctuations. As a medium of exchange, money enters into all transactions, and since prices adjust only sluggishly to changes in the supply of and demand for money, monetary disequilibrium alters the structure of prices and production and upsets the smooth functioning of a market economy. It is this nonneutrality of money that is the characteristic feature of what Clark Warburton (1949, p. 1) called the "doctrine of erratic money" or "theory of monetary disequilibrium."[4]

The Doctrine of Erratic Money

The key proposition of the doctrine of erratic money, as stated by Warburton (1949, pp. 1–2), is that "a departure in the quantity of

---

[2]Meltzer (1983, p. 252), in referring to a study he and Brunner conducted, states that for the 1953–80 period, the erratic nature of Fed policy "added more variability to nominal output growth than it removed." For the 1969–80 period, a constant money growth rule (holding the rate of money growth to a noninflationary rate) "would have removed as much as half the variance of GNP growth." For the full results of the study, see Brunner and Meltzer (1983).

[3]According to Brunner (1984, p. 206): "The elimination of uncertainty about the course of monetary affairs forms the crucial rationale of a monetary order."

[4]Warburton (1949, p. 1, n.1) uses the term "erratic money," or "theory of monetary disequilibrium," rather than "unstable money" because he wishes "to emphasize the effect of monetary aberrations upon business activity and employment rather than their effect upon the price level." He goes on to say that "[t]he doctrine of erratic money, or theory of monetary disequilibrium, might also appropriately be called the doctrine of unneutral money." But he avoids that usage "because the correlative term, 'neutral money,' has been used by Hayek [1931, 1935] . . . in a way which is inconsistent with the older theory of stable money."

money from a reasonable rate of growth, if of substantial proportion, will produce serious business maladjustment—price inflation if the quantity of money expands excessively; depression if it contracts or does not increase sufficiently." Proponents of the theory of monetary disequilibrium argued that erratic money effects business activity because prices do not adjust instantaneously to abnormal changes in the quantity of money; the process of adjustment to a new equilibrium price level takes time and during this process real economic variables deviate from their normal values. This belief—that ragged adjustment in the value of money (i.e., in the level of prices) causes money to be nonneutral—led proponents of monetary disequilibrium theory to emphasize "achievement of a stable value of money," notes Warburton (p. 2).

In the period prior to the Great Depression, economists widely discussed the importance of stable money. In particular, they examined the problems of how best to define stable money, how to measure monetary stability, and how to conduct monetary policy so as to achieve stable money and prices (Warburton 1949, p. 1). According to Warburton (1950b, p. 164), the pre-Depression, or pre-Keynesian, theory of monetary disequilibrium can be divided into two parts: an application of the principles of demand and supply to money; and a discussion of "the process by which the value of money becomes adjusted to changes in its quantity (relative to productive capacity), and of the disturbances to business and employment and the injustices in the distribution of the national income and product which result from the character of this process"—by far the more significant component of the doctrine of erratic money.

In the case of an actual shrinkage in the quantity of money, the nominal income stream will immediately fall, and without an offsetting increase in monetary velocity total spending will decline. Under these conditions, the general level of product prices must fall if normal production and employment are to be maintained. The problem is that business costs, especially wages, tend to lag behind changes in product prices because of custom and contracts. Thus, monetary deficiency is typically accompanied by falling profits and the postponement of new investment, even at relatively low interest rates.[5]

---

[5]Warburton ([1947] 1966, pp. 229–30) notes that under conditions of monetary deficiency, "a reduction in the 'pure' interest rate cannot function to adjust the volume of savings . . . and business takings of investment funds to each other, because the prospective profit margin normally arising from the reduced rate of interest is more than offset by increased risk of loss due to shrinking prices. Instead, it is business losses, together with the elimination or sharp reduction in savings by those individuals whose income

Businesses therefore have an incentive to reduce employment and wait for better times before resuming normal production. As monetary velocity falls, it reinforces the shrinkage in the quantity of money, producing a cumulative downward spiral in economic activity.

The pervasive influence of money makes it an ideal candidate for disrupting economic activity. As Leland Yeager (1973, p. 151) points out: money has no market or price of its own and when in disequilibrium can throw a "special snarl" into the market system. Joseph French Johnson (1905, p. 172), making an analogy between language and money, noted the confusion that would result if the stability of either were undermined:

> Just as language is a medium of exchange of ideas, so is money a medium of exchange of goods and services. Money performs its work by virtue of its exchangeability, and like language is in common use. Universal aphasia would have very much the same effect upon conversation that fluctuations in the value of money have upon the production and exchange of wealth.

The major tenets of the doctrine of erratic money, or theory of monetary disequilibrium, can be stated as follows: (1) circular velocity of money is relatively stable, though it may exhibit a downward trend; (2) significant changes in velocity occur only during periods of prolonged monetary disturbance and these changes in velocity are *subsequent* to the initial monetary disturbance; (3) monetary impulses operate primarily through their differential impact on prices, which vary sequentially over the adjustment process, thereby affecting business profits and prospects; (4) business conditions therefore tend to fluctuate as a consequence of abnormal changes in the quantity of money; (5) during the money-induced business expansion or contraction, changes in the rate of use of money (i.e., in velocity) will accentuate the business fluctuation; (6) monetary expansion or contraction is dominated by the decisions of banks rather than by the borrowing practices of business firms and households, with the central bank playing a key role; (7) price-level stability requires a reasonable rate of money growth, that is, a rate consistent with economic

---

has been cut off or reduced, which brings about the adjustment."

See also Warburton (1949, pp. 105–107) for a fuller discussion of the "chain of reasoning which connects the theory of value with the theory of employment and business fluctuations, under the traditional doctrine of the effects of monetary disequilibrium." According to Warburton (p. 107), "the duration and amplitude of a business depression resulting from monetary disequilibrium depends not only on the degree of that disequilibrium, but also on the tenaciousness of rigidities in the cost-price structure." The theory of monetary disequilibrium, therefore, may properly be called "a theory of the effect of price rigidities under an erratic supply of money."

progress and changes in the use habits of money (allowing for a secular decline in the circular velocity of money).[6]

The major policy implication of monetary disequilibrium theory is clear: the monetary authority can and should conduct policy so as to achieve a reasonable rate of money growth consistent with price-level stability. This policy should be clearly stated and enforced so as to create the expectation of long-run stability in money and prices. Such a rules-based or constitutional approach to monetary policy would remove the major cause of business fluctuations and allow market prices to efficiently perform their information, incentive, and coordinating functions.

The Importance of Stable Money: A Survey

The pre-Keynesian doctrine of erratic money, with its emphasis on monetary disequilibrium as the dominant cause of business fluctuations, has a long history dating at least back to the work of David Hume in the mid-18th century. According to Warburton ([1950c] 1966, p. 27):

> The historical fact is that the classical theory of equilibrium was accompanied in its development by a concomitant theory of disequilibrium, applying to the circumstances under which the monetary condition for the maintenance of equilibrium is not met in the real world. This theory of monetary disequilibrium was stated by David Hume two centuries ago and was developed in much detail by Ricardo's contemporaries, Attwood, Bollman[n], Joplin, and Thornton. It was recognized by Marshall in writings other than his *Principles*, and implicitly accepted in that great work. It was developed more thoroughly by Marshall's contemporaries in the United States. It was so widely understood that it is proper to say that it was not only a logical corollary of the classical theory of equilibrium but also as integral a part of the body of economic thought developed in the nineteenth century and the first quarter of the twentieth.

This section will illustrate the importance of stable money from the mid-18th century through the first quarter of the 20th century by

---

[6]Warburton (1966, pp. 4–6) outlines the analytical framework of the theory of monetary disequilibrium, which he refers to as the "dynamic theory of money" (a term he borrows from Eduard Heimann). My summary of the major tenets of monetary disequilibrium theory is based on Warburton's discussion. See also Warburton ([1950c] 1966, pp. 28–29) for a similar but more detailed listing. In a very useful note (p. 29, n.8), Warburton provides a list of references to the 19th- and early 20th-century literature on monetary disequilibrium theory and uses his list of postulates to categorize the various writers.

briefly surveying the writings of some of the more important monetary disequilibrium theorists.[7]

Writings of 18th- and 19th-Century Disequilibrium Theorists

The significance of stable money (and, hence, a stable value of the monetary unit) was widely recognized in the 18th and 19th centuries. David Hume, in particular, emphasized as early as 1752 that variations in the quantity of (metallic) money do not immediately or uniformly affect prices. Erratic money therefore alters the structure of prices during the transition process. Moreover, during excessive or deficient money growth, input prices typically change more slowly than product prices causing fluctuations in the rate of profit. These changes in the price and profit structure alter real economic behavior during adjustment to the new equilibrium price level. As Hume ([1752] 1955, p. 40) stated:

> [A]lterations in the quantity of money, either on the one side or the other, are not immediately attended with proportionate alterations in the price[s] of commodities. There is always an interval before matters [can] be adjusted to their new situation; and this interval is as pernicious to industry, when gold and silver are diminishing, as it is advantageous, when these metals are [i]ncreasing. The workman has not the same employment from the manufacturer and merchant; though he pays the same price for everything in the market. The farmer cannot dispose of his corn and cattle; though he must pay the same rent to his landlord. The poverty, and beggary, and sloth, which must ensue, are easily foreseen.

Hume's disequilibrium analysis was carried on in 19th-century America by a number of writers, including Erick Bollmann, Condy Raguet, Eleazar Lord, William M. Gouge, Charles Francis Adams, George Tucker, and Amasa Walker. Bollmann (1811, p. 255) presented an especially lucid statement of the importance of stable money by explaining the effect of monetary disturbances on economic calculation, incentives, and economic organization:

> It is of the utmost importance that extraordinary and general changes of prices, such as arise, not from occasional and natural variations in demand and supply, with regard to one or another commodity, but from a sudden and considerable diminution or increase of circulating medium, should be as much as possible avoided. . . . This should be attended to; not only from principles of justice, but also from motives of convenience and policy; because such revolutions in nominal value baffle all rational calculations, impair security,

---

[7]For a more exhaustive survey, see Warburton (1946c, 1949, 1950b, 1950c, 1973, 1981). See also Mints (1945) for a useful discussion of the literature and an extensive bibliography, and Miller ([1927] 1972).

destroy industry, and thus undermine the very foundation of national power and wealth.

To achieve stable money and prices, Bollmann (1811, p. 290) proposed limiting the quantity of high-powered money (in his example, Bank of England notes) by law:

> I can see no good reasons to hinder parliament from *confining by law* the issues of the bank within certain limits. The sum of twenty millions of pounds sterling I should suppose fully adequate to the exigencies of the public; but, if the amount actually in circulation considerably exceeds this sum, it may, in order to prevent distress, be limited at what it actually is. As soon as this has been done, the nominal prices of commodities, as far as they depend on the amount of currency in circulation, will *gradually* become *fixed* [i.e., the general level of prices stabilized].[8]

In response to the question of whether the stock of high-powered money could be controlled, Bollmann (1819, pp. 86–87) argued:

> If the first Bank-note, issued beyond the sum limited by law, were to blow up the whole board of directors as inevitably, as an electric spark would, applied to their seats, if they were seated on barrels of gunpowder, nobody in the nation would entertain the least apprehension of over-issues. And would not the security be equally great, if the breach of the law were rendered punishable with death, if you please, or the confiscation at least, of all the private property, of all the directors, and officers of the Bank, concerned in the transgression? Pass such a law, and let it be executed as rigorously, as has been hitherto the law against forgeries, and there will be no danger of its being frequently violated.

To monitor the Bank's compliance with his monetary rule, Bollmann (1819, p. 96) proposed that the Bank be required to provide "periodical and detailed accounts . . . of the amount of their notes in circulation." Thus, Bollmann appears to be the first American economist to propose using the force of law to limit the growth of high-powered money and stabilize prices, imposing strict penalties for violating the monetary law, and monitoring performance via frequent reporting of monetary statistics.

By the end of the 19th century the notion that stable money is a prerequisite for price-level stability and a smoothly functioning market economy was well established, as is evidenced by the following statement from the *Report* of the U.S. Monetary Commission of 1876 (1877, pp. 51–52):

---

[8]Bollman (1811, p. 289) recognized that "[t]he nominal price of things, which depends on [the] quantity of currency—is immaterial; but the *steadiness* of those prices, as far as they depend on a *uniform quantity* of that currency, is important."

It is in a volume of money keeping even pace with advancing
population and commerce, and in the resulting steadiness of prices,
that the wholesome nutriment of a healthy vitality is to be found.
The highest moral, intellectual, and material development of nations
is promoted by the use of money unchanging in its value. That kind
of money, instead of being the oppressor, is one of the great instru-
mentalities of commerce and industry. . . . It is only under steady
prices that the production of wealth can reach its permanent maximum, and that its equitable distribution is possible.

Writings of Early 20th-Century Disequilibrium Theorists

The theory of monetary disequilibrium was so widely accepted by
the early part of the 20th century that it was part and parcel of
elementary economics textbooks. These included texts by Francis A.
Walker (*Money in Its Relations to Trade and Industry*, 1883), Joseph
French Johnson (*Money and Currency in Relation to Industry, Prices,
and the Rate of Interest*, 1905), Irving Fisher (*Elementary Principles
of Economics*, 1912), Herbert J. Davenport (*Economics of Enterprise*,
1913), and Harry Gunnison Brown (*Economic Science and the Common Welfare*, 1923). All of these works accepted the importance of
stable money and discussed the effects of erratic money on economic
activity, taking into account rigidities in the cost-price structure.

Francis A. Walker (1883, pp. 87–88), for example, noted:

[A] progressive increase of the volume of money . . . raises prices,
but not equally and at once in all directions. . . . It proceeds not
only from one class of commodities to another, as Hume observed,
but also, as Professor Cairnes has shown in his *Essays on the Gold
Question*, from country to country, with appreciable intervals, which
permit of important economic efforts being produced meanwhile.
Those effects are various, but that which we are here particularly
concerned is the influence upon profits.

One of the most complete and clearest analyses of monetary disequilibrium—and of the interconnection between monetary and value
theory—was presented by Joseph French Johnson, a professor of
political economy at New York University. Johnson (1905, pp. 130–
31) emphasized the sluggishness of the adjustment process and the
misallocation of resources that results from erratic money:

[C]onsiderable time must elapse before a new level of prices, put-
ting commodities into the same exchange relations which they held
under the old, is established. During this transitional period there
exists what may be called a maladjustment of prices to values, the
exchange relations of commodities being disturbed by conditions
not primarily affecting their demand or supply. . . . [S]ometimes the
maladjustment is so great as to exert a powerful influence upon all
industry, diverting capital into channels into which it would not

otherwise flow, and bringing unexpected, if not undeserved, gains or losses to many *entrepreneurs.*

Although he did not deny the harmful effects of erratic money on relations between creditors and debtors, Johnson thought such redistributive effects, resulting from changes in the value of money, were less important than the effects of erratic money on production and resource allocation—with these latter effects stemming from the ragged adjustment in the level of prices following the monetary disturbance.[9] According to Johnson (1905, p. 171): "The worst effects of a change in the value of the standard are in the field of production. A depreciating standard tends to an overstimulated production and may lead to an unwise use of labor and capital. An appreciating standard, on the other hand, tends to discourage the production of wealth and so to bring hardship upon all."

Following in the Humean tradition, Johnson (1905, pp. 162–63) wrote:

> The level of prices . . . is itself of no importance; it does not matter whether prices are high or low, if there is perfect adjustment between prices and the supply of money. Whether the value of the dollar shall be much or little, whether prices, in other words, shall be high or low, is of no more consequence than the question whether the mile shall contain ten thousand or five thousand yards. But *changes* in the value of a dollar, that is, changes in the level of prices [occasioned by erratic money], are of the utmost importance, for they are always attended by an irregular readjustment of prices.

Another important contributor to the integration of monetary and value theory was Irving Fisher (1911, 1912, 1928). He recognized that the proportionality postulate of the quantity theory is a theoretical nicety that is unlikely to hold in practice, and that monetary disturbances typically have real effects. According to Fisher (1911): "periods of transition are the rule and those of equilibrium the exception, the mechanism of exchange is almost always in a dynamic rather than a static condition" (p. 71); "the 'quantity theory' will not hold true strictly and absolutely during transition periods" (p. 161); and erratic money affects the structure of prices and production because "practically prices never do move in perfect unison" (p. 184).

For Fisher (1912, p. 191), the transition to the new equilibrium price level could be quite long ("about ten years"), because "[w]hile the [commercial] pendulum is continually seeking a stable position,

---

[9]Johnson (1905, p. 163) attributed the "disturbing effects of a change in the value of the standard" to four factors: "(1) the use of credit, (2) the fact that production involves a period of time, (3) the fact that prices do not change uniformily, and (4) the psychology of confidence and depression."

practically there is almost always some occurrence to prevent perfect equilibrium. . . . The factors in the equation of exchange are continually seeking normal adjustment."

In tracing out the real effects of monetary disequilibrium, Fisher (1928, pp. 90–91) emphasized the effects of excessive and deficient money growth on the cost-price structure and, hence, on business profits:

> Monetary depreciation (rising price level) stimulates, and monetary appreciation (falling price level) depresses business. The reason is simple. When producers get higher prices they do not, at first, have to pay correspondingly higher costs; for instance, wages and salaries do not rise so fast, being fixed by contract for months or years in advance. Much less do they, at first, have to pay higher rent and interest. Such lagging of important expenses usually involves a lagging of total expenses behind total receipts. Consequently, profits, the excess of receipts over expenses, tend at first to increase. Conversely, a falling price level diminishes profits.
>
> Now the profit-taker is the captain of industry on whose decision depends the rate of output. Hence it follows that, when the price level rises and profits increase, industry is expanded and business booms; but when profits decrease, industry is contracted and business is depressed.

Fisher's statistical work supported the key proposition of monetary disequilibrium theory, namely, that erratic money is the major cause of business fluctuations. Referring to one of his studies, Fisher (1928, p. 92) notes: "almost every fall in the buying power of the dollar leads a little later to an increase in the volume of trade; while almost every rise in the dollar leads to a decrease in that volume. The statistics of bankruptcies and unemployment follow this same relation to the changes in the dollar."

In addition to considering the impact of erratic money on price differentials and profits—due to rigidities in the cost-price structure—Fisher (1911) employed a type of Wicksellian cumulative process model to show how monetary disturbances could cause the real rate of interest to deviate from its equilibrium value, causing "overinvestment" during periods of excessive money growth (because of an artificially low real rate of interest), and conversely for periods of monetary contraction or deficiency. Thus, for Fisher "maladjustments in the rate of interest" were of crucial importance in explaining the nonneutrality of money.[10]

---

[10]See Fisher (1911, pp. 55–73). For a useful summary of Fisher's disequilibrium theory of money and its parallels with the so-called Austrian theory of the business cycle, see Humphrey (1984, pp. 15–17). But compare Yeager (1986) who views the Austrian

Herbert Joseph Davenport (1913), like Fisher and other early 20th-century Americans working within the monetary disequilibrium paradigm, accepted the nonneutrality of money and emphasized the importance of sticky wage and price adjustments for prolonging the real effects of monetary impulses.[11] Moreover, like Fisher and others working within the framework of a commodity standard, Davenport (p. 297) recognized that excessive money growth would ultimately be reversed as bank reserves reached a critical point and profit margins narrowed.

Most significantly, Davenport realized that during a period of crisis or panic—caused by a monetary contraction or deficiency—individuals would form expectations of further declines in prices and profits. This state of expectations would show up as an increase in the demand for money, not as a medium of exchange for present goods but as "an option of delay" or "storehouse of value." The consequent decline in circuit velocity would then act as an accentuating force causing further declines in prices and profits, discouraging new investment and leading to business depression.[12]

Harry Gunnison Brown (1923) displayed a sound understanding of the real maladjustments caused by monetary disequilibrium. He dismissed the oversaving/overproduction theory of business depression and, instead, viewed "depression basically as a cumulative general disequilibrium touched off by monetary disturbance" (Yeager 1973, p. 161).[13] Like Davenport (1913, p. 291), Brown ([1923] 1926, p. 120) thought that "the immediate cause of depression is the credit crisis," with the accompanying contraction of deposit currency.

In explaining why monetary deficiency is a primary cause of business depression, Brown, like his contemporaries, noted that prices and wages adjust slowly because of fixed contracts, money illusion,

---

business cycle theory as a rival of the theory of monetary disequilibrium. Ludwig von Mises' *Theory of Money and Credit* (1912) was an early treatise on the integration of monetary and value theory, but it did not appear in the United States until 1934, when it was first translated into English. For a discussion of the doctrinal history of the cumulative process model, see Humphrey (1986).

[11]According to Davenport (1913, p. 299), during a period of monetary deficiency and reduced spending, workers will "angrily and persistently" resist wage cuts and "the employer often finds it not less profitable, and much more comfortable, to close his shop. . . . Inertia is a fact which must be reckoned with. Wages rise slowly and, when fall is inevitable, fall slowly and with painful struggle. . . . Were it possible for prices to fall evenly all along the line, the depression following upon panic would be less important and of shorter duration."

[12]On the ideas discussed in this paragraph, see Davenport (1913, pp. 300–21).

[13]See also Yeager (1973, pp. 159–62) for a general discussion of Brown's theory of monetary disequilibrium.

and the general reluctance of individuals to accept what they consider unreasonably low wages or prices (pp. 121, 127). However, if wages and prices were more flexible, the period of depression could be significantly reduced and perhaps avoided: "there need never be business inactivity or depression if only prices could become sufficiently low . . . so that the diminished dollars-expenditure of a low-spending period would nevertheless buy all available supplies of goods as rapidly as the goods could be put upon the market" (p. 105).

From a policy perspective, Brown no doubt favored greater wage and price flexibility, but his emphasis was on achieving price-level stability via the Federal Reserve's control of high-powered money. Thus, "to prevent the alternation of prosperity and depression," Brown (p. 129) recommended holding the Fed accountable for conducting monetary policy so as to achieve "stable business and a stable price level." He argued that the Fed's control over the volume of bank reserves could be used to achieve these policy objectives.

Keynes's Eclipse of Monetary Disequilibrium Theory and Warburton's Revival

With the Great Depression and the apparent failure of monetary policy, along with the publication of John Maynard Keynes's *General Theory* in 1936, the doctrine of erratic money lost much of its luster. As Phillip Cagan (1978, pp. 85–86) remarked:

> No one who was not in touch with the economics profession in the 1940s and early 1950s can quite imagine the state of thinking then in the profession at large on monetary theory and policy. The quantity of money was not considered important, indeed was hardly worth mentioning, for questions of aggregate demand, unemployment, and even inflation. . . . Textbooks in basic economics and even in money and banking mentioned the quantity theory of money, if at all, only to hold it up to ridicule. . . . [I]f you traveled among the profession at large, mention of the quantity of money elicited puzzled glances of disbelief or sly smiles of condescension.

It was within this hostile atmosphere that Clark Warburton waged a lonely intellectual battle to revive the theory of monetary disequilibrium. However, by 1966 he could write:

> The venerable theory that monetary disequilibrium—in the form of substantial departures from a stable or steadily-growing stock of money at a reasonable rate—is the major element in bringing about depression or inflation is now widely, though not universally, accepted, in contrast to its eclipse when the articles reprinted in this book [Warburton 1966] were written [1945–53].[14]

[14]Warburton (1966, p. 11).

This section discusses the Keynesian revolution, as it diverted attention from the pre-Depression doctrine of erratic money, and Warburton's counterrevolution.

The Keynesian Revolution

The Keynesian revolution successfully diverted attention from unstable money as the dominant cause of business fluctuations. Keynes's *Tract on Monetary Reform* (1923) was largely forgotten as the economics profession swung toward the Keynes of the *General Theory*. An avalanche of macro-Keynesian models devoid of the postulates of monetary disequilibrium theory flooded the literature; the "Keynesian diversion," to use Yeager's (1973) expression, was nearly complete. As Warburton ([1946c] 1966, p. 81) commented: "Perhaps the most remarkable feature of contemporary business-fluctuation theory is the unanimity with which economists have ignored the timing and amplitude of changes in the quantity of money in the United States relative to change in population, output, consumer spending, prices, and employment."[15]

In the *General Theory*, Keynes by-passed the long-standing theory of monetary disequilibrium and never attempted to test his saving-investment maladjustment theory of the Depression against its chief rival; the monetary disequilibrium hypothesis was assumed dead. For Keynes and the Keynesians, the movement from the prosperity of the 1920s to the depression years of the 1930s marked a sharp downturn in monetary velocity *prior to* the shrinkage of the quantity of money. In contrast to the monetary disequilibrium hypothesis, the Keynesian paradigm *assumed* velocity was unstable and posited this instability as the chief cause of business fluctuations. Moreover, since Keynesians viewed changes in velocity and changes in money as compensatory, monetary policy was viewed as an ineffective tool for restoring prosperity in the midst of depression. The pre-Keynesian theory of monetary disequilibrium, on the other hand, assumed that velocity varies "sequentially and directly with changes in the quan-

---

[15]Warburton ([1946c] 1966, n.10, pp. 81–83) lists dozens of well-known economists (both Keynesians and non-Keynesians) who neglected to carefully look at the sequence and importance of changes in money versus other variables in explaining business fluctuations. He notes that in the *General Theory* Keynes refers to the U.S. economic climate, but "has no reference to the data regarding the quantity of money" (p. 81). In perusing the major economics journals for the nine-year period following publication of the *General Theory*, Warburton notes: "I have not found a single article which reveals acquaintance with the factual data regarding the quantity of money in the United States, though the importance of monetary stability and reasonable growth is recognized in several of them" (p. 83).

tity of money except those accordant with the increase in output at full use of resources" (Warburton [1948b] 1966, p. 262).[16]

Warburton (1950a, p. 15) best sums up the state of the economics profession regarding monetary disequilibrium theory during the Depression years and in the midst of the Keynesian revolution:

> Abandonment of the doctrine of unstable money left a great gap in economic theory and in consequence produced bewilderment among economists when the new era crumbled and prosperity was lost. As the world was passing through a depression of greater severity and length than any in the 18th and 19th centuries there was no understanding of how it had come about. Observation of the slow velocity of money during the depression, together with the vacuum in theory produced by dropping the doctrine of unstable money, made economists receptive to new versions of old theories which had stressed idle money and oversaving as originating elements in lapses from full employment.

By abandoning the work of early 20th-century economists such as Walker, Johnson, Fisher, Davenport, and Brown, as well as the older tradition of the dynamic theory of money that was developed during the 18th and 19th centuries, "Keynesianism, with its worries about savings gaps and inadequate investment, was a backward step" (Yeager 1973, p. 162). This backwardness in monetary theory was also reflected in policy; the stable money policy of the U.S. Monetary Commission of 1876 was lost sight of and the Federal Reserve embraced the Keynesian doctrine.

The eclipse of the doctrine of erratic money was evidenced in the policy statement of the Board of Governors of the Federal Reserve System, as reported in the *Federal Reserve Bulletin* of April 1939 (p. 256): "The facts show clearly that the volume of money does not control the price level"; "Usually other things have a greater influence on prices than has the amount of money."[17] Moreover, Warburton ([1946d] 1966, p. 314) points out that the Board of Governors, in other publications in 1939 and 1943, accepted the Keynesian postulates that "monetary policy has little influence on economic stability" and that "the major cause of inadequate use of the country's economic resources and price fluctuations is variation in the rate of use of money."[18] It was left to Warburton and others to disprove the Fed's

---

[16]For a summary statement of these competing hypotheses regarding the relation between changes in money and changes in velocity, and their relationship to business fluctuations, see Warburton (1948a, pp. 294–95). Warburton notes that his empirical findings are consistent with the pre-Keynesian theory (p. 295).

[17]Quoted in Warburton ([1946d] 1966, p. 313).

[18]See Warburton ([1946d] 1966, pp. 314–15) for a summary of the Board's remarks.

fallacies and restore the doctrine of erratic money to the central position it held for nearly two centuries prior to the Keynesian revolution.

Warburton's Counterrevolution

Although Keynesian economics and its policy recommendations captured the imagination of most economists during the 1940s and early 50s, a minority of the profession continued to stay attuned to the pre-Keynesian doctrine of erratic money. Among these individuals Clark Warburton stands out, both for his development of the theory of monetary disequilibrium and for his testing of that theory against the prevailing Keynesian paradigm.[19]

Relying on his restatement of the monetary disequilibrium hypothesis and his tests of that hypothesis, Warburton provided the following rebuttal to the Federal Reserve Board's acceptance of the Keynesian paradigm. First, with respect to whether inflation and deflation are principally monetary phenomena, Warburton ([1946d] 1966, p. 314) wrote:

> An examination of the annual changes, during the period since 1918, in the supply of money relative to the need for money, and comparison of those changes with an index of prices of final products, lead to conclusions different from those stated by the Board of Governors. These statistical data give unqualified support to a conclusion closely approximating that of orthodox monetary theory prior to World War I, namely, that changes in the general level of prices depend principally upon changes in the quantity of money relative to the need for money, taking into account the productive capacity of the country and the established monetary habits of the population.

Second, with respect to whether monetary instability—as opposed to instability in the rate of use of money or monetary velocity—was the dominant cause of business fluctuations, Warburton (p. 315) states:

> When the appropriate statistical data are examined, the conclusions appear to be inescapable (1) that the reduction in the rate of use of money associated with the production and sale of goods and services

---

[19]For discussions of Warburton's contributions to monetary economics, see Bordo and Schwartz (1979), Cargill (1979), and Yeager (1981). According to Bordo and Schwartz (pp. 61–62):

Warburton revived monetary disequilibrium theory. His emphasis on variations in monetary growth as a key cause of business fluctuations and his systematic presentation of empirical evidence that turning points in money preceded those in economic activity paved the way for later research on money and business cycles by Friedman and Schwartz. His scathing theoretical and empirical attack on the alternative Keynesian view was a forerunner of the comparison of money and autonomous expenditure by Friedman and Meiselman.

during the great depression of the 1930's followed rather than preceded monetary contraction; (2) that the world-wide severity of that
depression was primarily due to monetary contraction in the United
States; (3) that monetary deficiency is the chief factor or[i]ginating
business depressions or amplifying minor recessions into severe
depressions; and (4) that the monetary deficiency preceding each
business depression since establishment of the Federal Reserve
System . . . has been produced by Federal Reserve action impinging
on the quantity of bank reserves.[20]

In concluding his review of the Board's policy statements, Warburton (p. 315) criticized the Fed for "inadequate examination of the
factual data" and viewed the Board's ineptitude as "an effective
barrier to the development of the kind of monetary policy needed
for full production without price inflation."

Based on his empirical findings, Warburton's confidence in the
traditional doctrine of erratic money grew while his confidence in
the new Keynesian economics waned. In the midst of the Keynesian
revolution, Warburton ([1946a] 1966, p. 257) wrote:

> To me the Keynesian ways of thinking—particularly the American
> versions and adaptations—seem quixotic. . . . [T]hat analysis seems
> to me to by-pass the central economic problem of recent years. The
> theoretical developments since the publication of Lord Keynes's
> *General Theory*, in my view, have shifted attention away from the
> policies which produced the great depression and other cases of
> large departure from full employment [namely, monetary distur-
> bances], and have laboriously diverted the energies of economists
> into fruitless directions.

Furthermore, while the profession at large continued to disregard
money in theory and policy, Warburton ([1950c] 1966, pp. 34–35)
predicted the demise of the Keynesian paradigm:

> As to the discard of earlier theoretical frameworks we can, I think,
> forecast the elimination from economic thinking, with respect to
> the origin of lapses from full employment and the conditions of
> recovery, of the current emphasis on governmental deficits and
> surpluses, the numerous structures described as "models," and a
> large part of Keynesian economics. These types of theory will be
> discarded because it will be found on close observation that the
> presence or absence of the factors emphasized by them is not closely

---

[20]See also Warburton ([1948c] 1966, pp. 40–41), where he presents a summary of his
statistical results showing that "deviations from trend in circuit velocity . . . lag behind
deviations from trend in quantity of deposits and currency, and except for this lag are
in the same direction"—a result that is consistent with the monetary disequilibrium
hypothesis but inconsistent with the Keynesian assumption that "idle money is an
independent or leading factor in the course of business fluctuations."

integrated with the presence or absence of business depression or price inflation, or with the beginnings of upswings and downswings.

Convinced that "a maladjusted supply of money" was the fundamental cause of the movement from prosperity to depression, Warburton (1946b, pp. 328–29) emphasized the need for a stable money growth rule. By allowing for reasonable growth in the quantity of money, he thought such a rule would maintain price-level stability and allow market prices and interest rates to efficiently perform their allocative function. According to Warburton (p. 329): "prosperity without inflation requires a monetary policy which does not interfere with a reasonable volume of investment by pulling interest rates out of adjustment with the basic conditions of the economy."

Warburton ([1952] 1966, pp. 366–67) also favored a stable money growth rule because he thought it would largely eliminate the need to offset changes in velocity with changes in money. He argued that with a known (noninflationary) growth of money, the cyclical component of velocity (due largely to erratic money) would disappear, leaving only secular movements in monetary velocity. But since the growth rate of money under his rule would be adjusted for secular changes in velocity, there would be no need to use monetary policy to compensate for changes in velocity.[21]

Like Bollmann, Warburton recognized that for a monetary rule to be credible, it must be enforced. Only then will a constant money growth rule be able to change expectations concerning the future price level so that individuals can engage in market activities with greater certainty about the future value of money. Indeed, for Warburton (p. 370) certainty was a key characteristic of a desirable monetary regime: "For economic stability with maximum output and employment, it is necessary to eliminate the erratic monetary fluctuations of the past, and also essential that a policy of maintaining a requisite but not excessive rate of growth be firmly adopted, and that it be known that such a policy will be maintained."

Although Warburton predicted the demise of Keynesian economics in 1950, it was not until the publication of Milton Friedman and Anna Schwartz's *Monetary History of the United States* (1963b)— and the rise of monetarism—that the seeds Warburton planted began to bear fruit. Numerous studies appeared supporting Warburton's

---

[21]Warburton ([1952] 1966, p. 367) recognized that even under a stable money growth rule variations in monetary velocity would occasionally have to be offset by "deviations in the quantity of money from the computed reasonable line of growth." However, he thought that "the degree of appropriate deviation is not likely to be more than a very small percentage" (p. 368).

early findings and Keynesian models began to lose much of their luster.[22] Once again money was coming to the center of the theoretical and policy debate, and even Keynesians had to admit that "money matters."

As the driving force behind the monetarist school, Friedman embraced many of the tenets of monetary disequilibrium theory.[23] He accepted the dominant role of erratic money in generating business fluctuations and recognized the importance of stickiness in the price adjustment process for prolonging the transition to the new equilibrium price level. Moreover, like pre-Keynesian monetary disequilibrium theorists, Friedman recognized that information costs and institutional rigidities help account for sluggishness in the adjustment process, as does the fact that individuals find it rational to hold off changing their pricing strategy until it is clear whether underlying conditions warrant a new wage-price vector.

In his 1976 Nobel address, Friedman (1977, pp. 469–70) clearly revealed his acceptance of the nonneutrality of money:

> [U]nanticipated changes in aggregate nominal demand and in inflation will cause systematic errors of perception on the part of employers and employees alike that will initially lead unemployment to deviate in the opposite direction from its natural rate. In this respect, money is not neutral. . . . [S]uch deviations are transitory, though it may take a long chronological time before they are reversed and finally eliminated as anticipations adjust.

---

[22]In addition to the monetarist attack on Keynesian economics, the work of F. A. Hayek and the neo-Austrian school, along with the work of W. H. Hutt and that of J. M. Buchanan and the public choice school has been instrumental in countering Keynesianism.

Special mention should be made of Hayek because he recognized at an early stage that monetary disturbances distort relative prices and production (Hayek 1931). However, he failed to see that the root cause of the Depression was insufficient money growth, not overinvestment caused by newly injected money. Also, unlike the monetary disequilibrium school, Hayek ([1931] 1935, p. 28) did not accept price-level stability as the primary goal of monetary policy. (But compare Hayek [1975] 1979, p. 17, where he states: "The primary aim [of monetary policy] must again become the stability of the value of money.") In his work, Hayek seems to have overlooked the disequilibrium components of traditional price and interest theory, especially as developed by Joseph French Johnson and his contemporaries (see Warburton 1966, pp. 84–94).

[23]See Friedman (1970, pp. 22–26) for a listing of the basic tenets of monetarism; and for a brief discussion of Friedman's recognition of the nonneutrality of money, see Humphrey (1984, p. 18). Commenting on the early work of Friedman and Schwarz (1963a), Warburton (1963) noted the importance of their work but also suggested that more attention should be paid to the transmission mechanism, especially the impact of erratic money on "prices and on business activity," and on "business anticipations and expectations" (p. 77). He also recommended "an analysis of the trends and cycles . . . in income velocity and the timing relationship between such cycles and those in the stock of money" (p. 78).

Because of the long transition process during the period of monetary disequilibrium and the distortions introduced into the pricing system, Friedman and other monetarists have long supported stable money as the predominant goal of monetary policy. Greater wage and price flexibility, of course, would reduce the transition period, but avoiding erratic monetary policy in the first place would help restore the resiliency of the price and profit system. With money of stable purchasing power, price and profit signals would be more attuned to the real underlying forces of demand and supply and individuals would not face the costs of removing monetary noise from the pricing system. Indeed, a key feature of monetary policy for Warburton (1946b, p. 328) was "to determine and to maintain at a fair degree of stability the equilibrium center of the price system." The reason being that "[u]nless such stability is achieved, there is no possibility of stability in the price and cost structure." This objective would be achieved by constraining the monetary powers of government so as to achieve a stable, noninflationary growth of the circulating medium. In this way wide swings in the value of money could be avoided and with them wide swings in business activity. Minimizing uncertainty of the future value of money, not perfect price stability, is the practical goal proponents of stable money were aiming at. This goal, however, is far from being realized.

Reforming the Monetary Regime

The high and variable rates of money growth over the last several years have occurred within a fully discretionary monetary regime.[24] Contrary to conventional wisdom, the Fed has never implemented and maintained a stable money growth rule. The so-called monetarist experiment (initiated in October 1979 by Chairman Volcker) was an illusion—there was no long-run commitment to price stability as the *overriding* goal of monetary policy, there was no credible monetary rule dictating a noninflationary money growth rate, and there was no

[24]According to David Fand (1985, p. 60), monetary policy under Volcker has been "wildly volatile and topsy-turvy. . . . One has to go back to the 1940s to find such erratic behavior in the money supply. Quarterly money growth shot up from minus four percent to 17 percent in 1980, and from three percent to 17 percent in 1982, while plummeting from 18 percent to three percent in 1983–84. In the six years before Mr. Volcker, the highest quarterly growth rate was only eight percentage points above the lowest." And this same pattern continues: M1 grew by about 16 percent in 1986, but from early December 1985 through early March 1986, M1 grew at an annual rate of about 8 percent; money growth then accelerated to nearly 19 percent by the end of June and stayed close to that path for the remainder of the year.

enforcement mechanism to hold the Fed accountable for failing to maintain stable money and prices.

The Fed has persisted with its roller-coaster monetary policy and maintained what Warburton ([1947] 1966, p. 233) called an "upside-down monetary policy"—one that attempts to stabilize interest rates rather than control high-powered money so as to achieve monetary stability and a stable price level. In such a policy regime, one would expect wide variability in money growth, monetary velocity, and interest rates, as predicted by the theory of monetary disequilibrium.[25] The chaotic nature of U.S. monetary law and the case for constitutional monetary reform will now be examined.

The Chaotic Nature of U.S. Monetary Law

Present monetary law in the United States incorporates neither the "convertibility theory" of monetary control nor the "responsibility theory."[26] Monetary law therefore remains in the same chaotic condition Warburton found it in 1946: "Monetary law in the United States is ambiguous and chaotic, does not contain a suitable principle for the exercise of the monetary power held by the Federal Reserve System, and has caused confusion in the development of Federal Reserve policy."[27]

The lack of any single policy objective under the current discretionary fiat money regime and the absence of an enforcement mechanism to ensure stable money growth and price-level stability are evident from a look at Section 2A of the amended Federal Reserve Act (Board of Governors 1984, p. 6):

> The Board of Governors . . . and the Federal Open Market Committee shall maintain long run growth of the monetary and credit

---

[25]Referring to the "monetarist experiment," Samuelson and Nordhaus (1985, p. 330) *assume* that a stable money growth rule was effectively implemented and then argue that "in the face of such a money rule—or more likely *because* of the money rule—velocity became extremely unstable." They also point to the erratic behavior of money and interest rates as evidence of the failure of monetarism. The inconsistencies in their argument should be obvious from an understanding of the theory of monetary disequilibrium.

[26]Warburton ([1946d] 1966, pp. 291–92) distinguishes between the convertibility principle of monetary control, which was incorporated into the original Federal Reserve Act of 1913 but discarded by the monetary legislation of the early 1930s, and the responsibility theory of monetary control, which has never become part of U.S. monetary law. Under the convertibility theory, the decisions of households and firms determine the optimal quantity of money and the government's role is to ensure convertibility among monies and of each money into the standard money. Under the responsibility theory, government is held accountable for controlling the stock of money and maintaining its value.

[27]Warburton ([1946d] 1966, p. 316).

aggregates commensurate with the economy's long run potential to increase production, so as to promote effectively the goals of maximum employment, stable prices, and moderate long-term interest rates. . . . Nothing in this Act shall be interpreted to require that the objectives and plans with respect to the ranges of growth or diminution of the monetary and credit aggregates disclosed in the reports submitted under this section be achieved.

By failing to limit the Fed's discretionary authority to the maintenance of price-level stability, Congress has violated its constitutional duty to safeguard the value of money as intended in Article I, section 8 of the Constitution. Instead of creating monetary institutions characterized by predictability, the present monetary regime thrives on uncertainty. As David Meiselman (1986, p. 573) notes: "To influence economic events and to achieve political power, the Fed must maintain uncertainty about its policies." And Brunner (1984, p. 187) states: "The creation of uncertainty appears in the prevailing context of policy institutions as a more or less deliberate instrument of monetary policy." Recent experience lends credence to the Meiselman-Brunner hypothesis.[28]

Constitutional Monetary Reform

In a recent policy statement, the Shadow Open Market Committee (1985, pp. 2–3) commented on the Fed's performance under the existing discretionary regime:

Money growth has shifted from high to low every three to five months since early 1984. This pattern increases uncertainty and discourages long-term planning. Further, the trend rate of money growth is rising, reopening the prospect of another round of inflation. . . . The only way to avoid the high costs of inflation and disinflation is to avoid inflation. Inflation will not be avoided unless the Federal Reserve and the pro-inflationists in Congress and the Administration accept a long-term commitment to achieve stability.

The problem, of course, is how to implement and maintain price-level stability (i.e., stable money) as a primary policy goal in a political democracy driven by the rent-seeking process.

---

[28]Warburton ([1958] 1959, p. 211) also was aware of the role of uncertainty in Federal Reserve policymaking. He stated:

[T]here appears . . . to have been a causal association, by way of business expectations, between the aura surrounding Federal Reserve policy, including the emphasis on variability and uncertainty, and the fact that the business fluctuations of the past few years, though moderate, have been sharper than would have been forecast from historical studies of the relation of monetary developments to business fluctuations.

The weakening of the constitutional fabric of modern democratic states has occurred alongside the abandonment of commodity money. The lack of any anchor to limit the inflationary drift of U.S. monetary policy—a policy Axel Leijonhufvud (1984, p. 23) has called a "random walk monetary standard"—continues to allow for the politicization of monetary policy, posing a danger to the stability of the entire economic system. Within a purely discretionary fiat money regime, there will be constant pressure to incur budget deficits and then reduce the real debt burden via inflation. Furthermore, in a modern democracy with downward wage rigidity, there will be continuous political pressure to achieve "full employment" by accelerating inflation. In the longer run, politically unacceptable rates of inflation will be met by mounting pressures for wage and price controls, with adverse effects on economic and personal freedoms. The lack of commitment to stable money in modern democratic states, therefore, reduces economic efficiency and undermines the democratic process as envisioned by the Founding Fathers.[29]

Irving Fisher (1911, chap. 13) was well aware of the difficulty of instituting fundamental monetary reform within a democratic setting; and although he favored a stable money growth rule from a theoretical viewpoint, problems of political economy led him to recommend alternative schemes to achieve stable money based on the convertibility principle. According to Fisher (pp. 329–30):

> It is true that the level of prices might be kept almost absolutely stable merely by honest government regulation of the money supply with that specific purpose in view. One seemingly simple way by which this might be attempted would be by the issue of inconvertible paper money in quantities so proportioned to increase of business that the total amount of currency in circulation, multiplied by its rapidity, would have the same relation to the total business at one time as at any other time. If the confidence of citizens were preserved, and this relation were kept, the problem would need no further solution.

---

[29]In modern democracies, says Haberler (1981, p. 19):

[G]overnments overreact even to comparatively low levels of unemployment and associated inflation—by excessive monetary-fiscal expansion, thus accelerating and perpetuating inflation; by ill-conceived regulations, by price and wage controls, and by import restrictions and subsidies in different forms to noncompetitive firms and industries. This leads to an enormous growth of government bureaucracy and stifling taxation—a potent discouragement of saving and investment—and to economic inefficiencies. Thus, the growth of productivity slows down and comes to a halt which makes it still harder to stop inflation. This vicious circle undermines the foundation of the capitalist, free market economy, and endangers the future of democracy itself.

But sad experience teaches that irredeemable paper money, while theoretically capable of steadying prices, is apt in practice to be so manipulated as to produce instability. In nearly every country there exists a party, consisting of debtors and debtor-like classes, which favors depreciation. A movement is therefore at any time possible, tending to pervert any scheme for maintaining stability into a scheme for simple inflation. As soon as any particular government controls a paper currency bearing no relation to gold or silver, excuses for its over-issue are to be feared.

By anchoring the dollar to gold, or a commodity bundle, Fisher hoped to gain public support for monetary reform. He also thought that the convertibility principle would limit the discretionary power of government in the monetary realm and make it relatively easy to detect government failure to maintain the value of money (see pp. 332, 345–46).

More recently, Friedman's recognition of the public choice problems surrounding the implementation and maintenance of a simple money growth rule has led him to propose freezing the monetary base, in effect, abolishing monetary policy (Friedman 1984). Although his new scheme differs from his earlier monetary rule, the rationale is much the same as that stated by Friedman over 20 years ago when in paraphrasing Poincaré he noted: "Money is too important to be left to the [discretion of] central bankers" (1962, p. 219). With respect to his recent proposal, Friedman (1984, p. 51) argues: "The great advantage of this proposal is that it would end the arbitrary power of the Federal Reserve System to determine the quantity of money and would do so without establishing any comparable locus of power and without introducing any major disturbances into other existing economic and financial institutions.[30]

F. A. Hayek, who has always been more concerned with the institutional characteristics of monetary reform than with the tactics of monetary policy, also has altered his strategy for reforming the monetary regime. Initially he favored an invariant money supply (though he did allow for adjustments due to changes in velocity and in the coefficient of monetary transactions) so as to make money "neutral" in the sense that it would have no effect on relative prices or the structure of production. Under this "neutral money" policy, however, the price level would not be invariant because Hayek would allow economic progress to lower the general level of prices.[31] Next, Hayek ([1975] 1979, pp. 15–18) moved to a Friedman-type

[30]See Friedman's essay in this volume (chap. 17) for a discussion of his proposal for freezing the monetary base.

[31]See Hayek ([1931] 1935, esp. pp. 31, 105–108, 131, 134).

constant money growth rule to achieve price-level stability. However, at present Hayek prefers denationalizing money and allowing private currency competition (see Hayek 1976a, 1976b). Like Fisher and Friedman, Hayek (1976a) thinks that "Our only hope for a stable money is indeed now to find a way to protect money from politics" and "to provide a framework of legal rules within which the people can develop the monetary institutions that best suit them" (pp. 16, 22).

Although a consensus might be reached that the present fiat money regime can be improved by an effective monetary rule, the questions about how the rule is to be specified, implemented, and maintained must still be answered. That is, after a constitutional monetary regime is chosen as superior to a discretionary regime, the type of rule must be specified (e.g., a constant money growth rule, a commodity standard, or a competitive money regime), and the problems of the political economy of monetary reform must be addressed. For unless the implementation and maintenance problems of constitutional monetary reform are solved, the desired reform cannot be realized.[32]

The relatively low current rate of inflation (2.8 percent in 1986 as measured by the GNP deflator) should not be allowed to become a red herring that diverts attention from the underlying weaknesses of a discretionary paper money regime. Erratic monetary policy continues to plague the monetary regime and interferes with rational economic calculation, misdirecting resources in the process. Moreover, the uncertainty of the present discretionary regime casts a long shadow on the future path of money growth; there is still no "stable and certain" monetary policy as proposed by Warburton some 30 years ago ([1958] 1959, p. 211). The characteristic feature of the present regime continues to be unpredictability.

At this juncture in U.S. monetary history, it is essential not to lose sight of the doctrine of erratic money and its implications for the importance of stable money. Ignoring the lessons of history can only increase the likelihood of repeating past policy errors. The chaotic state of U.S. monetary law calls for careful consideration of the institutional changes required to promote stable money, including the political framework necessary to implement and maintain a sound monetary constitution. By considering the economics and politics of monetary reform—and searching for those monetary regimes most

---

[32]On the importance of constitutional monetary reform and the implementation and maintenance problems, see especially the papers by Bernholz and Buchanan in this volume (chap. 5).

consistent with stable money—the essays in this volume help pave
the way for meaningful monetary reform.

References

Board of Governors of the Federal Reserve System. *Federal Reserve Act and Other Statutory Provisions Affecting the Federal Reserve System, As Amended Through April 20, 1983*. Washington, D.C.: Board of Governors, 1984.

[Bollmann, Erick]. "A Letter to Alexander Baring, Esq., on the Present State of the Currency of Great Britain." *American Review of History and Politics* 2 (October 1811): 243–95.

Bollmann, Erick. "A Letter to Thomas Brand, Esq., on the Practicability and Propriety of a Resumption of Specie Payments." London: J. Murray, 1819.

Bordo, Michael David, and Schwartz, Anna J. "Clark Warburton: Pioneer Monetarist." *Journal of Monetary Economics* 5 (1979): 43–65.

Brown, Harry Gunnison. *Economic Science and the Common Welfare*. [1st ed., 1923] 3d ed. (revised). Columbia, Mo.: Lucas Brothers, 1926.

Brunner, Karl. "Monetary Policy and Monetary Order." *Aussenwirtschaft* 39 (1984): 187–206. Reprint Series No. C-137. Center for Research in Government Policy and Business, Graduate School of Management, University of Rochester.

Brunner, Karl, and Meltzer, Allan H. "Strategies and Tactics for Monetary Control." *Carnegie-Rochester Conference Series* 18 (Spring 1983): 59–103.

Cagan, Phillip. "Monetarism in Historical Perspective." In *The Structure of Monetarism*, pp. 85–93. Edited by Thomas Mayer. New York: W. W. Norton & Co., 1978.

Cargill, Thomas F. "Clark Warburton and the Development of Monetarism Since the Great Depression." *History of Political Economy* 11, no. 3 (1979): 425–49.

Davenport, Herbert Joseph. *The Economics of Enterprise*. New York: Macmillan, 1913.

Dorn, James A. "A Historical Perspective on the Importance of Stable Money." Introduction. *Cato Journal* 3 (Spring 1983): 1–8.

Dorn, James A. "Reforming the Monetary Regime." Introduction. *Cato Journal* 5 (Winter 1986a): 675–84.

Dorn, James A. "Money, Politics, and the Business Cycle." Introduction. *Cato Journal* 6 (Fall 1986b): 353–64.

Fand, David. "Paul Volcker's Legacy." *Policy Review* 34 (Fall 1985): 58–63.

Fisher, Irving. *The Purchasing Power of Money*. (Assisted by Harry G. Brown.) New York: Macmillan, 1911. (Reprinted 1912.)

Fisher, Irving. *Elementary Principles of Economics*. New York: Macmillan, 1912.

Fisher, Irving. *The Money Illusion*. New York: Adelphi, 1928.

Friedman, Milton. "Should There Be an Independent Monetary Authority?" In *In Search of a Monetary Constitution*, pp. 119–243. Edited by Leland B. Yeager. Cambridge, Mass.: Harvard University Press, 1962.

Friedman, Milton. *The Counter-Revolution in Monetary Theory*. Occasional Paper 33. London: Institute of Economic Affairs, 1970.

Friedman, Milton. "Nobel Lecture: Inflation and Unemployment." *Journal of Political Economy* 85 (June 1977): 451–72.

Friedman, Milton. "Monetary Policy for the 1980s." In *To Promote Prosperity: U.S. Domestic Policy in the Mid-1980s*, pp. 23–60. Edited by John H. Moore, Stanford, Calif.: Hoover Institution Press, 1984.

Friedman, Milton, and Schwartz, Anna J. "Money and Business Cycles." *Review of Economics and Statistics* (Supplement) 45 (February 1963a): 32–64.

Friedman, Milton, and Schwartz, Anna J. *A Monetary History of the United States, 1867–1960.* Princeton: Princeton University Press, 1963b.

Haberler, Gottfried. "The Great Depression of the 1930s—Can It Happen Again?" In *The Business Cycle and Public Policy, 1920–80.* A Compendium of Papers submitted to the Joint Economic Committee, Congress of the United States, 28 November 1980. Reprint No. 118. Washington, D.C.: American Enterprise Institute, January 1981.

Hayek, Friedrich A. *Prices and Production.* [1st ed., 1931] 2d ed. (revised and enlarged). New York: Augustus M. Kelly, 1935. (Reprinted 1967.)

Hayek, Friedrich A. "Inflation, Misdirection of Labor, and Unemployment." 1975. Reprinted in *Unemployment and Monetary Policy*, pp. 3–19. Cato Paper No. 3. Washington, D.C.: Cato Institute, 1979. (Originally published in *Full Employment at Any Price*, Occasional Paper 45, London: Institute of Economic Affairs, 1975.)

Hayek, Friedrich A. *Choice in Currency.* Occasional Paper 48. London: Institute of Economic Affairs, 1976a.

Hayek, Friedrich A. *Denationalisation of Money.* Hobart Paper 70. London: Institute of Economic Affairs, 1976b.

Hume, David. "Of Money." In *Political Discourses.* 1752. Reprinted in *David Hume: Writings on Economics*, pp. 33–46. Edited by Eugene Rotwein. London: Thomas Nelson and Sons, 1955.

Humphrey, Thomas M. "On Nonneutral Relative Price Effects in Monetarist Thought: Some Austrian Misconceptions." Federal Reserve Bank of Richmond *Economic Review* 70 (May/June 1984): 13–19.

Humphrey, Thomas M. "Cumulative Process Models from Thornton to Wicksell." Federal Reserve Bank of Richmond *Economic Review* 72 (May/June 1986): 18–25.

Johnson, Joseph French. *Money and Currency in Relation to Industry, Prices, and the Rate of Interest.* Boston: Ginn and Co., 1905.

Keynes, John Maynard. *A Tract on Monetary Reform.* 1923. Reprinted in Keynes' *Collected Writings*, Vol. 4. London: Macmillan, 1971.

Keynes, John Maynard. *The General Theory of Employment, Interest, and Money.* New York: Harcourt, Brace, and Co., 1936.

Leijonhufvud, Axel. "Inflation and Economic Performance." In *Money in Crisis*, pp. 19–36. Edited by Barry N. Siegel. Cambridge, Mass.: Ballinger Publishing Co. for the Pacific Institute for Public Policy Research, 1984.

McCulloch, John Ramsay. *The Literature of Political Economy.* London: Longman, Brown, Green & Longmans, 1845.

Marget, Arthur W. *The Theory of Prices: A Re-examination of the Central Problems of Monetary Theory.* Vol. 1. New York: Prentice-Hall, 1938.

Meiselman, David I. "Is There a Political Monetary Cycle?" *Cato Journal* 6 (Fall 1986): 563–79.

Meltzer, Allan H. "Discussion [of paper by Benjamin M. Friedman]." In *Monetary Policy Issues in the 1980s*, pp. 249–55. A Symposium Sponsored by the Federal Reserve Bank of Kansas City, Jackson Hole, Wyoming, August 9–10, 1982. Kansas City, Mo.: Federal Reserve Bank of Kansas City, 1983.

Miller, Harry E. *Banking Theories in the United States Before 1860.* 1927. Reprint. Clifton, N.J.: Augustus M. Kelley, 1972.

Mints, Lloyd W. *A History of Banking Theory in Great Britain and the United States.* Chicago: University of Chicago Press, 1945.

Mises, Ludwig von. *The Theory of Money and Credit.* 1912. Translated from the German by H. E. Batson. London: Jonathan Cape, 1934. (Reprint, Indianapolis: Liberty Classics, 1980.)

Samuelson, Paul A., and Nordhaus, William D. *Economics.* 12th ed. New York: McGraw-Hill, 1985.

Shadow Open Market Committee. *Policy Statement and Position Papers.* PPS-85-2. Center for Research in Government Policy and Business, Graduate School of Management, University of Rochester, 22–23 September 1985.

U.S. Monetary Commission, 1876. *Report of the United States Monetary Commission.* Senate Report No. 703, 44th Cong., 2d sess., 1877.

Walker, Francis A. *Money in Its Relations to Trade and Industry.* New York: Henry Holt and Co., 1883.

Warburton, Clark. "A Reply to Dr. Arndt." *Review of Economic Statistics* 28 (May 1946a): 92–94. Reprinted in Warburton (1966, pp. 254–57).

Warburton, Clark. "The Problem of 'Full Employment'—Discussion" [Comment on A. R. Sweezy]. *American Economic Review* 36 (May 1946b): 326–29.

Warburton, Clark. "The Misplaced Emphasis in Contemporary Business-Fluctuation Theory." *Journal of Business of the University of Chicago* 19 (October 1946c): 199–220. Reprinted in Warburton (1966, pp. 73–102).

Warburton, Clark. "Monetary Control under the Federal Reserve Act." *Political Science Quarterly* 61 (December 1946d): 505–34. Reprinted in Warburton (1966, pp. 291–316).

Warburton, Clark. "Volume of Savings, Quantity of Money, and Business Instability." *Journal of Political Economy* 55 (June 1947): 222–33. Reprinted in Warburton (1966, pp. 217–33).

Warburton, Clark. "The Theories of John Maynard Keynes—Discussion" [Comment on L. Tarshis]. *American Economic Review* 38 (May 1948a): 293–95.

Warburton, Clark. "Monetary Velocity and Monetary Policy." *Review of Economics and Statistics* 30 (November 1948b): 304–14. Reprinted in Warburton (1966, pp. 258–75).

Warburton, Clark. "Bank Reserves and Business Fluctuations." *Journal of the American Statistical Association* 43 (December 1948c): 547–58. Reprinted in Warburton (1966, pp. 36–47).

Warburton, Clark. "Erratic Money: An Outline of the Theory of Monetary Disequilibrium." Box 16, Warburton Collection, Special Collections, George

Mason University Library, Fairfax, Va., 1949. (Unpublished book-length manuscript.)

Warburton, Clark. "The Role of Money in Business Fluctuations." American University lecture notes, Theory of Monetary Disequilibrium course. Box 15, Warburton Collection, Special Collections, George Mason University Library, Fairfax, Va., 11 February 1950a.

Warburton, Clark. "Monetary Theory and the Price Level Trend in the Future." In *Five Monographs on Business Income*, pp. 161–93. New York: Study Group on Business Income of the American Institute of Accountants, 1 July 1950b.

Warburton, Clark. "The Monetary Disequilibrium Hypothesis." *American Journal of Economics and Sociology* 10 (October 1950c): 1–11. Reprinted in Warburton (1966, pp. 25–35).

Warburton, Clark. "How Much Variation in the Quantity of Money Is Needed?" *Southern Economic Journal* 18 (April 1952): 495–509. Reprinted in Warburton (1966, pp. 353–70).

Warburton, Clark. "Adequacy of the Statistical Foundation for Monetary Policy Formation—Discussion" [Comments on J. J. Polak and R. A. Young]. *Proceedings of the Business and Economic Statistics Section*, American Statistical Association, December 27–30, 1958 (1959): 210–12.

Warburton, Clark. "Comment on Friedman's and Schwartz's 'Money and Business Cycles.'" *Review of Economics and Statistics* (Supplement) 45 (February 1963): 77–78.

Warburton, Clark. *Depression, Inflation, and Monetary Policy: Selected Papers, 1945–1953*. Baltimore: The Johns Hopkins Press, [1966].

Warburton, Clark. "The Theory of Monetary Disequilibrium, 1750 to 1970." Box 16, Warburton Collection, Special Collections, George Mason University Library, Fairfax, Va., 1973. (Unpublished book-length manuscript; the title was later updated to "The Theory . . . , 1750 to 1975"; a preface was drafted in 1973, and that is the date selected for reference purposes.)

Warburton, Clark. "Monetary Disequilibrium Theory in the First Half of the Twentieth Century." *History of Political Economy* 13 (Summer 1981): 285–300.

Yeager, Leland B. "The Keynesian Diversion." *Western Economic Journal* 11 (June 1973): 150–63.

Yeager, Leland B. "Clark Warburton, 1896–1979." *History of Political Economy* 13 (Summer 1981): 279–84.

Yeager, Leland B. "The Significance of Monetary Disequilibrium." *Cato Journal* 6 (Fall 1986): 369–99.

PART I

THE ERRATIC NATURE OF FEDERAL RESERVE POLICY

2

MONETARY CONTROL AND THE POLITICAL BUSINESS CYCLE*
William Poole

Introduction

This paper might equally well be entitled, "Political Control and
the Monetary Business Cycle." The observations I will offer reflect
25 years of following current events and studying economic policy
and a recent period of government employment of two and one-half
years. My observations are meant to be subject to empirical testing,
but that task lies outside the scope of this paper.

In casual conversations on economic policy, questions about the
objectives and motives of the policymakers almost always arise. Along
the spectrum of published work on economic policy, ranging from
abstract theoretical models to newspaper editorials, the mix of objective analysis and subjective speculation about the policymakers'
motives changes. Scholarly work by economists, though not by historians, usually avoids analysis of motives; the objectives of the policymakers are taken as given. Conversely, editorial writers often
speculate about the policymakers' motives, and if those motives are
judged "bad" the policy actions themselves are judged bad and objective analysis of policy deemed irrelevant.

I myself have always been uncomfortable when discussing motives,
for they are ordinarily not directly observable and subject to empirical verification. Moreover, it is very easy for policymakers to believe
that they have been unjustly attacked when observers discuss their
motives, for the policymakers may know that they did not have the
intentions ascribed to them.

In a paper on the interplay of politics and economics in the determination of Federal Reserve policy I cannot avoid discussing the
policymakers' motives. However, my commentary on motives should
be interpreted quite strictly in an "as if" sense. Economists are

*Reprinted from *Cato Journal* 5 (Winter 1986): 685–99.

The author is Professor of Economics at Brown University and a former member of
the Council of Economic Advisers.

accustomed to analyzing business behavior under the assumption that business firms produce at the point where marginal cost equals marginal revenue, and the fact that many businessmen deny they have any such intention or motivation in making their production decisions is irrelevant to the predictions of the economic theory based on the profit-maximizing assumption. My comments on the motives of policymakers should be interpreted in exactly the same "as if" sense; sometimes the calculations are conscious and well understood by the policymakers and sometimes they are not. I also want to emphasize that the behavior of the Federal Reserve is similar in many respects to the behavior of other government agencies and, for that matter, divisions of large private firms.

The paper is divided into five major sections. In the first I discuss the role of motives in public debates about policy, and in the second the objectives of the Federal Reserve System. Issues concerning policy myopia are taken up in the third section, and political gaming is discussed in the fourth. A final section contains some overall comments and conclusions.

Public Debates on the Policymakers' Motives

The role of policymakers' motives in public policy debates is underappreciated in scholarly work on economic policy. Motives are ignored because they are unobservable and would not seem to have any relevance to assessment of the objective effects of policy. But the role of motives ought to be examined more thoroughly because of their influence on public policy debates and on market expectations about future policy actions.

The motives of the policymakers are important for market participants because an understanding of the reasons for particular policy actions may provide information useful in predicting future policy actions. The great importance of predicting future policy actions is probably the reason why there are so many Washington seminars and "insider" newsletters purporting to uncover the "real story" behind policy actions that are themselves readily observable.

The rivalry among competing agencies, personalities, and political parties often leads to a great emphasis on the motives of the competing parties. Newspapers and their readers often seem more interested in the rivalries themselves than in the policy issues. Public perceptions of policy actions and assessment of the performance of agencies is very often dependent on issues of motivation. If the policymakers' motives are judged to be good ones, policy failures are often excused. Conversely, policy successes may be criticized if the motives are judged to be poor. For example, policy successes are often criticized as being "opportunistic."

Beyond the predictive value of understanding motives, public debates often focus on motives because the technical aspects of policy are ordinarily extraordinarily difficult to understand. Indeed, the implications of many policy actions are so complicated that it is difficult to explain them even to well-trained experts in the field. It is not surprising that public policy debates in the Congress and the op-ed pages of newspapers often focus on motives by default.

Because the electorate emphasizes motives, so also must the policymakers. Monetarist critics of the Federal Reserve often find themselves frustrated by this emphasis in the public policy debates. Efforts to put the debate on a basis that intelligent laymen can understand by emphasizing basic and first-order monetary effects gets nowhere because economists both within and without the Federal Reserve System argue that such analysis is "simplistic." But the layman cannot understand highly sophisticated economic arguments. Thus, the debates easily turn to matters of motivation; economics per se has little to offer on this subject, and the Federal Reserve defends itself by insisting that it is well-meaning, which it is, and interested only in serving the public interest. And that is where the debate then rests.

The Objectives of the Federal Reserve System

Officials of the Federal Reserve System pursue the traditional policy objectives laid out in the economic policy literature. These are the objectives of low inflation, full employment, financial stability, and so forth. At a personal level, Federal Reserve officials with very few exceptions care deeply about these objectives and often find themselves agonizing over the policy choices they must make. Many Federal Reserve officials have long careers in the System, and serve at very substantial financial sacrifice. There are, of course, compensations in the form of higher expected future income from employment after leaving the System, from extensive travel, and so forth, but it would be a misuse of language to ignore the deep sense of responsibility felt by most Fed officials by claiming that these compensations show that these officials in fact serve for purely "selfish" reasons.

Federal Reserve officials, almost without exception, have a deep conviction that Federal Reserve independence is essential to achieving the traditional economic objectives. Thus, maintaining independence from direct and continuous political control is itself an objective of the Federal Reserve System. Pursuit of this objective may at times lead the Federal Reserve to take policy actions that it knows are not in the interest of furthering the traditional economic objectives. The issue here is essentially the same as the possible conflict for the firm in pursuing short-run versus long-run profit maximization. There is certainly nothing wrong in principle about trading short-run economic performance against improved long-run economic performance. Indeed, economists are constantly emphasizing the dangers of policy myopia. The issue is not one of principle but of whether policy actions to further political independence in fact have the effect of improving long-run economic stability.

Another motivation for Federal Reserve officials to maintain political independence is to enjoy an easier and more comfortable life. It is perfectly natural for the Federal Reserve to want to maintain some of the comforts it enjoys compared to the typical government agency. This "bad" motive, though surely operative, is greatly overstressed in many of the debates about Federal Reserve independence precisely because it is such an easy shot by Federal Reserve critics. It is also, in my opinion, a criticism without much merit. The turnover rates among middle-level Federal Reserve employees suggest that the comforts of Federal Reserve employment are not all that great, and direct knowledge of the differences between Federal Reserve employment conditions and those of the civil service suggest that the Federal Reserve has been able to avoid only a few of the worst features of the civil service employment system.

The "Number One Problem" Syndrome

Public discussion of economic policy in the Congress and newspapers is dominated by the "number one problem" syndrome. Policymakers are expected to cure whatever it is that most afflicts the economy at the moment. This phenomenon is not quite the same as the one economists call "myopia." As generally discussed, myopia involves excessive attention to the short-run effects of policy, with too little attention being paid to the remote and/or long-run effects of policy. Because the effects of monetary policy show up first on employment and output, and only later on inflation, monetary policy myopia can be expected to impart an inflationary bias to the economy.

Myopia can explain a policy bias over time but cannot readily explain changes in policy over the course of the business cycle. Myopia fits the typical conditions in the early stages of a cyclical expansion when emphasis on raising employment can lead to excessively high money growth because the longer-run inflation costs are too heavily discounted. But an explanation involving myopia does not fit the situation where the Fed maintains a restrictive policy well into a recession. For example, monetary policy was very restrictive throughout 1974 as unemployment rose, and it was not until late 1974 and early 1975—only shortly before the business cycle trough in March 1975—that the Fed changed its policy stance. (After the cycle peak in November 1973, the Fed did not cut its discount rate until December 1974; the discount rate, of course, is not itself important except as a symbol of Fed intentions.) Similarly, Fed policy remained on a very restrictive course through the middle of 1982 despite the continuing rise of unemployment after the cyclical peak in July 1981.

In both of the above examples, public concern over inflation was so high that a very substantial increase in unemployment was required to switch the focus of concern away from inflation and toward unemployment. The policymakers' own views play a role here, but the constraint provided by public attitudes should not be underestimated.

The syndrome is in part the result of public misconceptions about economic policy. It is a fact of arithmetic that increasing money growth one year requires reducing money growth in some other year if the trend rate of money growth is not to rise. With high probability, higher average money growth will raise the inflation rate; thus, higher money growth in the short run will raise inflation unless there is an offset in the form of lower money growth later. Would the Federal Reserve have raised money growth in a year such as 1977 if it had been required at the same time to provide a plan for an offsetting reduction in 1978 or 1979? Conversely, would the Federal Reserve have been willing to forsake a period of lower money growth in a period such as 1981 if the price of doing so were a commitment not to permit higher money growth in some subsequent year?

This problem is not, of course, peculiar to the Federal Reserve. Would the Congress have been willing to cut tax rates in 1981 if it had been required either to cut spending at the same time or to legislate specific future tax increases or spending reductions?

The government can avoid commitment to future policy offsets because there is just enough truth to statements insisting that future offsets may not be necessary. Tax reductions need not be offset by future tax increases if there is sufficient economic growth to provide high enough revenues to cover the level of government expenditures. Changes in money growth need not be offset in the future if there are lasting changes in the income velocity of money.

The problem with the monetary policy claim is not that the appropriate velocity offsets *never* occur, but that they are infrequent and that on the average velocity and money growth change in the *same* direction. But offsetting changes in velocity do occur just often enough, as in 1975 and 1982–83, to make plausible Federal Reserve pursuit of monetary policies that do not involve commitment to offsetting money growth changes in the future. Occasional policy successes, therefore, are used to justify a procyclical monetary policy driven by a political process dominated by myopia and the number one problem syndrome.

Public concentration on the number one problem tends to push policymakers into time-inconsistent policies. In the literature on this subject time inconsistency is usually explained in terms of policymakers bidding for votes by breaking implied or actual past commitments. Common examples are rent control—there are more voting tenants than voting landlords; inflationary policies that reduce the real value of outstanding debts, transferring wealth from creditors to debtors; and the imposition of special taxes such as the windfall profits tax on oil.

Policymakers often feel aggrieved when they are charged with deliberate pursuit of time-inconsistent policies; to them the process often seems to be one of being forced by the politics of the situation to take such actions as a defensive matter. Politicians out of power press for adoption of time-inconsistent policies. Those in office find that they must respond in order to retain political support. The fundamental problem is not that devious officials plot these damaging policies but that they are driven to pursue them by the political appeal of such policies when political opponents offer them to the electorate.

However clear public officials may be in their understanding of the undesirable characteristics of the policies they are pursuing, it is nevertheless necessary that the policies be justified in the court of public opinion. Some justifications are genuine and some are stratagems designed to deflect criticism. In the case of time-inconsistent policies, it is essential that the inconsistency be hidden. Inconsistencies can be hidden by providing justifications involving great technical complexity and by insisting that rules, standards, and regularities designed to eliminate time inconsistency are undesirable because they reduce "flexibility" and eliminate optimal responses to changed circumstances.

Without rules and standards, there is great difficulty in demonstrating time inconsistency in public debates. The unwillingness of the Federal Reserve to adhere to a clear money growth rule reflects in part its difficult situation in these public debates. If the Federal Reserve were to adopt a rule before such a rule were generally supported in the body politic, how could it defend itself when political opponents attacked and argued that there would be manifest advantages to a different monetary policy? It must be emphasized that the essence of this problem is that the short-run gains really do exist. It is not easy to enter public debates on the side of an unchanged policy when unemployment has risen by several million over the last few months and your arguments depend on asserted long-run gains and abstract principles.

The observable consequences of the poor public understanding of monetary policy issues are several. There is a lag in adjusting monetary policy to changed business conditions. This lag produces the procyclical behavior of the money stock and of the spread between the federal funds rate and the discount rate. The procyclical behavior of monetary policy has been known for many years, but there is no sign whatsoever that the process is changing. The knowledge that economists have accumulated about the economics of this process has had little or no effect in changing the policy process itself. As a nation, we continue to make the same monetary policy mistakes over and over and over again.

There is a peculiar market expectations constraint on the way monetary policy is adjusted. When inflation is high, the Fed believes that it cannot allow interest rates to fall "too" quickly until unemployment has replaced inflation as the number one problem. Otherwise, market expectations about monetary policy would be violated and Fed credibility would suffer as it appeared that the "fight against inflation" was being abandoned. That appearance would create political problems for the Fed and might add to the difficulty of bringing down inflation in an orderly way. Similarly, when unemployment is the number one problem the Fed must tread gingerly in allowing interest rates to rise for fear that "too" big a change will lead to market expectations that the policy might not be politically sustainable.

Market expectations interact with the political constraints on policy. Roughly speaking, perhaps the best way to put the point is that maintaining political support requires that policy "look right"—policy must not be grossly counter-intuitive to the conventional intuition.

Finally, monetary policy often has asymmetrical characteristics that reflect the interplay of Fed intentions and market and political expectations. When unemployment is the number one problem, errors in controlling the money stock on the low side tend to be soon offset by higher money growth, but errors on the high side are not offset by lower money growth. In the terminology of the monetary targeting literature, base drift is asymmetrical with the upside deviations of money from target being accommodated and the downside deviations being offset. The same process is at work when inflation is the number one problem. In this case, base drift runs in the other direction, but for exactly the same analytical reasons. Examples of such periods are the second halves of 1974 and 1981.

These asymmetries are sometimes incorporated quite explicitly in the policy directive sent by the Federal Open Market Committee (FOMC) to the open market desk at the Federal Reserve Bank of New York. The desk may be instructed to accommodate money growth on the high side but to move promptly should money growth be lower than projected, or vice versa. When the market learns that the FOMC has introduced an asymmetrical instruction into the policy directive, interest rates may jump discretely up or down. The reason is that the asymmetry is equivalent to the Federal Reserve saying that it will, for example, permit interest rates to rise readily under certain circumstances but not to fall readily. That information changes the near-term expected value of money market interest rates by changing the shape of the probability distribution of interest rate changes.

Although the Federal Reserve would never make a flat announcement that interest rates should rise, an asymmetric policy instruction is the operational equivalent of such an announcement. The FOMC does not release to the public the policy directive adopted at one meeting until after the next meeting, at which time the new directive supersedes the old one. Nevertheless, it seems likely that the way in which the open market desk conducts open market operations provides clues to astute Fed watchers when an asymmetry has been introduced to the directive. Otherwise inexplicable interest rate changes may occur when the market guesses that the Fed has introduced or eliminated an asymmetry in its open market operations.

Political Gaming

Much of what is said and done in Washington can be understood only within the context of political gaming—the thrust and parry, move and countermove, of political rivals and agencies as they attempt to improve their political positions. Actions that seem peculiar become perfectly clear once the inside story of personal rivalries and of the deals that are struck becomes known.

One of the most obvious features of political gaming is the practice of scape-goating. The common human trait of resistance to admitting mistakes is especially important for government agencies. The political power and even survival of agencies depends on maintaining an image of competence. No one should underestimate the potential for quirky and fundamentally unimportant episodes to affect an agency's image and therefore its public support. All agencies, including the Federal Reserve, do their best to avoid damaging incidents, to take credit for the good things that happen, and to blame others, either openly or by inference, for the bad things that happen.

It is extremely difficult to obtain from the Federal Reserve a simple yes or no answer to a question such as: "In retrospect, and all things considered, would it have been better for the U.S. economy if M1 growth had been one percentage point lower than it actually was each year 1977–1979?" However, it is also worth emphasizing that questions of this kind are rarely asked of the Federal Reserve by the Congress.

Several reasons come to mind as to why such questions are so rarely asked. For one, a member of the Congress who pressured the Fed to hold interest rates down in the late 1970s is in a poor position to ask now why money growth was not lower. For another, members of Congress may want to retain their freedom to scape-goat the Federal Reserve in the future.

The present arrangements for congressional oversight of the Federal Reserve serve the political interests of both the Fed and the Congress because these arrangements permit both bodies a relatively easy escape from answering hard questions and taking real positions on important monetary policy issues. The present extensive congressional oversight hearings provide the appearance of careful congressional scrutiny of Federal Reserve policy without in fact changing very much what the Federal Reserve actually does.

There are considerable political rewards for the politician who takes on a "bad" agency and wins a highly visible battle. However, to win these political battles the public must have concerns about the competence of an agency, and the critics must maintain a "reform" image. However, the game is a tricky one because anyone attacking a "sound" agency may be viewed as irresponsible and as acting simply for "political" reasons. Such a person may be easily discredited by the agency claiming that the attacker is irresponsible and simply scape-goating. As emphasized earlier, the political combat is carried on largely at the level of intentions, motives, and integrity; the merits of a case are of distinctly secondary importance.

Over the years the Federal Reserve has been extraordinarily successful in maintaining the high ground in these political debates. One of the reasons is that many of the attacks on the Fed *have* been irresponsible. The focus of these political attacks is almost always on the level of interest rates, and the Federal Reserve has been extremely successful in fending off such attacks.

One of the principal stratagems pursued by the Federal Reserve has been to avoid appearing responsible for interest rate changes. After the Treasury-Federal Reserve Accord of 1951, the Fed adopted the "bills only" policy in its open market operations. By confining its open market interventions to the short end of the maturity spectrum, the Fed was able to claim that it had nothing to do with fluctuations of long-term interest rates. Increases in bond yields could not be the Fed's fault. That policy reduced a possible pressure point on the Fed to resume the pegging of long-term interest rates.

Federal Reserve market intervention to control short-term interest rates became increasingly explicit after the Accord. Starting in 1967 the FOMC set narrow limits on day-to-day fluctuations of the federal funds rate, and the numerical "tolerance range" for the funds rate was published with only a short lag after the mid-1970s. In October 1979 the Federal Reserve moved to a system it described as "nonborrowed reserves" control. Under this system much wider day-to-day fluctuations in interest rates were permitted, and the Fed insisted that interest rates were being set entirely by market forces.

After 1979 controversy grew about interest rate volatility, the high average level of interest rates, and the protracted 1981–82 recession. Responding to this criticism, in the fall of 1982 the Fed changed its policy procedures again by adopting what it described as a "borrowed reserves" target.

Under this new policy the day-to-day behavior of the federal funds rate has been almost identical to that under the earlier policy of explicitly pegging the funds rate in the short run. This outcome is not surprising. It is well known in the academic literature that if the bank borrowing function is stable a borrowed reserves target is *identical* to direct targeting of the federal funds rate. Nevertheless, the Fed has been at pains to insist that the policies followed after the fall of 1982 have not involved close control over money market interest rates on a day-to-day basis.

In addition to conducting open market operations in ways that minimize the appearance of influence over interest rates, the Federal Reserve has continuously emphasized the role of non-monetary causes of interest rate changes. This approach reflects the genuine professional views of the members of the Board of Governors and its staff. At least since the Accord, the Board has put much more emphasis on the role of budget deficits in determining nominal interest rates than monetarists think appropriate. There is a genuine difference of professional opinion here, but having said that it is also fair to observe that monetarists do not fare well on the Board staff. The monetarist emphasis on the role of inflation and inflation expectations—both of which are largely the result of money growth—in determining nominal interest rates is a threat to the institution. In public speeches and congressional testimony, Federal Reserve emphasis on fiscal policy influences on interest rates makes effective use of public myths about budget deficits to deflect attention away from Federal Reserve policy.

In all of these ways the Federal Reserve has been successful over the years in blunting the charges of critics who assert that the Fed is responsible for an unduly high level of interest rates. The defense appears credible to the public by virtue of the fact that the financial institutions themselves seem more directly involved with interest rate determination than does the Federal Reserve. For this reason the critics of high interest rates have often found the financial institutions a more tempting target of their charges than the Federal Reserve. Federal Reserve officials have on occasion made comments that tend to support these views and have rarely come out with ringing defenses of financial institutions when rates are rising. After all, if the institutions are not to blame, who is? There is no point to encouraging political enemies to ask that question.

The one visible interest rate set by the Federal Reserve is the discount rate. Here again the Fed has played its hand very successfully. Discount rate changes generally follow changes in market rates, making it possible for the Fed to claim that the discount rate is being adjusted to maintain alignment with market rates. However, the Fed has insisted on maintaining independent control over the discount rate—rather than tying it to market rates—in order to have a visible policy instrument to adjust when it appears necessary to broadcast a message about Fed concern and action to deal with unfortunate economic conditions. When the cry is abroad to "do something," a change in the discount rate is the ideal policy action.

These comments should most definitely not be read as reflecting a view on my part that the Federal Reserve should target interest rates. The point is that political pressures on the Federal Reserve are concentrated on interest rate issues. Barring scandal—and the Fed has an excellent record of avoiding both the actuality and appearance of scandal—the institution is politically safe as long as interest rates are trending down. In reconciling a sound monetary policy with the political realities, interest rates are *the* issue. To the extent that the Fed can avoid taking responsibility for interest rate changes it can avoid being backed into a political corner where it might be forced to attempt to limit interest rate increases. Its success in this enterprise is responsible for monetary policy being as good as it has

41

been. Monetarist critics, of course, believe that policy could have been much better.

As part of its effort to maintain its independence, the Federal Reserve engages in extensive efforts to explain economic conditions as being the result of disturbances beyond Federal Reserve control. Federal Reserve speeches and testimony generally devote far more space to analysis of fiscal policy and non-monetary influences on economic conditions than to monetary analysis. Space devoted to monetary analysis is ordinarily concentrated on why money demand shifts and other irregularities require a "flexible" monetary policy.

The Federal Reserve has been so successful over the years in maintaining the political high ground that alternative views are usually greeted skeptically in the public debates. Federal Reserve views are in fact often correct, and where they are not they always have a ring of great plausibility. Moreover, administration and congressional criticisms of the Fed are generally dismissed on the ground that they are politically motivated.

For a recent example of this phenomenon, the Reagan administration has quite obviously been on the political defensive on the budget deficit issue, and everyone knows that there is political advantage for the administration to deny that budget deficits cause high real rates of interest. Consequently, the administration's position that budget deficits are not responsible for high real rates of interest has lacked credibility and has been dismissed out of hand by many observers. Indeed, the case has been so lacking in surface plausibility and the political motivations for making it have seemed so obvious that many observers have never even considered the possibility that the position might have merit. The substantive conclusion has been decided on the basis of the administration's motives. For these reasons, the administration's attempts to pin the interest rate tail on the Federal Reserve donkey have never gotten very far in the public debates.

Another aspect of political gamesmanship has made it relatively easy for the Fed to maintain the high ground. On the principle that the "enemy of my enemy is my friend" the political party out of the White House almost always has an incentive to side with the Fed. The Fed has been very successful in pursuing policies that do not provide an opportunity for both political parties to line up on the same side of an issue with the Fed on the other side. For example, when interest rates are rising in a presidential election year the Fed almost invariably permits money growth to rise also. The party out of power can then attack the party in power for rising interest rates, and the party in power cannot deflect blame to the Federal Reserve by pointing to falling money growth. Conversely, when interest rates fall in a presidential election year, money growth usually falls also so that the opposition party cannot charge that the Fed is rigging the election for the party in power.

Discussing these political gaming issues almost always has an unseemly air about it. My purpose is not to disparage the Federal Reserve System, but to direct scholarly attention to how this process works. Successful political leaders and successful agencies must engage in political gaming. That is what politics is all about. Economists should not discuss economic policy entirely under the assumption that politics does not exist, or is unworthy of scholarly attention. There are, presumably, laws to political behavior in democracies, and those laws should be regarded as constraints that are every bit as important to the policymakers in pursuing their objectives as are the constraints imposed by the structure of the economy.

Conclusion

I am convinced that under the present institutional arrangements controlling monetary policy decisions there is no reason to expect that we have seen the last of stop-go monetary policy. I cannot predict whether the next episode will be stop or go. The case for go is that during the present business cycle expansion we have not yet seen a period of flat real growth and/or rising interest rates that could lead to great pressure on the Federal Reserve to raise money growth. Slow real GNP growth in 1962 and 1976 led to monetary policy decisions that accelerated money growth and eventually led to inflation. Rising interest rates in 1967, 1972, and 1977 led to higher money growth that accelerated inflation.

The case for stop is that the memory of the recent inflation is still very strong. Many observers are now willing to take risks on the side of restrictive monetary policy rather than take the chance of reigniting inflation. With these attitudes, a decline of inflation expectations leading to a decline of interest rates could generate excessively low money growth because of Fed concerns that interest rates not fall "too" rapidly. In the late 1950s public attitudes toward inflation produced a monetary policy biased on the side of restriction. The result was that the recovery from the 1957–58 recession was aborted by very low money growth in the second half of 1959. Later, of course, the memory of the back-to-back recessions in 1957–58 and 1960–61 created an inflationary bias to monetary policy.

There must be a better way. Greater congressional control over day-to-day monetary management would not, however, be useful.

The political process that has given us a procyclical monetary policy operates with a vengeance at the congressional level. We need monetary rules and standards rather than new management.

Some observers believe that greater Federal Reserve independence would prevent the political interference with monetary policy of the type described in this paper. But I do not see how anyone committed to democratic government could advocate a central bank completely free of democratic political controls. Greater independence is a nonstarter; it should not happen and it will not happen.

The crux of the matter, I believe, is that relying on political will and good management to improve monetary policy is like relying on the social responsibility of firms to clean up pollution. Just as the responsible firm in a pollution-prone industry will be driven out of business by less responsible firms, so also may responsible political officials be driven out of the political marketplace by less responsible officials when certain kinds of policy decisions are made on a case-by-case basis.

If this view seems farfetched, consider the position of the Federal Reserve System if, during a period of rising interest rates, the President were to make a strong public statement insisting that the Fed should not increase the discount rate. Is it imaginable that the Federal Reserve would increase the discount rate the very next day? Is it unimaginable that the President, or some other important official such as the Speaker of the House of Representatives, might correctly see short-run political advantage to making such a statement?

This example is not farfetched. In December 1966 there was a highly public battle between President Johnson and Federal Reserve Chairman Martin. If Johnson had attacked the Federal Reserve before the discount rate increase instead of after, the Fed would almost surely have delayed its action. For another example, it is well known that the Federal Reserve had great misgivings about President Carter's 1980 request that the Fed impose credit controls. Could the Federal Reserve have defied President Carter by refusing to impose controls? Could the Federal Reserve have cut its discount rate in September 1974 when President Ford was convening his "Whip Inflation Now" meeting in Washington?

The answers to these questions are obvious. And it is important to note that in the event of Federal Reserve defiance of the President or Congress the public debate would turn away from the merits of the policy action itself to the power of the Federal Reserve. In these situations the only responsible thing for the Federal Reserve to do is to acquiesce to the greater political power and to muddle along making the best of a bad situation. After a time, a changed climate of opinion opens up room for maneuver. The Federal Reserve can then argue that changed economic conditions rather than defiance of the President or the Congress justifies changing policy. But this process is obviously not without its costs. Needed policy actions may be delayed, and policy may for a time feed an inflation or depress an already contracting economy.

The end result of this political process is a sequence of monetary policy outcomes characterized by myopia and time inconsistency. These are not the results intended by the Federal Reserve, but at an abstract level they can be analyzed "as if" they were. This process will continue until a policy rule of some sort replaces policy discretion. I see no basis for a rule other than one specifying control of some monetary aggregate within some bounds. Only a rule constraining the creation of money can lead to a determinate price level and an end to the procyclical monetary policy that has afflicted the U.S. economy for so many years.

3

INHERENT CONFLICTS OF U.S. MONETARY POLICYMAKING*
Lawrence K. Roos

I have come to the realization that perhaps the best contribution I can make to the debate over monetary policy is to discuss the "inherent conflicts" of monetary policymaking as it is currently conducted in the United States. I do not presume to be able to discuss all the problems of policymaking, nor can I presume to prescribe acceptable solutions to the multitude of problems that have vexed so many for so long. Instead, I would like to present a few of the most meaningful impressions that I gathered during the seven years in which I participated in monetary policymaking. I will leave it to you to decide which of these impressions are valid and how the problems they suggest might be corrected.

In line with the present emphasis on "truth in labeling," I must remind you that my impressions are somewhat subjective. I anticipate that some of my colleagues in the policymaking process will, no doubt, disagree with each and every one of them, and that some may even have a totally different view of what the process is all about.

A Policymaker's View of the Policymaking Process

What Monetary Policy Should Be

First, let me state what I believe monetary policymaking should be. Under our institutional arrangement, the Federal Reserve System possesses, for all practical purposes, only one tool of policy implementation: open market operations that inject or withdraw bank reserves into and from the banking system. It follows that, if there is a primary goal, or a set of *consistent* goals that we desire to achieve, monetary policy must be, simply, a process for producing the changes in bank reserves necessary to achieve such goals. This, in turn, requires both a theory that describes the relationship between changes in

---

*Reprinted from *Cato Journal* 5 (Winter 1986): 771–76.
The author is a former President of the Federal Reserve Bank of St. Louis.

reserves and the achievement of goals, and empirical estimates of the magnitude of the impact of such changes and the timing involved. In addition, there must be some agreement among policymakers about whether and how to respond to "shocks" or "surprises" that might occur along the way to achieving desired goals.

Because we live in an open and free society—in the political sense—monetary policy goals must be agreed upon by, and known to, the public. And the method chosen by policymakers to achieve those goals must be clearly understood by the public. Policy actions must be easily observable, well explained, and, of course, consistent with the goals sought. And finally, it is essential that policymakers be held accountable for the achievement of their announced goals.

Shortcomings of the Policymaking Process

In reality, very few of these elements that I believe to be so crucial to policymaking currently exist. To start with, there are no clear, achievable goals promulgated by monetary policymakers. Never once in my participation in meetings of the Federal Open Market Committee (FOMC) do I recall any discussion of long-range goals of economic growth or desired price levels. It was like trying to construct a house without agreeing upon an architectural design. Instead of seeking a few achievable goals, the Federal Reserve is supposed to solve all sorts of problems, including inflation, unemployment, lagging real output growth, high interest rates, balance of payments disequilibrium, volatile exchange rates, depressed stock prices, a sagging housing industry, and the world debt crisis. Now, asking monetary policymakers to do all this is sheer nonsense. Such diverse goals represent a "wish list" designed for achieving utopian objectives; those who would have the Fed seek them pay no attention either to their consistency or to what monetary policy is capable of achieving. Imposing such a laundry list of goals and wishes on the Fed reflects a total lack of understanding as to what the Federal Reserve is able or not to do. This kind of thinking hampers the workings of the FOMC. For within the FOMC, there were usually as many goals as there were chairs around the table. In my experience at the Fed, I cannot recall any significant ranking of objectives or if the diverse goals considered were mutually consistent either with one another or with the policy actions being considered. To be sure, everyone agreed that they wanted full employment, stable prices, low interest rates, a booming housing sector, thriving farmers, and a prosperous financial community. But I recall no consensus on long-range goals nor do I recall serious efforts to set policy on other than the shortest time horizons.

One can, of course, say that at different times, different goals are appropriate; this has been the conclusion of those who delight in econometric estimations of Fed "reaction functions." However, the net result of such a disorderly pursuit of transitory goals is likely to be precisely what we have experienced over the past decade—namely, highly variable money growth, volatile financial markets, and real growth that has swung from boom to bust. Perhaps because there was no clearly defined set of long-range consistent goals, there has been no general agreement among policymakers as to the effects of policy actions.

The existence of the "eclectic" school of policymakers, which encourages shifting from one indicator to another and thus opts for having multiple indicators to choose from, reflects the fact that there are many different theories about the relationships between actions and goals. We are all familiar with past disagreements over whether interest rates, M1, M2, or M3 are the most appropriate indicators, and the heated discussions of such issues in the public press. I must agree that there may be some legitimate disagreements, as there always are when theories are compared. But as long as there is no consensus as to which goals are being sought or what theories are to be used in achieving them, there can be neither consistent monetary policymaking nor achievement of desired goals.

One of the most vexing problems in monetary policymaking is the question of timing. Substantial evidence exists that the timing of the impact of changes in bank reserves differs across various measures of economic activity. The price level, for example, is affected by changes in bank reserves, and associated changes in money, with a relatively long lag—upwards of three to five years, depending on whose empirics you trust. Output, on the other hand, is affected by changes in bank reserves, and the associated change in money, with a considerably shorter lag, perhaps only two to three quarters; and the output effect is only transitory. Thus, if one's goal is to achieve reduced inflation, or price level stability, one's policy horizon must be three to five years distant; on the other hand, if you want to achieve some transitory impact on output, you will lower your horizon to several quarters ahead. In reality, although policymakers discuss economic activity projections for a year in the future, there is little attention paid to formulating policy as a means of achieving clearly defined goals. Policy prescriptions are set, generally, from one FOMC meeting to another; thus, the span of these prescriptions is no longer than two or three months. As a result, we experience base drift, frequent violation of longer-term targets, and undesired variations in economic activity.

Moreover, by dealing with such very short time horizons, it is easy to come to believe that monetary policy has no effect on economic activity; that, instead, the reverse is true. Since over short periods of time much of economic activity is indeed predetermined, the only effect that monetary policy can have is on money market conditions. As a result, the focus of policymakers, and of policy itself, is channeled toward interest rates, especially short-term rates; the longer-term goals receive scant attention, except when inflation or output problems reach crisis proportions.

Finally, given a multiplicity of goals, targets, and indicators, there can be no real accountability to Congress or to the public in general. While a lack of accountability may be comforting to policymakers, it produces its own set of problems. There is an old saying that "thieves and gypsies never return to the same place twice"—presumably because they will have to account for their previous actions. Monetary policymakers, on the other hand, have no such qualms or constraints; they can, and do, return again and again to the same policies despite previously unsatisfactory results.

I would like to emphasize that, while these impressions are critical of the monetary policymaking process, I do not believe that they reflect on the conscious desires of policymakers. Policymakers want to do the right thing! The problem lies in the absence of a set of consistent goals for monetary policy to achieve. Without such goals, it is impossible to reach consensus about the theory to use or a specific monetary target to seek. Without these, it is uncharitable to demand accountability on the part of monetary policymakers.

Difficulty of Consensus and Persistence of Ignorance

Whether such clearly definable goals can be agreed upon in the present political environment is not at all clear. In a climate of diverse and differing philosophical beliefs, it is difficult to achieve a consensus. Another major stumbling block is the "plain ignorance" of economics that seems so widespread. For example, it is commonly believed by the public, and thus by politicians, that the Federal Reserve can control interest rates at will. Despite reams of evidence to the contrary, such erroneous beliefs inevitably produce political pressures on monetary authorities to lower interest rates by speeding up money growth, even at the expense of all other goals.

In sum, my main point is simply that we must have clearly defined and achievable goals on which to base policymaking decisions. Furthermore, it is not enough to hammer out clear and consistent goals if public and political pressure is expected to be exerted on the Fed to abandon them whenever it seems like "the politically expedient thing to do." Finally, there must be a clear recognition by the public of what the Fed can and *cannot* do. Without such a consensus, even the best conceived goals will not stand a chance of surviving.

Addendum: Economic Forecasting and Monetary Targeting*

In theory, there is a direct relationship between M1 growth and output in the short run and prices in the long run, after a lag period. I do not think the FOMC ever really tries to set, within its own closed-door deliberations, specific targets for output in the future or for the price level. When the discussion is held, I have always had the feeling that the discussion was "Where do you think the economy will be a year or two in the future, and how can we best set targets so we won't have egg on our face if this doesn't come about?" Most of the people I knew in the FOMC did not really feel that policy-making could have an impact on what was going to happen. Instead, it was viewed as being reactive and defensive. In terms of policy-making, whatever was done was not too far out of sync with what was going to happen economically due to all of these uncontrollable (in their mind) factors that move the economy. In other words, poli-cymaking was not looked at as I interpreted it—as a means of getting from here to there. Rather, it was looked at as a means of trying to defensively protect the Fed from being out of step with what most of the members felt would happen despite monetary policy decisions.

Moreover, I do not think that the leaders and the staff of the Federal Reserve actually feel that money growth can be controlled, even over a one- or two-year period. I can tell you without violating any confi-dences that more than once when we met, when the money growth M1 figure was disclosed since the previous FOMC meeting, someone would say that we lucked out this time. There is not a serious belief that this machine can be guided by controlling money. Indeed, I do not believe that the control of money growth ever became the primary priority of the Fed. I think that there was always and still is a preoc-cupation with stabilization of interest rates.

*This addendum is Mr. Roos's reply to the following questions asked by Godfrey Briefs of the House Banking Committee during the Cato Institute's third annual monetary conference (21–22 February 1985): "Mr. Roos, could you tell us more about the rela-tionship between the forecast of the economic outlook and the manner in which the monetary aggregates are decided? Is there a cause-and-effect relationship? Is there mutual interdependence? What is the role of the forecast in arriving at the monetary aggregates?"—EDS.

When anything goes haywire, the Fed does the most convenient thing. When M1 grew too quickly, all of a sudden the Fed in its brilliance said "M1 has been distorted." M1 was not really distorted all that much. They adopted other multiple targets instead of M1. When something is not working, you gather a bunch of other things. If you have enough "other things" when you go to Congress, you are bound to hit the target on one or two of your objectives even though they have no relevance to output or the price level.

4

THE IMPORTANCE OF STABLE MONEY: THEORY AND EVIDENCE*

Michael D. Bordo and Anna J. Schwartz

The importance of monetary stability derives from the significant independent influence of monetary change on the subsequent course of economic activity. If money did not matter at all or were of only secondary importance in affecting the flow of spending, income, and prices, monetary stability would be of little relevance.

Our views reflect theoretical models and the empirical evidence testing them that establish a close relation between economic stability and monetary stability, and between inflation and monetary growth in excess of the rate of real growth. Hence a stable monetary environment is crucial to achieve economic stability encompassing both stable prices and real growth immune to wide swings. The essential element required to generate a stable monetary environment is systematic policy, so as to minimize monetary shocks to the expectations of economic agents. Discretionary policy is unsystematic, hence fails this test. Increasing the variability of money growth in an attempt to fine-tune the economy will make the variance of real output greater than it would otherwise have been. An economy in which countercyclical policy is followed will end up with unstable money and unstable real output.

Postwar developments in monetary theory have shifted the issues that were the original centerpieces of analysis supporting the case for stable money. Correspondingly, the kinds of evidence suggested to test the analysis have changed to reflect the nature of the issues that are highlighted. We examine the developments in chronological order, beginning with Friedman's case for stable money, based on a theoretical argument against the pursuit of countercyclical stabilization policy (Section I). Section II then examines the opposing

*Reprinted from *Cato Journal* 3 (Spring 1983): 63–82, with revisions.

Michael D. Bordo is Professor of Economics at the University of South Carolina and both he and Anna J. Schwartz are Research Associates of the National Bureau of Economic Research. The authors are indebted to Milton Friedman, Gottfried Haberler, and Joseph Whitt for helpful comments on an earlier draft.

theory of economic policy associated with Theil and Tinbergen and the Phillips curve analysis. That theory holds that countercyclical policy can be employed to stabilize the economy and that stable monetary policy is not decisive for that purpose. Successful countercyclical policy would achieve a standard deviation of money growth that would precisely offset the standard deviation of real economic growth that would otherwise occur, and thereby reduce the variance of real output below that of money. The section concludes with a discussion of the natural rate hypothesis that was the culmination of the Phillips curve analysis. The latest development we cover is the rational expectations hypothesis (Section III). In each section we examine the implications of the theory for the stable money view and report the available evidence. In Section IV we summarize the case for a legislated rule and present some new evidence for a monetary growth rule. Section V concludes with a brief discussion of the role that a constant monetary growth rule plays in the views of the schools of global monetarism, of Austrian economics, and of the new monetary economics.

I. The Case Against Discretionary Monetary Policy

The general rule case against discretionary monetary policy formulated by Friedman (1953) is that, to function well, stabilization policy must offset random disturbances to economic activity; that is, it should remove the variation in income due to those disturbances. To achieve such a goal, two conditions must be satisfied: one involving timing, and the other involving the magnitude of the policy action. The timing of the policy action should conform to that of the disturbance, and the size of the policy action should be congruent with the size of the disturbance. If both conditions are not satisfied, the policy response will be insufficient and may even be destabilizing.

Friedman (1948, 1953) went on to argue that the lags in the effect of discretionary monetary policy are likely to be long and variable, reflecting both an "inside lag"—the time that elapsed before the monetary authority responded to the disturbance—and an "outside lag"—the time that elapsed before changes in monetary growth affect economic activity. As a result, discretionary policy actions might exacerbate rather than mitigate cyclical disturbances. In addition, Friedman contended that there was no basis for believing that policymakers (and the economics profession) possess the detailed knowledge of the economy's complex interactions and of the lag structure requisite for the pursuit of successful countercyclical policies or for fine-tuning. Furthermore, in his view, even well-meaning monetary authorities were likely to respond to political influences. Politically advantageous, short-run actions by the authorities would ignore the long-run destabilizing consequences. The conclusion Friedman drew from this array of circumstances and from evidence to be considered in what follows was that monetary policy should be based on a legislated rule instructing the Federal Reserve to increase the quantity of money, or high-powered money, on a year-to-year basis at a steady known rate of growth.

Friedman did not allege that such a prescription would yield nirvana. He allowed for the possible accretion of knowledge of the operation of the economy once the rule was adopted that would permit improving it. Adoption of the rule would not eliminate cyclical change, but the rule would remove disturbances arising from erratic fluctuations in the supply of money. The effect would be to reduce the amplitude of the random shocks to real economic growth inherent in the operation of the economy.

Several types of evidence have been used to evaluate the case for a monetary rule, namely: the statistical record of changes in money growth rates and their relation to changes in economic activity; qualitative historical data; and simulations of the hypothetical path of economic activity under an assumed monetary growth rule, compared with the actual path. We first report the statistical and historical evidence.

One body of evidence, of which Clark Warburton was the author, predated Friedman's theoretical case against discretionary monetary policy. Warburton's writings from the early 1940s, when the Keynesian revolution was in full swing, until the end of his life in 1980, were in the quantity of money tradition and stressed the importance of monetary disequilibrium as the fundamental cause of business fluctuations. At the time that Warburton's views first appeared, attention to the role of money had all but vanished from professional work. His main evidence was based on deviations from trend of quarterly money data for the period 1918–65. He demonstrated that turning points in money preceded those in business and concluded: "[A]n erratic money supply [was] the chief originating factor in business recessions and not merely an intensifying force in the case of severe depressions" (1966, Intro., p. 9). Warburton also cited, as prime examples of the harmful effects of discretionary policy, the mistakes of the Federal Reserve System that produced the great contraction of 1929–33 and the contraction of 1937–38:

> Since the time of the establishment of the Federal Reserve System, annual deviations in the quantity of money from a reasonable rate of growth have ranged from more than 30 percent excess to nearly

> 20 percent deficiency. There is no known need for annual variations
> in the quantity of money, from the estimated reasonable rate of
> growth, of more than 2 percent, and annual variations in the quantity
> of money outside this range have been invariably associated with
> business instability and with inflation or depression. The range of
> additional variation for seasonal purposes is probably not more than
> three percent [1966, chap. 17 (1952), pp. 368–69].

The dismal record of the Federal Reserve led Warburton to strongly
favor a legislated monetary rule that would limit the growth rate of
money, for a given definition, to 3 percent per annum.[1]

The evidence provided by Friedman and his associates also utilized statistical and qualitative historical data. Unlike Warburton,
who expressed the data as deviations from trend, Friedman and
Schwartz used first differences of the logarithms of the money series.
They then selected turning points in the series from 1867 to 1960,
and compared the peaks and troughs in the percentage rate of change
of the money stock with peaks and troughs in general business as
dated by the National Bureau of Economic Research reference cycle
chronology. On average, of the 18 nonwar cycles since 1870, peaks
in the rate of change of the stock of money preceded reference peaks
by 16 months, and troughs in the rate of change of the stock of money
preceded reference troughs by 12 months. On this basis, they argued
strongly that: "Appreciable changes in the rate of growth of the stock
of money are a necessary and sufficient condition for appreciable
changes in the rate of growth of money income"; and, "this is true
both for long secular changes and also for changes roughly the length
of business cycles" (1963a, p. 53). Using a different methodology
over the same period, William Poole (1975) found that the evidence
supported the Friedman and Schwartz conclusion.

To the question whether money changes conformed positively to
the business cycle with a lead or inversely with a lag, the answer
Friedman and Schwartz gave was that the dispersion (measured by
the standard deviation) of the leads and lags, as computed under the
two interpretations, is uniformly lower when the money series is
treated as conforming positively. Serial correlations, furthermore, of
expansions with succeeding contractions and of contractions with
succeeding expansions display the same patterns for the money change
series and a proxy indicator of physical change in general business.

[1]Warburton (1964, p. 1328). In earlier studies, in the 1940s and 1950s, Warburton
advocated a 5 percent annual growth rate in the money stock, inclusive of an adjustment
for a projected steady secular decline in velocity of 1.5 percent per year. The shift to a
lower proposed growth rate for money incorporated the assumption that the reversal
in the trend of velocity in the 1950s—from negative to positive—would continue.

Expansions in both series are not systematically correlated with the succeeding contractions, whereas contraction in both series are highly correlated with the succeeding expansions. This evidence supports the positive interpretation of the relation of money *changes* to the business cycle. Otherwise, if inverted conformity were the case and changes in business produced later changes in the opposite direction in money, then the correlations with the succeeding reference cycle phase for money and the physical change in general business measure should be opposite. But the pattern for business *does* reflect, with a lag, the pattern for money.

Statistical evidence provided by Friedman and Schwartz (1963b, p. 594) matched periods with a low standard deviation of year-to-year percentage changes in monetary growth with comparable periods in velocity, real income, and wholesale prices. They also matched periods with a high standard deviation of year-to-year changes in monetary growth with comparable periods in the other magnitudes. In the nine decades, 1869–1960, four periods of comparative stability in money growth were accompanied by relative stability of the rate of growth of output and the rate of change of prices: 1882–92; 1903–13; 1923–29; 1948–60. All other periods were characterized by unusually unstable money growth rates and unusually unstable rates of growth of output and rates of change of prices.

The qualitative historical evidence that Friedman and Schwartz examined also supported the conclusion that erratic money changes, as a result of discretionary actions by the authorities, were accompanied by economic changes in the same direction. Moreover, in a number of episodes when monetary changes had led changes in economic activity, the evidence that the monetary changes were independent of the changes in activity was irrefutable.

We now turn to the simulation studies that compare the hypothetical behavior of the U.S. economy under an assumed constant money growth rate rule with actual economic performance. The evidence is mixed. Friedman (1960) found that a rule would have outperformed discretionary policy in the interwar period, but that the case for the post-World War II period was less clear-cut. For the postwar period, at least until the mid-1960s, most studies (Bronfenbrenner 1961; Modigliani 1964; Argy 1971) concluded that discretionary policy outperformed a 3 or 4 percent monetary growth rate. One inference might be that the Federal Reserve had learned from its "mistakes" in the interwar period. Recently, however, Argy (1979) found that for the period from the late 1960s to the late 1970s, a simulated monetary growth for a sample of nine industrial countries would have reduced the variance of real growth considerably below its actual variance.

Finally, Kochin (1980) found that over much of the postwar period U.S. monetary policy was destabilizing. His study, based on an interpretation of the results of several economic models, followed Friedman's (1953) procedure for evaluating stabilization policy.

II. Keynesian Riposte and Return Sally

An analytical development that favored intervention along Keynesian lines was the Theil-Tinbergen theory of economic policy. That approach provided policymakers with an array of instruments—monetary, fiscal, incomes policies—to achieve multiple goals by matching instruments to goals following the principle of comparative advantage. This theory of economic policy combined with the use of optimal control procedures led to a strong case for fine-tuning. It was held that policymakers could devise feedback rules between real economic activity and monetary and fiscal policy that could be applied to offset disturbances to the private sector.

Another development that apparently advanced the case for countercyclical policy was the Phillips curve tradeoff. Phillips (1958), Samuelson and Solow (1960), and Lipsey (1960) reported evidence of a stable inverse relationship for the U.K., the U.S., and other countries between the rate of change of money wages (alternatively, the rate of change of the price level) and the level of unemployment. The findings led to the view that policymakers could choose, based on a social preference function, between high inflation and low unemployment, or low inflation and high unemployment, the desired choice to be achieved by discretionary monetary and fiscal policy.

The upshot of these developments was that many economists came to believe that the economy could be stabilized at any desired level of activity. Friedman's objections to fine-tuning seemed to have been circumvented.

Friedman's response came in his 1967 presidential address to the American Economic Association. He arged that the Phillips curve tradeoff was a statistical illusion arising from the failure to account for inflationary expectations. Monetary and fiscal policy could stabilize the economy at some arbitrary level of output or employment, but only temporarily and, even then, only at the expense of accelerating inflation or deflation. Both Friedman (1968) and Phelps (1968) modified the Phillips curve approach by applying the concept of the natural rate of employment—that rate consistent with the microeconomic decisions of firms and workers active in the labor force. The natural rate of employment reflects the optimal choice of workers between labor and leisure and the optimal mix of labor and other factors of production for firms in a dynamic economy. According to the "natural rate hypothesis," the natural rate of employment is determined by the intersection of the demand and supply curves for labor, given demographic factors and labor market institutions. Hence deviations of employment from the natural rate are produced only by imperfect information and the costs of acquiring information that affect job search.

One explanation given for such imperfections in information was that employers and workers have different perceptions of changes in real wage rates. It was argued that firms always have perfect information on the prices of their output so that for them actual and expected real wages are always equal. In contrast, workers base their evaluations of prospective real wage rates on their expectations of what the rate of inflation will be over the duration of their contracts. For example, suppose inflation is rising and workers' expectations do not fully reflect the higher inflation rate. Faced with lower real wage rates, firms will be willing to expand employment, which will put upward pressure on nominal wages. The result will appear as a movement along the (short-run) Phillips curve. However, once workers adjust their expectations to the higher inflation rate, they will demand higher money wages. The resultant rise in real wage rates will cause firms to reduce employment to its previous level. The economy will then return to the natural rate of employment consistent with labor market forces, *but at a higher rate of inflation.*

The *measured* unemployment rate is thus assumed to depend on the natural unemployment rate and the difference between the actual and expected inflation rates; that is, on the inflation forecast error, with some rate of adjustment of the employment rate to the forecast error. As long as the actual and expected inflation rates differ, measured unemployment can differ from th natural rate. However, in the *long run*, actual and expected inflation rates converge, and hence, measured unemployment reverts to the natural rate, though this adjustment process may be sluggish.

The theory of search is an alternative way of explaining unemployment. This theory posits that the natural rate of unemployment is determined by long-run demographic forces, but that deviations from the natural rate are caused by short-run factors affecting the costs and duration of search.

The policy implication that emerged from the natural rate hypothesis was that stabilization policies aimed at reducing unemployment below the natural rate would have only temporary success. Any attempt to achieve permanent results would produce accelerating and, ultimately, runaway inflation. In addition, policies designed to peg the unemployment rate at the natural rate could lead easily to an explosive inflation or deflation if the forces determining the natural rate were to change. Such forces include changes in the labor force skill mix and demographic determinants of the labor force. Thus, the natural rate hypothesis strengthens the case for monetary stability, since monetary instability would produce deviations between the expected and actual inflation rates, causing fluctuations in unemployment and output.

III. The Rational Expectations Hypothesis and the Case for Stable Money

Recent advances in the treatment of expectations supplement the case for monetary stability implied by the natural rate hypothesis. According to the rational expectations hypothesis, economic agents act rationally with respect to the gathering and processing of information, just as they do with respect to any other activity (Muth 1961). This proposition implies that agents will not make persistent forecast errors. If their forecasts turn out to be wrong, agents will learn the reason for their errors and revise their methods of forecasting accordingly. Such an approach seems more reasonable than alternative approaches commonly used to model expectations, such as static expectations that simply extrapolate existing conditions, or adaptive expectations that have the property of yielding continuous forecast errors. Additionally, in contrast to the adaptive expectations approach that uses only past values of the variable about which expectations are to be formed, the rational expectations hypothesis also uses other relevant information.

The rational expectations model assumes that private agents form expectations about the rate of inflation based on their understanding of the economic model that generates the inflation rate, as well as on the policy rule followed by the monetary authorities.

In a model based on rationally formed expectations, Sargent and Wallace (1975) demonstrated that systemic monetary policy would be completely ineffective in influencing real variables. They argued that if the monetary authorities devised a monetary feedback rule, using optimal feedback techniques, according to which the authorities systematically altered the money supply to offset disturbances in real economic activity, then private decision-makers would learn the rule and incorporate it into their rational expectations. The thrust of this model—where deviations of output from its full employment (or natural) level can only be produced by an inflation forecast error— is that if expectations are formed rationally, the forecast error cannot be manipulated by systematic (and, therefore, anticipated) monetary or fiscal policy. Indeed, the only way output or unemployment can be altered from its natural rate is by an *unexpected* shock. However, unexpected shocks—monetary or other—have the negative attribute of increasing the level of uncertainty in the economy.

If a negatively sloping Phillips curve were observed, it might result from constant price expectations in a period with *ex post* fluctuations in actual inflation due to unanticipated random shocks that are negatively correlated with *ex post* fluctuations in measured unemployment (Begg 1982, p. 141). Lucas (1973) offered a variant explanation, in a world of rational expectations, for a negatively sloped short-run Phillips curve or, alternatively, a positively sloped short-run supply curve for output, which is determined by lagged output and the discrepancy between actual and expected inflation. Lucas assumed that the economy is characterized by uncertainty, and that competitive firms cannot readily discern whether a change in the price of their output reflects a change in the price level or a change in relative prices. He then demonstrated that other things equal, the greater the variance of the aggregate price level, owing to greater monetary variability, the more likely it is that firms will mistake a price level change for a change in relative prices. Expansion of output in response to an increase in the level of prices, holding relative prices constant, will ultimately lead to accumulation of inventory, cutbacks in output, layoffs, and more inelastic supply curves and also a more inelastic aggregate supply and Phillips curve. In addition, greater price level variability will be associated with greater resource misallocation because price level variability impairs the ability to perceive the information that prices convey in a market economy.

Brunner, Cukierman, and Meltzer (1980) perceive the problem of extracting the signal from prices somewhat differently from Lucas. For them, the distinction that needs to be made is not the sorting out of aggregate from relative price changes. It is rather the distinction between transitory and permanent price changes. Firms will wait to learn whether a change is permanent before reacting to it and, with great price variability, that process is made more difficult and prolonged than would otherwise be the case.

In any event, price variability reflecting discretionary money variability clearly has negative effects on the economy and reinforces the case for monetary stability. Moreover, the entire enterprise of selecting discretionary policies by simulation of econometric models has been challenged by Lucas (1976). His critique was based on the kinds of equations that are used in econometric models. These are reduced forms of effects on the economy of existing policy arrangements that incorporate the private sector's expectations of policy effects on economic variables. Were the authorities to change the policy rule, the public would adjust its expectations accordingly. Consequently, attempts to forecast the effects of alternative policies without accounting for changes in private agents' expectations are bound to lead to inappropriate policies.

Discretionary policy (defined as policy reacting to the current situation) based on optimal control techniques has been shown by Kydland and Prescott (1979) to be suboptimal and possibly destabilizing in a world of rational expectations. The policy chosen at each point in time may be the best, given the current situation. In the authors' terminology, the policy may be consistent, but it will be suboptimal because the policymaker has failed to take into account the optimizing rules of economic agents. The decisions of agents will change as they come to recognize the change in policy. The example Kydland and Prescott cite is that agents may expect tax rates to be lowered in recessions and increased in booms and make decisions in light of those expectations. Over successive periods, it is not optimal to continue with the initial policy because control theory is not the appropriate tool for dynamic economic planning. Current decisions of economic agents are affected by what they expect future policy to be. A government that attempted to reduce unemployment by increasing the money supply without attention to the rational inflation expectations of private agents would end up with a suboptimal mix of the natural rate of unemployment and positive inflation, despite the fact that it sought to maximize its "social welfare function" by combining the desirability of full employment and zero inflation. The authors conclude (1977, p. 487):

> The implication of this analysis is that, until we have . . . [a tested theory of economic fluctuations], active stabilization may very well be dangerous and it is best that it not be attempted. Reliance on policies such as a constant growth in the money supply and constant tax rates constitute a safe course of action. When we do have the prerequisite understanding of the business cycle, the implication of our analysis is that policymakers should follow rules rather than have discretion. The reason that they should not have discretion is not that they are stupid or evil but, rather, that discretion implies selecting the decision which is best, given the current situation. Such behavior either results in consistent but suboptimal planning or in economic instability.

Oversimplification by certain proponents of the rational expectations hypothesis should be noted. A number of factors could lead to nonneutral effects of anticipated monetary growth even in the presence of rational expectations. First, anticipated monetary growth can have effects on the natural rate of unemployment (output) through a real balance effect on the aggregate expenditure function, or by changing the steady-state capital-labor ratio and thus affecting the real rate of interest (Buiter 1980).

Second, if the assumption that both government and the private sector have equal access to information is violated when there is a rule for systematic monetary policy, then it is possible for the government to change its policy after the private sector has formed its expectations and thereby affect the inflation forecast error. As a result, output and unemployment can deviate from the natural rate. Such an outcome is also possible in cases where wages are determined by multi-period overlapping contracts (Fischer 1977). In that situation, even if private agents form their expectations rationally, the government can systematically affect output and employment between contract negotiating dates. Third, if the assumption of market clearing is abandoned, yet the assumption of rational expectations is maintained, then it is possible for output to be affected by stabilization policy. Explanations for price stickiness range from the Keynesian disequilibrium approach (Buiter 1980) to price-setting behavior in a world of high coordination costs (Cagan 1980).

Fourth, evidence of persistence—that unemployment does not rapidly disappear and bring the economy to full employment—or alternatively, the existence of serial correlation of output and employment over the business cycle, has been advanced as contradicting the rational expectations approach. On the other hand, McCallum (1980) explains persistence within the rational expectations context as reflecting real costs of adjusting the fixed capital stock and other factors of production. For Lucas (1975), persistence occurs because of information lags that prevent "even relevant past variables from becoming perfectly known" (p. 1114), and an accelerationist effect of physical capital. Finally, the rational expectations approach fails to explain how private agents learn from their forecast errors in forming rational expectations (De Canio 1979).

We now turn to the evidence for the rational expectations hypothesis. The evidence most generally cited is that by Barro (1977a, 1977b, 1981) and Barro and Rush (1980). Barro and Rush regressed the unemployment rate over the 1949–77 period on lagged values of a measure of unexpected monetary growth and of expected monetary growth. Expected monetary growth was estimated from a regression of current monetary growth on past monetary growth, the deviation of government spending from its trend, and past unemployment. Such a regression was designed to capture the monetary rule that economic agents perceived. The predicted values of the regression were employed to represent expected monetary growth, and the residuals were used to represent unexpected monetary growth.

Barro and Rush found most of the variation in unemployment was explained by unexpected monetary growth, and that expected monetary growth was not statistically significant. They concluded that expected monetary growth is neutral and that only unsystematic elements of monetary policy affect the unemployment rate—a finding that is supportive of the rational expectations hypothesis.

The evidence that Barro has presented—that only unexpected monetary growth explains variations in unemployment—has been challenged. Cagan (1980) argued, following a more traditional approach, that most variations in output and employment can be explained by deviations in money growth from a long-run trend, without invoking rational expectations. Sargent (1976) demonstrated that it is difficult to distinguish Barro's results from those produced by a more traditional approach because of the observational equivalence of natural and unnatural rate theories. For Sargent, the only way to test a refutable hypothesis is to be able to isolate periods involving a change in clear-cut policy rules. Gordon (1976a, 1976b, 1979) argues that, unless it can be shown that the full effect of a change in nominal income is absorbed by price change, the case for the neutrality hypothesis is not confirmed. In his view, to the extent that some of the effect of expected monetary growth is absorbed by output change, scope remains for stabilization policy. Mishkin (1982) also finds that anticipated movements in monetary growth have effects on output and unemployment that are larger than those of unanticipated movements, but his evidence confirms that expectations are rational.

The rational expectations approach appears to be firmly established, despite unresolved questions including those mentioned above. A clear implication of the literature is that active monetary intervention is likely to lead to large price level changes with little favorable effect on output or employment. Unpredictable policies are likely to increase the degree of uncertainty in the economy and enlarge the fluctuations around the natural rate. The aim of policy should therefore be to establish predictable monetary rules, preferably rules that are easily understood, with full consideration of all the relevant costs and benefits.

IV. The Case for a Legislated Rule

Modigliani's presidential address to the American Economic Association (1977) disputed monetarist views that (a) the economy is sufficiently shockproof that stabilization policies are not needed; (b) postwar fluctuations resulted from unstable monetary growth; (c) stabilization policies decreased rather than increased stability. He finds that "Up to 1974, these [stabilization] policies have helped to keep the economy reasonably stable by historical standards, even though one can certainly point to some occasional failures" (1977, p. 17). He attributes the serious deterioration in economic stability since 1973 to "the novel nature of the shocks that hit us, namely, supply shocks. Even the best possible aggregate demand management cannot offset such shocks without a lot of unemployment together with a lot of inflation. But, in addition, demand management was far from the best." The failure, he contends, was the result of ineffective use of stabilization policy "including too slavish adherence to the monetarists' contant money growth prescription."

Modigliani's defense of stabilization policies amounts to acknowledging specific failures while asserting overall success, except when exogenous supply shocks occur which "we had little experience or even an adequate conceptual framework to deal with" (1977, p. 17).

Table 1 shows the standard deviations of quarter-to-quarter deviations of a two-quarter moving average from a 20-quarter growth rate of M1. The standard deviations are a proxy for unexpected monetary change (shocks) that, according to both older and newer approaches,

TABLE 1

COMPARATIVE VARIABILITY OF MONETARY GROWTH AND RATES OF CHANGE OF REAL GNP, POSTWAR SUBPERIODS QUARTERLY, 1952I–1986II

	Standard Deviation of Quarter-to-Quarter Percentage Changes in:	
Period	Deviations from a 20-Quarter Moving Average of M1 of a 2-Quarter Moving Average (1)	Annualized Real Output Growth (2)
1952I–1960IV	1.79	4.54
1961I–1971II	1.74	3.49
1961I–1973III	1.67	3.56
1973IV–1979III	1.56	4.64
1979IV–1986II	3.02	4.49

Note: We are indebted to the division of research of the St. Louis Federal Reserve Bank for the data underlying col. 1.

should be associated with consequent effects on real output and, once fully anticipated, on prices. The table, therefore, also shows the standard deviation of quarter-to-quarter annualized real output growth rates for four postwar subperiods: 1952I to 1960IV; 1961I to 1971II (alternatively, 1973III); 1973IV to 1979III; and 1979IV to 1986II.

The variability of the (unexpected) money series declined moderately during the 1960s and until the quarter preceding the Nixon price controls or, alternatively, the quarter preceding the 1973 oil price shock. Over the same subperiods, real output variability also declined, but substantially more than the decline in money variability. In the subsequent subperiod, though money variability declined modestly, real output variability rose to a level exceeding the one prevailing in the initial subperiod.[2] In the final subperiod, money variability nearly doubled and output variability remained high but somewhat lower than in the preceding subperiod.

Modigliani's attribution of the serious deterioration of economic stability since 1973 to "too slavish adherence to the monetarists' constant money growth rule" is not apparent in Table 1. The inability of stabilization policy to cope with unexpected developments *supports* monetarist views. If policymakers are thought to have an informational advantage over private agents and so are able to reduce fluctuations of output around its natural rate, they must be able to make correct inferences about the precise character of current shocks. That does not seem to be the case.

Theory and evidence strongly suggest that a systematic monetary rule is superior to discretion. A fixed rule with no feedback from the current situation to policy instruments, a rule that is simple and preannounced, is the most favorable condition for stabilizing the economy. Any feedback rules that involve government manipulation of the private sector's forecast errors are doomed to failure. There is no information available to authorities that is not also available to the private sector.

A fixed, simple, preannounced rule can take a number of forms. For some who are opposed to discretionary policy, the preferred

[2]Paul Evans (1984) reports that, based on a modification of Barro's model, he finds "no evidence that money growth volatility affects output at all. In contrast, interest rate volatility is an important determinant of output" (p. 206). Evans's study deals with the level of output, whereas we report the variability of changes in output. Evans's work is also subject to McCallum's (1983) criticism that it is invalid to use money stock innovations to represent the surprise component of monetary policy actions since the Federal Reserve has relied on operating procedures that require manipulating the federal funds rate. Unsystematic monetary policy actions show up in interest rates in addition to or instead of the money stock. Interest rate innovations pick up the explanatory power lost by M1 innovations when the former variable is added to the system.

sytematic rule is the gold standard rule, for others, an interest rate or price rule. We do not examine the reason such rules have won support from their adherents. The rule we favor is a constant monetary growth rule. It satisfies the requirement for a systematic preannounced policy or regime that economic agents can incorporate in their expectations. It is a rule which can easily be implemented. The case for it, as stated initially by Friedman, is that economists lack adequate knowledge to conduct discretionary policy successfully. A monetary growth rule would obviate monetary policy mistakes. When physicians take the Hippocratic oath, they pledge not to do harm to their patients. Economists should take a similar oath with respect to the instruments that they may be in a position to administer.

The development of the rational expectations approach suggests that public response to stable monetary growth would contribute to the stabilization of the economy. Constant monetary growth will not make the business cycle obsolete. But avoidance of the mistakes of discretionary monetary policy will reduce the amplitude of fluctuations inevitable in a dynamic economy.

V. Divergent Views on a Constant Monetary Growth Rule

Economists who accept the primacy of monetary change in producing changes in economic activity do not all agree that the policy solution is to adopt a rule for constant monetary growth. We may distinguish the views of adherents of global monetarism, Austrian economics, and the new monetary economics.

Global monetarism emphasizes that the world economy is highly integrated with respect both to commodity and capital markets, international price and interest rate arbitrage serving to coordinate national economies. The appropriate unit of analysis, therefore, is not the individual national economy but rather the world. The elements of the doctrine were constructed for a world of fixed exchange rates where the domestic rate of inflation is determined exogenously by the world rate of inflation, and the domestic money stock is determined by the rate of growth of domestic nominal income, set by the world inflation rate. For such an approach, prescribing a rule for domestic monetary growth is pointless. Under a flexible rate regime, however, domestic monetary authorities can control their money supplies *if they choose*. Regardless of the exchange rate regime, global monetarism has not supported a monetary rule for a single nation.

Austrian economics acknowledges the role of monetary policy in producing inflation and shares the monetarist view that the result of monetary attempts to reduce unemployment below its natural level is accelerating inflation. The chief emphasis, however, is less on these propositions than on the distortions in the production process resulting from monetary expansion. Moreover, in Austrian economics, flexible exchange rates are not the path to domestic monetary control. Hayek, for example, favors fixed exchange rates as a constraint on the government's overexpansion of the domestic money supply. The preferred solution, however, is the abolition of central banks, and the establishment of a commodity money. Hayek recently has advocated the denationalization of money and giving private producers freedom to offer alternative kinds of money. The market would then choose the money that would prove to be stable. Hence no legislated rule would be required.

The new monetary economics enters under the free-market banner. In the system that we are familiar with, money is the product of pervasive government regulation. Had free-market policies prevailed for transactions services, economists of that persuasion argue, a more efficient banking system would have been created and velocity would have been much different. The new monetary economics therefore opposes a constant monetary growth rule on the ground that macroeconomic performance, under free-market provision of money, could be much better than a rule would have produced. Different schemes have been elaborated by members of this school to replace an inefficiently regulated money stock, but as Hall (1982, p. 1555) writes: "None of them would rely on the concept of a money stock or its stability relative to total income. Whether their macroeconomic performance would equal that of a simple money growth rule is still a matter of controversy."

Proposals to change utterly root and branch the existing monetary system strike us as ignoring the enormous attachment of the private sector to arrangements that have become customary. Imposing a system that appeals to visionaries as far more satisfactory than the one markets have adjusted to, given the existing network of regulations, is not the historical way in which alterations in the monetary system have occurred. A complete breakdown in existing arrangements as a result, say, of the catastrophe of hyperinflation would be a prerequisite to the adoption de novo of one of the schemes the new monetary economics espouses.

The new monetary economics, by proclaiming that results superior to those of a monetary growth rule are within reach, shares some of the confidence of interventionists. Advocates of a monetary growth rule are skeptical not only about demand management or fine-tuning by interventionists, but also about the prospects that new schemes for settling transactions can be as easily implemented as they can be devised.

Some observers predict that the deregulation process now under way will obscure the quality of moneyness of assets and hence render control by the central bank problematical. We regard this apocalyptic view as unduly alarmist. Not so long ago, it was commonly argued that payment of interest on demand deposits would mean the end of their use as transactions balances. That has not happened and we do not foresee radical changes on the horizon in the operation of the payments system. The alternatives are not the creation *de novo* of a set of monetary arrangements or the preservation unchanged of the existing set.

For all the talk of the adoption of monetarism by central banks, their performance gives little indication that they in fact have been influenced by the central message of the doctrine—monetary instability is a potent source of unstable economic performance. The wide swings that are observed even in a smoothed two-quarter moving average of the U.S. money growth rate from 1980 through the second quarter of 1982—supposedly the period of the Fed's "monetarist experiment"—and certainly in the following four years belie the notion that they represent monetarism.

A legislated rule has *never* been tried. It is a modest step towards restraining monetary authorities, but both theory and evidence suggest that it could be a giant step toward achieving economic stability.

References

Argy, Victor. "Rules, Discretion in Monetary Management, and Short-term Stability." *Journal of Money, Credit, and Banking* 3 (February 1971): 102–22.

Argy, Victor. "Monetary Stabilization and the Stabilization of Output in Selected Industrial Countries." Banca Nazionale del Lavoro, *Quarterly Review* 129 (June 1979): 155–66.

Barro, Robert J. "Unanticipated Money Growth and Unemployment in the United States." *American Economic Review* 67 (March 1977a): 101–15.

Barro, Robert J. "Long-term Contracting, Sticky Prices, and Monetary Policy." *Journal of Monetary Economics* 3 (July 1977b): 305–16.

Barro, Robert J. "The Equilibrium Approach to Business Cycles." In his *Expectations and Business Cycles.* New York: Academic Press, 1981.

Barro, Robert J., and Rush, Mark. "Unanticipated Money and Economic Activity." In *Rational Expectations and Economic Policy.* Edited by Stanley Fisher. Chicago: University of Chicago Press, 1980.

Begg, David K. H. *The Rational Expectations Revolution in Macroeconomics: Theories and Evidence.* Oxford: Philip Allan, 1982.

Bronfenbrenner, Martin. "Statistical Tests of Rival Monetary Rules: Quarterly Data Supplement." *Journal of Political Economy* 69 (December 1961): 621–25.

Brunner, Karl; Cukierman, Alex; and Meltzer, Allan H. "Stagflation, Persistent Unemployment and the Permanence of Economic Shocks." *Journal of Monetary Economics* 6 (October 1980): 467–92.

Buiter, Willem H. "Real Effects of Anticipated and Unanticipated Money: Some Problems of Estimation and Hypothesis Testing." *Journal of Monetary Economics* 11 (March 1983): 207–24.

Cagan, Phillip. "Reflections on Rational Expectations." *Journal of Money, Credit, and Banking* 12 (November 1980): 826–32.

De Canio, Stephen J. "Rational Expectations and Learning from Experience." *Quarterly Journal of Economics* 93 (February 1979): 47–57.

Evans, Paul. "The Effects on Output of Money Growth and Interest Rate Volatility in the United States." *Journal of Political Economy* 92 (April 1984): 204–21.

Fischer, Stanley. "Long-term Contracts, Rational Expectations and the Optimum Money Supply." *Journal of Political Economy* 85 (February 1977): 191–205.

Friedman, Milton. "A Monetary and Fiscal Framework for Economic Stability." *American Economic Review* 38 (June 1948): 245–64. Reprinted in *Essays in Positive Economics*. Chicago: University of Chicago Press, 1953.

Friedman, Milton "The Effects of a Full Employment Policy on Economic Stability: A Formal Analysis" (1951). Reprinted in *Essays in Positive Economics*. Chicago: University of Chicago Press, 1953.

Friedman, Milton. *A Program for Monetary Stability*. New York: Fordham University Press, 1960.

Friedman, Milton. "The Role of Monetary Policy." *American Economic Review* 58 (March 1968): 1–17.

Friedman, Milton, and Schwartz, Anna J. "Money and Business Cycles." *Review of Economics and Statistics* 45 (February 1963a, Supplement): 32–64. Reprinted in *The Optimum Quantity of Money*. Chicago: Aldine, 1969.

Friedman, Milton, and Schwartz, Anna J. *A Monetary History of the United States, 1867–1960*. Princeton: Princeton University Press, 1963b.

Gordon, Robert J. "Recent Developments in the Theory of Inflation and Unemployment." *Journal of Monetary Economics* 2 (April 1976a): 185–219.

Gordon, Robert J. "Can Econometric Policy Evaluation Be Salvaged?—A Comment." In *The Philips Curve and Labor Markets*. Edited by Karl Brunner and Allan H. Meltzer. Supplement 1 to the *Journal of Monetary Economics* 1 (1976b): 47–58.

Gordon, Robert J. "New Evidence That Fully Anticipated Monetary Changes Influence Real Output After All." *Journal of Political Economy* 90 (December 1982): 1087–1117.

Hall, Robert E. "Monetary Trends in the United States and the United Kingdom: A Review from the Perspective of New Developments in Monetary Economics." *Journal of Economic Literature* 20 (December 1982): 1552–56.

Hayek, Friedrich A. *Denationalisation of Money*. London: Institute of Economic Affairs, 1978.

Kochin, Levis. "Judging Monetary Policy." *Proceedings of Second West Coast Academic/Federal Reserve Economic Research Seminar.* Federal Reserve Bank of San Francisco, 1979.

Kydland, Finn E., and Prescott, Edward C. "Rules Rather Than Discretion: The Inconsistency of Optimal Plans." *Journal of Political Economy* 85 (June 1977): 473–91.

Lipsey, Richard G. "The Relation Between Unemployment and the Rate of Change of Money Wage Rates in the United Kingdom, 1862–1957: A Further Analysis." *Economica* 27 (February 1960): 1–31.

Lucas, Robert E. "Some International Evidence on Output-Inflation Trade-offs." *American Economic Review* 68 (June 1973): 326–34.

Lucas, Robert E. "An Equilibrium Model of the Business Cycle." *Journal of Political Economy* 83 (December 1975): 1113–44.

Lucas, Robert E. "Econometric Policy Evaluation: A Critique." In *The Phillips Curve and Labor Markets.* Edited by Karl Brunner and Allan H. Meltzer. Supplement 1 to the *Journal of Monetary Economics* 1 (1976): 19–46.

McCallum, Bennett T. "Rational Expectations and Macroeconomic Stabilization Policy." *Journal of Money, Credit, and Banking* 12 (November 1980): 716–46.

McCallum, Bennett T. "A Reconsideration of Sims' Evidence Concerning Monetarism." *Economic Letters* 13 (1983): 167–71.

Modigliani, Franco. "Some Empirical Tests of Monetary Management and Rules Versus Discretion." *Journal of Political Economy* 72 (June 1964): 211–45.

Modigliani, Franco. "The Monetarist Controversy or, Should We Forsake Stabilization Policies?" *American Economic Review* 67 (March 1977): 1–19.

Muth, John F. "Rational Expectations and the Theory of Price Movements." *Econometrica* 29 (July 1961): 315–35.

Phelps, Edmund S. "Money-Wage Dynamics and Labor Market Equilibrium." *Journal of Political Economy* 78 (July/August 1968): 678–711.

Phillips, A. W. "The Relation Between Unemployment and the Rate of Change of Money Wage Rates in the United Kingdom, 1861–1957." *Econometrica* 25 (November 1958): 283–99.

Poole, William. "The Relationship of Monetary Decelerations to Business Cycle Peaks: Another Look at the Evidence." *Journal of Finance* 30 (June 1975): 697–712.

Samuelson, Paul A., and Solow, Robert M. "Analytical Aspects of Anti-Inflation Policy." *American Economic Review* 50 (May 1960): 177–94.

Sargent, Thomas. "The Observational Equivalence of Natural and Unnatural Rate Theories of Macroeconomics." *Journal of Political Economy* 84 (August 1976): 631–40.

Sargent, Thomas, and Wallace, Neil. "Rational Expectations and the Theory of Economic Policy." *Journal of Monetary Economics* 2 (April 1976): 169–83.

Warburton, Clark. "Variations in Economic Growth and Banking in the United States from 1835 to 1885." *Journal of Economic History* 18 (June 1958): 283–97.

Warburton, Clark. "Monetary Disturbances and Business Fluctuations in Two Centuries of American History." In *In Search of a Monetary Constitution*, pp. 61–93. Edited by Leland B. Yeager. Cambridge, Mass.: Harvard University Press, 1962.

Warburton, Clark. "Four Statements." In *The Federal Reserve System After Fifty Years*, vol. 2, pp. 1314–42. Hearings before the Subcommittee on Domestic Finance of the Committee on Banking and Currency, House of Representatives, 88th Cong., 2nd sess. Washington, D.C.: Government Printing Office, 1964.

Warburton, Clark. *Depressions, Inflation, and Monetary Policy: Selected Papers, 1945–53*. Baltimore: The Johns Hopkins Press, 1966.

COMMENT

MONEY, MARKETS, AND STABILITY*
Gottfried Haberler

It is a great pleasure to comment on the excellent paper by Michael Bordo and Anna Schwartz. It covers a large area and a vast literature. I can touch only on some highlights.

Let me first mention areas of agreement. Surely money, monetary policy, and monetary mismanagement account for a very large part of economic instability. There has never been a significant inflation, prices rising say 4 or 5 percent for two or more years without a significant increase in the quantity of money, and practically all serious cyclical depressions have been due largely to monetary mismanagement.

The situation is a little different for mild recessions. The authors admit that when they say that the business cycle would still exist, even if the steady monetary growth rule which they recommend were strictly followed, it would presumably be a milder cycle.

The authors argue convincingly that fine-tuning will not work and they reject discretionary monetary and fiscal policies. I fully agree if by fine-tuning we mean an attempt to iron out by discretionary financial measures all ripples or minor recessions in economic activity. But I submit that discretionary measures cannot be ruled out altogether. Let me illustrate what I have in mind by the Great Depression of the 1930s.

In their "truly great book" *A Monetary History of the United States, 1867–1960* (if I may use the words of the eminent Keynesian, Sir Roy Harrod[1]), Milton Friedman and Anna Schwartz have demonstrated convincingly that the exceptional severity and length of the depression were due to errors of commission and omission of monetary policy—commission, deflationary measures taken during the depression (e.g., in 1931 after Britain dropped the gold standard

*Reprinted from *Cato Journal* 3 (Spring 1983): 83–91, with new title.

The author is Resident Scholar at the American Enterprise Institute and Professor Emeritus at Harvard University.

[1]See his review of *A Monetary History of the United States*, *The University of Chicago Law Review* 32 (Autumn 1964): 186–96.

which put pressure on the dollar)—and errors of omission, failure to stop the deflationary spiral by sufficiently large open market operations. Let me also mention that Sir Roy Harrod defended the Friedman-Schwartz view against the criticism of other Keynesians who argued that the disaster could not have been avoided by monetary measures. Sir Roy said, "Monetary policy has not been tried."

For example, Nicholas Kaldor argued that monetary expansion would merely have led to a decline in the velocity of circulation of money and not to an increase in the flow of spending.[2] He tried to support his theory by pointing to Canada where there was no collapse of the banking system, but a sharper decline in velocity of money than in the United States. He did *not* point out that Canada was forced to depress its economy to about the same level as in the United States, whatever its monetary policy, because the Canadian dollar was rigidly linked to the U.S. dollar by the gold standard.

The point I want to make is that if an economy has sunk into a severe recession or depression, either as a consequence of monetary mismanagement as in the 1930s, or possibly for some other reason, there can be made a strong case for discretionary expansionary action. As far as the 1930s are concerned, I would go one step further. I think Keynes was right at that time to ask for deficit spending. Monetary expansion alone surely would have eventually led to an increase in the flow of spending, but it would have taken a long time and in the process a large amount of liquidity would have been created which later would have caused inflationary troubles. Therefore, a strong case can be made for injecting money directly into the income stream by government deficit spending. I once heard Milton Friedman say on television that in circumstances such as in the 1930s government deficit spending can be recommended.

Let me mention that these monetary causes of the Great Depression have been widely stressed in the literature. For example, Joseph A. Schumpeter, whose theory of the business cycle was not a monetary one, said that the collapse of the U.S. banking system and the deflation involved "turned retreat into a rout"; what otherwise would have been a recession became a catastrophic depression.[3]

[2]Nicholas (Lord) Kaldor, "The New Monetarism" *Lloyds Bank Review* 97 (July 1970). He argued that, since in July 1932 the monetary base (what Friedman calls high-powered money) was 10 percent higher than it was in July 1929, the monetary explanation of the extraordinary severity of the depression is invalid. He evidently thinks that the monetary authorities had done their duty by keeping the monetary base barely stable in the face of a massive decline of the money supply as a consequence of the stock exchange crash and several waves of bank failures.

[3]See *Essays of J. A. Schumpeter*, Richard Y. Clemence, ed. (Cambridge, Mass.: Addison-Wesley Press, 1951), p. 214.

The second section of the Bordo-Schwartz paper deals with what the authors call the "Keynesian Riposte and Return Sally." The Keynesian reposte was the Tinbergen-Theil theory of economic policy and the Phillips curve. I shall not say much about these two theories. It would mean flogging a dead horse.

Let me make only two brief remarks. First, that there is no stable tradeoff between inflation and unemployment has been known for a long time. Long before Phillips, the Harvard economist Sumner Slichter argued that the Federal Reserve should not try to stabilize the price level but should stabilize the inflation rate at, say, 5 percent. The answer was that you cannot stabilize a significant rate of inflation or, more precisely, that a stable rate of inflation would soon lose its power to contain unemployment. Only an unanticipated *increase* of inflation could temporarily reduce unemployment.

The second remark is that one should not call the Phillips theory the Keynesian reply to Friedman's criticism of fine-tuning. True, some Keynesians embraced it, notably Samuelson and Solow. But Keynes himself would surely have rejected it if he had been alive. He always was concerned with inflation both before and after the *General Theory*. For example, in 1937, one year after the publication of the *General Theory*, he wrote in three famous articles in *The Times* that inflation had again become a serious problem and that policy should be changed accordingly.[4] He did so despite the fact that the rate of inflation at that time was not particularly high by post-World War II standards and unemployment was still about 10 percent. The fact is that he changed his position so quickly that many of his followers could not keep pace with him.

The key concept in Friedman's reply to the Keynesian criticism is "the natural rate of unemployment," which in the authors' words is "determined by the intersection of the demand and supply curves of labor." The natural rate of unemployment is a rather elusive concept. Nobody really knows for sure what the natural rate of unemployment

[4]It can be argued that Keynes consistently was concerned about inflation, although in the 1930s, when he wrote *The General Theory*, he rightly concentrated his fire on deflation. Keynes's three articles in *The Times* are reprinted in T. W. Hutchison, *Keynes Versus the Keynesians? An Essay on the Thinking of J. M. Keynes and the Accuracy of Its Interpretation by His Followers* (London: Institute of Economic Affairs, 1977). For details see also T. W. Hutchison, *On Revolution and Progress in Economic Knowledge* (Cambridge: Cambridge University Press, 1978), especially chap. 6, "Demythologizing the Keynesian Revolution," pp. 175–99. In a letter to *The Times* (July 28, 1933) Keynes went out of his way to emphasize his agreement with Pigou on policy. (See T. W. Hutchison, "The Keynesian Revolution," p. 187.) For Keynes's view on inflation see Thomas M. Humphrey, "Keynes on Inflation," Federal Reserve Bank of Richmond *Economic Review* 67 (January/February 1981): 3–13.

is at any one time. This plays into the hands of the monetarist policy prescription. Since we do not know at any time what the natural rate of unemployment is, it makes no sense to say that the actual rate of unemployment should be pushed to the natural rate by discretionary monetary or fiscal measures.

There is no time to go into details.[5] All I can do is to indicate very briefly the reasons for my doubts about the usefulness of the concept.

To say that the wage is determined by demand and supply of labor implies that there is perfect competition in the labor market. The theory that unemployment is compatible with perfect competition has been brought out very clearly in an important paper by Karl Brunner, Alex Cuikerman, and Allan Meltzer[6] which has attracted much attention. The authors insist that *persistent* unemployment can and does occur in economies where "all markets instantaneously clear," that is to say, under perfect competition. That seems to contradict one of the most basic principles of economics. If supply of labor exceeds demand, the price, the wage, should fall and equilibrium with full employment be restored.

The solution of the puzzle is that the authors have a rather odd definition of unemployment. They distinguish between positive and negative unemployment. Negative unemployment is what usually is called over-full employment; for example, people working longer hours than they really want. This is described as the "substitution of future leisure for present leisure." By the same logic positive unemployment has to be defined as the "substitution of present leisure for future leisure."

To say that the unemployed choose leisure makes it quite clear that the authors really speak of spurious, voluntary unemployment. But the indispensable distinction between voluntary and involuntary unemployment is alien to this school of thought. That the words

[5]I discussed these problems in greater detail in my book *Economic Growth and Stability: An Analysis of Economic Change and Policies* (Los Angeles: Nash Publishing, 1974). See also my paper "The Economic Malaise of the 1980's: A Positive Program for a Benevolent and Enlightened Dictator," *Contemporary Economic Problems 1981–82* (Washington, D.C.: American Enterprise Institute), and my paper prepared for the Accademia Nazionale dei Lincei, Rome, on the occasion of the Antonio Feltrinelli Prize, 1980, "The World Economy, Macroeconomic Theory and Policy—Sixty Years of Profound Change," to be published by the American Enterprise Institute, Washington, D.C., 1983.

[6]Karl Brunner, Alex Cukierman, and Allan Meltzer, "Stagflation, Persistent Unemployment and the Permanence of Economic Shocks," *Journal of Monetary Economics* 6 (October 1980): 467–92.

come from Keynes's *General Theory* has probably made the distinction suspect.

Actually, the distinction has often been made, though using other words, in serious discussions of the unemployment problem, both theoretical and empirical. An excellent discussion can be found, for example, in Pigou's *Theory of Unemployment* (London, 1930) and compilers of unemployment figures have to struggle to prevent voluntary unemployment from contaminating their statistics, no doubt without complete success. The published unemployment figures surely contain significant numbers of spurious, voluntary unemployment; high unemployment benefits and welfare payments partly account for that.

Let me elaborate a little, for the wage problem is of paramount importance. Consider the case of the U.S. steel or auto industry. Wages in those industries are more than 50 percent higher than the U.S. average, and unemployment is very high. Does it make sense to say that the unemployed steel or auto worker, because of a "forecasting error," chooses leisure? One could perhaps say that from the standpoint of the *union* the unemployment is voluntary, that the union bosses are willing to pay the price of high unemployment to keep the wage level high. But for the unemployed steel and auto workers the situation is quite different. They surely would be happy to work at the ruling wage or even a slightly lower one, if jobs were available.

To my mind the plain fact is that wages have become very rigid even in non-union industries. I am fond of quoting Frank H. Knight, who like Henry Simons, Jacob Viner, and other members of the older generation of the Chicago school, did not ignore or minimize the great importance of the growing rigidity of wages and prices for the smooth working of the monetary system. Knight wrote, "In a free market these differential changes [between prices of 'consumption goods' and 'capital goods' on the one hand, and the prices of 'productive services, especially wages,' on the other hand] would be temporary, but even then might be serious, and with important markets [especially the labor market] as unfree as they actually are, the results take on the proportion of a disaster."[7] Knight wrote with the deflation of the 1930s in mind, but what he says about wage and price rigidity applies equally to the case of disinflation and recession.

[7]Frank H. Knight, "The Business Cycle, Interest and Money," *Review of Economic Statistics* 23 (May 1941). Reprinted in Frank H. Knight's *On the History and Methods of Economics* (Chicago: University of Chicago Press, 1956), p. 224. See also p. 211: "Wages are notoriously sticky, especially with respect to any downward change of the hourly wage rates."

Since then the situation has become much worse. Government policies, generous unemployment benefits, welfare payments, minimum wages, etc., have, of course, greatly contributed to the rigidity of wages. Needless to add that the labor unions are not the only culprits. Other pressure groups, such as organized agriculture, with the help of governments, keep prices of their products high and rigid, causing a drop in output and employment, or alternatively causing labor to be used to produce huge unsalable surplus stocks, held by the government at the taxpayer's expense.

In recent years more and more economists have come to the conclusion that a decisive recovery from the worldwide recession requires a reduction of the level of real wages. Two years ago a large group of prominent German economists, several of them of monetarist persuasion, urged a wage freeze to let inflation bring down the real wage. Recently *The Economist*, a stronghold of Keynesianism, in two articles recommended a wage reduction—a recommendation which shocked many of its readers.[8] It might be mentioned that this recommendation is entirely in line with what Keynes taught. In *The General Theory* Keynes accepted the classical proposition that marginal productivity of labor declines when more labor is employed and that therefore the real wage has to decline. The trouble is that after many years of inflation the Keynesian policy to bring the real wage down by inflation does not work so well any more. Widespread indexation of wages and other incomes and inflationary expectations have made the Keynesian method to reduce real wages increasingly ineffective.

Herbert Giersch has argued in several important papers that all industrial countries suffer from excessively high real wages and too low profits. He thinks it will take several years to bring about the necessary adjustment in the income distribution.[9]

I find myself in substantial agreement with what the authors say about the rational expectations theory. The basic idea that people on the whole do not simply extrapolate the current situation or the recent trend but try to form a rational judgment of how the situation is likely to develop, including the actions of the policymakers, is undoubtedly correct. This fits in very well with the monetarist prescription of steady monetary growth.

But the rational expectations theorists often spoil their case by overstatements, by assuming that people on the whole reach the

[8]"Work on a Pay Cut," *The Economist*, London, November 27, 1982, pp. 11–12, and "Wage Cuts," *The Economist*, London, December 18, 1982, pp. 14–15.

[9]See Herbert Giersch, "Prospects for the World Economy," *Skandinaviska Enskilda Banken Quarterly Review*, Stockholm, 1982, pp. 104–10.

same, correct conclusion about future developments, including the future course of monetary and fiscal policy.

In the final section of their paper the authors critically examine the views of three groups of economists who accept the proposition that "monetary change" is of primary importance for changes in economic activity, but reject the rule of steady monetary growth.

The first group is the "global monetarists," the second the proponents of "Austrian economics," and the third the "new monetarists."

The authors do not say who the global monetarists are, but they seem to have advocates of the gold standard in mind. Under the gold standard there is indeed no room for the rule of steady monetary growth. The exchange rates are fixed and monetary growth is exogenously determined. The authors are right that all this is different under floating. If there were time I would say something on the recent criticism of floating.

Let me mention, however, that I can think of only one well-known economist who is not an advocate of gold who can be called a global monetarist. Ronald McKinnon argued recently that for the United States the flow of spending, etc., is better explained by changes in the world money supply than by the changes in the U.S. money supply. But his statistics have been convincingly challenged by Henry Goldstein.[10]

One more remark: It should not be forgotten that for the numerous countries that peg their currency to the dollar, the deutsche mark or some other currency or basket of currencies, the rule of steady monetary growth obviously is not applicable. An example: The Austrian schilling is pegged to the deutsche mark, and the Austrian National Bank, unlike the German or Swiss banks, does not set monetary growth targets. This has been interpreted to mean that Austria follows a Keynesian rather than a monetarist policy. As I have explained elsewhere, the correct interpretation is that the German Bundesbank provides the monetarist basis for Austria.[11]

The term "Austrian economics" is not easy to define. Professor Machlup has tried to clarify the problem in an excellent article in the *New Encyclopedia of the Social Sciences*. As far as money is concerned, the older members of the Austrian school, including Ludwig von Mises, were staunch supporters of the gold standard. This is also

[10]Henry Goldstein, "A Critical Appraisal of McKinnon's World Money Supply Hypothesis," Federal Reserve Bank of Chicago, November 1982 (Mimeographed).
[11]See my paper on "Austria's Economic Development After the Two World Wars: A Mirror Picture of the World Economy," in *The Political Economy of Austria* (Washington, D.C.: American Enterprise Institute, 1981) and "Austro-Keynesianism or Austro-Monetarism," pp. 67–69.

true of the so-called Neo-Austrian school that flourishes at New York University. The members of this school are largely disciples and followers of Mises. (I might mention that the only real Austrian at New York University, Fritz Machlup, is not a member of the Neo-Austrian school.)

In his earlier writings Hayek supported the gold standard and argued that from the theoretical standpoint the ideal rule would be to keep the quantity of money constant.

I don't know whether he still believes that. But his latest radical proposal to get the government entirely out of the business of money creation, to eliminate central banks, to "denationalize" money, should be regarded as a counsel of despair, that the modern democratic government cannot be entrusted with such a complicated task as that of regulating the money supply in an acceptable way. He therefore wants to turn over the creation of money to the forces of free markets. Banks should be free to create money, and the forces of free competition will lead to the survival of the fittest; that is to say, those banks that issue the stablest money will survive.

This sounds rather strange to put it mildly. I still think that Bagehot was right when he said that "money cannot manage itself."

I agree with the authors that Hayek's proposal, as well as similar proposals of the new monetarists, to "change utterly root and branch the existing monetary system ignores the enormous attachment of the private sector to arrangements that have become customary." I would add that these proposals also ignore the enormous importance of having a common unit of account and medium of exchange. If the moneys issued by different banks competed freely in the market, the result would be either the emergence of a private monopoly or oligopoly of money creation, or the circulation, side by side, of several kinds of money with fluctuating exchange rates between them. Either one of these two outcomes would be intolerable. The immediate result would be to bring the government back into the business of money creation.

I therefore agree with the authors that a steady monetary growth rule is the best policy, but I hope they will agree that discretionary measures cannot be ruled out altogether. In addition to the situations mentioned earlier, there is the fact that the steady rate of growth of the money supply will have to be changed from time to time. The rate of monetary growth cannot remain unchanged for long periods irrespective of institutional changes in the monetary area and surrounding conditions. A change of the growth rate is an act of discretion. I conclude that the present practice of many central banks to have narrow target ranges rather than a single monetary growth target is a reasonable compromise.

PART II

CONSTITUTIONAL MONETARY REFORM

5

THE IMPLEMENTATION AND MAINTENANCE OF A MONETARY CONSTITUTION*
Peter Bernholz

The Inflationary Bias of Government and Problems of Monetary Constitutions

The present age of discretionary monetary policies, which began in 1914, has turned out to be an age of permanent inflation. Inflation rates have ranged from low and moderate to hyperinflationary, but have scarcely anywhere and mainly only during the Great Depression been absent. It is true that countries with rather independent central banks have enjoyed lower rates of inflation (Parkin and Bade 1978), but the long-term effects in those countries still have been substantial.

This development stands in strong contrast to what prevailed before 1914, when sound monetary constitutions provided an anchor for the value of money, using either pure gold or silver standards (see Table 1). An inflationary bias, however, is not the only characteristic by which different monetary constitutions can and should be judged. The variance of such real factors as unemployment, business activity, or real interest rates may well be as important. And it is possible that in some countries these variances were higher under the gold standard than under the present discretionary system (Bernholz 1983; Meltzer 1986). Nevertheless, many economists are now convinced that to eliminate permanent inflation we have to return to a monetary constitution that binds the hands of government and the central bank.

Proposals for a sound monetary constitution are wide-ranging. They include proposals for stabilizing the monetary unit in terms of a price index (Fisher 1912; Simons 1948), constraining the issue of fiat money by a constitutional growth rule (Friedman 1968), introducing a com-

---

*Reprinted from *Cato Journal* 6 (Fall 1986): 477–511.
The author is Professor of Economics at the University of Basle.

CONSTITUTIONAL MONETARY REFORM

TABLE 1
PRICE-LEVEL CHANGES IN SELECTED COUNTRIES, 1750–1980

Wholesale Price Index

Year	Great Britain	Germany	France	Switzerland	United States
1750	107.95	—	—	—	—
1790	—	—	—	—	100
1792	100	100	100[d]	—	—
1800	171.5	173.1	100	—	143
1810	173.9	169.2	140.7	—	146
1820	130.7	115.4	77.8[e]	—	118
1830	107.4	100	67.4	—	101
1840	116.5	102.6	69.1	—	106
1850	83.5	91.0	95.9	—	93
1860	112.5[a]	120.5	124.4	—	103
1870	109.6	118.0	114.9	—	150
1880	107.6	111.5	103.7	—	111
1890	86.3	110.9	86.4	—	91
1900	83.4	115.4	85.5	—	91
1910	90.2	119.2	93.3	—	115
1913	—	134.6	100.2	—	113
1914	97.9	—	101.9	134.6[f]	111

1921	195.8	2,318.1	341.8	263.6	159
1930	119.7	167.7[b]	521.7	168.8	141
1938	121.0	133.4	617.6	144.1	128
1950	313.4	244.1[c]	12,225	295.6	258
1960	423.1	293.7	20,376	311.0	299
1970	566.5	325.3	27,271	378.4	348
1980	2,136.8	534.9	59,305	528.3	739

Period	Average Annual Rate of Inflation (%)				
1750–1914	-.0006	—	—	—	—
1790–1914	—	—	—	—	0.08
1792–1913/14	-.0002	.25	.00009[g]	—	—
1890/92–1914	.53	—	.69	—	0.83
1914–50	4.58	—	20.22	3.07	2.37
1950–80	6.61	2.65	5.41	1.95	3.57
1970–80	14.2	5.1	8.08	3.39	7.82

[a]The index for 1860 has been calculated by using the change of the German index from 1850–51, since the base of the British index has been changed for that year.
[b]After devaluation 1:10[12] in 1923.
[c]After devaluation 1:10 in 1948.
[d]Index for 1796.
[e]The index for 1820 has been calculated by using the change of the German index from 1819–20, since the base of the French index has been changed for that year.
[f]The index number for 1914 set equal to that of Germany.
[g]Average annual inflation rate for 1798–1914.
SOURCES: Mitchell (1976, pp. 735–47); U.S. Dept. of Commerce (1975, Part 1, pp. 199–202); Statistisches Bundesamt (1981, pp. 704–707).

85

modity money (Yeager 1962), and instituting free banking with no governmental control (Hayek 1976). No agreement thus exists on the type of sound monetary constitution to be introduced. But as Geoffrey Brennan and James Buchanan (1981, p. 64) have emphasized: "The proponents of free market money, competitive monies, commodity money, or rule-constrained fiat issue all agree on the desirability, necessity, acceptability of some monetary constitution."

My discussion (Bernholz 1983) of the political and economic reasons for the inflationary bias of unrestrained government shows that this bias can only be contained for an extended period by adequate monetary constitutions.[1] The idea that sound monetary constitutions are necessary to limit the inflationary tendencies of unfettered government dates to at least 1800, and has been favored by many economists. To quote from Ludwig von Mises (1912, p. 288):

> As soon as only the principle has been accepted that the state is allowed and has to influence the value of money, be it even only to guarantee its internal stability, then the danger of mistakes and exaggerations again at once emerges.
>
> These possibilities and the memories of the financial and inflationary experiments of the recent past have pushed into the background the unrealizable ideal of a money with an unchangeable intrinsic value as compared to the postulate: that at least the state should refrain from influencing in any way the intrinsic value of money [my translation].

Even though the reasons for the inflationary bias of central banks and governments and the possible alternatives restricting them by sound monetary constitutions have been widely discussed by economists, little attention has been paid to an equally important problem. In particular, the problem of implementing and maintaining a sound monetary constitution, given the political forces working in favor of inflation. This paper, therefore, aims to treat the problem of how to introduce and to maintain a sound monetary constitution and to give some preliminary answers. Possible solutions to this problem may also bear on which monetary constitution to select. For example, a particular constitution may be judged excellent for its consistency and potential to prevent inflation and reduce the variance of real variables of the system, but if it cannot be introduced or maintained, then a more limited but still satisfactory alternative must be substituted.

---

[1]See Frey and Schneider (1981) and Schmidt (1983) for the behavior patterns of independent central banks.

Returning to a Sound Monetary Constitution: Historical Patterns

Four distinct patterns emerge when looking for historical patterns of the introduction of sound monetary constitutions. These patterns can be categorized as follows: (1) the return to a stable monetary constitution following hyperinflation; (2) the restoration of a sound monetary constitution at the old (gold or silver) parity following periods of war, during which convertibility has been abolished; (3) the introduction or reintroduction of a sound monetary constitution at a lower parity following moderate inflation; and (4) the introduction of stable monetary systems occasioned by the example of such constitutions in other countries.

For the first two categories, there are certain public choice mechanisms that facilitate a transition to a sound monetary constitution. These will be discussed in the remainder of this section. In the following section, I focus on the third category, which is the most puzzling from a public choice perspective. The fourth category is not considered in this paper.

Restoration Following Hyperinflation

A return to sound monetary conditions is inescapable after a system has entered hyperinflation. Hyperinflation has to end in collapse and, consequently, either a reform or the replacement of the current money by commodity or foreign money has to take place. In organized modern states the reform alternative has usually been chosen.

It is well known that during a hyperinflation and even during an advanced inflation individuals reduce their real cash balances and no longer use money as a unit of account. The declining real stock of money leads to a liquidity crunch and reinforces the replacement of the national currency by foreign currencies and other stores of value. As a consequence, the government obtains fewer and fewer resources from inflating the money supply, while normal tax revenues decrease because of the misallocation of resources brought about by inflation and the lag in collecting and spending taxes. The fact that people have now learned about inflation checks any expansionary effect of increasing rates of inflation on the demand for labor. On the contrary, the disorganization and misallocation of resources leads to rising unemployment.

Given this situation, the governing party(ies) or the opposition can gain the support of a broad majority of voters by introducing a currency reform. At this juncture, faith in the government and the monetary authorities is absent. Thus the introduction of a new monetary constitution, which at least appears to be a reliable safeguard against further inflation, is inescapable. Otherwise the reform will falter, as in the cases of the replacement of the assignats by the mandats in France or the Chinese currency reform of 1948 (see Table 2).

Restoration Following War

Turning to the second category—the restoration of the old parity after wars before or during which convertibility had been abolished—the question arises as to what political forces allow a return to a sound monetary constitution (usually to the gold or silver standard). The most important factor has been the perception that the war period was extraordinary and that with its end everything, including the currency and thus the monetary constitution, should return to normality. Obviously politicians responded to this widely shared feeling. National prestige also has played a part in resurrecting the old system and parity. A world power like Great Britain would have lost status had it not returned to the prewar parity after the Napoleonic wars and after World War I. Finally, for a world financial center like London, the absolute trustworthiness of a stable currency employed in worldwide contracts was essential. Competition with the emerging financial center of New York was also an important consideration after World War I (Kindleberger 1984, ch. 18).

Some political forces opposed the return to the old system and to prewar parity. Those dependent on export and import-competing industries were mostly against the deflation and the unfavorable exchange rates necessitated by the reform. The coal strike of 1925 and the general strike of 1926 in Great Britain show that forces are emboldened by the recession or depression that paves the way to the old parity. It is thus not surprising that David Ricardo and John Maynard Keynes favored the introduction of a lower parity (Ricardo at least under certain conditions). In contrast to Ricardo, Keynes preferred the replacement of the gold standard by a more discretionary system (Silberman 1924, pp. 437–38; Kindleberger 1984, pp. 337–42).

Since the strength of the social and political forces opposing reform is related to the necessary degree of disinflation, a return to the old parity is possible only if the devaluation of the currency and the rise in the price level are not far out of line with the cost and price levels of the main trading partners who have preserved or reintroduced the stable monetary constitution and the old parity. This view is confirmed by the League of Nations (1946, p. 92) report on the monetary experience of various countries following World War I:

TABLE 2
CASES OF HYPERINFLATION AND STABILIZATION

Country	Inflation Period	Base Period	Increase over Base Period (multiple)		Highest Velocity of Circulation of Money	New to Old Currency Units (conversion factor)
			Money Stock	Price Level or Exchange Rate[a]		
Germany	1914–23	Jan. 1914	319.2×10^8 (Nov. 1923)	$7{,}330 \times 10^8$ (Nov. 1923)	22.96	1: (1×10^{12})
Hungary	1914–24	Dec. 1920	229.12 (July 1924)	488.61 (July 1924)	1.91	1: (15×10^3)
Hungary	1945–46	Dec. 1945	226.03×10^{11} (July 1946)	702.28×10^{22} (July 1946)	310.71×10^9	1: (828×10^{27})
Austria	1914–22	July 1914	2,526.24 (Aug. 1922)	5,932 (Aug. 1922)	2.35	1: (15×10^3)
Poland	1914–Jan. 1924	July 1919	60.05×10^3 (Dec. 1923)	264.08×10^3 (Dec. 1923)	4.40[b]	1: (1.8×10^6)
China	1937–May 1949	Sept. 1945	302×10^6 (May 1949)	105×10^9 (May 1949)	347.68	1948, currency reform faltered; 1949, communist take-over.
France	1789–Mar. 1796	1790	89.49 (Mar. 1796)	255.3 (Mar. 1796)	2.85[b]	1795, currency reform[c] faltered; return to gold standard.

[a]Exchange rate against U.S. dollar for Poland and against Dutch guilder for France.
[b]Calculated using exchange rate.
[c] A new money (mandats) was introduced in 1795.

Of the six countries which ultimately stabilized their currencies at the pre-war gold parity, five, namely Sweden, Norway, Denmark, the Netherlands and Switzerland, were neutral during the war and had been spared such fundamental dislocations of their national economies and finances as were experienced by most of the belligerent countries. All of them, including the United Kingdom, were countries whose currencies had not depreciated by more than one-half in relation to the dollar.

As the maxima of relative price indices show (Table 3), the countries with only relatively low maximal indices were the ones that did return to their prewar parities (cf. Table 4).

Economic and Political Characteristics of Moderate Inflation and Stabilization

All the cases belonging to the third category exhibit moderate inflation before the reintroduction of a sound monetary constitution. In contrast to the second category, however, some cases were not

TABLE 3

CASES OF MODERATE INFLATION AND STABILIZATION AT THE PREWAR PARITY

Country	Period of Inflation before Stabilization	Maximum of Domestic over Foreign Price Level[a]	Year of Maximum
Sweden	1750–1772	200[b]	1764
Great Britain	1797–1823	143[c]	1813
United States	1861–1879	174[b]	1864
Great Britain	1914–1925	129	1921
Netherlands	1914–1924	233	1918
		160[d]	1919
Sweden	1914–1922	141	1921
Switzerland	1914–1924	135	1919
Norway	1914–1928	165	1921
Denmark	1914–1926	139	1921

[a]Normal = 100 for base year.
[b]Index for domestic price level only.
[c]Wholesale price indices.
[d]The relative cost of living index seems to be rather high for 1918; hence, the highest value for the years after World War I (up to 1924) has also been given.
SOURCES: Table 1 and Appendix Tables A1–A6; Bernholz (1982).

connected with wars and all of them restored a lower parity than the old one. These two facts are not unconnected. In the absence of an earlier war, no perceived necessity was felt to return to normalcy after an extraordinary period and to restore national prestige to its former status. Given these facts, why has it been possible to reintroduce sound monetary constitutions after moderate inflation not connected with wars? Why could stable monetary constitutions with a lower than the old prewar parity be introduced, given the fact that a restoration of the old parity was politically not possible?

The answer is that the same political forces that opposed a return to prewar parity in cases of the second category favored a restoration of a sound monetary constitution in cases of the third category. And in those third-category cases connected with wars, political forces were strong enough to prevent a return to the old parity because inflation had risen to such levels that a drastic disinflation would have been required. Indeed, Table 4 shows that the relative cost of living index for third-category cases moved to higher levels in the case of war-connected inflations than for second-category cases (cf. Table 3). To understand the political forces leading to a sound monetary constitution in cases of the third category, it is necessary initially to discuss the economic and political characteristics connected with moderate inflations and their stabilization.

If, after a long period of monetary stability, a country enters a path of moderate inflation, its initial impact is on demand in goods and labor markets, in the form of increasing incomes and perhaps, through some early bottlenecks in one or the other sector of the economy, a few rising prices. But no general rise of the price level is perceived or expected in this early stage of moderate inflation. Consequently, demands for compensating wage increases are slow to come. All these facts are usually reflected in the statistical observation that the price level is increasing less strongly than the nominal stock of money, if there has been no prior inflationary experience in the country during the last generation (cf. Appendix Tables A2, A4–A6).

Whereas domestic prices and wages react slowly in the early years of a new and moderate inflation, foreign exchange rates move up more rapidly and strongly, even if they usually first lag the movement of the money stock. Exchange markets are better organized and market participants are usually better informed about changes affecting the whole economy. It follows that the beginning of a moderate inflation (if it is relatively higher than that of the trading partners) leads to an undervaluation of the currency compared to other currencies. Consequently, export industries benefit from prices (expressed in domestic currency) that have increased more strongly than the

TABLE 4
CASES OF MODERATE INFLATION AND STABILIZATION AT A LOWER PARITY

Country	Period of Inflation before Stabilization	Maximum of Domestic over Foreign Price Level[a]	Year of Maximum
Netherlands	1864–1875. No real inflation. Fall of silver price leads to abandonment of silver standard (1873) and adoption of gold standard (1875).	103.58[b]	1873
Austria-Hungary	1864–1896. No real inflation. Fall of silver price leads to denial of private rights to demand minted silver coins at parity (1879) and to adoption of gold standard (1892/96).	130[c] 121[d] 144[e]	1887 1890 1896
Argentina	1884–1899	255[f] 161[g]	1891 1896
Czechoslovakia	1914–1927	818	1921

France	1914–1928	290	1916
Belgium	1914–1927	459	1927
Poland	1914/1924/–1927. Stabilization after hyperinflation (1924), and second stabilization after moderate inflation (1926).	235.10	Dec. 1924

[a]Normal = 100 for base year.
[b]Price of silver in London in terms of gold. This price fell further after 1873 (see Appendix Table A1), so fears of future devaluation and inflation were justified had the Netherlands remained on a silver standard.
[c]Maximum of relative prices until 1892, the year of the currency reform (see Appendix Table A1).
[d]Lowest relative price between 1892 and 1896.
[e]Maximum for 1864–1904 period (see Appendix Table A1). In 1896 the new gold parity became effective in setting a lower limit to the value of the Austrian guilder.
[f]Index for domestic price level only, as measured by export price index (see Appendix Table A2).
[g]Index for domestic price level only, as measured by Wage Index (see Appendix Table A2).
SOURCES: Table 1 and Appendix Table A1–A6; Bernholz (1982).

prices of most of their inputs. Similarly, import-competing sectors of the economy enjoy better competitive positions in domestic markets than before the inflation. On the other hand, the stronger rise of import prices than of the prices of goods produced at home leads to a positive feedback effect on inflation, a kind of "imported inflation." These relationships are rather long lasting, as can be seen from Figures 1 and 2 and Appendix Tables A2, A4–A6. Moreover, they seem to occur in most historical cases. The same is true for the qualitative characteristics associated with stabilizing moderate inflations relative to important trading partners.[2]

FIGURE 1
INDICES OF MONEY SUPPLY, PRICES, AND EXCHANGE RATES IN SWEDEN, 1755–68

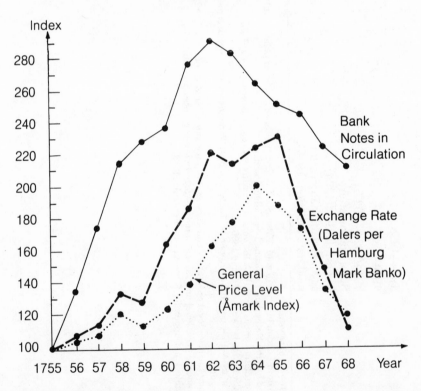

SOURCE: Eagley (1971, pp. 115–17).

[2]For a fuller description of these qualitative characteristics and other historical evidence for 17 cases see Bernholz (1982) and Bernholz, Gärtner, and Heri (1985). The latter article also presents a model that attempts to explain these characteristics.

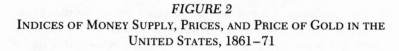

FIGURE 2
INDICES OF MONEY SUPPLY, PRICES, AND PRICE OF GOLD IN THE
UNITED STATES, 1861–71

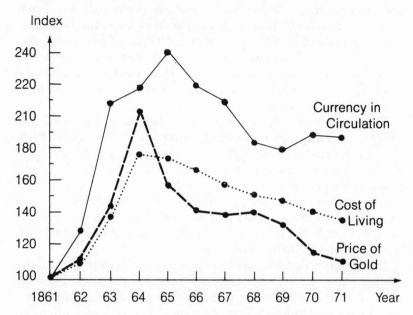

SOURCES: For money-supply and cost-of-living indices, U.S. Dept. of Commerce
(1975, Series X, Part 2, p. 993, and Series E, Part 1, p. 212); for gold-price index,
Mitchell (1908, Table 1, p. 4).

Stabilizing inflation relative to another country requires reducing
the growth of the domestic money stock, at least compared with that
of any given trading partner. Such a development took place in all
cases shown in Figures 1 and 2 and Appendix Table A2. The respective reference countries were either on a pure gold standard or the
gold premium itself was used to measure the movement of the exchange
rate. Also, in the cases shown in Appendix Tables A4 and A6, the
indices for the ratios of the money stocks fell, or at least did not
increase, for some years. Although in the case of Belgium (Appendix
Table A5) the annual figures do not show this movement, it is visible
in the monthly figures for the second half of 1926.

The consequences of the relative stabilization of the money stock
are shown in the respective figures and tables. First, the real stock
of money moves back toward normal. The index for the price level
is in accord with the index for the nominal stock of money. Second,
the exchange rate falls more strongly than the price level, which still

95

may be increasing. Undervaluation of the currency vanishes, and purchasing power parity is nearly restored. In fact, even some overvaluation may result. These facts depict nothing other than a kind of stabilization crisis. Export and import-competing industries lose accustomed advantages of undervaluation and may even be hurt by some overvaluation. The disinflationary impact of the decrease in the growth rate of the money stock is reinforced by the downward movement of foreign exchange rates. How strongly these consequences will spread to other sectors of the economy depends on overall economic conditions.

The experience of the U.S. economy between 1973 and 1985 provides a good illustration of such stabilization (Corden 1984). First, the U.S. inflated more strongly than, say, Germany or Switzerland. As a consequence the values of the mark and Swiss franc increased much more than the relative U.S. cost of living index. However, when relative stabilization occurred in the United States, these exchange rates dropped, whereas the cost of living index increased further, though at a slower rate. Undervaluation of the dollar eventually turned into an overvaluation.

The political consequences of such recent developments in the United States are representative for the historical cases discussed here. Export industries, import-competing industries, and their employees feel the disciplining forces of foreign competition—of shrinking sales, profits, and employment. As such, interest groups feel pressure to increase their lobbying for protection from foreign competition, for price supports and/or subsidies. Politicians respond to those pressures in the hope of gaining or preserving the votes of people employed in those sectors of the economy. Although consumers will be hurt by trade restrictions, the costs are widely dispersed and usually are not associated with the protective political actions. An exception occurs if the expenditures for a given good (say, automobiles) amount to a substantial share of household expenditures in which cases it may pay for consumers to inform themselves and thus for politicians to be reluctant or unwilling to adopt trade restrictions (see Bernholz 1966).

Establishing a Sound Monetary Constitution after Moderate Inflation

What is the influence of the relationship just sketched on the possibility of introducing a sound monetary constitution after a moderate inflation? The sectors hurt by disinflation—certainly the export and import-competing industries and the people employed by them—

will soon exert pressure for protective legislation and administrative intervention. The accustomed benefits of undervaluation decrease and may even change into the competitive disadvantages of overvaluation as a result of the stabilizing measure.

Given this situation, governments can take quite different measures. For example, intervention could take the form of protective tariffs, import quotas (perhaps agreed on with foreign countries), and anti-dumping duties, or it could take the form of interventions in foreign exchange markets combined with an increase of the money supply. Interventions of this latter kind were pursued by the German Bundesbank and the Swiss National Bank in 1978 and by the British Exchange Equalization Account after April 1932 to depress the external value of the pound (see Kindleberger 1984, pp. 382–84).

Another possible course of action would be to introduce a stable currency with a fixed but still undervalued exchange rate. Such a proposal would readily gain support from export and import-competing industries, which would be hurt by further strengthening of the foreign exchange rate and thus a loss of undervaluation. In fact, export industries would prefer this over import duties and import quotas. And such stabilization would also be judged by export and import-competing industries to be preferable to subsidies. Moreover, politicians could even boast that they had finally provided an inflation-proof currency.

It remains to be shown that the foregoing factors were, in fact, instrumental in creating the sound monetary constitutions found in cases of the third category, that is, in episodes following moderate inflations. Argentina in the 1890s is a case not connected with war (see Bernholz 1984). After years of inflation and mounting foreign debts that were used to finance an unsustainable development boom, a general collapse in 1890 resulted in the Baring Crisis in London. The Argentinean national government, its 14 provinces, and many municipalities defaulted. Bank runs in 1891 ended with the liquidation in April of the Banco Nacional and the Bank of the Province of Buenos Aires. The panic reached its highwater mark that summer, and a general moratorium was declared from July 4 to October 18.

The situation swiftly turned around after the stabilizing measures were taken. The Rothschild Committee and the Argentinean federal government agreed on the following measures: a moratorium on the payment of foreign debt for several years; a funding loan of £15 million; no new foreign debts to be incurred by the Argentine government and no increase in national obligations in any arrangements with the provinces; and a reduction by the government of the stock of bank notes in circulation. The consequences of these measures and the earlier developments are shown in Appendix Table A2. Undervaluation of the peso was an obvious consequence of the inflation and, after stabilization, the rate of undervaluation declined. Agriculture and such new domestic industries as sugar, paper, and textiles, which had been stimulated by the undervaluation, were hurt by this reversal.

In this situation, in which a further revaluation of the peso or even an overvaluation were expected, banker Ernesto Tornquist proposed in 1898 to return to the gold standard and to fix the exchange rate between paper and gold at a parity of 2.5:1. His suggestion was taken up by the government and passed by Congress in 1899, and was known as the Conversion Law.[3] This law fixed parity at 227.27 paper pesos for 100 gold pesos. At this parity the *Caja de Conversión* was obliged to exchange gold against paper in unlimited amounts. Scarcely any gold was available to secure the conversion of paper pesos into gold, but this really did not matter, since parity had been fixed at an undervalued level. Thus a balance of payments surplus resulted, gold had to be bought with paper money to maintain the parity, and the amount of paper money in circulation increased (see Appendix Table A3). By 1914 Argentina enjoyed the highest per capita gold stock in the world.

France is another case of the (re)introduction of a gold standard. Inflation and undervaluation, compared with the U.S. dollar, resulted from events of World War I (Appendix Table A4). Finally, after a renewed crisis, especially in foreign exchange markets, the new Poincaré government eliminated the low fixed interest rate on floating debts, increased taxes, cut expenditures, and began to refund the floating debt. Bank notes in circulation were reduced from 56 billion francs in July 1926 to 52.8 billion a year later. Consequently, the dollar exchange rate fell from an index value of 793.3 in July 1926 to 487.4 in January 1927, and French undervaluation rapidly dwindled.

Political forces in France, however, began to operate, limiting the revaluation of the franc. According to Charles Kindleberger (1984, p. 358):

---

[3]President Roca's message accompanying the Conversion Law revealed the government's motivations for currency reform:

[T]he instability of all values caused by the rapid increase of the values of the paper currency . . . strongly damages our most important branches of production. . . . These disadvantages are especially felt by the producers and manufacturers. The rise in the value of the currency changes the economic conditions under which we have lived for years, and disturbs the equilibrium of the value relationships, especially between wages, rents and production costs, which are changing extremely slowly, and the prices of products following world market prices [Quoted from Wolff 1920, pp. 56–57, my translation].

[P]ressure began to come from businessmen, especially in the exporting automobile industry, not to let the rate get too high. In its report of 3 July, the Committee of Experts had warned against a high rate (of exchange or parity) which would produce a deflation like that being experienced in Britain. . . . In November, when Léon Juhaux, head of the Confédération Générale de Travail, the national trade-union federation, protested about rising unemployment in export industries, the franc was stabilized *de facto* at close to the rate recommended by Rueff, 124 francs to the pound and 25.51 to the dollar. . . . At this rate, however, the franc was seriously undervalued.

When stabilized the franc was indeed undervalued. The return to the gold standard in June 1928 did not change the de facto parity established in 1927. Thus the balance of payments remained in surplus for years, and gold and foreign exchange reserves, bank notes in circulation, and the price level all increased until 1933 (Appendix Table A4).[4]

Similar developments took place in Belgium, Poland, and Czechoslovakia at about the same time (Appendix Tables A5–A7). The return to the gold standard at undervalued parities took place in these countries with results similar to those for France. Belgium, however, allowed the index of the exchange rate for the dollar to drop only from 794 in July 1926 to 693.96 in October—much less than the increase of the French franc vis-à-vis the dollar. In Czechoslovakia, on the other hand, the index of the exchange rate decreased even more than in France, namely, from 1,628 in 1921 to 691 in 1923, when stabilization occurred. In Poland a second stabilization took place in 1926, after a new moderate inflation had followed the 1924 stabilization of the hyperinflation. Obviously the new exchange rate fixed at 8.917 zloty per U.S. dollar (the rate selected in 1924 was 5.184 zloty per dollar) was undervalued and, until 1928, led to a substantial increase of gold and foreign exchange reserves (see Appendix Table A7 and League of Nations 1946, pp. 108–11).

Patterns fitting into the third category are also found in the cases of Austria-Hungary (1872–92, see Appendix Table A1) and the Netherlands (1864–75).[5] Although the movements of exchange rates were very small, they led to strong political reactions. For example, the

[4]For other accounts of the Poincaré stabilization in France, see Sargent (1983) and Makinen and Woodward (1985).

[5]See Mises (1907, 1912) for a pioneering discussion of these cases along the lines of the present paper. Also, on the case of the Netherlands, see the early work of Ludwig Bamberger (1876), Ottomar Haupt (1886), and P. Kalkmann (1901). These studies demonstrate that in the history of economic thought, the discovery of certain relationships has often shown that similar facts were already stated by pioneers in earlier cases.

value of the Austrian guilder in pound sterling increased by merely 8.4 percent between 1886 and 1891 (see Appendix Table A1). The movement of the real exchange rate was somewhat stronger, 14.6 percent, from 1882 to 1891 (if the figures can be trusted), but even this figure is small compared with today's standards. The movement of the Dutch exchange rate that led to the currency reform of 1875 was even less pronounced, at 3.1 percent. One explanation of why such small movements of exchange rates were able to generate such strong political reactions is that people in the latter half of the 19th century were accustomed to relative monetary stability and therefore were quite sensitive to inflationary pressures. Moreover, Mises (1907, pp. 561–62) points out that all experts expected a further revaluation of the Austrian guilder: "The generally shared belief in a persistent 'advance' of the Austrian currency was one of the most effective motives for the rapid beginning of the reform" (also see Menger 1892).

The introduction of the gold exchange standard in British India seems to have followed the same pattern as in Austria-Hungary and the Netherlands. The colonial government ended silver convertibility in June 1893, after the exchange rate of the Indian rupee had fallen from 22.5 pence sterling in 1873 to 14.625 pence in May 1893. At the same time the government announced that it would buy gold in any amount against rupees at 16 pence per rupee, but would not buy rupees with gold. Given that the fall of the rupee was the result of the declining price of silver, it is remarkable that the new parity was not set higher, and that no convertibility of the rupee into gold was guaranteed. It is at least probable (though I lack direct evidence) that even the colonial government took into account the interests of export and the import-competing industries (Heyn 1904).

After the termination of silver convertibility, the exchange rate of the rupee fluctuated for some time and reached a low of 12.5625 pence sterling in January 1894. But it became obvious that an undervalued gold parity had been selected as the upper limit for the value of the rupee. After 1898 the exchange rate reached 16 pence, and it remained a little above this parity only because of government intervention (Heyn 1904, pp. 163–65). Gold and sterling exchange reserves were accumulated, and the balance of payments showed a surplus (Heyn 1904, pp. 314–15).

It is perhaps revealing that legislation in Austria-Hungary (1892), in the Netherlands (1875), and in British India (1893) merely set an upper limit on the parity for the value of the domestic currency. Only the purchase of gold against domestic currency was guaranteed by law at the legal parity.[6] In Austria-Hungary full de facto convertibility was reached only when the Austrian-Hungarian bank began, in 1896, to follow the initiative of the government and the wishes of the business world and sell gold at the new parity (Mises 1907, p. 582). The political situation in the Netherlands and India was probably similar. The Bank of the Netherlands as early as 1875 began to sell gold at 1,653 guilders per kilogram of fine gold (Kalkmann 1901, p. 56). Finally, the British Indian government, too, was ready if not legally bound to exchange rupees into gold at parity in 1899 (Heyn 1904, p. 316).

Why Stabilization after Moderate Inflation?

The historical evidence clearly shows that the introduction of sound monetary constitutions is politically feasible if stabilizing measures have been undertaken following moderate inflations. It is, however, not clear why stabilization was undertaken at all, given the opposing political forces.

We have discussed the reasons for stabilizations following abnormal periods of war (cases of the second category), but how can we explain the stabilizations that occurred following moderate inflations and the absence of wars? The Dutch and Austrian guilders and the Indian rupee decreased externally because of the fall of the price of silver. In the case of Argentina, inflation and foreign credit supported a development boom that led to a liquidity and credit crisis. None of these factors had anything to do with war. Thus other political factors must have been at work permitting a move toward stabilizing fiscal and monetary policies.

The realization that the inflationary process is, or may be, getting out of control is a major force working against expansionary policies. As the inflation proceeds, a larger number of people, including wage-earners and their unions, will correctly perceive inflation. Consequently, spending increases, bottlenecks develop, and workers and unions begin to include the expected rate of inflation in their wage demands. Once this happens, the political benefits from inflation—namely, lower unemployment and greater tax receipts—begin to fade while the costs of inflation become more pronounced, as creditors

[6]As Mises (1907, pp. 581–82) explained:
> [I]t seems as certain that the victory of the reform project was assisted by just the fact that accepting the bills of the government only prohibited, at the moment, a further increase of the value of the currency and that the chance of its eventual decrease, if such existed, was left open. By agreeing to the currency reform the friends of easy money lost nothing but gained much, namely, the fixation of an upper limit for the value of the currency.

and those with relatively fixed incomes suffer real-income losses. Government officials and opposition leaders then find it politically rewarding to propose and enact anti-inflationary measures. A comparison with other countries that have greater monetary stability may also engender a widespread public belief (which politicians find it beneficial to respond to) that a stabilization policy is necessary. The prevention of capital flight, moreover, induced by outside stability, may be an additional motive to turn away from inflationary policies.

Although stabilization efforts may be expected after the main advantages of moderate inflation have been exhausted, this does not mean that politicians will persist in stabilization efforts until an inflation-free situation has been reached. Indeed, as we have shown, disinflation itself awakens political forces opposing further pursuit of stabilization policies. Thus, another turnaround may be expected if the propitious moment of mounting pressures on export and import-competing industries is not used to introduce a sound monetary system posited on conditions acceptable to the political forces opposing further stabilization. If this opportunity is missed a further round of expansionary and/or protectionist policies can be expected. These hypotheses have ample support, especially in Latin America (Paldam 1985) and, for the last several decades, also in Western industrialized countries (see Table 1). After the first turnaround, an even higher level of inflation is often reached, since the expansionary process begins from an inflationary base that is already established. Hence, economic systems giving discretionary powers to governments or central banks can never be inflation-free in the long run.[7]

The Maintenance of Monetary Stability

Long-term monetary stability—an inflation-free monetary system—can be maintained only if politicians and central bankers have no discretionary authority to influence the stock of money. No currency in history has ever maintained its long-term stability without constitutional constraint. History also shows, however, that even the best monetary constitutions cannot be maintained indefinitely. Periods of a century or more of price stability have been experienced in recent history only by several countries during the 19th century, and therefore seem to be rare accomplishments. Moreover, major wars have always been the biggest danger for the survival of sound monetary constitutions.

[7]This statement does not deny that independent central banks are more likely to produce lower rates of inflation than dependent central banks. Both, however, operate subject to the economic demands of political forces and so will, at best, be able to maintain a low average rate of inflation but never an inflation-free system.

What can be hoped for given these observations? First, apart from avoiding major wars, the rare opportunities for introducing sound monetary constitutions must be seized with courage and determination. Furthermore, to implement and maintain a constitution with characteristics best suited to prevent inflation over the long run, a concrete plan has to be present at the right moment. Such a plan should include the following six measures:

1. A constitutional restriction on the power of governments to create budget deficits;
2. A constitutional safeguard that prevents governments and central bankers from influencing the stock of money;
3. A mechanism limiting the stock of money;
4. A requirement that the monetary constitution can be amended only by qualified majorities, say, by two-thirds in both chambers;
5. An obligatory popular referendum to validate all changes of the monetary constitution passed by qualified majorities;
6. No emergency clauses empowering the cabinet to make changes under certain conditions.

The enactment of these measures would narrowly limit discretionary policy, but they are not sufficient to control inflation. The pure gold and silver standards had one clear advantage. The rule of convertibility of bank notes against the precious metal and vice versa, at a fixed parity, could always be tested by everybody and could not be easily reinterpreted by governments, central banks, or supreme courts. The latter condition would not be true for a constitutional rule prescribing, say, an annual monetary growth rate of 2 or 3 percent. First, the public would neither be able to test the rule nor determine if it had actually been followed. Second, it would be difficult to decide which monetary aggregate should grow by which percentage in which period against which base. Here there would be ample room for various interpretations, so that the constitutional rule would be of little value if it were not clearly defined. True, it would not be impossible to define the monetary aggregate, the base, and the relevant period in the constitution. But what would happen if the money aggregate selected became less and less relevant because of financial innovations? Moreover, the observance of the rule could still not be monitored by the public. Who should control the central bank? Another government agency? Or would individual persons have a right to sue government or the central bank for violating the rule?

Stabilizing a weighted price index would lead to similar problems. The prices and thus the index could be manipulated by the government. And if the weights and commodities of the basket were fixed in the constitution they might lose their relevance over time, because of substitution and other factors.

Given these difficulties, there seems to be good reason to favor a simple monetary arrangement such as the pure gold standard. To return to a gold standard, however, would require greater flexibility than prevailed before World War I to prevent the higher variance of real variables, as mentioned in the first section of this paper. Moreover, during World War I no European country with notes issued by the government or a central bank monopoly maintained the gold standard. This was true even for neutral countries. Only Albania, which had neither government notes nor a central bank, stayed on the gold standard (League of Nations 1946, p. 93). Albania is perhaps not a good example, but it seems that only a removal of the monetary system from the sphere of the state may be sufficient to maintain a stable monetary constitution under adverse conditions.

My own tentative proposal to solve these problems would be to abolish the central bank, institute a pure gold standard, and allow free banking. The monetary constitution would only postulate that each creditor had the right to demand payment from each debtor in gold at the fixed parity. Any violation of this rule would be severely punished by private and/or public law. Moreover, the constitution would grant the right of any bank fulfilling certain conditions—including unlimited liability of its shareholders—to issue bank notes and to create any type of claim preferred. Finally, any government owned or controlled banks would be outlawed by the constitution.

These are radical proposals. But the Scotch free banking system combined with the gold standard seems to have worked quite well without a central bank as a lender of last resort (White 1983). And the Swiss system seems not to have experienced too many problems before the foundation of the national bank in 1907. But the most important feature of the proposal would be the complete removal of government influence from the monetary system and the opening up of the path of innovation in the field of money.

APPENDIX TABLE A1

MONEY, PRICES, AND EXCHANGE RATES IN AUSTRIA-HUNGARY

Year	P_s[a]	M[b]	CPI[c]	PI*[d]	CPI / PI*	ER[e]	CPI / PI*·ER
1864	100		100	100	100	100	100
1865	99.94		92.01	98.32	93.58	93.97	99.59
1866	99.59	100	91.58	100.84	90.82	103.74	94.80
1867	98.68	110	91.14	99.16	91.91	108.61	84.63
1868	98.57	115	89.31	96.64	92.42	100.44	92.01
1869	98.47	120	91.04	89.92	101.25	106.69	94.90
1870	98.68	130	93.95	92.44	101.63	106.94	95.04
1871	98.57	138	96.87	96.64	100.24	104.68	95.76
1872	98.27	139	103.89	107.56	96.59	95.29	101.36
1873	96.54	141	106.16	106.72	99.48	95.74	103.90
1874	95.01	128	104.86	101.68	103.13	95.71	107.75
1875	92.67	127	101.62	98.32	103.36	96.40	107.22
1876	85.95	130	100.11	96.64	103.59	104.62	99.02
1877	89.31	126	100.43	92.44	108.64	105.40	103.08
1878	85.64	131	96.54	84.87	113.75	101.64	111.92
1879	83.50	126	96.44	82.35	117.11	100.55	116.47
1880	85.13	131	96.98	85.71	113.15	101.59	111.38
1881	84.22	135	95.03	83.19	114.23	101.65	112.38
1882	84.11	144	94.28	84.87	111.09	103.14	107.71
1883	82.38	146	93.95	84.87	110.70	103.52	106.93
1884	82.48	146	92.87	79.83	116.33	105.16	110.63
1885	79.22	140	89.42	73.95	120.92	107.78	112.19
1886	73.87	143	86.39	69.75	123.86	109.16	113.46
1887	72.68	146	88.55	68.07	130.09	107.10	121.46
1888	69.59	153	87.26	70.59	123.61	103.07	119.93
1889	69.62	158	88.66	70.59	125.60	103.07	121.85
1890	77.72	163	88.77	73.11	121.42	100.05	121.36
1891	73.42	167	89.20	72.27	123.43	100.70	122.57
1892		173[f]	84.88	68.91	123.18	102.87	119.74
1893			85.42	68.91	123.96	106.73	116.14
1894			84.88	62.18	136.51	107.50	126.98
1895			86.93	60.50	143.69	105.13	136.67
1896			83.37	61.34	135.91	103.60	131.19
1897			84.02	62.18	139.12	103.24	130.88
1898			84.67	65.55	129.17	103.76	124.49
1899			86.39	70.59	122.38	104.05	117.62
1900			86.82	76.47	113.53	104.41	108.74
1904		228[f]	88.34	69.75		105.24	120.35

[a]Price of silver in pence sterling.
[b]Bank notes and government notes in circulation.
[c]Cost of living index in Austria.
[d]Rousseaux' overall price index for Great Britain.
[e]Exchange rate, Austrian guilders per £10 sterling.
[f]Rough estimate.
SOURCES: P_s and ER until 1885: Soetbeer (1886); P_s and ER, 1886–91: Menger (1936, pp. 259–61); M until 1891: Lexis (1893), for later years: Mises (1907); ER from 1892–1904: Kaiserliches Statistisches Amt (1903); CPI: Oesterreichisches Statistisches Zentralamt (1979, pp. 676–79); PI*: Mitchell (1962).

APPENDIX TABLE A2

PAPER MONEY IN CIRCULATION, BORROWINGS ABROAD, PRICE
OF GOLD PESOS, EXPORT PRICE AND WAGE INDICES IN
ARGENTINA, 1884–1900

Year	Paper Money in Circulation[a]	Borrowings Abroad[b] Public	Total	Price of 100 Gold Pesos[c]	Export Price Index	Wage Index
1884	61,739		39,732	100		
1885	74,820		38,732	137		
1886	89,198	41,587	67,580	139	100	100
1887	94,071	45,548	153,498	135	97	
1888	129,505	91,760	247,796	148	93	
1889	163,648	30,833	153,612	191	118	
1890	245,101	11,420	45,395	251	165	125
1891	261,408	2,506	8,242	387	255	
1892	281,609	0		332	232	138
1893	306,743	0		324	207	
1894	298,703	0		357	209	146
1895	296,743	0	184,106	344	216	
1896	295,166	0	(annual	296	204	161
1897	292,704	0	average:	291	179	
1898	292,047	0	20,460)	258	177	
1899	291,342	0		225	138	
1900	295,166	0		231	154	

[a]Millions of paper pesos.
[b]Millions of gold pesos.
[c]In paper pesos.
SOURCE: Williams (1920).

APPENDIX TABLE A3

ARGENTINEAN BALANCE OF PAYMENTS, 1884–1904 (MILLIONS OF GOLD PESOS)

Year	Exports	Imports	Balance of Trade[a]	Borrowings	Interest	Balance of Borrowings[b]	Balance of Payments[c]
1884	68,030	94,056	−26,026	39,732	27,574	12,158	−13,856
1885	83,879	92,222	−8,343	38,732	22,637	15,522	6,179
1886	69,835	95,409	−25,574	67,580	26,764	40,816	15,242
1887	84,422	117,352	−32,930	153,498	37,305	116,193	83,263
1888	100,112	128,412	−28,300	247,796	49,523	198,273	169,973
1889	90,145	164,570	−74,425	153,612	59,802	93,810	19,385
1890	100,819	142,241	−41,422	45,395	60,241	−14,846	−56,268
1891	103,219	67,208	36,011	8,242	31,575	−23,333	12,678
1892	113,370	91,481	21,889	—	—	−15,873	6,016
1893	94,090	96,224	−2,133	—	—	−20,130	−22,263
1894	101,688	92,789	8,889	—	—	−30,577	−21,688
1895	120,068	95,096	24,971	17,197	38,149	−20,952	4,019
1896	116,802	112,164	4,638	37,144	39,863	−2,719	1,919
1897	101,169	98,289	2,880	38,295	43,985	−5,690	−2,810
1898	133,829	107,429	26,400	46,063	50,530	−4,467	21,934
1899	184,918	116,851	68,067	24,966	54,698	−29,732	38,335

APPENDIX TABLE A3 (cont.)

ARGENTINEAN BALANCE OF PAYMENTS, 1884–1904 (MILLIONS OF GOLD PESOS)

Year	Exports	Imports	Balance of Trade[a]	Borrowings	Interest	Balance of Borrowings[b]	Balance of Payments[c]
1900	154,600	113,485	41,115	27,540	58,575	−31,033	9,082
1901	156,716	113,960	42,756	—	—	—	—
1902	179,487	103,344	76,143	—	—	—	—
1903	220,985	131,207	89,778	—	—	—	—
1904	264,158	187,306	76,852	—	—	—	—

[a]Exports minus imports.
[b]Borrowings minus interest.
[c]Balance of trade plus balance of borrowings.
SOURCES: 1884–1900: Williams (1920); 1901–1904: Wolff (1905).

APPENDIX TABLE A4

MONEY SUPPLY, COST OF LIVING, AND EXCHANGE RATES:
FRANCE RELATIVE TO UNITED STATES, 1914–34

Year	M^a	CPI^b	M^{*c}	CPI^{*d}	$\dfrac{M}{M^*}$	$\dfrac{CPI}{CPI^*}$	ER^e	$\dfrac{CPI}{CPI^*{\cdot}ER}$	Gold and FE^f
1914	100	100	100	100	100	100	100	100	100
1915	168	120^g	96	104	175	115.38	107.58	107.25	
1916	212	129^g	105	118	202	109.32	113.73	96.12	
1917	257	138^g	113	142	227	97.18	111.50	89.88	
1918	376	206^g	127	174	295	118.39	108.61	109.00	
1919	474	238	141	177	336	134.46	140.57	95.65	
1920	521	342	157	217	332	157.60	278.90	56.51	114.79
1921	514	309	142	180	362	171.67	260.10	66.00	108.61
1922	496	296	129	167	384	177.25	237.90	74.51	108.24
1923	510	334	138	170	370	196.47	320.10	61.38	109.66
1924	545	369	139	169	395	218.34	373.00	58.54	109.55
1925	602	400	138	174	436	229.89	405.02	56.76	109.68
1926	716	505	142	174	504	290.22	595.59	48.73	115.35
1927	731	514	138	170.31	530	243.09	491.64	49.44	160.55
1928	872	519	138	168.13	632	308.70	490.20^h	62.97	338.16

APPENDIX TABLE A4 (cont.)

MONEY SUPPLY, COST OF LIVING, AND EXCHANGE RATES: FRANCE RELATIVE TO UNITED STATES, 1914–34

Year	M[a]	CPI[b]	M*[c]	CPI*[d]	$\dfrac{M}{M^*}$	$\dfrac{CPI}{CPI^*}$	ER[e]	$\dfrac{CPI}{CPI^* \cdot ER}$	Gold and FE[f]
1929	936	556	134	167.63	699	331.68	492.11	67.40	353.82
1930	1043	582	134	161.26	778	360.91	491.08	73.49	417.39
1931	1170	569	157	145.34	745	391.50	491.37	79.68	477.48
1932	1160	526	158	130.25	734	403.84	490.39	82.35	465.59
1933	1128	520	162	125.39	696	414.71	492.26	84.25	416.93
1934	1116	516	200	133.10	558	387.68	491.81[i]	78.83	

[a]Bank notes in circulation in France.
[b]French consumer price index.
[c]Currency held by public plus demand deposits in United States, end of year.
[d]U.S. consumer price index.
[e]Exchange rate, francs per dollar.
[f]Foreign exchange reserves.
[g]Index for food only.
[h]On 25 June 1928 France returned to a fixed gold parity that was equivalent to a U.S. dollar parity of 25.52 francs per dollar. The index figure is an average of the first half of the year up to this date.
[i]On 30 June 1934 the devaluation of the U.S. dollar in terms of gold led to a new parity of 15.075 francs per dollar. The index figure for 1934 is given in terms of an unchanged parity. Taking the change into account leads to an index figure of 290.52. Thus the franc was still undervalued before but overvalued after the devaluation of the dollar.
SOURCES: Statistisches Reichsamt (1921–22, 1924–25; 1936).

APPENDIX TABLE A5

MONEY, PRICES, AND EXCHANGE RATES IN BELGIUM, 1913–33

Year	M[a]	M*[b]	$\frac{M}{M*}$	CPI[c]	CPI*[d]	$\frac{CPI}{CPI*}$	ER[e]	$\frac{CPI}{CPI*\cdot ER}$	Gold & FE[f]
1913	100	100	100	100	100	100	100	100	100
1919	534	141	379	390	156	250			78
1920	537	159	338	455	200	228	263	87	71
1921	613	144	426	400	174	230	259	89	69
1922	643	131	491	374	169	221	252	88	69
1923	700	139	504	428	173	247	370	67	69
1924	763	141	541	501	172	291	416	70	73
1925	757	142	533	533	178	299	406	74	73
1926	841	143	588	639	176	363	589	62	185
1927	958	144	665	789	172	459	693	66	216
1928	1,159	138	840	817	169	483	694	70	206
1929	1,341	135	993	867	169	513	693	74	246
1930	1,640	135	1,215	890	165	539	695	78	329
1931	1,825	158	1,155	799	151	529	693	76	358
1932	1,811	159	1,139	721	137	526	693	76	369
1933	1,707	162	1,054	715	131	546	559[g]	98	384

[a]Notes in circulation in Belgium, end of year.
[b]Currency held by public plus demand deposits in United States, end of year.
[c]Cost of living index, Belgium.
[d]Cost of living index, United States.
[e]Exchange rate, Belgian francs per U.S. dollar.
[f]Foreign exchange reserves.
[g]In 1933 the U.S. dollar was devalued against gold.
SOURCES: Statistisches Reichsamt (1928; 1925, 1934).

APPENDIX TABLE A6

MONEY, PRICES, AND EXCHANGE RATES IN CZECHOSLOVAKIA, 1913–27

Year	Mᵃ	M*ᵇ	$\frac{M}{M*}$	CPIᶜ	CPI*ᵈ	$\frac{CPI}{CPI*}$	ERᵉ	$\frac{CPI}{CPI*\cdot ER}$	Gold and FEᶠ
1913	—	100 ⎫	100	—	100ᵍ ⎫	100	100 ⎫	100	—
1914	100ʰ	⎭	100	100	⎭	100	⎭	100	—
1919	1850ⁱ	143	1298	—	156	—	—	—	—
1920	2431	159	1529	—	200	—	1343	—	100
1921	3099	144	2152	1423	174	818	1628	50	235
1922	2783	131	2124	1289	169	763	891	86	436
1923	2544	139	1830	918	173	531	691	77	667
1924	2273	141	1612	914	172	531	696	76	471
1925	2122	142	1494	951	178	534	687	78	465
1926	1997	143	1397	938	176	533	686	78	654
1927	2057	144	1428	976	172	567	684	83	787

ᵃNotes in circulation in Czechoslovakia, end of year.
ᵇCurrency held by public plus demand deposits in United States, end of year.
ᶜCost of living index, Czechoslovakia.
ᵈCost of living index, United States.
ᵉExchange rate, Czechoslovakian crowns per U.S. dollar.
ᶠForeign exchange reserves.
ᵍMarch–December 1913.
ʰEstimated for 1914 as a percentage of the Austrian-Hungarian circulation, corresponding to the figures given by Amonn (1923, pp. 3–4) for this year and for February 1919.
ⁱFebruary 1919 following Amonn (1923, pp. 3–4).
SOURCES: Statistisches Reichsamt (1928; 1925–34).

APPENDIX TABLE A7

MONEY, PRICES, AND EXCHANGE RATES IN POLAND, 1914–33

Year	M[a]	M*[b]	M/M*	CPI[c]	CPI[d]	CPI/CPI*	ER[e]	CPI/(CPI*·ER)	M/CPI	Gold & FE[f]
1914		116		100	100	100	100	100		
1915		111		206	99	208				
1916		123		341	112	304				
1917		131		1,029	143	720				
1918	252	148	170	1,424	165	863			18	
1919	1,310	164	799	2,016	182	1,108			65	
1920	12,165[g]	182[g]	6,684	12,165	200	6,083			100	
1921	56,569	165	34,284	46,843	150	31,229	1,512	73	121	100
1922	195,540	149	131,235	231,000	139	166,187	5,312	115	85	361
1923	30,897,559	161	19,191,030	119,656,600	143	83,675,944	76,839	41	26	384
1924							413,901	40		
March	146,942,673		90,705,354	287,296,800		200,906,853	117,859,147	71	51	
Dec.	244,370,351	162	150,845,896	336,600,000	143	235,384,615	221,915,198	91	73	1,203
Dec.	299,433,263[h]		184,835,348				223,214,286	105	89	
1925	361,537,940	162	223,171,568	262,800,000	154	170,649,351	241,072,971	71	138	658
1926	452,920,535	165	274,497,294	205,818,213	158	130,264,692	377,780,735	34	220	977
1927	582,009,542	162	359,265,149	227,927,147	156	146,107,146	378,811,134	39	255	702
1928	682,976,225	160	426,860,141	229,072,510	154	148,748,383	380,728,607	39	298	2,503
1929	709,635,849	156	454,894,775	232,279,525	154	150,830,860	381,070,306	40	306	2,301
1930	696,164,732	157	443,417,027	216,244,449	149	145,130,503	381,641,169	38	322	1,829

APPENDIX TABLE A7 (cont.)

MONEY, PRICES, AND EXCHANGE RATES IN POLAND, 1914–33

Year	M[a]	M*[b]	$\frac{M}{M*}$	CPI[c]	CPI*[d]	$\frac{CPI}{CPI*}$	ER[e]	$\frac{CPI}{CPI*·ER}$	$\frac{M}{CPI}$	Gold & FE[f]
1931	647,555,665	183	353,855,555	196,773,286	137	143,630,136	381,946,330	38	329	1,526
1932	587,924,775	184	319,524,334	179,134,703	124	144,463,470	382,099,093	38	328	1,198
1933	596,968,323	189	315,856,256	163,099,627	118	138,220,023	274,885,273[i]	50	366	1,058

[a]Bank notes issued by the Polish State Loan Bank until May 1924, and then by the Bank of Poland. From the second figure for December 1924, currency in circulation including bank notes of the Bank of Poland, token coins, and token notes (with denominations up to five zlotys) issued by the government; end of period figures.

[b]Currency in circulation in the United States, end of year.

[c]Until 1920 Polish wholesale price index (Fiedorowicz); from 1921. Polish cost of living index 1921–24 figures are for December (except in March 1924); in other years figures are annual averages.

[d]U.S. cost of living index, annual averages.

[e]Polish marks per U.S. dollar until March 1924. Thereafter, Polish zlotys per U.S. dollar (1,800,000 marks = 1 zloty). Average for July and December in 1918, average of December for 1921–24, annual averages for all other years.

[f]Foreign exchange reserves.

[g]1920 set equal to figure for CPI (1920) or CPI* (1919); since CPI* figure refers to end of period), respectively, 12,165 and 182. 1920 thus serves as a base, since Polish monetary figures for 1918–19 are probably too low.

[h]The figure refers to currency in circulation, including coins and state cash notes (Staatskassenscheine).

[i]In 1933 the U.S. dollar was devalued against gold.

SOURCES: Statistisches Reichsamt (1928; 1924/25, 1934). For foreign exchange rates additionally: Young (1925) and Karpinski (1921/22).

References

Alemann, R. T. *Goldmenge, Silberpeso and Papiergeld*. 150 Jahre Argentinische Währungen, Buenos Aires, 1966.

Amonn, Alfred. "Die tschechoslovakische Währung und Währungsreform." *Schriften des Vereins für Sozialpolitik* 165 (1923): 1–21.

Bamberger, Ludwig. *Reichsgold*. Leipzig: Brockhaus, 1876.

Bernholz, Peter. "Economic Policies in a Democracy." *Kyklos* 19 (1966): 48–80.

Bernholz, Peter. *Flexible Exchange Rates in Historical Perspective*. Princeton Studies in International Finance No. 49. Princeton University, 1982.

Bernholz, Peter. "Inflation and Monetary Constitutions in Historical Perspective." *Kyklos* 36 (1983): 397–419.

Bernholz, Peter. "Inflation, Over-Indebtedness, Crisis and Consolidation: Argentina and the Baring Crisis (1884–1900)." *Zeitschrift für die gesamte Staatswissenschaft* 140 (1984): 669–84.

Bernholz, Peter; Gärtner, Manfred; and Heri, Erwin. "Historical Experiences with Flexible Exchange Rates: A Simulation of Common Qualitative Characteristics." *Journal of International Economics* 19 (1985): 21–45.

Brennan, Geoffrey, and Buchanan, James M. *Monopoly in Money and Inflation*. Hobart Paper No. 88. London: Institute of Economic Affairs, 1981.

Corden, Warner M. *The Revival of Protectionism*. Group of Thirty, Occasional Papers No. 14. New York, 1984.

Eagley, R. V. *The Swedish Bullionist Controversy: P. N. Christiernin's Lectures on the High Price of Foreign Exchange in Sweden*. Philadelphia: American Philosophical Society, 1971.

Fisher, Irving. *The Purchasing Power of Money*. New York: Macmillan, 1912.

Frey, Bruno S., and Schneider, Friedrich. "Central Bank Behavior. A Positive Empirical Analysis." *Journal of Monetary Economics* 7 (1981): 291–315.

Friedman, Milton. "The Role of Monetary Policy." *American Economic Review* 58 (March 1968): 1–17.

Haupt, Ottomar. *L'histoire monétaire de notre temps*. Paris and Berlin, 1886.

Hayek, F. A. *Denationalization of Money*. 2d ed. Hobart Paper No. 70. London: Institute of Economic Affairs, 1976.

Heyn, O. "Das Steigen des Rupienkurses nach der Aufhebung der indischen Silberwährung und seine Ursachen." *Jahrbücher für Nationalökonomie und Statistik* 28, 3d ser. (1904): 160–79, 289–318.

Kaiserliches Statistisches Amt. *Statistisches Handbuch für das Deutsche Reich*. Berlin, 1903.

Kalkmann, P. "Hollands Geldwesen im 19. Jahrhundert." *Jahrbuch für Gesetzgebung, Verwaltung und Volkswirtschaft im Deutschen Reich* 25 (1901): 33–66.

Karpinski, Z. "Die Währungs und Finanzverhältnisse Polens." *Weltwirtschaftliches Archiv* 19 (1921/22): 347–58.

Kindleberger, Charles. *A Financial History of Western Europe*. London: George Allen and Unwin, 1984.

League of Nations. *The Course and Control of Inflation: A Review of Monetary Experience after World War I*. Paris, 1946.

Lexis, Wilhelm. "Papiergeld." *Handwörterbuch der Staatswissenschaften* 5 (1893).

Makinen, Gail E., and Woodward, Thomas G. "Some Sadly Neglected Monetary Aspects of the Poincaré Stabilization of 1926." Paper presented at the Monetary and Financial History Conference, Federal Reserve Bank of Minneapolis, 24 October 1985.

Meltzer, Allan H. "Some Evidence on the Comparative Uncertainty Experienced under Different Monetary Regimes." In *Alternative Monetary Regimes*, pp. 122–53. Edited by Colin D. Campbell and William R. Dougan. Baltimore: The Johns Hopkins University Press, 1986.

Menger, Carl. *Der Uebergang zur Goldwährung.* Wien and Leipzig: Wilhelm Braumüller, 1892.

Menger, Carl. "Aussagen vor der Währungs-Enquête-Kommission." 1892. Reprinted in *The Collected Works of Carl Menger*, vol. 4: *Schriften über Geldtheorie und Währungspolitik*, pp. 257–86. London: London School of Economics and Political Science, 1936.

Mises, Ludwig von. "Die wirtschaftspolitischen Motive der österreichischen Valutaregulierung." *Zeitschrift für Volkswirtschaft, Sozialpolitik und Verwaltung* 16 (1907): 561–82.

Mises, Ludwig von. *Theorie des Geldes und der Umlaufmittel.* München and Leipzig: Duncker and Humblot, 1912.

Mitchell, Brian R., ed. *Abstract of British Historical Statistics.* Cambridge: Cambridge University Press, 1962.

Mitchell, Brian R. *European Historical Statistics, 1750–1970.* New York: Columbia University Press, 1976.

Mitchell, Wesley C. *Gold, Prices and Wages under the Greenback Standard.* Berkeley: University of California Press, 1908.

Paldam, Martin. "Inflation and Political Instability in Eight Latin American Countries 1946–83." Memo No. 3. Institute of Economics, Aarhus Universitet, Denmark, 1985.

Parkin, Michael, and Bade, Robin. "Central Bank Laws and Monetary Politics: A Preliminary Investigation." In *The Australian Monetary System in the 1970s*, pp. 24–39. Edited by M. A. Porter. Melbourne, Australia: Monash University, 1978.

Sargent, Thomas J. "Stopping Moderate Inflations: The Methods of Poincaré and Thatcher." 1981. In *Inflation, Debt and Indexation*, pp. 54–96. Edited by Rudiger Dornbusch and Mario H. Simonsen. Cambridge: MIT Press, 1983.

Schmidt, P. G. "Die Zentralbank in der Demokratie." *Jahrbuch für Neue Politische Oekonomie* 2 (1983).

Simons, Henry C. *Economic Policy for a Free Society.* Chicago: University of Chicago Press, 1948.

Soetbeer, Adolf. *Materialien zur Erläuterung und Beurteilung der wirtschaftlichen Edelmetallverhältnisse und der Währungsfrage.* 2d ed. Berlin: Puttkammer and Mühlbrecht, 1886.

Statistisches Bundesamt. *Statistisches Jahrbuch für die Bundesrepublik Deutschland 1981.*

Statistisches Reichsamt. *Die Wirtschaft des Auslands 1900–1927.* Berlin: Reimar Hobbing, 1928.

Statistisches Reichsamt. *Statistische Jahrbücher für das Deutsche Reich.* Berlin: Reimar Hobbing, 1921–22, 1924–34.

Statistisches Reichsamt. *Statistisches Handbuch der Weltwirtschaft.* Berlin, 1936.

U.S. Department of Commerce. Bureau of the Census. *Historical Statistics of the United States.* Bicentennial ed. Washington, D.C.: Government Printing Office, 1975.

Vazquez-Presedo, V. *El Caso Argentino. Migración de Factores, Comercio Exterior y Desarollo, 1875–1914.* Buenos Aires: Eudeba, 1979.

White, Lawrence H. *Free Banking in Britain: Theory, Experience and Debate, 1800–1845.* Cambridge: Cambridge University Press, 1984.

Williams, John H. *Argentine International Trade Under Inconvertible Paper Money 1880–1900.* Cambridge, Mass.: Harvard University Press, 1920.

Wolff, J. "Die argentinische Währungsreform von 1899." *Staats- und Sozialwissenschaftliche Forschungen* 24, no. 5 (1905): I–XV, 1–131.

Yeager, Leland B., ed. *In Search of a Monetary Constitution.* Cambridge, Mass.: Harvard University Press, 1962.

Young, J. P. *Foreign Currency and Exchange Investigation.* Prepared for the U.S. Senate Commission of Gold and Silver Inquiry, serial 9, vol. 2. Washington, D.C.: Government Printing Office, 1925.

COMMENT

CONSTITUTIONAL STRATEGY
AND
THE MONETARY REGIME*
James M. Buchanan

It would be erroneous to interpret Peter Bernholz's paper as another argument for a commodity-based monetary standard, and it would also be amiss to interpret the paper somewhat more generally as an argument for monetary rules (that is, for some monetary constitution) as opposed to nonconstrained discretionary authority on the part of modern central banks. The paper is, of course, both of these; it does contain a powerful argument for monetary rules, and it does come down in favor of a commodity-based standard. These two strands of discussion are imbedded in a genuinely massive array of data from the monetary histories of many nations, an array that will in itself insure the paper's longevity. Peter Bernholz has established himself as perhaps the world's leading authority on the comparative history of inflations.

I want in my comment, however, to emphasize a feature of the Bernholz paper that is more important than any of those noted above. I refer to the innovative integration of what we may call "constitutional strategy" into the discussion. Also, I want to raise some general points regarding monetary research, monetary rules, and monetary regimes—points that are relevant to the rules-versus-authority set of issues in monetary discussion.

A Methodological Schema

I propose to examine the Bernholz discussion in terms of a general methodological schema that can then be used in particular applications, including monetary policy. There are two categorically distinct

---

*Reprinted from *Cato Journal* 3 (Spring 1983): 143–46 and *Cato Journal* 6 (Fall 1986): 513–17, with added title and revisions.

The author is Harris University Professor of Economics and General Director of the Center for Study of Public Choice at George Mason University. He is the recipient of the 1986 Nobel Memorial Prize in Economics.

classifications: *the theory of economic policy on the one hand and constitutional political economy* on the other. In the first category, analysis (whether positive or normative) is limited to the constraint that the basic institutions through which policy actions are taken are considered invariant. In the second main category, these institutions are considered to be variable, and alternative regimes are subject to examination.

There is a further breakdown within the two main categories. Within each category, I separate positive analysis from normative, and, further, I distinguish two types of positive analysis and two types of normative analysis under each main category.

Theory of Economic Policy

Consider first, subcategory IA–1 of the schema (see below), the domain of the traditional theory of monetary policy. Here the analyst examines the effects of alternative policy actions that the authorized agents may take under existing institutions. This sort of analysis is conceptualized as offering potential input into the actual policy choices of agents empowered to make decisions. Bernholz is essentially unconcerned about this type of inquiry.

At the outset of his discussion, Bernholz focuses on the inquiry under subcategory IA–2, namely, an analysis of the incentive structure faced by agents empowered to act within existing institutions and an explanation-prediction of those agents' behavior. Bernholz suggests that existing monetary regimes exhibit an inflationary bias due to the vulnerability of agents to the unidirectional political pressures toward inflation. He backs up his prediction with a carefully prepared exhibition of data drawn from the experience of many countries over long periods of time.

As the shift is made into the normative theory of policy, Bernholz pays little or no attention to the idealized policy pattern that might characterize perfect adherence to the dictates of some agreed-on or postulated social welfare function. The possible content of discussion under IB–1 does not interest him because it is deemed to be irrelevant. The prior analysis under IA–2 offers the essential input into that of IB–2, and here the normative argument comes down clearly for rule-directed behavior of monetary agents.

Constitutional Political Economy

The second major category, constitutional political economy, is subdivided analogously to the first category. Under subcategory IIA–1, I have included positive analyses of the operations of alternative sets of rules, arrangements, or regimes. In monetary matters, this area

A METHODOLOGICAL SCHEMA

I. Theory of Economic Policy
  A. Positive
    1. Incidence and effects of alternative policy choices under given institutional arrangements.
    2. Analysis of the predicted behavior of agents empowered to make choices under given institutional arrangements.
  B. Normative
    1. Argument in support of policy choice norms preferred by analyst independently of possible constraints derived from analysis under IA-2.
    2. Argument in support of policy choice norms preferred by analyst as constrained by behavioral predictions derived in IA-2.

II. Constitutional Political Economy
  A. Positive
    1. Incidence and effects of alternative rules, regimes or institutions within which policy choices are made by designated agents.
    2. Analysis of the predicted behavior of persons and groups involved in making changes in the basic rules or institutions.
  B. Normative
    1. Argument in support of rules or institutions preferred by analyst independently of possible constraints derived from analysis under IIA-2.
    2. Argument in support of rules or institutions preferred by analyst as constrained by behavioral predictions derived from analysis of IIA-2.

of inquiry involves comparisons of the predicted working properties of commodity-based standards, competitive money regimes, discretionary fiat issue by governmental agencies, rule-constrained fiat issue, and others. Analyses here must, of course, draw on and use that summarized under IA-2. Most of the positive analysis that has emerged under constitutional economics could be classified as falling within this subcategory IIA-1.

The innovative feature of the Bernholz paper lies in the specific inclusion of the inquiry that I have labelled under subcategory IIA-2, that is, the attempt to explain and predict the choices among regimes, and the analyses of the processes through which constitutional-institutional changes or reforms are made. Almost no research has been devoted to this area of inquiry. As I have noted in the schema, the analysis in IIA-2 is analogous to that in IA-2, where an attempt is made to explain and predict choices among policy actions within existing institutions. In IA–2, analysis concentrates on the incentive structure faced by agents empowered to make choices, and it is from this structure that the prediction of the inflationary bias emerges. In IIA–2, by comparison, analysis concentrates on the pressures toward constitutional changes in existing institutions.

Toward a Positive Theory of Constitutional Choice

Why has this area of inquiry (under IIA–2) been neglected? In part the answer lies in the generalized failure of economists to consider constitutional rules, that is, to examine the institutions through which policy must be implemented, and to undertake the research summarized in the second major category of the schema. Modern public choice theory has been instrumental in correcting this neglect, but within public choice itself, we may still ask why so little attention has been paid to what may be called the "positive theory of constitutional choice."

The answer to this more specific question is complex. Those of us who have long held that policy reform can only come through changes in the rules of politics and who have called on economists to shift their attention to the constitutional stage have implicitly assumed that such a shift, in itself, largely eliminates the dilemma-like setting that prevents preferred policy patterns from emerging at the level of choices dictated by given institutional arrangements. In a sense, we have implicitly assumed that there is a total transformation in the choice setting when we shift from choices within given institutional regimes to choices among the regimes themselves. If the incentive structure for persons in identified roles is such as to prevent normatively preferred patterns of outcomes from being realized, then it is deemed necessary to change the incentive structure by placing choosers in positions where precise identification of roles becomes impossible. The Buchanan-Tullock veil of uncertainty and the Rawlsian veil of ignorance are familiar devices that tend to accomplish this total transformation of the choice setting as between the two levels.

In effect, Bernholz pulls us up short and suggests that, after all, we are caught up in our own histories. We cannot consider constitutional change *carte blanche*, and, hence, we will tend to react to proposals for changes in the rules in terms of an incentive structure that can be subjected to examination by economists. While we may want to acknowledge that there are categorical differences between choices among alternative policy actions within existing institutional arrangements and choices among the arrangements themselves, we need not go all the way to postulate that there is no positive analysis relevant to institutional choices—that is, to the choices of rules shaping individual choice sets. We need not presume, as our practice might have suggested, that subcategory IIA–2 is empty of potential content. If, however, we bypass IIA–2, there is no relevant content in subcategory IIB–2, the second of the normative subcategories that I have included under constitutional political economy. If the second major category here is restricted so as to eliminate IIA–2, then analysis in IIA–1 allows the analyst to shift directly to IIB–1 when he seeks to advance arguments in support of preferred rules, quite independently of the rule-feasibility set that the analysis of IIA–2 might allow him to define.

Monetary Research, Monetary Rules, and Monetary Regimes

The general points raised by Bernholz's paper are pertinent to the wider rules-versus-authority set of issues already touched upon. I now want to sketch out in further detail what I consider to be three major areas of difficulty with current discussion of the rules-versus-authority set of issues and offer an alternative research strategy.

Misuse of Data

I have long considered it a major error in monetary research to use empirical data accumulated in a period when there existed no monetary rule as evidence for or against the efficiency of such a rule, had such a rule been in existence. In part, this error has been motivated by the apparent urge of modern economists to carry out empirical tests independently of relevance to the problem at hand. I think that philosophers would refer to my criticism as counter-factual argument.

Do we really want to assume that individual behavior in the holding and usage of money and its substitutes would remain invariant as between two quite distinct monetary regimes? Do we want to suggest, for example, that a monetary growth rule tied to the monetary base would not have worked well over the period 1929–33 because, over that historical period, in fact, the base moderately increased at the same time that M1 fell dramatically? Would this sort of relationship have been observed under a rule that was tied directly to the monetary base? The fact is that there was no such rule then in existence; there was basic and pervasive uncertainty about monetary policy, as it was implemented by the authorities. There was a wholly different monetary constitution or regime from one that would have embodied an effective monetary rule, whether tied to the base or anything else.

If we do assume that behavior with respect to the holding and use of money would have been invariant, it is always possible to demonstrate that no rule could possibly have worked so well as an ideally omniscient authority. Further, it is also always possible to use the data in the historical record to construct, *ex post*, a complex rule that would have worked better than any simpler rule. I am not sure here just what limit those who play such games would want to place on the mathematical order of the fitted "optimal" rule.

My criticism is, of course, a simple and obvious one. Presumably, the error continues to be made because the only data we have is historical, and we really do not have much history of rule-oriented regimes. Further, modern economists do not feel really "with it" until and unless they can somehow refer to empirical data.

Misplaced Emphasis in Monetary Discussion

My second main point refers to the setting of the debate-discussion on monetary reform. I think that this debate-discussion is prematurely joined when we start referring to the advantages and disadvantages of this rule or that rule, this regime or that regime, all within the set of monetary regimes that are alternatives to that which is in existence. I share the view of those who suggest that any monetary reform must ultimately replace the existing uncontrolled monopoly authority with *one* alternative that, in the process of the dialogue, emerges as the "winner." Debates about which of the alternative regimes is to be preferred must take place. But, prior to this discussion, we should try to attain consensus on the need for *some* alternative regime that will embody greater predictabililty than the unconstrained monetary authority that describes that which now exists. The familiar analogy is with the traffic chaos that would exist if there were no rules. The first requirement is that there be some rules of the road. Whether or not these rules require driving on the left or the right is of secondary importance to the requirement that there be a rule.[1]

In our monograph, *Monopoly in Money and Inflation* (1980), Geoffrey Brennan and I distinguished among three stages or levels of monetary argument. First, debate about the appropriate direction of policy under an existing regime is, of course, where most attention has been centered until very recently. Second, there are or should

[1]See Brennan and Buchanan (1985) for a general discussion of the reasons rules are needed and in what settings.

be debates about whether or not the unconstrained monetary regime works as well as alternatives that would embody more predictability, even if less flexibility.[2] In other words, the debate at this level is over whether there should or should not be a shift in regimes, in the basic monetary constitution. Here the debate is properly joined between the nonconstitutionalist (the supporter of continued discretionary authority) and the constitutionalist (the supporter of some alternative regime). Third, there are the debates already mentioned above, between the supporters of this or that option among the set of alternatives to the existing monetary arrangements.

There seems to be continuing confusion and shifting between the second and third levels of discussion. Careful distinction would allow the supporters of money growth rules, commodity-based monetary systems, and competitive currency systems to join in arguments against those who support unconstrained discretionary monopoly. In other words, the central issue is not one of "rules versus authority"; the central issue is one of "alternative monetary constitutional regimes versus unconstrained monopoly." Let us first agree, as Bernholz does, that genuine constitutional reform is needed before wasting our energies in arguing with each other as to the merits of our own preferred alternatives.

The Stagflation Dilemma

My final point applies to the effects of the foreshortened time horizon in generating the stagflation dilemma of the 1970s, which seems likely to recur in the late 1980s. If and when the pressures for inflation are renewed, we shall be back in a classic dilemma. Attempts to reduce the rate of inflation will generate unemployment that is not acceptable politically; the short-run Phillips curve is too flat. Yet we all recognize that there is no advantage whatever, while there are major disadvantages, in rekindling inflation at or near the rates of the 1970s. Then we were politically motivated by prospects of moving up short-run Phillips curves, and we kept doing so even as these curves shifted successfully outward and upward.

Have we really learned the lessons from the 1970s? What assurance do we have that the Federal Reserve Board will react "properly" during the periods when the exchange value of the dollar falls and upward pressure is placed on domestic prices? Can we predict that the authority will withstand the domestic political pressures (from

---

[2]See Buchanan (1962) for a detailed discussion of predictability as a criterion of sound monetary institutions.

both parties) motivated by myopic overweighting of short-term constituency interests?

I do not think that the workings of ordinary politics in the United States, whether at the level of the Federal Reserve authority, the Congress, or the Presidency, offer much grounds for optimism in these respects. It is this conviction that, for me, offers the strongest argument for genuinely *constitutional* change, for a shift in regimes. I am referring here to reform that must extend any announced adoption of a rule by the monetary authority that exists and also beyond any mere congressional instruction to the existing authority. I am referring to a change in the constitutional setting for monetary arrangements.

Prospects for dramatic constitutional change may seem dim in the political climate of 1986, but it is possible that the central bankers themselves can begin to sense the desirability of basic reform in the rules. We clearly suffer from an absence of credibility in the pious pronouncements of policy direction. Credibility can be restored, as Bernholz makes clear in his paper, only if the monetary authorities are bound constitutionally. And should not these very authorities, like Ulysses, agree to be so bound in their *own* long-term interests?

Unless we can get an effective change in monetary regimes, we cannot expect our politicians or our central bankers to resolve the incipient stagflation dilemma. Until and unless we begin to take the long-term perspective in our private and in our public capacities, including the adoption of new and binding constitutional constraints on the fiscal and monetary powers of government, we are doomed to remain mired in the muck of modern politics.

Conclusion

Let me conclude by summarizing the Bernholz argument. There is an inflationary bias in the operation of existing monetary arrangements. This bias stems from the incentive structure that agents confront when making policy choices. Analysis of alternative institutional structures suggests that such bias can be eliminated only under some commodity-based monetary standard. As historical examples and analysis indicate, reforms in monetary rules in the direction indicated to be preferred can be predicted to occur only in specific circumstances defined by the incentives faced by relevant interest groups in modern democracies. In particular, Bernholz suggests, only after periods of moderate but not hyperinflations can sufficient political support be mustered for the directionally preferred basic shifts in monetary rules.

The domain of strategy for constitutional reform must be opened up for intensive inquiry by constitutional economists. In a very real sense, the strategy of constitutional reform must be prepared well in advance so that when circumstances are right, those who recognize them to be such can indeed "seize the day."

References

Brennan, Geoffrey, and Buchanan, James M. *Monopoly in Money and Inflation*. London: Institute of Economic Affairs, 1980.

Brennan, Geoffrey, and Buchanan, James M. *The Reason of Rules*. New York: Cambridge University Press, 1985.

Buchanan, James M. "Predictability: The Criterion of Monetary Constitutions." In *In Search of a Monetary Constitution*, pp. 155–83. Edited by Leland B. Yeager. Cambridge: Harvard University Press, 1962.

6

CONSTITUTIONAL CONSTRAINTS ON THE MONETARY POWERS OF GOVERNMENT*

Axel Leijonhufvud

The Current Problem

In a memorable Peanuts cartoon of quite some years ago, Peppermint Patty was shown in school struggling with a true-false examination. Her efforts to divine the malicious intent of capricious authority went something like this: "Let's see, last time he had the first one False, so this time it should be True." "He wouldn't have just one false, after a single true, so False, False." "Ok, now we've got True, False, False, True, ..." "Looks reasonable so far," she says with a contented smile.

If this sounds vaguely familiar, it may be because you read the business and financial pages. "This quarter should be Go, because they want interest rates down before the election." "Next quarter will be Stop again, though, because otherwise we risk a revival of inflationary psychology." "Quarter after that is probably Stop too, but then it is bound to be Go because something will have to be done about unemployment." "So, now we've got Go, Stop, Stop, Go." "Looks reasonable so far."

But not much further. It is possible sometimes to muster considerable confidence in Peppermint Patty divination for the first few steps into the future. But a few more steps and it falters and then disappears altogether. You cannot build up a firm expectation of the price level three years hence this way. Your price-level expectations for 1995 or 2000 will be so diffuse that, if possible, you would rather not write contracts the real outcome of which will depend significantly on your guesses being in the right ballpark.

*Reprinted, by permission of the publisher, from *Constitutional Economics*, edited by Richard B. McKenzie (Lexington, Mass.: Lexington Books, D.C. Heath and Co., Copyright 1984, D.C. Heath and Co.), pp. 95–107, with revisions. This paper was originally presented at the Conference on Constitutional Economics: The Emerging Debate, sponsored by the Heritage Foundation, Washington, D.C., November 18–19, 1982.

The author is Professor of Economics at the University of California, Los Angeles.

In order to understand the case for constitutional constraints on the monetary authorities, we need first to understand what is wrong with the monetary regime that we have allowed to evolve in the United States over the last 20 years.

Constitutional Monetary Regimes

A *monetary regime* is, first, a system of expectations governing the behavior of the public. Second, it is a consistent pattern of behavior on the part of the monetary authorities such as will sustain these expectations. The short-run response to policy actions will depend on the expectations of the public, which is to say, on the regime that is generally believed to be in effect. A policy designed to slow down the growth rate of nominal aggregate demand may, for example, drastically increase unemployment without much effect on inflation or, with different expectations ruling, it may slow down inflation without much effect on unemployment. Since the predicted consequences of the same action may differ between regimes, we need a different macromodel for each regime.[1]

Different monetary regimes will show different patterns of macroeconomic behavior. We can choose among different possible monetary regimes by choosing behavior rules for the fiscal and monetary authorities. By choice of regime, it is possible to select systems with more or less desirable macroeconomic performance.

A *constitutional regime* is one in which the discretion of the policymaking authorities is constrained, at least in the short run.[2] The scope for discretionary policy allowed by a monetary constitution may be wide or narrow. The "constitutional" requirement to defend a fixed exchange rate, for example, leaves a rather wide choice of permissible policies in periods when foreign reserves are adequate. The requirement to follow a Friedman rule, in contrast, leaves hardly any discretionary authority of consequence (unless the privilege to fiddle with Regulation Q be so regarded). Most monetary constitutions will have *escape clauses*. Under the gold standard, for instance, the temporary suspension of convertibility in the face of banking panics or in case of a major war escapes the constitutional rules of

---

[1]That the predicted consequences of the same action may differ sounds slightly paradoxical perhaps. But the consequences of policy actions depend on how they are *interpreted* by the public and on how the public therefore reacts.

[2]The U.S. Constitution is far too difficult to amend for the purposes here discussed. A more appropriate degree of constraint on short-run discretion is that common in European constitutions where a constitutional article can only be changed or amended by majority votes in two consecutive sessions of the legislative body, usually with the proviso that the two sessions be separated by a general election.

the standard. Misuse of escape clauses, of course, will destroy the system of expectations characteristic of the regime in question and, consequently, spell its abandonment.

Why then should we put constraints on the exercise of discretion in monetary management? Opponents to monetary constitutions make two major points that need to be answered. First, they argue, a binding rule is "undemocratic" if it prevents elected officials from responding as best they can to the wishes of the electorate. Second, a constitutional constraint such as a Friedman rule means that policy will not take current information on the system's behavior into account; but, the critics object, control theory tells us that it will always be possible in such cases to find a feedback governed rule that will improve on the system's performance.[3]

The answer to both objections is at bottom the same. Consider the control theoretic point first. It assumes that the system that is the object of control is structurally "the same" whether run on a constitutional basis or on an unconstrained discretionary basis. Systems exist for which this is a valid presumption. Rational expectations theory has made it a familiar point to us, however, that it is not a valid assumption for economic systems. Discretionary policy will not just "correct the course" of the same system using the latest available information on its performance; it will impinge on a system that behaves differently from a system under a monetary constitution. Consequently, one cannot be confident that relaxing previously existing constraints on discretionary policymaking will bring a net social benefit.

Consider how the systemic interaction between the public and policymakers might deteriorate. Suppose an economy already such that the private sector resorts to Peppermint Patty divinations of future monetary policies. Transactors have to base their decisions (especially their investment decisions) on highly unreliable guesses about future money prices. These expectations that will guide the public's behavior are in turn unobservable to the policy authorities. Since the expectations are unreliable, they are also likely to be volatile and to change in ways that are difficult for policymakers to infer. But the results of policy actions depend on these expectations. Thus, both parties rely on unreliable information and consequently their decisions are vulnerable to error. Macroeconomist observers would find that their ability to predict the path of the system has deterio-

---

[3]Most monetary constitutions, of course, do not eliminate short-run discretionary policy totally. But all must have constraints that are sometimes binding—and when they are, behavior governed by feedback is ruled out.

rated. Policymakers, the business community, the general public—
and, not to forget, the economists—all do badly in a regime of this
sort.

What is required to improve the situation is that the policymaking
authorities change over to a less complex pattern of behavior. This
will improve the private sector's ability to forecast future price levels.
Economists will be able to assume that the public's expectations bear
some stable relation to the pattern of policy in effect. Better economic
predictions mean that policymakers can at least know what they are
doing, although their choices of what to do are more circumscribed.[4]

One of the arguments for constitutional constraints on democratically elected officials is exactly the one just given. By restricting
"arbitrary" actions (even when majority support can at least temporarily be mustered for them), a more reliable framework is created
for private activity.[5]

The Cost of Inflation

The argument for constitutional constraints on the discretionary
powers of the monetary authorities that was sketched above puts
much stress on the unreliability of price-level forecasts when the
pattern of monetary policy becomes difficult to foresee. A constitution could make future values more predictable. Many advocates of
unbridled discretion would certainly see this argument as a very
weak one. The simple truth is that economists have had trouble
figuring out why unstable or unpredictable nominal values should
be damaging. "Inflation is a monetary phenomenon." "Money is
neutral." "When people adapt to it, inflation probably becomes very
nearly neutral." ("So, why worry?") Those who do not see a significant social cost in inflation also will not find the case persuasive for
constraints on discretion.

In order to understand the case for a monetary constitution, therefore, one needs first to understand the costs and consequences of

---

[4]On the last two paragraphs, see Ronald A. Heiner, "The Origin of Predictable Behavior,"
American Economic Review 83 (September 1983): 560–96.

[5]An example (also due to Ron Heiner) from another sphere may help illustrate the
general principle involved. Consider some team sport, such as basketball. Some of the
rules of the game have been imposed to prevent intentional injuries. Leave those intact.
But imagine successively abolishing more and more of all the others, leaving behavior
to the "discretion" of finely tuned athletes. At some point the quality of play will begin
to deteriorate. In the absence of rules restricting their behavior, sufficiently reliable
interaction is not possible and the athletes will not be able to show their skills to best
advantage.

inflation.[6] The problem comes in two parts: (1) the effects of inflation, given predominantly nominal contracting in the economy in question, and (2) the reasons why the private sector does not eliminate nominal contracting and neutralize erratic inflationary policies by generalized indexing. This paper will not resolve this second part of the problem.

The usual analysis of the costs of inflation starts from the neoclassical anticipated inflation model. This is a seriously misleading model which assumes that we know how to make future price levels predictable and that a credible constitution fixing the price path is in effect. The question asked of it is how the social cost of inflation would vary with the rate of inflation *under such a regime*. The answer is that, since, under the conditions assumed, inflation is nothing more than a tax on real money balances, the social costs are those of the various little inefficiencies that occur as a consequence of the attempts that people make to avoid the tax by economizing on real balances. This puts inflation as a social problem in the class of milk subsidies or sundry excise taxes. Another conclusion to be drawn from the model is that an inflation of this sort could be cured overnight with no more trouble or disruption of the economy than usually accompanies changes in taxes.[7]

A corollary of that point says that it is not the rate, but the regime that is the relevant inflation problem. The anticipated inflation model is a bad model precisely because it misdirects our attention to the rate of inflation (which is easily changed) and away from the inflationary regime (which is not easily reformed).

What kind of regime will make people engage in Peppermint Patty prediction? What are the consequences of making people live under such a regime?

Elsewhere, I have called the present American regime the "Random Walk Monetary Standard" (RWMS). I should add that this is meant metaphorically, not as a technical, statistical description. Under the RWMS, the authorities decide one period at a time whether to

---

[6]What I have to say on this subject simply paraphrases what I have written elsewhere. See Axel Leijonhufvud, "Costs and Consequences of Inflation," in *The Microeconomic Foundations of Macroeconomics*, ed. G. C. Harcourt (London: Macmillan, 1977), pp. 265–312, reprinted in my *Information and Coordination* (New York, Oxford University Press, 1981); also "Theories of Stagflation," *Revue de l'Association Française de Finance* (1980): 185–201, and "Inflation and Economic Performance," in *Money in Crisis: The Federal Reserve, the Economy, and Monetary Reform*, ed. Barry N. Siegel (Cambridge, Mass.: Ballinger, 1984), chap. 1.

[7]The way to do so is by a type of currency reform which I have called the "blueback scheme" and described in "Inflation and Economic Performance."

accelerate, keep constant, or decelerate the rate of money stock growth. Only current economic conditions and immediate political pressures (and, perhaps, the latest macroeconomic fad to reach public notoriety) enter into the decision. Future money growth rates are left to the future. Whoever will be in charge when the time comes will accelerate or decelerate as he sees fit. The only "rule" governing the process is that at each point in time you choose what seems the most convenient and expedient thing to do.

There is no "scientific" way to forecast future price levels in this system. For price levels relatively close to the present, I may generate expectations by telling myself some Peppermint Patty tale, reassured by the hope that the system will not wander too far away from where it is today.[8] Other people will tell somewhat different Patty tales, so even short-term expectations are likely to be somewhat *incoherent*.[9] The uncertainty attaching to any individual forecast of the price level will grow exponentially with distance from the present. The price level 10 years into the future is a subject for joking, not for rational discussion. Yet, of course, in an economy such as ours *people are forced to bet on it all the time*.

What will be the consequences? I have written on this at length elsewhere, so I will only briefly state the effects here. They may be grouped in somewhat rough and ready fashion into three categories.

1. Long-term bond markets will thin out and markets for some types of contracts might even disappear. The raggedness of price adjustments in an inflation puts "noise" into the relative price mechanism and makes it more difficult to coordinate current resources efficiently. Frequent turn-arounds in monetary policy will mean more frequent mistakes in output decisions. Such mistakes affect current profits adversely, and the expectation of their continuance under this regime reduces the incentive to invest in long-term capital. The increased risk of long-term nominal financing reinforces this ten-

---

[8]Suppose a new monetary authority comes in determined to be "tough" on inflation and starts braking it down more abruptly than has been tried by previous authorities. If this is interpreted as a return to constitutional money, all may go well. But if nothing is done to actually institute a constitution, it is really rather more likely that the "tough" policy is perceived (a) to increase the "step-size" of policy changes in the RWMS process, and (b) to increase the probability of a near-future reversal of disinflation. *That* would not be a good way to go!

[9]See my "Keynesianism, Monetarism, and Rational Expectations," in *Individual Forecasting and Aggregate Outcomes: "Rational Expectations" Examined*, ed. R. Frydman and E. S. Phelps (New York: Cambridge University Press, 1983), where the term "coherence" (of the state of expectations) is used to denote a situation where everybody has the same expectations (although the variance of individual expectations might be great).

dency. So, we expect that both productivity and capital accumulation will be adversely affected by the RWMS.

2. Under the Random Walk standard the ability to forecast inflation and to hedge against it when it cannot be forecast with any accuracy becomes more important to the success and survival of firms than efficiency and competitiveness in the production and distribution of goods and services. The rules of the economy's "natural selection" of individuals for fame and fortune change: finance people are favored over marketing people, lawyers over product designers, accountants over production managers. People, especially ambitious people, will reallocate their efforts and ingenuity accordingly.

In the late 1960s and 70s, playing the inflation right was the way for ambitious Americans to make it big. But an entire people cannot improve their living standards by playing this game. Who takes care of making productivity growth happen while the rest of us take care of our real estate deals and tax shelters?

3. In the RWMS environment, the real outcome of private contractual agreements becomes more uncertain. Contracting becomes a less effective, less reliable method for reducing the risks particularly of long-term ventures to manageable proportions. When contracting increasingly fails, political lobbying becomes a substitute strategy for many groups. Random Walk monetary mismanagement will bring in its wake efforts by all sorts of groups to obtain by public compulsion what private cooperation failed to achieve. Legislatures will be swamped by demands to control this price or that rent, to regulate his or her way of doing business, to tax X and subsidize Y. In trying to cope with it all they will themselves become less efficient, just as the economy has become less efficient, in carrying out their proper business. The political system thus loses legitimacy—and a generation of politicians will come to face the *ultimate indignity:* the public demand for *new* constitutional constraints on government—constraints not imposed on a previous generation of legislators.

Monetary Control

If you are persuaded by the case for a monetary constitution, the big question becomes, of course, what kind of monetary constitution we ought to strive for. The two proposals that recent debates have made familiar to us all are to adopt a Friedman rule fixing the growth rate of some monetary aggregate or return to the gold standard. These proposals are examples of constitutions built on the basis of contrasting conceptions of how price-level control is best to be accomplished.

For brevity, we may refer to these conceptions as the *quantity principle* and *convertibility principle,* respectively.

The quantity principle aims at control of the price level through control of some monetary aggregate, usually referred to as the "quantity of money." In its logically tidiest form, such a system will be on a pure fiat standard. It requires central banking. It is not a system, therefore, that you would leave in private profit-motivated hands. It virtually implies government control of the banking system. With some over-simplification, perhaps, we may say that the government sets the quantity of money and the private sector then decides the level of prices.

The convertibility principle, in contrast, requires the government to set the legal price of a commodity (such as gold) and let the private nonbank sector decide the quantity of paper money and bank deposits it desires to hold. If overissue of bank monetary liabilities were to raise the market price of the standard commodity above the legal conversion rate, the commodity would be more cheaply obtained at the banks. Redemptions of bank money would eliminate the overissue. The nonbank public, rather than the government, polices the banking system so as to protect the economy from inflation.

Early banking history shows us systems relying altogether on convertibility for monetary control. Until recently, modern monetary systems have generally been compromises between the two principles. The present U.S. system, however, retains no shred of convertibility. We rely completely on governmental quantity control. This system has already failed us badly.

It is important to understand the reasons underlying the gradual movement away from convertibility as the main regulating principle of nominal values. Aggregate demand in a gold reserve standard system (for example) is subject to monetary disturbances (1) through changes in world gold production and through the decisions of countries to join or secede from the international gold standard, (2) through balance of payment deficits or surpluses, and (3) through expansions and contractions of bank credit and, most particularly, banking panics. From the first two, we used to protect ourselves by sterilization of reserve flows. More recently, of course, the final elimination of gold from our monetary system and the move to flexible exchange rates have perfected our "protection" against disturbances from these sources. But the main motive behind the historical trend away from convertibility control to pure quantity control has been the desire to insure the monetary system against runs on fractional reserve banks.

The method of monetary control does not complete the description of a monetary regime. A corresponding characterization of the nominal expectations of the public is also required. In a gold standard system, the public would learn to expect some long-term drift of the price level determined basically by the growth of the world gold stock in relation to the growth in output. Cyclical fluctuations of the price level around this trend are also to be expected, but their amplitude would be confined to that of the relative value of gold in terms of other commodities.[10] In this system, finally, transactors must be prepared for occasional threats to the solvency of banks.

Nominal expectations under a pure fiat system depend entirely, of course, on how it is being run. The most important question in this regard is probably whether or not the desideratum of monetary stability is allowed to dominate government fiscal requirements. Virtually all the worst inflations of this century have been the result of making monetary policy subservient to the public finances rather than *vice versa*. The Random Walk Monetary Standard is a less virulent form of the fiat quantity-control system—or at least our experience until now makes it seem so.[11] The entire evolution of the fiat system has been a story of striving for added discretionary powers, so that a very restrictive constitutional version of it may not be a very realistic political possibility. But, in principle, a Friedman rule could stabilize price-level expectations and reduce the uncertainty attaching to them much as would a convertibility system and with the important added advantage of a very much reduced risk of banking collapses.

The system of public expectations associated with the respective regimes determine what can be expected from central bank policy. Consider the effects of monetary policy *when the public knows perfectly well what is going on*. Under the fiat-quantity regime, a fully anticipated increase in the monetary base should have no effects on real aggregate demand, if distribution effects can be ignored. Admit-

---

[10]Cyclical expansions in an old-fashioned gold standard system would be financed by expansions of bank and nonbank trade credit. There is a limit to how far nominal income can be bid up in such fashion. When the process begins to put upward pressure on the market price of gold, redemption of paper money will put an end to the banking system's ability further to extend credit.

[11]A particularly interesting hybrid is the one investigated by Thomas J. Sargent and Neil Wallace in their "Some Unpleasant Monetarist Arithmetic," *Federal Reserve Bank of Minneapolis Quarterly Review* 5 (Fall 1981): 1–17. Sargent and Wallace deal with the timely example of a system that is under some monetary discipline presently but is committed to fiscal deficits so large that they will have to be monetized later. They show this to be a recipe for very high current real rates of interest.

tedly, the qualification can be important.[12] But it is to invite confusion if one lets possible exceptions obscure the rule: that exogenous fiat money is basically neutral. A central bank controlling only a nominal quantity cannot normally expect to exert much control over real magnitudes. A history of volatile fiat-quantity manipulation will give the private sector strong incentives to watch the central bank closely at all times. This causes the effectiveness of monetary policy to diminish and, in the New Classical limit, to vanish.

Under the fiat-quantity regime, the authorities can sooner or later make nominal income whatever they want (although to little constructive purpose). This is altogether outside the powers of a central bank constrained by convertibility on a commodity standard. It has no control at all over the price level in the longer run. By the same token, however, it can within the limits of the standard operate on real magnitudes.

This becomes most obvious if we imagine the logically extreme (and correspondingly impractical) case of a multi-commodity standard such that convertibility would insure not just the fixity of the price of gold but the virtual fixity of the price level. Variations in central bank credit change the volume of "real" credit in such a system. If, despite the absence of exogenous nominal shocks, the economy experiences business cycles, the central bank can play a useful role by restricting its credit in booms and extending credit in recessions. It is likely to use the "price of credit" (the bank rate) as its main instrument. The interest rate is, of course, a "real" rate in this setting, and reducing it and keeping it low does not carry the imminent danger of an explosion of nominal values, since the price level *and price expectations* are kept in check by convertibility.

The analysis is considerably more complicated for the gold standard case[13] and will not be carried through here. The point remains that a central bank, operating within the constraints of convertibility, can affect the price and availability of "real" credit and, thereby, also real activity levels. The effectiveness of stabilization policy of this brand is no doubt rather limited, but it depends for its effects neither on redistributing wealth arbitrarily nor on fooling everybody by doing

---

[12]Indeed, quite a bit of old-fashioned Keynesian theory could be hidden behind this innocuous phrase. If, for example, in a recession, important sectors were "liquidity constrained" because they had ended up with larger than anticipated real debt burdens, inflation might stimulate these sectors to increased real activity. It would do so by redistributing wealth, of course, that is, by swindling others.

[13]See Gertrud M. Fremling, "Monetary Policy Under a Gold Standard: How Effective Is It?" (Ph.D. dissertation, UCLA, 1983).

the unanticipated. This kind of central banking is at its most effective when fully anticipated.

Monetary regimes constructed on the convertibility principle in the manner just discussed have been gone for 50 years. It is an even longer time since we had a well-functioning regime of this type. In discussing monetary reform today, it would be dangerously irresponsible to forget that the attempt to restore a world monetary order after World War I on a gold standard basis was relatively short and absolutely disastrous. For the understanding of our own times, the compromise regime that emerged after 1933 and at Bretton Woods is much more important.

This regime removed gold convertibility for the public and retained it only between central banks. As such, the Bretton Woods regime reduced the risk of banking panics directly and made feasible a system of deposit insurance that virtually guaranteed that panics would not recur on the scale of 1931–33. But without the redemption privilege the private sector could no longer protect itself against "debauchment of the currency." This, in effect, put the United States on governmental quantity control (while small open economies did not gain much scope for autonomous policy unless they restricted the international convertibility of their currencies). The Bretton Woods system was a perennial target of academic criticism. What seems most interesting about it in retrospect is that a system of expectations basically appropriate to an economy with convertible money was sustained by quantity control and with the central convertibility mechanism removed.

A system of price-level expectations consistent with the convertibility principle means, most importantly, that people expect prices to revert to the longer term trend if and when they go above or below trend. For such expectations to be maintained when the economy is not in fact on a commodity standard, the central bank must, in effect, "mimic" the behavior of such a standard, that is, contract above trend and expand below it. It must also maintain the faith that this pattern of behavior will be continued indefinitely. An (at least implicit) constitution will be of help in this regard. For small open economies, a habit of defending a fixed exchange rate may be the way to accomplish this task.

In the United States, monetary stability was maintained in this way for 20 years. With the private sector firmly expecting a quite low, and not very variable, rate of inflation, the Federal Reserve System could affect the availability and price of "real" credit to some extent. Thus monetary policy could play a limited, but constructive role in attempts to stabilize aggregate employment. The continuance of this regime depended, however, on the authorities not overreaching themselves. The old Keynesian doctrine of the "ineffectiveness" of monetary policy—a doctrine fitting a true commodity standard—may have served, inadvertently, as a myth protecting the regime. When the monetarist doctrine that the quantity of money was an effective regulator of nominal income gained acceptance, it was inevitable that advocates of discretionary policy would put it to use. This was particularly so insofar as they also believed in the stickiness of nominal wages, for that suggested that the stock of money (if Friedman was, perchance, right?) would serve as an effective regulator of employment. But vigorous manipulation of the supply of nominal money will destroy the system of expectations that makes nominal prices relatively inflexible. When the private sector comes to watch the central bank's base figures week by week, even the limited usefulness of monetary policy under the Bretton Woods dollar exchange standard would seem destroyed. We then end up in a situation where even when, for some stretch of time, base money is made to follow a path that is not in fact much more volatile than in the stable regime, this may nonetheless produce price-level movements of far greater amplitude than before, as the market tries to second-guess the intentions of the authorities and attaches extrapolative rather than mean-reverting expectations to various short-run wiggles in the base.

Constitutional Proposals

What kind of constitution should we then aim for? I do not come fully armed with my own proposal for the monetary order of the 21st century. I have, however, two suggestions for discussion—and more public discussion is exactly what we need.

A Peel-Friedman System

For the time being, we are stuck with the problem of getting some order back into a monetary system relying on fiat-quantity control. From the previous discussion, I conclude that discretionary quantity policy will do us little good when the price level is perceived as having no constitutional anchor. For providing an anchor, I see no substitute for a Friedman rule. Of the several possibilities, a rule imposed on the monetary base seems preferable. The previous discussion also suggests however that, when the price level does have an anchor, central bank "credit" policy might have a quite limited, but still potentially useful role to play. With unlimited discretion, we want a rule; given a rule, we want discretion. Combining the two is the trick.

We might borrow a leaf from Peel's Bank Act of 1844. You will recall that it divided the Bank of England into an Issue Department and a Banking Department. The Issue Department operated on a rule, albeit on a gold standard rule (as understood by the Currency School) rather than a Friedman growth-rate rule; it issued Bank of England notes as a simple linear function of its gold holdings. The Banking Department could then engage in discretionary stabilization policy with the note issue as the base for the rest of the banking system. The total amount of Issue Department note liabilities would set the upper limit on feasible Banking Department expansionary ambitions at any time.

Veterans on both sides of the "Rules versus Authority" battles will detest such unprincipled compromise. But if some advocates of discretion could bend this far, perhaps we could muster enough support in the profession for monetary reform with some constitutional stability built into it.

A Peel-Friedman system would split the Fed into an Issue and a Stabilization Department.[14] The Issue Department would be responsible for making base money grow according to rule. The rule in question would determine once and for all how much government debt will be monetized in any given year. The Stabilization Department would be obliged to treat this base money as if it were its foreign reserves in a fixed exchange rate world. It could pursue an expansionary policy only as long as it had excess reserves on hand, and it would have to rebuild its reserves before it could do it again.

Two problems with this approach may deserve brief mention. First, as has been pointed out with some frequency, we cannot choose a growth rate of some monetary aggregate from today until the end of this century with much confidence that we will be satisfied with the consequences. Financial innovation is proceeding at a great pace and with unpredictable consequences for the future demand for base money. I would approach this problem by amending the Federal Reserve Act so as to make price-level stabilization over the longer term *the* basic and overriding responsibility of the Federal Reserve System. Other goals of social policy should be eliminated from the Act. This provision of the Act should then be seen as stating the basic intent of the monetary constitution and would serve as the escape clause under which changes in the Friedman rule could be made. If, for instance, the originally chosen growth rate for the base turns out

---

[14]Compare Jurg Niehans, *The Theory of Money* (Baltimore: The Johns Hopkins University Press, 1978), chap. 12, pp. 286 ff.

to be quite inflationary in a few years, it could be adjusted downward for this reason—but for this reason *only*.

Second, the unilateral decision of the United States to stabilize the purchasing power of the dollar will create an incentive for other countries to fix their exchange rates with the dollar. A possible transitional problem would be a "dollar shortage" for them and a deflationary excess demand for base dollars for us. The United States might agree to limited issues by the IMF of Special Drawing Rights convertible into dollars to cope with this problem.

A System Based on Convertibility

My second suggestion can be made more briefly. It is simply that monetary economists should start seriously to study the possibility of constructing a new system of monetary control based essentially on the convertibility principle. The reason for this suggestion is simply the fear that unchecked financial innovations and computerization of the payments mechanism will eventually (indeed, before too long) make monetary control on the quantity principle no longer feasible.[15] An illustrative nightmare will make the point. Suppose that all debits and credits in the economy arising from current resource transfers are fed into a clearinghouse computer programmed to hunt for closed loops of indebtedness and to clear all such loops up to the largest common numerator. Debts and claims are systematically settled without the use of a medium of exchange. The monetary base might become the "small change" of such a system. Contracting the supply of small change will not stop an inflation; it merely creates a "coin shortage," as we know.

The convertibility idea, to repeat, is to fix a price and let the private sector endogenously determine monetary and financial aggregates. If quantity control becomes increasingly tenuous and unreliable, some sort of composite-good convertibility system might offer a preferable alternative. Some schemes of this sort have been discussed in the literature, but I have not come across any that are *obviously* workable. The subject deserves more thorough exploration.

Conclusion

I have not committed myself to a particular constitution. One reason for this is that I am not certain what the best scheme would be. But I also happen to believe that we need a monetary constitution.

[15]As I was writing this paper, Philip Cagan came to the UCLA Money Workshop with a paper arguing the same point. See Phillip Cagan, "The Report of the Gold Commission (1982)," *Carnegie-Rochester Conference Series on Public Policy* 20 (1984): 247–68.

What type of constitution we would individually prefer is a secondary matter and should be kept in the background. If too many of us start peddling our own favorite schemes, we will fail as a group in helping to get an effective movement for monetary reform off the ground. The late lamentable Gold Commission should convince us of this, if we did not know it already.

The Reagan administration has done as much as could be hoped to bring down the rate of inflation in this country. Some would say they have done more. But the administration has done *nothing at all* to ensure for us a future of relative monetary stability. Indeed if those looming future deficits will have to be monetized, the present government will be seen as having taken us farther down the road toward South American monetary arrangements.

Reducing the current rate of inflation and building a new framework for monetary stability are two distinct tasks. Doing one's utmost on the first does not necessarily contribute to the accomplishment of the second. It is more than just plausible that the failure to tackle monetary reform has already been a costly one. Disinflation undertaken and understood as an orderly transition to new and stable monetary arrangements should be less costly in terms of unemployment than disinflation, the pace and persistence of which must be the object of speculation. The President ought to appoint a National Monetary Commission. But this one had better be a worthy successor to the commission that laid the groundwork for the Federal Reserve System and to the Commission on Money and Credit of 20-some years ago.

7

A NEW MONETARY CONSTITUTION*
Thomas D. Willett

Fundamental Monetary Reform

The serious inflationary problems of the American economy of the past two decades clearly highlight the need for serious reevaluation of our monetary institutions. Poor harvests, oil shocks, and militant unions can all make contributions to stagflation. Likewise, fluctuations in money multipliers and the velocity of money keep the monetary authorities from being able to control monetary conditions perfectly in the short term. However, few economists would argue that longer run inflationary trends are not primarily monetary phenomena, at least in the sense that monetary accommodation is required for inflation to continue at a significant pace.

Despite the recent success in substantially reducing inflation in the United States we have little basis for confidence that the inflationary roller coaster of the preceding two decades will not reappear. Many of the political and economic factors that contributed to the escalation of inflation in the past still remain in place.[1] Furthermore, the technical aspects of implementing monetary reforms are generally much easier when one starts in a non-inflationary environment. We should not be lulled by momentary price stability into postponing

---

*Portions of this paper draw on the author's working paper, "Theories of Central Bank Behavior and Implications for Monetary Reform" (coauthored with John McAuthur), which was presented at the June 1984 meetings of the Western Economic Association. An earlier version with the current title was presented at the Hoover-Claremont conference on Constraining Federal Spending held at Stanford University in October 1981.

The author is Horton Professor of Economics at Claremont McKenna College and Claremont Graduate School and Director of the Claremont Center for Economic Policy Studies. He is indebted to the participants at the Hoover-Claremont conference and the WEA session, and particularly to Keith Acheson, King Banaian, Thomas Borcherding, Milton Friedman, Robert Hall, Harold McClure, Thomas Mayer, Gary Smith, and Richard Sweeney for helpful comments. However, not all of these individuals support the policy recommendations offered here.

[1]See Hirsch and Goldthorpe (1978), Lindberg and Maier (1985), and Willett (forthcoming) for discussions of the political and economic factors that generated the escalating inflation of the 1960s and 70s.

145

serious debate over proposals to implement safeguards to reduce the likelihood of future repetitions of the inflationary bouts of the recent past.

The concern of this paper is not with specific technical proposals for the implementation of monetary policy, such as procedures for targeting the federal funds rate or moving to contemporaneous reserve accounting, but with proposals for more fundamental reforms in the nature of the process through which monetary policy is determined, that is, for changes in our effective monetary constitution. Such changes need not always take the form of actual constitutional amendments. One of the most important institutional aspects of the U.S. monetary regime is the "independence" of the Federal Reserve, which was established by legislation rather than constitutional amendment. Existing ground rules for the discretionary fiat regime have clearly taken on the character of a special type of legislation now thought to be institutionalized and not subject to frequent revision. While the actual legal forms proposed changes in our monetary regime might take is an important issue, it is secondary to the debate over the basic nature of alternative monetary regimes.

In contrast, the vast majority of normative treatments of monetary policy regimes have focused on the development of optimal, or at least technically desirable, strategies for the implementation of monetary policy. However, since reputable economists have adopted a variety of theoretical points of view, a wide range of often conflicting critiques and prescriptions have been offered. Given the disputes among economists over optimal strategies and the technical details of monetary policy, it is not difficult for the Federal Reserve to defend its highly discretionary policymaking.[2] Such debate provides a convenient set of rationales for diffusing criticisms of mistakes. Of course technical analysis of the details of policy and proposals for optimal strategies are legitimate and useful activities. It is important, however, to clearly distinguish between such optimal policy exercises and the alternative type of institutional-political economy analysis that addresses the question of whether monetary policy outcomes are heavily influenced by political pressures.

While perhaps being desirable on other grounds, the available evidence does not give a basis for optimism that inflationary tendencies will be substantially dampened by relatively mild institutional reforms such as having Congress set the budget for the Federal Reserve or making the Federal Reserve directly responsible to the Treasury. Such reforms might help reduce some of the bureaucratic

---

[2]See, for example, Kane (forthcoming).

incentives for inflation but will leave basically intact the powerful political incentives for policy actions which result in inflation. The majority of central banks in the industrial countries are already directly responsible to their governments and their inflation rates have generally been higher than those in the United States.[3] More fundamental types of reforms need to be seriously considered.

The following section discusses desirable characteristics of a monetary constitution. By this is meant the fundamental institutional environment under which monetary policy is conducted. Important aspects of this structure may be set by the legislative or executive branch rather than by constitutional change, as, for example, the current "independence" of the Federal Reserve.

Desirable Characteristics of a Monetary Constitution

There has been considerable discussion of what types of considerations should and should not be included in a constitutional framework. Unfortunately, review of both actual constitutional provisions and the normative literature on this subject fails to yield a clear-cut guide. As Craig Stubblebine (1984, pp. 219–20) has argued:

> Constitutions, including the federal, typically address a wide variety of subject matter and contain detailed provisions on specific subjects (as well as fundamental principles). If there is a cogent criterion for delimiting the proper subject matter of constitutions it would appear to be the following: a constitutional provision is appropriate whenever the body politic perceives that the outcomes of the decision making process in the absence of that provision largely fail or would fail to comport with the outcomes desired by that body politic.

Changes of a formal or informal constitutional nature are costly and should be considered only if serious problems exist and, once implemented, should not be subject to frequent revision. Desirable characteristics or criteria of a monetary constitution include:
1. Limiting the scope for undesirable policy outcomes;
2. Allowing desirable policy strategies to be followed;
3. Providing enforceable provisions;
4. Being as simple and widely understood as possible; and
5. Securing considerable support and not being based on a particular point of view subject to widespread dispute.

[3]On the comparative inflationary experiences of countries with dependent and "independent" central banks, see Banaian, Laney, and Willett (1983). For critical analysis of the arguments by Toma (1982) and Shughart and Tollison (1983) that efforts to increase Federal Reserve budgets have been a major contributor to U.S. inflation, see Banaian, Laney, McArthur, and Willett (forthcoming).

147

Of course tradeoffs may be necessary among the different criteria, for example, between objectives one and two. For a particular regime the fewer constraints, the greater the scope for following optimal policies, but the greater also is the scope for undesirable policies. Likewise, the best technically feasible tradeoffs between objectives three and four might require complicated procedures that would conflict with the objective of simplicity.

The search for the best can easily be the enemy of the good. The wait for the development of a consensus among mainstream macro-economists, much less Austrians, Marxists, and supply-siders, is likely to be long, if not infinite. A major aim of this paper is to stimulate discussion of whether, despite the strength of their disagreements over optimal policy strategies, there may be scope for the development of a much broader range of agreement among members of these opposing camps about the outlines of a reasonable second-best approach to removing or constraining some of the worst dangers of our current monetary system. For such constitutional-type considerations a considerable degree of risk aversion and willingness to compromise seem appropriate. This suggests that more emphasis be placed on the development of safeguards against the worst possible types of outcomes than on the possibilities of achieving one's perception of the best conceivable outcome.[4]

Evaluation of Traditional Proposals for Monetary Reform

James Buchanan, in commenting on proposals for monetary reform, has argued (1983, pp. 144–45):

> [T]he debate-discussion is prematurely joined when we start referring to the advantages and disadvantages of this rule or that rule,

---

[4]Largely on these grounds I do not consider proposals for free currency competition (see, for example, Hayek 1978), which would eliminate government's monopoly over money, as viable candidates for monetary reform. As an intellectual matter I do not believe that such proposals should be dismissed out of hand. Recent studies suggest that free currency competition might prove more workable than most economists have traditionally assumed. Still I believe that there is a substantial danger that market participants will fail to sharply distinguish brandname quality among issuers and that this will create incentives for overissue and subsequent financial instability (see Melvin, forthcoming). For an analysis of this process in the first half of the 19th century in the United States, see Willett (1968). It should be noted that several reinterpretations of U.S. experience with free banking have recently appeared. These have argued that losses to note holders were a less serious problem than had been previously thought and that state regulation of banks' bond holdings were a contributor to this problem (see, for example, White 1983 and references cited therein). These new conclusions, however, do not address directly the macroeconomic problems generated by monetary instability during this period.

> this regime or that regime. . . . Debates about which of the alternative regimes is to be preferred must take place. But, prior to this discussion, we should try to attain consensus in the need for *some* alternative regimes that will embody greater predictability than the unconstrained monetary authority that exists. . . . Let us first agree that genuine constitutional reform is needed before wasting our energies with each other as to the merits of this or that regime.

While I certainly sympathize with Buchanan's comment, I believe it is important to combine discussion of the merits of alternative monetary regimes with discussion of the need for fundamental reform. Many professional economists view negatively all of the best-known proposals for fundamental monetary reform. It is therefore important to see if approaches can be devised that meet the principal objectives raised against these pure approaches. For example, there may be many economists who could be persuaded of the absolute desirability of monetary reform but who would continue to opt for the status quo if the only available alternatives were a gold standard and a Friedman-type monetary rule.

In considering the advantages and disadvantages of alternative monetary regimes it is useful to distinguish between issues concerned with (1) the growth of aggregate demand (nominal income) and (2) the desirability of generating or accommodating deviations from a constant growth path in the face of various types of shocks.

In considering the first issue, it is now well understood by economists that the effectiveness of alternative policy strategies to maintain a steady growth of spending are a function of the types (and relative magnitudes) of the shocks to which the economy is subjected. Buchanan (1983) has noted in this context that we must keep the Lucas econometric policy critique in mind when looking at the historical evidence; behavior may not be independent of the existing policy regime. Surely the generation of inflation in a regulated environment made a nontrivial contribution to the financial innovations and fluctuations in velocity that we have seen in recent years. With a more stable policy regime velocity would have been less volatile. By the same token, we should not necessarily expect the pattern of disturbances in the future to closely resemble those of the past. Thus, for example, even if we conclude that the gold standard provided considerable price stability in the last century, this fact would not provide conclusive evidence that a gold standard would provide the same stability in the future.[5]

---

[5]For recent analyses and references to the literature on the performance of the gold standard, see Bordo and Schwartz (1984), and Briggs, Christiansen, Martin, and Willett (forthcoming).

For the adoption of an international gold (or commodity-bundle) standard to provide a relatively stable growth of nominal income in a particular country there must be relative stability in the aggregate demand and supply of gold (or the commodity bundle) at a noninflationary price path, and in the equilibrium real exchange rate.[6] Thus unless shifts systematically offset each other (an unlikely occurrence) we would need stability both in the demand and supply of gold (or the commodity bundle) and in the demand and supply of foreign exchange. Where we had the latter without the former, the case for an international fixed exchange rate system would remain strong, but the gold (commodity) anchor would have to be replaced with some type of aggregate monetary control.

Fixed exchange rates alone, even if genuinely permanent, would not be a guarantee against inflation. Such a regime guarantees only the longer run correction of deviations from average rates of inflation. In the short run under such a system, there may be political incentives to try to export inflation which could ratchet up inflation for the whole system (see Willett and Mullen 1982). The problem of inflationary bias for the system could be handled by Ronald McKinnon's proposal to combine fixed exchange rates among several major countries with prohibitions or limitations on sterilized intervention in the foreign exchange market and the adoption of coordinated national monetary growth rules.[7] The desirability of this approach rests, however, on the assumption that the equilibrium real exchange is relatively constant. The available empirical evidence suggests that this is not a safe assumption to make.[8] The need to maintain constant nominal exchange rates would generate substantial fluctuations in national incomes, especially for large economies such as the United States. The major industrial countries do not constitute an optimal currency area.[9]

The other simple type of monetary regime is a constant money-growth rule. This will provide a relative constant rate of nominal income growth if velocity (the demand for money) is relatively stable. Keynesians, of course, have traditionally argued against the view that there is sufficient stability in the demand for money to justify a constant money supply rule as a guide to constant nominal income growth. Recently this view has also been adopted by global mone-

[6]See Mayer and Willett (forthcoming).
[7]See, for example, McKinnon (1984).
[8]See Arndt, Sweeney, and Willett (1985) for evidence and references.
[9]See Tower and Willett (1976) and Willett (1985) on the concept of optimal currency areas and its relevance to exchange rate issues.

tarists who argue that international currency substitution has under-cut the stability of the demand for money at the national level (while maintaining it at the global level).[10] Concerns with recent financial innovations and shifts in the demand for money have led other leading monetarists to abandon their advocacy of simple monetary rules (while holding that most of the basic tenets of monetarism remain intact).[11]

As the basis for a longer run constitutional guide, both prudent reasoning and efforts at consensus building require an approach that does not depend on an extremely high degree of constancy of any of these key parameters just discussed. However, concerns about enforceability suggest that it would be insufficient to mandate that the monetary authorities just target nominal income or the price level. Thus we are left with no simple proposal which we can argue with great confidence would assure a reasonable steady growth in aggregate demand. Furthermore, many economists favor at least some degree of adjustments in national income in response to some types of shocks such as the OPEC-sponsored oil price shocks.

These considerations require rejection of all of the simplest proposals for constitutional monetary reform; maximization with respect to the criterion of simplicity must therefore be abandoned. There is still scope, however, for developing multipart approaches to monetary reform that are relatively simple and easy to understand.

Multipart "Compromise" Approaches to Monetary Reform

There have been a number of proposals for softened versions of the traditionally pure types of proposals for monetary reform. Various schemes for loosened linkages of gold to money-supply determination and forms of shorter run exchange rate fixity are cases in point. In general, however, these "compromise" proposals are inefficient approaches that often dictate undesirable policy responses in the short run without providing longer term guarantees against substantial inflationary trends. Particularly dangerous in this regard are gold- or commodity-based price rules that provide for short-term feedback from prices to monetary behavior. Given the wide range of possible shocks and lags in the effects of money-supply changes, the likelihood of dynamic instability from such proposals is quite high. It is

---

[10]For recent discussion and references, see Miles (1984). For critical analysis of this review, see Radcliffe, Warga, and Willett (1985) and references cited therein.

[11]See, for example, Laidler (1981).

indeed ironic that some of these gold-based proposals can be subjected to the same type of criticism as Keynesian fine-tuning.[12]

Several economists have proposed that money growth be adjusted for changes in velocity.[13] Again there is a danger of dynamic instability in this approach if it were applied to short-term changes in velocity and rates of money growth. Thus this approach should focus on longer run developments. One such version was proposed several years ago by Robert Weintraub (1983). In Weintraub's proposal M1 growth would be held constant at 2 percent "unless the rate of growth in M1 velocity falls below one percent per year or rises above five percent per year for two consecutive years" (p. 180). If such changes in velocity occurred the money growth rate would be adjusted up or down until the four-quarter velocity increase returned to within the original zone. This should be an appealing proposal for monetarists who are concerned about possible changes in velocity. But it would have little appeal to Keynesians who still see some scope for demand management and short-run cushioning of shifts in the demand for money.

To achieve broader support it would be necessary to combine short-run discretion in monetary policy with constraints on long-run behavior that assure against the development of a cumulative inflationary (or deflationary) trend. Jurg Niehans (1978) has suggested a three-part proposal which is consistent with this approach.[14] He suggests that monetary policy activities of the central bank be divided into three sections. The *price department* is held responsible for the central bank's entire portfolio and given the objective of achieving a long-run average rate of inflation of zero plus or minus some small margin. It is also given freedom to decide what monetary policy actions to use to achieve this objective. The *output department* is given responsibility for Keynesian stabilization policy and may engage in an unlimited volume of open market operations subject to the constraint that any open position be closed out within a period of five years. The *liquidity department* is given the same type of constraint, but with the proviso that open positions be closed out within six months.

This is an interesting approach and deserves careful attention. I believe that several parts of the proposal require clarification or

[12]See Brunner (1983, p. 43) for similar criticism of these proposals.
[13]Recent examples are McCallum (1984), Meltzer (1984), and Weintraub's (1983) proposal which will be discussed below. For a useful review of the historical development of different versions of monetary rules see Macesich (1984).
[14]See also the discussion of this proposal by Carl Christ (1983, pp. 131–32) and the proposal by Leijonhufvud (1984).

modification, however. The initial proposal does not discuss procedures for ensuring the enforceability of the price stabilization department. One approach to this issue will be discussed below. A second difficulty involves the complete rebalancing provision. The idea of avoiding sustained cumulative increases on these accounts is certainly attractive, but I suspect that provisions for complete rebalancing would be too strong for the tastes of many Keynesians. While complete rebalancing would seem plausible for dealing with cyclical fluctuations, for supply shocks many Keynesians would recommend nonreversible monetary accommodations. If this could be limited to partial one-shot accommodation that avoided longer run acceleration in monetary expansion, this would be a major accomplishment. Some loosening of the complete rebalancing provision could be done without seriously undercutting the ability of this approach to substantially constrain long-run average rates of inflation.

Another important issue is how the policy targets should be specified. The three leading candidates proposed so far have been stabilization (typically within a range) of the price level; the average rate of inflation (at zero or some low level); and the growth rate of nominal income. Stabilization of the inflation rate within a range would allow a substantially greater increase in the price level over time than with the first target. For this reason, strong anti-inflationists would tend to prefer targeting the price level. However, given the need for developing a strong consensus for monetary reform, a movement to inflation rate targets might be necessary to secure the support of economists with less staunch anti-inflationist views. On technical grounds I do not see at this point a clear-cut choice between stabilization targets for the inflation rate and the growth of nominal income, but I am sympathetic to Robert Hall's argument that ". . . targeting nominal GNP is the best compromise between price targeting and real targeting" (1983, p. 102).[15]

In the absence of the development of technical analysis showing the definite superiority of one over the other, this choice might best be made on "political" grounds. Here there may be a major conflict. Targeting nominal income has been discussed favorably by some leading Keynesians and thus might be preferred on political consensus-building grounds among economists.[16] On the other hand, it would probably be easier to secure public support for a price stability objective that could then be technically defined in terms of a specified bound for the average inflation rate over a period of time.

[15]See also Hall's (1984) proposal for an elastic price target.
[16]See, for example, Tobin (1983).

Greater scope for the range of short-run discretionary actions can be provided both by widening the target range and lengthening the period over which the target variable is averaged. Presumably monetarists would argue for narrower limits and Keynesians for wider ones. It is important to remember, however, that the views of the technical authorities on how to identify and offset exogenous financial disturbances and the desirability of monetary accommodation of supply shocks to reduce transitional unemployment are not the only relevant factors in deciding on the allowable scope for discretionary actions. Wider limits could also give greater scope for short-term political business cycle manipulation. A loose set of rules might result in curing the secular inflationary bias predicted by political business cycle models without eliminating the generation of short-term instability. For those who consider this source of danger to be much greater than possible losses from discretionary adjustment to economic shocks, a pure velocity-adjusted monetary rule would be the most desirable regime.

For those who believe that both considerations are important, a tough tradeoff must be faced. One way of constructing more favorable terms for the tradeoff would be to impose tighter limits on the possibilities of monetary acceleration in periods preceding elections. This would require careful attention to the likely timing of policy behavior motivated by the political business cycle. For interest rate considerations this time period would be quite short, while for employment effects the lags would be longer. Perhaps the most important difficulty with this approach, however, is that it would further complicate the reform plan, further reducing its score on the simplicity criterion.

Another important consideration in analyzing the most appropriate range for discretion is that a looser rule is likely to have greater durability than a tighter one. Hence, up to some point a greater degree of looseness might well be expected to provide a more effective constraint over the long run than the adoption of a tighter constraint that would be more likely to be overthrown.[17] On the other hand, if the regime is too loose, little will be gained and it could even be counterproductive. A monetary reform that contained few effective constraints on the inflationary bias of government, however, could temporarily generate a false sense of security and undercut efforts to initiate substantive reform. Indeed, advocacy of a very loose regime could be a clever political strategy for those who prefer dis-

---

[17]See Viner's cogent comments on this point (1962, p. 258).

cretionary policy as a way to substitute symbols of concern for the substance of reform.

The tradeoffs between the tightness of the rule and the provisions for overrides in "emergency" circumstances and the provisions for enforcement will also need to be carefully considered. Enforcing the mandated targets is another important issue. Analysis of the likely effects of different degrees of tightness and of the possible scope for meaningful compromise between monetarists and Keynesians should be an important area for future research.

One approach to the enforcement issue would be to impose civil and/or criminal penalties on top officials of the monetary authority if the targets are violated, perhaps on a progressive scale linked to the severity of the violation. While ultimately there must be some such underlying penalty structure for noncompliance (including dismissal), I am attracted to the idea of specifying required actions in terms of variables over which the monetary authorities have a reasonably high degree of control. On these grounds, use of the monetary base is probably preferable, but the use of M1 or M2 would also be feasible to control average rates of money growth over somewhat longer time periods and might have greater political appeal.

Proposal for a Two-Part Rule

Concerned with possible instabilities in velocity, Viner (1962) proposed a rule to set the rate of monetary expansion at that rate which would have yielded price stability over the previous five years. In this exact form the proposal is technically deficient in that it would not handle well the problem of continued increases or decreases in velocity over time. However, Viner's proposal can be easily adapted to a forward-looking perspective. A two-part rule would specify that if the target variable range were violated, then the growth rate of some specific monetary variable under the control of the monetary authorities would be adjusted until the target variable was brought back within its specified range. Only if the monetary authorities failed to carry out the prescribed adjustments would direct penalties be imposed.

This approach has the advantage of providing a strong safeguard against substantial inflation while giving the monetary authorities scope for managing the economy in the short run on the basis of the best technical advice they could obtain. It would not preclude the adoption of presumptive rules for their monetary actions as recommended by many economists. Given some scope for discretion, the monetary authorities would not be freed entirely from short-term political pressures. However, a self-corrective mechanism is built in. As the monetary authorities engaged in more accommodative measures (whether due to public interest concerns or political pressures), their remaining scope for discretion in that direction would be lessened. Their own desires to maintain some scope for discretion could be harnessed to provide increasingly strong back-stiffening as the target variable range was approached. The two-part rule, therefore, should operate much like procedures for "leaning against the wind" with exchange market intervention, procedures that call for progressively less forceful intervention the longer the wind continues to blow in the same direction.

The two-part rule would clearly be a defective prescription as a direct guide to policymaking, if no attention were paid to the target variable until it was hit. Indeed, in terms of short-term operating guidelines, a good case can be made for just the reverse procedure: holding to a constant growth rule except in the case of clearly discernible shocks.[18] Yet, there is no necessary inconsistency when it is recognized that the proposed rule is for a set of constraints on short-term monetary policy behavior, not a strategy for optimal short-run policy.[19]

If monetary authorities expect to benefit as bureaucrats by achieving greater discretion, then this expectation would act as a shadow price of accommodation. The shadow price would increase as higher levels of accommodation pushed the target variable closer to its limit, providing incentives for the monetary authorities to become increasingly less accommodative the further they moved above the middle of their target range. While we should have no illusions that such an incentive structure could be relied on to generate optimal policy behavior, eliminating all possible scope for political business cycles, such a constraint could produce reasonably sensible outcomes on average while offering considerable protection against the generation of a cumulative inflationary (or deflationary) spiral.

Technically, the two-part rule would state that the monetary authorities are required to keep the y-year average of the target variable T (which could be the price level, domestic price index, inflation rate, growth rate of nominal GNP, etc.) within a range of t_1

---

[18]See, for example, Fischer (1980), who has called this a modified activist policy (MAP) strategy.

[19]Failure to distinguish between the desirability of rules as operational procedures versus constraint systems was also common in the discussion of the use of stock versus flow measures of reserve indicators for exchange rate adjustments during the negotiations on international monetary reform following the breakdown of the Bretton Woods pegged rate system. See the discussion and references in Willett (1977, pp. 113–20).

to t_2. If this range were violated on the up side, then in the absence of a two-thirds vote by Congress to suspend or rebase the system, the quarterly (or semiannual) growth rate of the monetary base (or some other designated monetary aggregate) would be limited to a fraction f (say, 0.5) of its average growth rate over the preceding y years. This restriction would stay in effect until T was brought back into its target zone.

While failing to meet the Washington dictum that "if it's too long to fit on a bumper sticker it won't sell," the concept could still legitimately be given a simple label such as the monetary rule or monetary control act or amendment. The technical provisions could be kept as short as or shorter than those of many of the recent proposals for balanced budget amendments. Thus I do not believe that the somewhat more complex forms of multipart compromise proposals need undercut their political feasibility.

The much more serious obstacles are to get economists to look at institutional reform from a constitutional perspective in order to develop interest in and support for such an approach and then to gain sufficient political support to force such a reform on those whose special interests it does not serve. These are clearly difficult tasks, but the recent popularity of "tax revolts" suggests that such constitutional monetary reform may not be impossible.

Conclusion

While a definitive case cannot be made, there is a strong basis for concern that our monetary regime needs fundamental reform and for believing that we can devise approaches that avoid the major criticisms raised against traditional proposals for reform. There is little hope for reaching agreement about optimal policy rules, but there should be a better basis for securing agreement about a reasonable system of constraints. This would require a substantial reorientation in the way most economists have approached the debate over monetary policy regimes.

Initial responses to efforts to contribute to such a reorientation suggest that this will be a slow process. While the success in bringing inflation down technically makes reforms much easier to implement (there is less need for special transitional provisions), the immediate political pressures for monetary reform are reduced. The cost of lowering inflation, however, has been high and it is important to develop safeguards against its reemergence.

The two-part monetary rule may not be ideal, but it is realizable—and along with other possible multipart "compromise" monetary

157

regimes should be the subject of increased professional analysis and debate. It is my hope, but not my prediction, that this will occur before rather than after another round of inflationary acceleration is generated. A new monetary constitution may then emerge that provides for greater monetary and price-level stability than under a purely discretionary regime.

References

Arndt, Sven; Sweeney, Richard J.; and Willett, Thomas D. *Exchange Rates, Trade, and the U.S. Economy*. Boston: Ballinger Press, 1985.

Banaian, King; Laney, Leroy O.; and Willett, Thomas D. "Central Bank Independence: An International Comparison." Federal Reserve Bank of Dallas *Economic Review* (March 1983):1–13.

Banaian, King; Laney, Leroy O.; McArthur, John; and Willett, Thomas D. "Subordinating the Fed to Political Authorities Won't Control Inflationary Tendencies." In Willett (forthcoming).

Bordo, Michael D., and Schwartz, Anna J., eds. *A Retrospective on the Classical Gold Standard, 1821–1931*. Chicago: University of Chicago Press for the NBER, 1984.

Briggs, John; Christenson, Dana; Martin, Pamela; and Willett, Thomas D. "The Decline of Gold as a Source of Monetary Discipline." In Willett (forthcoming).

Brunner, Karl. "Has Monetarism Failed?" *Cato Journal* 3 (Spring 1983): 23–62; reprinted (with revisions) in this volume.

Buchanan, James M. "Monetary Research, Monetary Rules, and Monetary Regimes." *Cato Journal* 3 (Spring 1983): 143–46; reprinted (with new title and revisions) in this volume.

Christ, Carl. "Rules vs. Discretion in Monetary Policy." *Cato Journal* 3 (Spring 1983): 121–41.

Fischer, Stanley. "On Activist Monetary Policy with Rational Expectations." In *Rational Expectations and Economic Policy*. Edited by S. Fischer. Chicago: University of Chicago Press for the NBER, 1980.

Hall, Robert E. "Macroeconomic Policy Under Structural Change." In *Industrial Change and Public Policy*, pp. 85–112. Symposium sponsored by the Federal Reserve Bank of Kansas City, Jackson Hole, Wyoming, 24–26 August 1983.

Hall, Robert E. "Monetary Strategy with an Elastic Price Standard." In *Price Stability and Public Policy*, pp. 137–60. Symposium sponsored by the Federal Reserve Bank of Kansas City, Jackson Hole, Wyoming, 2–3 August 1984.

Hayek, F. A. *Denationalisation of Money*, 2nd ed. London: Institute of Economic Affairs, 1978.

Hirsch, Fred, and Goldthorpe, John, eds. *The Political Economy of Inflation*. Cambridge, Mass.: Harvard University Press, 1978.

Kane, Edward J. "Fedbashing and the Role of Monetary Arrangements in Managing Political Stress." In Willett (forthcoming).

Laidler, David. "Monetarism: An Interpretation." *Economic Journal* 91 (March 1981):1–29.

Leijonhufvud, Axel. "Constitutional Constraints on the Monetary Powers of Government." In *Constitutional Economics: Containing the Economic Powers of Government*, pp. 95–107. Edited by Richard B. McKenzie. Lexington, Mass.: Lexington Books, 1984; reprinted (with revisions) in this volume.

Lindberg, Leon, and Maier, Charles, eds. *The Politics of Inflation and Economic Stagnation*. Washington, D.C.: Brookings Institution, 1985.

McCallum, Bennett T. "Monetarist Rules in the Light of Recent Experiences." *American Economic Review* 74 (May 1984):388–91.

McKinnon, Robert I. *An International Standard for Monetary Stabilization*. Washington, D.C.: Institute for International Economics, 1984.

Macesich, George. *The Politics of Monetarism*. Totowa, N.J.: Rowman and Allanheld, 1984.

Mayer, Thomas, and Willett, Thomas D. "Evaluating Proposals for Fundamental Monetary Reform." In Willett (forthcoming).

Meltzer, Allan H. "Overview." In *Price Stability and Public Policy*, pp. 209–22. Symposium sponsored by the Federal Reserve Bank of Kansas City, Jackson Hole, Wyoming, 2–3 August 1984.

Melvin, Michael. "Monetary Confidence, Privately Produced Monies, and Domestic and International Monetary Reform." In Willett (forthcoming).

Miles, Marc A. *Beyond Monetarism*. New York: Basic Books, 1984.

Niehans, Jurg. *The Theory of Money*. Baltimore: Johns Hopkins University Press, 1978.

Radcliffe, Christopher; Warga, Arthur; and Willett, Thomas D. "International Influences on U.S. National Income." In Arndt, Sweeney, and Willett (1985).

Shughart, William F., and Tollison, Robert D. "Preliminary Evidence on the Use of Inputs by the Federal Reserve System." *American Economic Review* 73 (June 1983):291–304.

Stubblebine, W. C. "Practical Problems of Constitutional Reform." In *Constitutional Economics*, pp. 213–23. Edited by Richard B. McKenzie. Lexington, Mass.: Lexington Books, 1984.

Tobin, James. "Commentary on Hall." *Industrial Change and Public Policy*, pp. 113–22. Federal Reserve Bank of Kansas City, 1983.

Toma, Mark. "Inflationary Bias of the Federal Reserve System: A Bureaucratic Perspective." *Journal of Monetary Economics* 10 (1982): 163–90.

Tower, Edward, and Willett, Thomas D. *The Theory of Optimum Currency Areas and Exchange Rate Flexibility*. Special Papers in International Economics. Princeton, N.J.: Princeton University Department of Economics, 1976.

Viner, Jacob. "The Necessary and Desirable Range of Discretion to Be Allowed to a Monetary Authority." In *In Search of a Monetary Constitution*, Chap. 9. Edited by Leland B. Yeager. Cambridge, Mass.: Harvard University Press, 1962.

Weintraub, Robert E. "What Type of Monetary Rule?" *Cato Journal* 3 (Spring 1983): 171–84.

White, Lawrence H. "Competitive Money, Inside and Out." *Cato Journal* 3 (Spring 1983): 281–99; reprinted (with revisions) in this volume.

Willett, Thomas D. "International Specie Flows and American Monetary Stability, 1834–1860." *Journal of Economic History* 28 (March 1968):28–50.

Willett, Thomas D. *Floating Exchange Rates and International Monetary Reform*. Washington, D.C.: American Enterprise Institute, 1977.

Willett, Thomas D. "Macroeconomic Policy Coordination Issues Under Flexible Exchange Rates." *ORDO* 35 (1985): 137–49.

Willett, Thomas D., ed. *Political Business Cycles*. San Francisco: Pacific Institute, forthcoming.

Willett, Thomas D., and Mullen, John. "The Effects of Alternative International Monetary Systems on Macroeconomic Discipline and the Political Business Cycle." In *Political Economy of International and Domestic Monetary Relations*, pp. 143–59. Edited by R. E. Lombra and W. E. Witte. Ames: Iowa State University Press, 1982.

PART III

MONETARISM AND THE SEARCH FOR STABLE MONEY

8

HAS MONETARISM FAILED?*

Karl Brunner

I. The Content of Monetarist Analysis

The alleged "failure of monetarism" can hardly be assessed, or its possible meaning understood, without an explicit framework of reference. This reference is provided by the writings of leading monetarists over the past decades including, in particular, the semiannual assessments and statements prepared by the Shadow Open Market Committee (SOMC) since September 1973. The SOMC has offered evaluations of current and future trends in monetary policy and has advanced specific proposals that can be examined in retrospect. I begin by exploring the content of monetarist ideas (Brunner 1971).

The difference between Keynesian and monetarist analysis reaches beyond some narrow "technical" issues. The two intellectual positions are separated by fundamentally different visions of the economy and substantially different views about the political economy of institutions and policymaking. They also determine very different approaches to the range of macro-economic problems. The sharp contrast between the alternative visions, however, allows some variations on the basic theme with occasionally common strands in some particular dimension of vision or analysis.

Both visions recognize the social process as a vast system of interacting agents. Keynesians are inclined to suggest that this complexity of the phenomenon must be matched by a correspondingly complex analytic schema. Their cognitive context emphasizes that all macrophenomena are a function of this complex interaction. An understanding of macro-theoretic issues thus requires that the economic process be represented by a huge model. Several crucial properties attributed to the economy need be incorporated into the model. The

*Reprinted from *Cato Journal* 3 (Spring 1983): 23–62, with revisions.

The author is Fred H. Gowen Professor of Economics and Director of the Center for Research in Government Policy and Business at the University of Rochester. He gratefully acknowledges detailed and patient comments by Allan H. Meltzer and Anna J. Schwartz on an earlier draft.

economic process is swayed by shocks and suffers either from a dynamic instability or an inherent disposition to settle around states substantially below "full employment." Belief in instability of the process, at least with respect to a "full employment" solution, is combined with a belief about the comparative invariance of the system's deterministic structure. Together with an essentially sociological view of political institutions, these properties justify an activist approach to policymaking. Such activism is both a sufficient and necessary condition for maintaining economic performance within a tolerable range.

The interaction between an IS and LM relation represents a rough approximation of the relevant aspects of the complex process. In the standard diagram the IS-LM curves are moved by the dynamics of the total process and disturbed by ongoing shocks. Nevertheless, many Keynesians implicitly, and sometimes quite explicitly, assert that they possess knowledge about the position and movements of these curves. Indeed, they proclaim to possess specific knowledge about the mix of fiscal and monetary policies that at any moment would guide the curves to a "full employment" equilibrium. This presumed knowledge about the IS-LM curves and the deviation from "full employment" determines the required path of activist policy.

The monetarist vision, in contrast, emphasizes the shock-absorbing property of the economic process. It also rejects the comparative invariance of a deterministic structure and emphasizes the inherent improbability of successfully formulating a large model with stable parameters.[1] This also means that the knowledge proclaimed by many Keynesians is judged to be thoroughly unrealistic, and this unrealism extends to the political economy of Keynes ("the Harvey street syndrome").

We can now view the monetarist position in somewhat more detail by considering five topics: the nature of the transmission mechanism, the internal stability of the system, the impulse problem, the money-supply process and monetary policy, and aspects of political economy.

The Nature of the Transmission Mechanism

Monetarists argued at an early stage that the paradigm formulated in terms of an IS-LM diagram was not well suited to cope with important aspects of monetary mechanisms (Brunner 1961, 1976; Friedman and Schwartz 1963; Brunner and Meltzer 1968, 1972, 1976). Two strands constituting the traditional Keynesian framework obstruct

---

[1] It is somewhat ironic to note that monetarist views on this point may be more closely attuned to Keynes' than are those of the "Keynesians."

an adequate explanation of important monetary problems. These strands bear on the emasculated representation of financial markets and the treatment of price-wage determination. The Keynesian analysis can be consistently developed under either one of two alternative assumptions: Only nonmoney financial assets are substitutes for money or all nonmoney assets (financial and real) form a Hicksian composite good that substitutes for money. Both assumptions reduce the representation of financial markets to a single equation. This representation neglects important issues associated with the interaction between credit markets and the money market.

The restriction to two assets in the context of an IS-LM world (Brunner 1971) involves more than an esoteric exercise or analytic convenience with little consequence. The Keynesian analysis and the alternative approach that regards both financial and nonfinancial assets as substitutes for money yield very different implications bearing on the role of money demand disturbances, the choice of monetary strategy, the real effects of monetary impulses, the nature of "reverse causation," and the questions formulated to guide empirical research on monetary policy effects.

The nature of the transmission mechanism surrounding price-wage adjustments explored in monetarist writings also implies that monetary impulses do not produce permanent real effects on output, employment and real interest rates, apart from longer-run real effects exerted via the expected inflation rate or distortionary institutional constraints (e.g., tax rates specified in nominal terms). This means, in particular, that recognized monetary growth patterns are fully absorbed by movements of the price level. Real effects can only be produced by monetary accelerations (or decelerations). This idea was further explicated by the rational expectations analysis (Lucas and Sargent 1981). That analysis also clarified the nature of another major difference with the Keynesian tradition with respect to the interpretation of (apparently) inertial processes shaping price-wage movements. Monetarist thought emphasizes the operation of feedbacks over an intermediate run from the state of the economy and the perceived policy regime to the structure of the inertial process. Keynesians, in contrast, deny that there is such a feedback or assert its irrelevance because its effect is spread over decades.

The Internal Stability of the System: Occurrence of a Normal Level of Output, Employment, and Unemployment

Monetarist analysis stresses the shock-absorbing character of the economic system. This property assures the internal dynamic stability of the system, but does not imply absence of economic fluctuations. The market adjusts to all ongoing shocks producing fluctuations in aggregate output and employment. The observation of such fluctuations, moreover, offers no prima facie evidence of inefficiency in the utilization of available resources.

The question concerning the system's internal stability is probably more usefully addressed as the occurrence and relevance of a normal level of output. That level depends on underlying preferences, technology, and the prevailing institutional structure. The economy's shock-absorbing property holds it within some range around the normal level of output. Sustained and large deviations (the Great Depression) thus require a succession of serially correlated shocks.

Monetarist analysis also emphasizes that the production function is not simply a description of technology. It is conditioned by institutional arrangements, especially by the range of admissible organizational forms and the structure of property rights. Institutional changes modify the space of production possibilities expressed by the normal level of output (Jensen and Meckling 1979). This level of normal output, of normal employment and normal unemployment, reflects the incentives built into the prevailing institutional structure.

The underlying differences in the approach to supply behavior and the price-wage process determine the specific Keynesian vision about the stability of the economic system. Keynes emphasized the occurrence of a stable underemployment equilibrium (Meltzer 1981) substantially below a "maximum employment" determined by preferences and technology, with the economy globally (i.e., relative to maximum output) unstable. The notion of a normal level of output does not fit the Keynesian scheme of a persistent underemployment equilibrium, and Keynesian maximum output (or employment) cannot accommodate the notion of institutional conditioning of the normal level of output. Some neo-Keynesians generalized Keynes's idea to posit multiple underemployment equilibria. A stable process controls the system's behavior over each position of underequilibrium. But the system is not stable with respect to movements between underemployment equilibria or relative to the maximum position. Its global stability around "full employment" can only result from the deliberate design of an activist policy regime.

The Keynesian concept of "full employment" determined by technology and preferences has no room in monetarist analysis, or else must be redefined. Keynesian "full employment" emerges from technology and preferences in an institutional vacuum inherited from the full information world of general equilibrium theory. In contrast, monetarist analysis stresses institutional conditions that shape the level of normal output. Keynesians and monetarists, therefore, approach employment policy from very different perspectives. Keynesians typically are inclined to exploit apparent opportunities for "demand management" to push the system towards "full employment." That level of employment, however, remains an extraneous element not specified by the analysis. Monetarists, on the other hand, emphasize a non-activist regime. Aggregate normal demand supplemented by an "institutional policy" is designed to adjust normal employment and normal output to a social optimum. This social optimum could be defined as "full employment."

The Impulse Problem

Attention to the impulse problem originated with the discussion of the comparative thrust of monetary and fiscal impulses. Monetarist analysis typically asserted the relative dominance of monetary impulses with respect to short-run (temporary) output movements. Fiscal policy was acknowledged to have real effects. The *aggregate* real effects, however, were considered to be comparatively small and temporary, except with respect to the real rate of interest and the long-run stock of real capital.

Subsequently, analysis differentiated between the results bearing on price-level and output effects. Elementary price theory informs us that a wide array of real conditions jointly with the money stock determines the movement of the general price level. But *persistent* monetary impulses dominate the inflation rate. The movement of output, meanwhile, reflects interaction of monetary and real shocks. Real shocks probably dominate the stochastic trend determining the evolution of normal output. Monetary conditions may contribute to this trend, especially as a result of distortionary taxes imposed on nominal values and the pattern of uncertainty associated with the prevailing policy regime. The stationary component of output movements reflects the joint impact of monetary and real shocks. The recession of 1973–75 exemplified the interaction between the shocks. A crucial difference between the monetary conditions shaping the stochastic trend and the stationary component is that the latter is controlled by unanticipated and misperceived monetary shocks evolving within a given policy regime, whereas the trend properties are greatly conditioned by the *characteristics* of the *regime*. Acceptance of a stochastic rather than a deterministic trend lowers the contribution of the cyclical component to the observed fluctuation in output and directs attention away from the role of short-run stabilization policy towards longer run "institutional policy" (Nelson and Plosser 1982).

167

MONETARISM

The Money Supply Process and Monetary Policy

Money and the Money Supply Process. Monetarist analysis has examined the nature of money and the money supply process. Money appears to be a social device that lowers both transaction and information costs (Brunner and Meltzer 1971; Alchian 1977). The analysis implies in particular that the social productivity of money is hardly represented by the "shoe-leather theory" interpretations implicit in some inventory approaches. Monetarist analysis offers a different interpretation of the role of real income in money demand functions. Variations in real income (including the "nonmonetized" part of an economy) raise the marginal productivity of money. The underlying analysis, moreover, emphasizes that money emerges, like many social institutions, from the spontaneous interaction between optimizing agents (Schotter 1981). The analysis establishes that there exists no *unique* solution to the social-coordination problem fostering the emergence of "transaction dominating assets." Theoretical questions directed to the *specific* items forming money at any particular time or in the future are thus in principle unanswerable and pointless, in contrast to questions about the existence of some assets with the characteristics of money.

More detailed attention to the money supply process grew naturally from contentious problems associated with specific issues. Keynesians usually disregarded the money supply process and its interaction with the real sector. The reader may compare Tobin-Buiter (1976) with Brunner-Meltzer (1976). It is hardly a coincidence that "A Monetary History of the United States" did *not* emerge from *Keynesian* explorations. Some of the issues motivating the analysis include: the role of "reverse causation"; the importance of the properties and disturbances associated with money demand; the role of various institutions; the comparative role of public, banks, and monetary authorities in the money supply process; the role of the public demand for credit; the role of interest rates; and, specifically, the controllability of monetary growth. Keynesians did not hesitate to offer opinions on all these issues even in the absence of systematic work by them on the money supply process.

Reverse causation is of course consistent with the persistent correlations between income and money. A detailed analysis of the money supply process establishes that a policy of interest rate targeting is the most important condition contributing to "reverse causation." Interest rate policy converts the monetary base, and consequently the money stock, into an endogenous magnitude sensitively exposed to all ongoing shocks affecting market rates of interest. These shocks are transmitted via interest targeting into accelerations or decelerations of monetary growth. This effect may, by good fortune, offset the simultaneous effect of the shock on velocity. But this *possible* offsetting depends on a very specific shock mixture at most very transitory in character and offering poor justification for an interest targeting policy. Other institutional arrangements may create additional channels of reverse causation without contributing to (more or less contemporaneous) *positive* correlation between income and money. A secondary influence operates via the "Hawtrey effect" on the currency ratio and the monetary multiplier over the cycle. But this channel of reverse causation cannot explain the positive money-income correlation. Prevailing policy institutions thus determine the comparative magnitude and also the direction of reverse causation. The latter is consequently very sensitive, in contrast to the "direct" causation, to variations in institutional arrangements controlling the supply function of base money.

The deterministic and stochastic properties of money demand were usually assigned a major influence by the Keynesian tradition of the Federal Reserve System. However, once portfolio processes move beyond the single LM equation—so that the money stock and interest rates emerge from the joint interaction of asset markets—the role of money-demand properties is much altered (Brunner 1973). It also follows that shocks operating on the credit and money markets influence the money supply process very differently. A relatively large variance of shocks affecting credit market conditions strengthens the case for monetary targeting, whereas a relatively large variance of money market shocks supports interest rate targeting. This aspect is neglected by the IS-LM tradition. The analysis of a policy tradeoff between the variance of monetary growth and the variance of "interest rates" also fails once we move beyond the standard IS-LM framework. Asset market interaction incorporating the rudiments of a term structure of interest rates reveals the flaws of the traditional argument (Brunner and Meltzer 1983; Mascaro and Meltzer 1983).

Lastly, much work has centered on the controllability of monetary growth. No monetarist ever expected or asserted that monthly or even quarterly magnitudes could be very closely controlled. The extensive studies prepared for the SOMC by Johannes and Rasche (1980–82), as well as the work of Bomhoff (1977) and Büttler et al. (1979), uphold the monetarists' central contention that monetary growth can be controlled over two quarters to one year within a small margin of error compared to the results produced by the Federal Reserve over the past 12 years.

Monetary Policy. The controllability of monetary growth is a necessary but not a sufficient condition for the monetarist case for a nonactivist regime characterized by a constant monetary growth rate (Brunner 1981b). Other conditions are required to complete the case. A second condition bears on the information required for the rational execution of an activist regime. Every single argument advanced in support of an activist regime postulates the policymakers' full knowledge about the deterministic and stochastic structure of the economy. Such knowledge does indeed offer the possibility of exploiting it for stabilization purposes. Monetarist analysis emphasizes in contrast that such detailed and reliable knowledge is not available (Friedman 1953). In fact, the nature of the economic process, continuously modifying the accumulated information capital, will never afford policymakers detailed and reliable knowledge. But an activist policy proceeding with uncertain information just as likely will reinforce instead of offset covariance between monetary and real shocks. A constant monetary growth rate regime under the circumstances is an optimal risk-minimizing strategy in a state of uncertain and shifting information (Brunner 1981b).

Aspects of Political Reality

A third condition supporting the case for non-activist regimes involves considerations of political economy. Advocates of activist policymaking combine the required information assumption with a "goodwill or public interest theory" of government. They may accept the core of economic analysis in relation to market phenomena but adopt an essentially sociological view in relation to the behavior of non-market institutions. A public interest theory of governmental behavior takes for granted that the full information available will be faithfully exploited for the social benefit. Full information and a public interest theory are thus sufficient conditions for socially productive activist regimes. *But both components of the sufficiency condition are thoroughly contradicted by relevant observations.* Political reality, especially, can hardly be described in terms of a "public interest" theory. Policy bureaucracies and politicians are entrepreneurs in a political market in which information is costly. These political entrepreneurs are deeply involved with their own political interests and influence. Their own preferences dominate the pattern of activist discretion (Brunner 1983; Cukierman and Meltzer 1983). A monetary standard, and most particularly a constant monetary-growth rate rule, is an institutional arrangement constraining the behavior of monetary authorities. The constraint raises the predictability of the regime and lowers the level of monetary shocks produced by an unconstrained discretionary policy.

The rationale for a monetary standard is a special case of a more general approach to political economy. The analysis of monetary and "socio-political" phenomena is *systematically* linked in the monetarist vision and not the chance product of Milton Friedman's idiosyncratic behavior (Tobin 1981). Both fields involve the systematic application of economic analysis, and most particularly, the unifying perception of man underlying economic analysis (Brunner and Meckling 1977). Many Keynesians, in contrast, resort to an implicit sociological view in discussions bearing on aspects of political economy. They frequently "explain" the monetarists' approach to the political economy of a society as an expression of "ideological" commitment or personal idiosyncrasy. This "explanation" simply reflects the failure to recognize (or acknowledge) an essentially *cognitive* issue, namely that monetarists at least attempt to provide a systematic and unified framework for the understanding of social reality.

II. The Media and the Political Market

The "voices of failure" in the past year have increasingly dominated the news. "Monetarism" is alleged on various grounds to have failed. But the array of castigations and objections to monetarism advanced by "supply-siders," Keynesians, or socialists exhibits no coherent pattern. They are not systematically addressed to the basic core of monetarist analysis or to the published statements of monetarists. A recently published book written by a businessman exemplifies this class of purported failure. The author finds the monetarists "wonderfully correct in defining inflation's underlying causes." But he finds them "less than efficient in their efforts to curb it without excessive and unnecessary pain" (*Wall Street Journal*, 4 January 1983, p. 29). The nature of the failure or its criterion frequently remains obscure. Alternatively, the failure is claimed relative to an irrelevant ideal state or without adequate examination of crucial data or the comparative severity of recent recessions.[2] Still, many allusions

[2]The media usually deplore the recent occurrence of the "largest recession or depression" since the 1930s. They hardly notice that total private employment fell *less* than in the recessions of 1953–54 and 1957–58. Real GNP dropped in 1981–82 by 2.6 percent over the recession, but fell 3.4 percent in 1953–54 and 1957–58. Industrial production declined in 1981–82 by about 12 percent, exceeding the 8.8 percent of 1953–54 and the 10.5 percent of 1957–58. The relative divergence of real GNP and industrial production reveals the difference between the early 1980s and the 1950s in the prevailing mix of more permanent allocative adjustments (steel, automobiles) and transitory cyclical movements. A similar problem applies to the rate of unemployment. The much higher level observed in 1982 is associated with an increase measured in percentage points practically equal to the increase in 1953–54 and 1973–75.

and allegations of failure involve a range of issues associated with monetarist analysis. The following sections examine the most common assertions and their relations to monetarist propositions. This examination seems particularly important as the alleged failure is rarely, if ever, supported by juxtaposing the underlying monetarist analysis with relevant facts.

The Recession of 1981–82

The Failure That Wasn't and the Success That Was. The Shadow Open Market Committee in March 1981 appraised the economic prospects of the U.S. economy. Its members argued at the time and during the spring and summer of 1981 that the shift to an anti-inflationary monetary policy expressed by a retardation (in the average) of monetary growth would initiate a recession in 1981. They also predicted a larger decline of inflation in 1982 than the consensus forecast and a lower inflation rate for late 1982 than most other forecasters. Some voices in the chorus shouting "failure" of monetarism in 1982 failed to recognize the direction of the economy, even by late summer of 1981, that was initiated with the monetary policy advocated by the Reagan administration. Shifting from an accelerating to lower monetary growth made a recession (almost) inevitable. The Shadow Open Market Committee, moreover, publicly criticized the optimistic forecasts published by the administration in early 1981 and in 1982.

The SOMC's assessment was certainly confirmed on all these points by actual developments. The media, however, did not acknowledge this confirmation; instead, they reported a recession "unforeseen, not forecasted" that surprisingly emerged on the economic horizon and attributed it to "monetarist" policies. Such policies were indeed, as we recognized before the event, the cause of a recession. But for the media the very *occurrence* of the recession became the prima facie, immediate, and direct evidence of a failure of monetarism. In the media's view, no policy should ever be adopted that risks a recession and rising unemployment. Of course, such a view is inherently flawed. Whatever one's emotional reaction may be, the analysis could still be correct and even the associated policy proposal the best choice in a very bad world. The occurrence of a recession offers, per se, no support for the allegation of the failure of monetarism. Nevertheless, some supply-siders and Keynesians also joined forces in questioning the "necessity" of a recession.

The Supply-Side Story. Some supply-siders had no interest in changing the course of monetary policy. A lower monetary growth was apparently for them not a necessary condition to achieve a decline in inflation. On the contrary, they contended that monetary growth at a high rate would produce an increase of about 13 percent per annum, in nominal GNP. Inflation could be lowered "without tears" (without a recession) as a result of the supply-side incentives unleashed by lower private and corporate taxes. Lower tax rates were expected to raise the rate of real growth and thus squeeze the inflation margin in a given rate of increase of nominal GNP. Monetary *acceleration* was actually *required* in order to allow the expected output expansion. Control of monetary growth along a declining path endangered the results promised by the supply-siders.

If there was a "failure," it rested with the miraculous output effects promised by the supply-side story. But that story was quite incomplete. Expenditure programs and regulatory policies do indeed produce important supply-side responses shaping the behavior of normal output—effects that were systematically neglected in the supply-side story some advocates told. But even a complete and competent account of the welfare-raising effects produced by supply responses, due to the radical change in fiscal policy (including both expenditure and tax programs), would not make a declining monetary growth irrelevant as an instrument of anti-inflationary policy, as some "supply-siders" appeared to believe.

The Keynesian Case. The Keynesian objection to monetarist anti-inflationary policy, best expressed by James Tobin, centers on the social cost of this policy. Three strands compose the Keynesian claim of "monetarist failure." One strand involves Tobin's accusations (1981) that "monetarist propaganda" promised a *costless transition* to a non-inflationary world solely with the instrument of monetary control. The second strand emphasizes the exorbitant level of social costs associated with a disinflationary monetary control strategy compared with the social costs of permanent inflation. Tobin phrased this idea by stressing the large number of "Bailey triangles" fitting into an "Okun gap." The third strand is that a disinflationary monetary policy supplemented by a "tax-based income policy" would effectively lower the social cost of the transition.

The first strand should be recognized as a remarkable fabrication. It thoroughly distorts monetarist arguments bearing on the social costs of disinflation—arguments that the SOMC has consistently stated.

Monetarist analysis, however, differs from Keynesian analysis with respect to the conditions controlling the social cost of disinflation. A Keynesian view of an inertial price-wage process embedded in the social fabric beyond the relevant influence of monetary regimes necessarily associates high social costs with *any* disinflationary policy.

The association occurs irrespective of the history of monetary policymaking and the mode of executing the policy shift. Monetarist arguments, on the other hand, emphasize the importance of the credibility of "disinflationary announcements." Credibility depends, at least in part, on the history of policymaking and the behavior of the policy institution. Low credibility offers little incentive to modify price-wage setting behavior, and the social cost of disinflation rises correspondingly. According to monetarist analysis of the transmission mechanism, the social cost of a disinflationary policy is not predetermined by the magnitude or duration of monetary retardation. It may vary substantially even between episodes exhibiting the same pattern of monetary deceleration. The social cost depends crucially on the public's belief in the persistence of the disinflationary action.

The second strand of the Keynesian objection juxtaposes the costs of a steady, permanent inflation compared with the disinflationary loss of output. But the political reality of a policy of permanent inflation is associated with intermittent and temporary phases of "anti-inflationary" policies (remember 1969, 1971, 1974–75, and now possibly 1981–82). The relevant comparison thus involves the social cost of a single disinflation on the one side and the discounted value of the social costs associated with a series of disinflationary phases in the future. This point has been emphasized repeatedly in position papers prepared for the SOMC. The public interest theory of government or policy institutions that guides much Keynesian thinking may subtly influence the nature of the comparison made. A policy of permanent monetary expansion, executed in accordance with the "public interest," as expressed by a social cost function, in that view could be relied upon to produce a steady inflation.[3]

According to the third strand, monetarists are accused of opposing price-wage controls on essentially ideological grounds without looking at the merits of each individual case. A charitable interpretation of such "ideological condemnations" would attribute them to a failure to recognize the difference in the underlying *theory* of political economy. Tobin's proposal of income policies to supplement anti-inflationary monetary policy seems conditioned, on the one hand, by the inertial price-wage process, and on the other, by the public inter-

---

[3]The unsubstantiated sociological view underlying this Keynesian strand is only one of its empirical problems. It disregards an empirical regularity connecting the rate of inflation and price dispersion (Cukierman 1983). This pattern produces a more diffuse uncertainty about relative prices, the general price level, and market conditions. It makes it more difficult for agents to infer the mix of more transitory and more permanent shocks shaping the economic scene. The real effects of this increased uncertainty add to the social costs of inflation.

est theory of government. The first component, in contrast to the Keynesian position of the 1950s or early 1960s, now attributes to monetary impulses a dominant and rather durable role with respect to output movements. Monetary decelerations (even when accompanied by "massive tax cuts"?) produce a large cumulative loss in output, a loss that can be lowered by price controls. The second component—that incomes policies will operate just for the purpose designed and will be dissolved after this purpose is satisfied—is assured by the public interest theory of political processes. But the analysis of a society's political economy, accepted by at least some monetarists, yields a different evaluation. It implies that irrespective of official motivation for establishing price controls, their operation is only marginally directed to the inflation problem. The price control apparatus will be dominated by groups that seek the redistribution of wealth. Moreover, the political reality lowers the likelihood that the price control system will ever be dismantled once it has been set up. "Monetarist" analysis thus recognizes social costs associated with "supplementary price controls" that are not recognized by some Keynesians.

From its inception in September 1973 the SOMC has expressed concern about the social cost of an anti-inflationary program. This concern, combined with advocacy of a risk-minimizing and predictable course of policy, increasingly induced the SOMC to emphasize the "institutionalization" of monetary policy in contrast to the whims and fragile judgments made by specific persons under "discretionary" policymaking.

The High Level and Volatility of Interest Rates

The behavior of interest rates has for good reasons attracted public attention over the past three years (1979–82), when nominal and real rates moved to levels never observed in the past. The variance of interest rates over the whole spectrum of the yield curve was unprecedented. The experience was generally attributed, with some encouragement by the Federal Reserve authorities, to the change in policy officially announced on October 6, 1979. The "monetarist conversion" of the Fed was seen to be the cause of high and erratic interest rates. The Fed's intellectual tradition anchored in a standard IS-LM paradigm supports this view (Board of Governors 1981). The IS-LM framework implies, as shown in the Fed's staff work, a trade-off between the variance of monetary growth and the variance of "interest rates" represented by a single rate. The "failure of monetarism" thus became clearly visible; interest rates "misbehaved" *after* the Fed instituted a "monetarist" policy of monetary control. So it follows, *post hoc ergo propter hoc.*

The following questions require our attention: Did the Fed pursue a "monetarist policy"? Is there a tradeoff between the variances of interest rates and monetary growth? Does a monetary deceleration systematically raise real rates of interest over a long period?

The first question will be investigated later in a broader context, but some comments may be made at this point. A reliable answer to the question, of course, requires some reference point characterizing a "monetarist policy." Fortunately, a reference point is provided by the writings of Milton Friedman, my paper on monetary policymaking (Brunner 1981b), and the statements or position papers offered over the past eight years by the SOMC. On various occasions the SOMC presented the detailed tactical procedure required for an effective and reliable policy of monetary control. The SOMC, moreover, argued with increasing emphasis that the tactical aspects, while necessary, were not sufficient. They needed to be integrated into a strategic conception expressed by the "institutionalization" of monetary policy. A constant monetary growth standard was the institutionalization advocated by members of the SOMC. When measured against this reference point, little remains of the "monetarist content" of Fed policy. What remains is the *rhetoric* of monetary targeting and the observed average decline of U.S. monetary growth from the end of 1979 until last summer. From 1979 to the summer of 1982, the strategic conception expressed by determined adherence of the Fed to discretionary policymaking (Brunner 1983) persisted with an unbridgeable difference relative to monetarist ideas. And so did the tactical procedures preferred by the Fed. The media may experience difficulties in recognizing and appreciating this substantive fact behind the rhetoric. But any comparison between the record of the Fed and the policies advocated by monetarists yields little support for an affirmative answer to the first question.

The alternative answers to the next two questions are crucially conditioned by the intellectual paradigm controlling the Keynesian view. The view is well represented by the IS-LM framework and its characterization of the transmission mechanism. But an affirmative answer to questions two and three is difficult to reconcile with two important observations cast up during the last three years. First, there occurred *no* tradeoff between the variances of monetary growth and interest rates; they both increased simultaneously. Second, the co-movements between interest rates over the whole spectrum of the yield curve were higher than ever before. The first fact immediately rejects the implication of the standard IS-LM model. The second fact is inconsistent with the proposition that the Fed pursued an anti-inflationary policy of monetary control that had achieved substantial credibility. Such a policy would have produced at most some variability at the *shortest* end of the yield curve with vanishing correlation over the yield curve (SOMC position papers; Brunner and Meltzer 1983). The IS-LM analysis fails to integrate aspects of the term structure and its interaction in response to transitory and permanent shocks. Reliance on this analysis precludes a proper understanding of the events observed since 1979.

The answer to the last question is similarly dependent on the view about the transmission mechanism. A standard IS-LM model will tell us that a retardation of monetary growth raises real interest rates for a long time. The inertial properties of the system assure this result. Older monetarist analysis implied a *temporary* effect concentrated mostly on *short-term* rates. Even this "moderate" position is increasingly questioned by apparently "neutral" economists (Mishkin 1981; Shiller 1980). There is little empirical support for a thesis that monetary retardation produces *persistently* high (short- and long-term) real rates of interest. So what accounts for the behavior of interest rates? The SOMC offered a tentative answer consistent with the evidence of the last three years. The *low credibility* and *diffuse uncertainty* associated with financial policies generated a high and volatile risk premium that was built into gross real rates of interest (Brunner, Shadow position papers 1981–82). A detailed theoretical and empirical study supports this analysis (Mascaro and Meltzer 1983).

The "Definability" and Controllability of Money

Regulations and inflation encourage financial innovations. Such innovations modify the composition of "money" and possibly change the substitution relations between money and non-money financial assets. A host of voices have asserted in the past three years that financial innovations have destroyed the concept of money, made it undefinable or unmeasurable, or measurable with a large error. Monetary control has thus become impossible or exceedingly unreliable, making "monetarist ideas" obsolete.

The fact of innovation is incontestable. But financial innovation is not a new experience. It characterized the 1950s when shares in savings and loan institutions grew much more rapidly than the stock of money did (remember Gurley and Shaw?). But the observation of financial innovation by itself establishes very little. It does not establish undefinability or unmeasurability; neither does it establish uncontrollability of the money supply, or if controllable, the irrelevance of such controls.

Let us turn first to the contention so blithely advanced that we (!) do not know what money is, or that money and credit lack individual qualities. This point covers both the definition and measurement of money, failure to distinguish between the two producing much confusion. Financial innovation does not affect the definition of money, but does require adjustments in measurement procedure. The definition remains basically the same: Money consists of any item which is used with great regularity to settle transactions, i.e., as a generally accepted medium of exchange. The relevance of this definition rests on two observations. First, in most societies a small group of goods or assets satisfies this *general* exchangeability criterion in contrast to most other assets, and second, economic agents do not behave randomly with respect to "transaction dominating assets" and other assets. Innovations over time change the composition of items satisfying the condition laid down by the definition. The composition was indeed affected by recent developments, and measurement procedures have been adjusted by the Fed, as they will have to be intermittently adjusted in the future.

Every measurement, no matter how closely it conforms with the definition, will involve an error. Such errors certainly crept into measures of M1 and M2 by the late 1970s. No evidence has been adduced, however, to support massive errors in the measures of these magnitudes in the past three years, whereas the error in the defunct M1A was probably quite large. It is interesting to note that those who find money undefinable and unmeasurable hardly hesitate to use the CPI or components of national income accounts that are probably subject to substantially larger measurement errors.

It should be emphasized that a constant or proportionate measurement error poses no problem for monetary control. A volatile measurement error together with an array of other conditions is alleged, on the other hand, to have lowered or destroyed the controllability of money. If so, the result would be revealed by the behavior of the money multiplier. Lowered controllability of monetary growth in particular implies that the stochastic process governing the money multiplier has changed in recent years. This change would lower its predictability or raise the variance of the forecast error of the money multiplier.

James Johannes and Robert Rasche have prepared ex ante forecasts of the money multiplier for each semiannual session of the SOMC for the last five years. The accumulated pattern of forecast errors offers no support for the contention of lowered controllability. The patterns, on the contrary, support the monetarist assertion of controllability with a small margin of error within one year. This controllability also is confirmed by the Board of Governors (1981) staff studies.

The relevance of controllability of monetary growth has been questioned on the ground that financial innovations have modified the behavior of monetary velocity. The link between money and national income expressed by velocity, it is argued, has become more uncertain in recent years. Has the stochastic process controlling velocity changed over the last several years? Some preliminary time-series studies described in recent position papers of the SOMC report two crucial statistics. The trend estimate increased somewhat over the 1970s compared with previous decades. But this appearance of an increasing trend is quite tenuous. The 95 percent confidence intervals for the trend parameters derived for the 1950s, 1960s, and 1970s overlap. The overlapping is consistent with the hypothesis that the trend parameter remained unchanged. However, even an increasing trend would pose no real problems for the relevance of monetary control. More interest attaches in this respect to the variance of the innovation expressing unforeseen changes in the velocity of several monetary aggregates. The variance of the innovations in base velocity and M1 velocity measured over the 1970s does not exceed the level estimated for the 1950s, whereas the variance of the innovation in the velocity of M2 rose slightly in the 1970s. Projections of innovations into 1980 and 1981 beyond the sample period (terminated at the end of 1979), moreover, yield no patterns that are substantially improbable (say, at most 5 percent) under the maintained hypothesis of an invariant stochastic process. The regulatory changes initiated in the winter of 1982–83 may affect velocity and permanently modify its level, trend, or variance. Neither of the first two modifications pose any serious problem for long-term monetary policymaking once the pattern is recognized. And speculative adjustments in the transition period with substantial ignorance offer no support for "stabilizing actions." Moreover, suppose that it were confirmed at some point in time that the link between money and national income "became looser" and the variance of the innovation significantly larger. We cannot rationally deduce from this fact that monetary control, and most particularly a constant monetary growth control, is irrelevant. A discretionary policy would probably produce a larger variance of monetary innovations with an unlikely offsetting (i.e., negative) covariance between the innovations that would otherwise occur (Brunner 1983). Well-meaning intentions expressed in flexible actions that are dependent on erroneous information and speculative assumptions cannot be expected to lower the variance of aggregate nominal demand. Lastly, the fact that velocity is well approximated by a random walk implies that discretionary policies attempting to offset observed or anticipated changes in velocity, on the average, most probably raise the variability of changes in nominal GNP.

Monetary Rules and Monetary Standards

The marketing ingenuity of some "supply-siders" has been remarkable. As their story based on tax cuts faded, they shifted attention to monetary problems. They claimed that the "gold standard" or price rules offered a superior arrangements to exorcise both inflation and deflation than monetarist emphasis on the "quantity side." They juxtaposed the "quality" to the "quantity" of money.

Quality Versus Quantity of Money. Termination of inflation required no control over the quantity of money with the corollary danger of recession. Policymakers needed only to improve the *quality* of money to end inflation. By instituting a gold standard the "quality of money" would be radically improved and the price level would be stabilized.

The rise in quality can only mean, at least in the context of economic analysis, an increase in money demand. The increase is produced by the institution of a gold standard which induces expectations of a stable price level. The price level, of course, adjusts to the interaction between money supply and money demand. It may deserve some emphasis that monetarists originally pioneered most of the empirical studies of money demand. A large increase in money demand relative to monetary growth would indeed dampen inflation *temporarily* and lower the price *level* permanently. Still, raising the "quality of money" in the sense defined *irrespective* of the behavior of monetary growth offers no assurance of a stable price level. The policymakers still need to control the magnitude of monetary growth.

The Gold Standard. The invocation of "quality" is not a sufficient argument for a gold standard. This standard must also constrain the behavior of monetary growth. In the absence of an effective constraint, expectations of a stable price level and a "quality jump" would not occur. But even the occurrence of a quality jump does not remove the need for a reliable and persistent monetary constraint. The "quality jump" is at best a once and for all event whereas inflation depends on the *persistent* monetary growth pattern.

A survey of the discussion concerning the gold standard, whether in the media or the political market (U.S. Gold Commission), offers little enlightenment. Advocates of a gold standard are quite vague about the institutional arrangements of a "gold standard." They also leave rather unclear how the arrangements would function to confine monetary growth on the average to a non-inflationary level. Some proponents visualize the gold standard as the definition of the *unit of account* in terms of a quantity of gold. It remains a mystery how this specification affects any transactions and thus the behavior of the money stock and the price level.

Price Rules. The political debacle of the supply-side story required some diversionary action on the media market. This was achieved with the promise that a monetary standard anchored by some price rule could be expected to improve our economic prospects. Some argued that monetary growth should be adjusted inversely to the movement of the gold price. Others argued on behalf of a general price index rule or an index of sensitive commodity prices. These proposals did not emerge from a careful analysis of their consequences. No supporting analysis was ever produced in a professional context or referred to. Some analytic probing establishes unambiguously that a price rule of the kind proposed and based on a general index would produce a non-stationary drift of the price level. It would not assure the prevalence (on the average over time) of a non-inflationary state. The use of price rules based on specific price groups would actually worsen the situation. Allocative or real shocks affecting the relative position of these price groups would be translated into monetary shocks and aggravate the non-stationary drift of the general price level. It should perhaps be noted at this stage that an *indirect* price rule is indeed built into the constant monetary growth regime. The benchmark guiding the choice of monetary growth is determined with the view to assure on the average (say, over four years) a stable price level. The benchmark depends on the trend in velocity and in normal output. The crucial difference between this "indirect price rule" and the "supply-siders' price rule" is this: The latter involves an activist short-run feedback from movements in specific price measures, whereas the former rejects such a feedback and modifies the benchmark only after substantial evidence of *permanent* changes in the underlying determinants.

General Remarks on the Nature of the Discussion

The questions addressed thus far all involve empirical issues. Any answer to these questions can conceivably be false. In particular, monetarist analysis could be empirically untenable, but so could the critics' views. The major thrust of my discussion does not address the correctness or empirical falsehood of the contentions advanced. My emphasis is rather on the quality of the arguments encountered.

They hardly satisfy professional standards. The level of impression-istic language occasionally appearing corresponds to arguments advanced by members of the Flat Earth Society. Similar arguments could "conclusively" establish that the sun rotates around the earth or that the universe is recreated at the beginning of each millenium. The quality of the typical argument is probably most revealing in discussions bearing on definability, measurability, and controllabil-ity of money.[4]

III. The Academic Market

No clean white line separates the political from the academic market. A simple criterion may suffice for our purposes, however. This part of my paper uses arguments advanced in a professional context. Two papers constitute my material: one presented by Harry Johnson (1971) to the American Economic Association and a paper by James Tobin (1981) evaluating the monetarist counter-revolution. My discussion is organized into four sections.

"Monetarism" and Monetarism

A Distorted Focus. Harry Johnson's Richard T. Ely lecture on "The Keynesian Revolution and the Monetarist Counter-Revolution" addressed the problem of changing paradigms, particularly the con-ditions favoring the "marketability" of a new paradigm. Among these conditions, Johnson assigned particular weight to the existence of a dominant socioeconomic problem. In his view, the marketing of the Keynesian Revolution was facilitated by prevailing mass unemploy-ment, while the marketing of monetarist ideas was aided by the drift into an apparently permanent inflation. Johnson may have correctly sensed the conditions favoring monetarist ideas, but I believe his argument projecting the long-run victory of Keynesian ideas focused on the wrong conditions. This issue, however, may be suspended for the moment.

Independently of the truth or falsity of Johnson's argument, it contributed to a limited vision of monetarist thought, covering little beyond money, inflation, and some technical aspects of monetary policymaking. Tobin essentially reinforces this view when he com-plains that Friedman turned "exclusively monetarist" after he had published a more broadly conceived "A Monetary and Fiscal Frame-

---

[4]Articles in the *Wall Street Journal* by Frank Morris, President of the Federal Reserve Bank of Boston, and Irving Kristol on monetary control and monetary policy, published in 1982, are noteworthy examples of the quality of the product offered in the public arena.

work for Economic Stability" (1948). This attribution is unfortunately a distortion of monetarist ideas. Those ideas, bearing on socioeconomic and socio-political issues *as a whole,* were an alternative to the Keynesian vision, whatever the dimension that appealed to the market. The general survey in Section I was deliberately incorporated to make this point. Some of the following discussion elaborates aspects of this broader range related to specific criticisms advanced by Tobin.

The Transmission Mechanism. Two issues appear under this heading—the price-output responses to nominal shocks and the role of asset markets. Tobin (1981) raises the first issue with the claim that monetarists "defined away" the problem of the "missing equation" and "escaped the messy groundwork in which Johnson expected them to lose their identity" (p. 37). Tobin thus repeats, without apparent regard for the professional discussion over the past 20 years, Johnson's (1971) view about monetarists' "abnegation of responsibility for explaining the division of the effects of monetary change between price and quantity movement" (p. 10).

Johnson's evaluation missed important strands of monetarist thought. His forecast of the "identity loss" was falsified by subsequent experience and reveals, once more, the distorted focus on the structure of the monetarist vision that obscures its central *cognitive* thrust.

1. *The "Missing Equation" and Unemployment.* Monetarist analysis presents a view of the transmission mechanism centered on the play of relative prices in asset and output markets. Supply responses thus form an integral part of the view that money substitutes in all directions over all goods. This view implied the monetarist proposition bearing on price and output responses advanced in the early 1960s: Persistent monetary growth approximately determines the movement of the price level and monetary acceleration (or deceleration) conditions output movements relative to normal output. This proposition has survived the facts of the past decades substantially better than did the Keynesian Phillips Curve with its implicit denial of a normal level of output or its explicit (associated) denial of the accelerationist thesis. The rational-expectations analysis, pioneered by Jack Muth and Robert Lucas, subsequently provided an analytical approach to tighten the original idea. It offered in the logician's sense a careful explication for the initial explicandum. That analytical approach should not be understood to depend on the standard market-clearing assumption.

Tobin's recent remark appears even more peculiar when contrasted with the discussion of monetarism in the middle of the 1970s.

Tobin co-authored a paper with Willem Buiter "defining away" any price-level problem (Tobin and Buiter 1976). In contrast, Brunner and Meltzer integrated output *and* price-level responses into the analysis (Brunner 1976; Brunner and Meltzer 1976). Their analysis also stated the conditions under which nominal shocks would be fully absorbed by the price level or partly by output. A first complete formulation of this output-price and asset-market interaction was presented in 1970 at the first Konstanz Conference (Brunner and Meltzer 1972).

It is difficult to fault Johnson for lack of perfect foresight, but Tobin's hindsight should have been better. Monetarists engaged in detailed empirical work bearing on price behavior (implicitly on the "division" of shocks) and also explicitly on output responses. Such work was developed by economists at the Federal Reserve Bank of St. Louis, by the Manchester group of economists, and by an international group associated with Allan H. Meltzer and myself.[5] Tobin's assertion, advanced with astonishing carelessness, is thoroughly contradicted by the facts. And so is Johnson's prediction about the "identity loss" suffered by monetarist analysis as a result of work on the price-output response problem. This statement reveals a subtle misconception of the structure of monetarist thinking. The broad structure of monetarism had been sufficiently delineated in the writings referred to by Johnson. He failed, however, to recognize the interrelations between crucial strands of this thought, as summarized in Section I.

The basic structure of monetarist thought defines an "identity of vision" hardly affected by the *fact* of empirical work on price-output responses. The crucial aspect remains that explicit attention to price-output responses actually sharpened, in contrast to Johnson's prediction, the conflicting interpretations offered by Keynesians and monetarists of the inertial process. The evolution of monetarist analysis, including the most recent extensive work by Milton Friedman and Anna Schwartz, contradicts Johnson's speculation. Subsequent events also contradict his forecast that "we will vanquish inflation at relatively little cost or we will get used to it" (Johnson 1971, p. 12). We

[5]The studies prepared at the Federal Reserve Bank of St. Louis include papers by Karnosky (1976) and by Rasche and Tatom (1977a, 1977b). The work of the Manchester group is summarized by Laidler and Parkin in an *Economic Journal* piece, "Inflation: A Survey," and related work listed in the bibliography of this piece. The studies resulting from the international group associated with Brunner and Meltzer are contained in The Universities-National Bureau Conference Volume published by the *Journal of Money, Credit, and Banking* in February 1973, and the Carnegie-Rochester Conference Series volume on "The Problem of Inflation" published in 1978.

have neither vanquished it nor have we become used to it. This dilemma, built into the political process, creates incentives to persist with a stop-go pattern of highly *erratic* but *permanent* inflation.

"Mass unemployment" is cited by Johnson, with Tobin's approval, as the social problem that will undermine the relevance of monetarist thought. We need to appraise this point very carefully. In some sense, as I interpret Johnson, we should agree. The current state of the economy seems to confirm his judgment. But it is important to understand that Johnson refers to the *political* marketability of monetarist ideas. "The key determinant to success or failure lies not in the academic sphere, but in the realm of policy" (1971, pp. 11–12). Political marketability depends, however, very little on the cognitive relevance of the ideas to be marketed. Apart from the reality of comparative and shifting political appeal there is still the cognitive issue bearing on the employment-unemployment problem. The historical motivation of Keynesian analysis yields neither assurance nor confirmation for its approach to the unemployment problem. A "demand deficiency" that is widely recognized by Keynesians and monetarists indeed occurred in the early 1930s. The recognition of such a problem does not support, per se, the Keynesian approach to unemployment. It can be subsumed under a monetarist framework (Friedman and Schwartz 1963; Brunner 1981a). Finally, the unemployment pattern that has evolved over the past decade in Western nations seems to a large extent beyond the scope of traditional Keynesian analysis. A large portion of current unemployment (in 1983) and the rising trend observed over many years cannot be intelligently interpreted as a result of "demand deficiency." It is essentially a relative-price problem produced by demographic and institutional changes supplemented by major allocative shocks that have raised the level of normal unemployment. The cyclical component of unemployment over the past two years, on the other hand, is indeed a consequence of monetary deceleration. The intellectually remarkable event in this context is the surreptitious conversion of the Keynesians expressed by their "single-minded" attention to the effects of restrictive monetary policy and their hope for salvation by monetary expansion. This "conversion" reveals both their persistent emphasis on independent inertial processes and a noteworthy shift in their assessment of the relative role of monetary policy, compared to the 1950s or 1960s.

2. *Asset Markets and the Substitution Realm of Money.* The reader of Tobin's (1981) article will encounter some surprising allegations and comments when examined against the background of the structure of monetarist thought. "[M]onetarists made quantity leaps from

general asset preference theory to special monetarist propositions. However stable 'the' money demand function may be, equating it to money supply cannot describe the whole economy if the function contains more than one endogenous variable. How Friedman and Brunner-Meltzer could turn multi-asset systems of equations into single equation monetarism remains a mystery I do not fathom" (p. 40). We further read: "Popular rational expectations macro-models, from which strong propositions about policy are derived, are underdeveloped on the financial side. They too neglect to describe the monetary transmission process. They assume a single sovereign M, unspecified as to concept, properties and measure" (p. 41).

These statements grotesquely distort the pertinent facts of monetarist work. The survey of the constituent strands of monetarist thought in Section I emphasized the role of an open-ended substitution process of money over the whole spectrum of assets. This emphasis motivated our insistence on moving beyond the IS-LM paradigm and on stressing the interaction between money, non-money financial assets, and real assets. This interaction radically modifies the nature of the transmission mechanism compared with the standard properties of the IS-LM model. Some tentative empirical work based on this view was explored in the 1960s (Brunner and Meltzer 1966, 1968). More extensive work along the same lines was developed in Europe (Korteweg and van Loo 1977). Tobin's statement is even more inexplicable when confronted with his own work represented, for example, by the paper he co-authored with Willem Buiter (1976), for the conference on monetarism in 1975. Tobin-Buiter presented a standard IS-LM framework with a fixed price level (over parts of the paper) and a *single* portfolio equation expressing the narrow Keynesian substitution assumptions. Brunner-Meltzer, in contrast, argued at great length that this "single equation approach" to financial markets misrepresented the transmission mechanism. In particular, they discussed a list of problems obscured by this *Keynesian* procedure. It is noteworthy that Tobin has recently elaborated, in contrast to his prior Keynesian commitments, the need for a less emasculated analysis of financial markets (1981). Tobin's comment that the rational expectations literature relies on an "undeveloped financial market" ignores the fact that this literature proceeds within the framework extensively advocated by Tobin but augmented by a supply function.

What is the "unfathomable" mystery mentioned by Tobin? He attributes to monetarists "a quantity leap" from asset preference to specific monetarist propositions or a mysterious reduction of multi-asset equations to a single equation. But the latter procedure typically characterizes Keynesian work and not our multiple asset-market analysis, which explicitly includes the interaction between a credit market and the money market. The meaning of the "quantity leap" is not clear and what proposition is leapt to by monetarists remains obscure. No references help the reader, as Tobin's whole paper omits references to any supporting material. As we have in all our analysis used a multi-asset equation system, as contrasted with Tobin's usual lapse into a single-asset equation system when discussing output-money interaction, I am at a loss to understand the nature of the "leap" attributed to us. One possible interpretation may involve the proposal of a "monetarist monetary rule." Should this be the case, then Tobin's assertion is bizarre. We did not derive this rule just from asset preferences. A paper I presented at a conference, with Tobin as a discussant, developed the two necessary and sufficient conditions for an activist regime. The empirical falsehood of these conditions determines the case for a non-activist regime represented by a constant monetary growth standard (Brunner 1981b). This analysis does not depend on specific assumptions about asset preferences, but depends crucially on the diffuse uncertainty bearing on the detail of the economy's response structure. A risk-minimizing strategy pursued under these conditions yields a constant monetary growth policy.

One last clarification of a long-maintained misinterpretation that Johnson's article reinforced: Friedman's discussion of the quantity theory within the frame of a money demand function has frequently been interpreted as a simple "generalization of Keynes." The critique overlooks Friedman's use of a full array of asset yields as arguments of money demand. Aspects of term structure are explicitly recognized. His formulation thus rejects the Keynesian substitution assumptions enshrined in textbooks. His formulation is not subsumable under a Keynesian view of the transmission mechanism.

Normal Output and Impulses. Some of the arguments contained in Tobin's (1981) text address the joint topics of normal output and impulse forces essential to monetarist analysis. We read: "With stable policies, they (i.e., monetarists) say, the economy itself will be stable. Exogeneous non-policy shocks, including entrepreneurial expectations and spirits, are assigned comparatively little empirical importance" (p. 34). This contrasts with another statement deploring the emerging emphasis on real shocks as possibly major influences on business cycles. Regarding "entrepreneurial spirits": Monetarists would say that, in the absence of any reliable theory about their occurrence and behavior, these kinds of real shocks can hardly be dealt with by fine-tuning monetary policy. Fine-tuning under a state of ignorance or uncertainty raises the likelihood of a destabilizing regime, whatever the degree of dynamic stability of the economy may otherwise be.

But consider specifically the assertion that monetarists assign little importance to non-policy shocks. Once again the facts seem to be inverted. The SOMC was among the first groups to emphasize in 1975 that the "quantum jump" in the real price of oil simultaneously caused a permanent increase in the price *level*, a temporary increase in the rate of inflation, and a permanent reduction in normal output. Tobin denies this effect, as he has on previous occasions denied that the OPEC real shock severely lowered normal output. But it happened to be the monetarists who emphasized the role of this non-policy real shock. It also follows that Tobin vastly overestimates the *cyclical* decline in 1974–75.

Money and Money Supply Theory. A variety of *obiter dicta* bear on the nature of money and the structure of the money supply process. Tobin complains that "concept, properties and measures" of money are unexamined and left obscure by the monetarists. They (i.e., the monetarists) "were impatient with requests to define conceptually the 'money' whose quantity was the alleged fulcrum of the economy. What properties of liabilities payable in the unit of account are essentially monetary? What characterizes money?" Tobin continues with some other questions and ends the series with the assertion that "monetarists preferred not to hear these questions." Beyond the nature of money Tobin addresses the structure of the money supply process. He argues that strong swings in the demand for money and credit produce variations in monetary growth. "Sometimes these were 'IS' shocks whose accommodation intensified boom or recession. Sometimes they were "LM shocks that, according to William Poole's paradigm, should be accommodated." He continues his comments on cyclical behavior: "The inevitable short-run pro-cyclical elasticity of money supplies gives ready alibis to those monetarists who are not actually running Central Banks." Lastly, we note Tobin's claim that the short-run relation of M's and MV's to reserve stocks, as subsequent events illustrate, are no tighter than their relation to the Federal Funds rate.[6]

In summary, the quoted material bears on the nature of money and on the money supply process. These are matters to which Keynesians, including Tobin, hardly contributed very much. Consider the first quote referring to "concept, properties and measure." Monetarists have substantially explored these questions, unlike Tobin who occa-

[6]References in this paragraph are to Tobin (1981, pp. 32–33).

sionally commented, without further analysis, on the inherent difficulties in recognizing "money" in the array of "liquid assets." This
should be contrasted with his use of a "single sovereign M" in the
context of an IS-LM approach. We start from the observation that
most people find little difficulty in distinguishing items which *are* a
generally accepted medium of exchange from those which are not.
Most agents easily distinguish between claims representing credit
which are *not* used in general to make payments and those which
are so used. The ability to distinguish is clearly revealed by agents'
behavior expressed by a non-perfect substitutability between items
with different "exchange-ability properties."

But there is more to be said in this context. More than 10 years ago
Allan H. Meltzer and I published an article on "The Uses of Money"
(Brunner and Meltzer 1971). This paper explored the conditions of a
monetary economy and explained money as a social device that
reduces information and transaction costs. It explained in particular
the nature of money's social productivity and the consequences of
hyperinflation and hyperdeflation on the search for new types of
money. An article by Alchian subsequently explored similar lines
(Alchian 1977). Neither Tobin nor the Keynesians, in general, made
any attempt to analyze the nature (concept and properties) of money.

The quoted statements that bear on the money-supply process are
similarly noteworthy. Tobin seems totally oblivious to the discrepancy between the effort invested by monetarists into analytical and
empirical studies of the money supply process and the comparative
disregard of the subject in Keynesian literature. His attribution of
inevitability to pro-cyclical movements of money supplies is without
foundation in analysis and fact pertaining to the money supply process. Systematic pro-cyclicality results from deliberate policy or the
institutional choices made by policymakers (e.g., the structure of
refinancing arrangements for banks). The cavalier attribution of alibi-
seeking by monetarists (which ones? the SOMC?) in order to cover
up the failure of "their policy" ignores the results of the Johannes-
Rasche forecasts of the monetary multiplier. These forecasts yield
serially uncorrelated errors and establish that monetary control within
a band of two percentage points centered on the target is quite
feasible over one year. Monetarist studies have yielded important
insights into the role of the Central Bank, the public, and the banks
in shaping the behavior of monetary growth and the growth rate of
bank credit. This analysis establishes that in the absence of an interest-rate policy, shocks to money demand exert a negligible effect on
monetary growth in the context of the interaction between credit and
money markets. We note as a curiosity Tobin's reference to swings

in M's due to swings in demand for money *and credit* in relation to Poole's analysis. But Poole's IS-LM model contains no credit market. An explicit incorporation of such a market yields implications bearing on credit-market shocks radically different from the results obtained for money-demand shocks. A large variance of credit-market shocks produces a result with respect to the choice of monetary strategy which is opposite that produced by a large variance of money-demand shocks. Monetary policy analysis proceeding within the IS-LM framework disregards this issue. Lastly, Tobin asserts that the relation between the monetary base and monetary growth is no tighter than the relation between the latter and the federal funds rate. The results of the Johannse-Rasche analysis, compared with the historical record of the Fed based on either strategic or tactical use of the federal funds rate, contradict this assertion.

Rewriting History

The most astonishing portion of Tobin's diatribe against "monetarism" is the asserted historical record of failure produced by "monetarist" policymaking. The section opens with one of the most remarkable sentences of his piece: "It is not surprising that the Central Bank fraternity embraced monetarism." This assertion is followed by a singularly shallow supporting argument. "Monetary targeting" became last decade, after the collapse of the Bretton Woods system, "the vehicle of discipline." Central Banks were, so we are told, increasingly influenced by monetarist principles and "sensitive to monetarist criticisms." Tobin finds the record of performance produced by an obviously monetarist policymaking simply "dismal." "Monetarists are," moreover, "in a poor position to shift blame to the inflationary legacy of the 1960s, or to OPEC or to fiscal policy." We also learn that the Fed was "not wholly monetarist." It "moved its short-run money growth target with eyes on national and international economic variables, actual and projected, and did not completely abandon its old strategy of 'leaning against the wind' . . . ."[7]

The assertion that the Fed and all other Central Banks pursued a monetarist regime remains a flagrant falsehood even if propagated in the media and by academic Keynesians. But the prevalence of this assertion justifies a more detailed discussion.

Tobin admits that the Fed "pragmatically modified" its "monetarist policy" but staunchly maintains that this offers no excuse for "alibi-seeking monetarists." We should note in passing the subtle questioning of motives which erodes the possibility of rational dis-

---

[7]The quotes in this paragraph are from Tobin (1981, pp. 30–34).

course. But the "pragmatic modification" involving changes in target, an *ex post facto* adjustment of targets to overshoots, a systematic positive bias in realizations, and the generally inflationary drift of monetary policy, reveals the truth of the matter. *Monetary targeting was a hoax,* a tactical device to defuse outside pressure on the Fed to initiate a policy of monetary control (Brunner 1983). The tactical use of targeting designed to protect the traditional range of discretionary policy is well understood by former members of the Fed's staff and close observers of the scene. This fact explains the prompt appearance of a multiplicity of M's, the weights assigned to specific M's shifting with the perceived political convenience and the "target drift" mentioned above.

Other aspects of the Fed's behavior may be considered. Its strategic conception centered on activist policymaking, and its tactical procedures anchored by the federal funds rate essentially were unchanged. The Fed's dominant conception remains anchored until this day by a very traditional IS-LM framework supplemented by a Phillips relation representing a process with massive inertia (Board of Governors 1981; Lombra and Moran 1980). This Keynesian vision reminiscent of the 1960s conflicts on all counts with the monetarist analysis summarized in Section I. The changes introduced after October 1979 actually offered even better protection for the traditional policymaking with the aid of a more subtle rhetorical curtain to filter outside pressures (Brunner 1982, Shadow position paper; Brunner and Meltzer 1983). A careful and honest observer would want to compare the actual behavior of the Fed with the record (in the public domain) of the SOMC. The comparison would show that the Fed adamantly opposed any constraint on its "discretionary tradition" by any kind of "institutionalized policy," and most particularly by a predictable monetary control policy. Any precommiting regime remained anathema to the Federal Reserve bureaucracy. The Fed refused to supply a useful discussion in its publication of the arguments advanced by the SOMC (Brunner and Meltzer 1983). The hypothetical observer also would want to compare the tactical implementation favored by ·the Fed with the specific proposals advanced by the SOMC and some of its members (Brunner 1981b). This comparison would reveal that monetary targeting exercises cultivated by the Fed contained a good measure of public-relations efforts.

The institutional behavior of the Fed reinforces my argument. The Fed religiously, and with remarkable effort and effectiveness, opposed any appointments to the Board or to the presidency of regional Federal Reserve Banks of persons with known "monetarist contamination." This fact is well established. One should also mention that the game of regular meetings with outside consultants was hardly designed to present "balanced views." Sufficient information about the control of dissent inside the Federal Reserve System has filtered to the outside. The control does not bear so much on disagreements within the FOMC as on any sign of serious, independent questioning, or any work that might drift too much toward aspects reflecting monetarist thought or emphasis. A staff member with monetarist interest will find his survival in the organization difficult indeed.

A comparison of the SOMC's statement, or Friedman's columns in *Newsweek*, with the reality of policymaking exhibits one last but fundamental discrepancy ignored by Tobin. The 1970s exhibited a rising trend in the rate of inflation produced by repeated and increasing accelerations of monetary growth. This crucial observation of *actual* policymaking proceeding under the targeting game thoroughly conflicts with monetarist proposals. The Shadow insistently argued *against* this trend and explicitly objected to the target drift engineered by a pattern of discretionary policymaking favored by our Central Bank. Such policies cannot be reconciled with monetarists' proposals without a radical distortion of the facts. A characterization of actually experienced "monetary targeting" as a "vehicle of discipline" is really a strange description of reality. Similarly strange is the innuendo that monetarists blamed the inflation of the 1970s on the "legacy of 1960s," "OPEC," and "fiscal policy." None of these assertions is true, and Tobin will not find any evidence in Friedman's columns or articles, the SOMC statements, or position papers to support his contention. It was a Keynesian, President Carter's chairman of the Council of Economic Advisers, who attributed a part of the inflation occurring at that time to the Vietnam War. So much about alibi-seeking. The inflation in the 1970s was never attributed by monetarists to fiscal policy and certainly not to a legacy of the 1960s. And most particularly, the SOMC objected to interpretations of *persistent* inflation in terms of OPEC price actions.

Nothing has been mentioned so far about other Central Banks. With the exception of the Swiss National Bank, the situation is quite similar to that at the Fed. The Bank of England's strategy and tactics remain far removed from monetarist ideas. The Bank's tactical implementation of "monetary control" revealed their opposition to monetarists' central policy ideas. Likewise, the Banque de France, the Banco de España, the National Bank of Belgium, and the Swedish Riksbank are not moved by monetarist proposals. Even the Bank of Canada and the German Bundesbank cultivate some rhetorical association that is not extended to the substance of policymaking. Quite generally, whatever the differences among the many Central Banks may be, they share a basically *discretionary approach* even to monetary targeting and most particularly to its execution. They uniformly oppose, explicitly or tacitly, any precommiting strategy. Lastly, the fact of worldwide monetary retardation since 1979–80 is clearly established. This retardation does indeed correspond to monetarist proposals, but not its speed, magnitude, or erratic execution. Some Keynesians also agreed that such retardation was a necessary condition for a declining rate of inflation. Monetarists, however, remained deeply worried about the discretionary, and thus essentially unreliable, context of the policymaking process. This concern seems justified once again by the most recent shift (in the late fall of 1981) in the Fed's strategy back to interest rate control. This concern is reinforced by the events observed since July 1982.

IV. Johnson's Prediction and the Relevant Failure of Monetarism

Johnson's prediction offers a good point of departure for a final assessment of the alleged failure of "monetarism." The reader may be reminded that according to Johnson, a decline of monetarist ideas and a corresponding reemergence of Keynesian analysis would occur with the reappearance of a stubborn unemployment problem.[8] It was noted before that this statement requires some interpretation because it is unclear whether it refers to the cognitive content or the "political marketability" of monetarist analysis.

The cognitive issue associated with the so-called "Keynesian character" of the unemployment problem was discussed in Section III, where it was shown that there was little reason to recognize in the current state of the labor market the *dominance* of a "Keynesian problem." Other dimensions, associated with relative prices and wages, probably constitute the major portion of the measured rate of unemployment and of the rising trend of normal unemployment experienced in most Western nations. But this trend is hardly explainable in terms of the Keynesian framework. The unemployment problem that has evolved over the past 15 years thus offers no good

---

[8]Johnson (1971, p. 13) also argued that monetarist attempts to correct their alleged neglect of price-output problems would lure them "into playing in a new ball park, and playing according to a different set of rules than it [monetarism] initially established for itself." Johnson seriously misunderstood the *logical* issues involved in this context. The *rules* he attributes to monetarists were essentially an invention of the Keynesians who bothered little to appreciate the conditions under which reduced forms offer valid tests for propositions bearing on *classes* of hypotheses. The projected "loss of identity" was thus based on a substantial analytic confusion.

grounds to embrace Keynesian theory as a guide to understanding the real world.

The cognitive interpretation of Johnson's prediction is further eroded by intellectual developments over the past 10 years. The monetarist position described in my old paper (Brunner 1971) has changed in several aspects. The analysis of the transmission mechanism benefited from the emergence of rational expectations models. The analysis of impulse shocks and the operation of a normal level of output were altered in response. And quite importantly, increasing concern about the background of policymaking led monetarists into a more extensive analysis of a society's political economy and the political economy of political institutions. All this involved a systematic evolution of earlier ideas even while it required much change in detail and technology of analysis. It can hardly be described as a "fading away," expressing a gradual "loss of identity" in a "Keynesian mainstream." This applies in particular to the reconciliation of "equilibrium analysis," associated with a generalization of "market clearing," with institutional facts surrounding price-and wage-setting behavior. Monetarist analysis from its inception accepted Henry Thornton's emphasis on comparatively "inflexible" prices or wages; i.e., it argued that prices and wages *do not fully* reflect all current shocks. Older monetarists found the "flexible price equilibrium model" of the younger generation a useful device to introduce and elaborate the idea of rational expectations, but also quite problematic as an approach to the observable world. It would appear that at this stage professional research has shifted again in the direction of the initial intuitive stirring of monetarist ideas, namely, to integrate institutional aspects of price-wage setting into a generalized equilibrium analysis. This would still be far removed from the traditional Keynesian approach expressed by a comparatively invariant inertial process controlled by institutional patterns that are hardly subject to feedback from the process described or the pattern of evolving shocks.

The Keynesian position has also experienced major modifications. Common ground emerged between many Keynesians and monetarists in their respective approach to inflation. A core with correspondingly small variance determined by a longer-run monetary regime is distinguished from more transitory components suffering a higher short-run variance associated with an array of real shocks. Modigliani's 1977 presidential address to the American Economic Association hardly expresses the Keynesian position of the 1950s or even the 1960s. Tobin (1981) recognizes, at least in principle, the relevance of our critique addressed to the IS-LM framework. He seems to accept at this stage the accelerationist thesis and the general idea of rational expectations.[9] Governor Wallich (1982) recently presented ideas pertaining to anti-inflationary policies and interest-control policies which are centerpieces of monetarist policy analysis.

It is an interesting question whether Johnson's "loss of identity" should rather be addressed to the Keynesian position. Keynesians need not worry, however. Leading Keynesians implicitly reject the extension of economic analysis to the working of the political process or the functioning of political institutions. They are basically committed to some version of a sociological vision of the socio-political process (Brunner and Meckling 1977). This strand appears most explicitly in Okun's (1975) work, but also is exemplified in Tobin's and Modigliani's arguments concerning the political sector and government policy. That approach to political institutions and the assessment of the role of government differs basically from the approach and assessment developed by a systematic extension of economic analysis. This difference moreover reflects, in contrast to the standard response of some Keynesians, substantive issues beyond ideological considerations.[10] In my judgment it will increasingly affect the discussion of public policy. "Keynesians" and "non-Keynesians" basically offer a radically different vision (both normatively and "positively") of the future course of Western societies. This will be the central issue in the future. Questions of monetary control and stabilization policies form incidental aspects of the basic problem.

At this point we acknowledge the ultimate and permanent failure of monetarism, in the sense that policymakers will not constrain themselves by its principles. Keynesian political economy combined with major strands of Keynesian macro-analysis provides a highly marketable product to the political market. The Keynesian approach offers an excellent framework for the rationalizations of activist pursuits of redistributive schemes under one guise or another. Keynesian ideas do not sway the political market with their cognitive force. They find a political constituency because they fit so well the interests of agents in the public arena. Monetarist thought, in contrast, has little marketability politically and little persistent appeal to the

---

[9]Herschel Grossman recognized these changes in his review of Tobin's *Asset Accumulation and Economic Activity: Reflections on Contemporary Macroeconomic Theory*. Review in *Journal of Monetary Economics* 10 (July 1982).

[10]Tobin's (1981) ambiguous use of the word "ideology" is noteworthy in this context. When he speaks about the "ideology of monetarism," his use of the word could be usefully replaced by a more neutral term, e.g., by Carnap's reference to an explicandum idea. Such usage would require a balancing contraposition with "the ideology of the Keynesians." The meaning of the term, however, shifts on occasion to the standard pejorative use applied by the intelligentsia. This shift can be observed in oral discussions.

intelligentsia. It therefore has little to offer any potential political constituency.

The story of inflation and anti-inflation policies illustrates this point. The benefits of inflation are generally well understood by the beneficiaries, whereas the costs are widely dispersed. The costs of disinflation, meanwhile, are well recognized by the social groups involved, but the benefits accrue gradually, are diffuse, and are not clearly or immediately visible to the public. Sustained inflation thus creates political interests favoring policies of permanent inflation. Against this background of political circumstances monetarist proposals of anti-inflationary monetary policy have at most temporary political appeal and arouse at best a passing interest among the media. The combination of costs and benefits of inflation and disinflation obstructs the emergence of a sustained political constituency actively supporting the monetarist approach to the inflation problem.[11]

Monetarist thought, with its dominant constitutionalist emphasis on limited government and with its emphasis on "institutionalization" of policy, offers no saleable product to political entrepreneurs acting in the public arena. Such entrepreneurs need a supply of new programs or modifications and extensions of already existing programs for their strategy of competitive survival. In contrast to the failure of monetarism to penetrate the political market, the longer-run political success of Keynesian thought seems assured by the nature of this market and by the competing intellectual product. Monetarism does involve a *political* failure as envisioned by Johnson, but, in my judgment, for entirely different reasons. The monetarist analysis, however, will better explain the long-run consequences of the Keynesian *political* victory that may be expected to dominate the rest of this century.

References

Alchian, Armen. "Why Money?" *Journal of Money, Credit, and Banking* 9 (February 1977): 133–40.

Board of Governors of the Federal Reserve System. *New Monetary Control Procedures*. 2 vols. Federal Reserve Staff Study. Washington, D.C.: Board of Governors, February 1981.

[11]The Swiss exception in the middle 1970s and its "fall from grace" in the winter of 1978–79 deserve some attention in this context. Anti-inflationary policy found a constituency encompassing employers' associations and labor unions. This constituency was ruptured for a while by the threat to Swiss exports caused by the fall of the deutsche mark and the dollar. The conditions shaping this constituency and the role of the Central Bank as a leader of this coalition, together with its temporary rupture, invite a detailed exploration. In retrospect, this coalition will probably appear by the end of this decade as a passing and peculiar historical episode.

Bomhoff, Eduard J. "Predicting the Money Multiplier: A Case Study for the U.S. and the Netherlands." *Journal of Monetary Economics* 3 (July 1977): 325–45.

Brunner, Karl. "The Report of the Commission on Money and Credit." *Journal of Political Economy* 69 (December 1961): 605–20.

Brunner, Karl. "The Monetarist Revolution in Monetary Theory." *Weltwirtschaftliches Archiv* 5 (1970): 1–30.

Brunner, Karl. "Survey of Selected Issues in Monetary Theory." *Schweizerische Zeitschrift für Volkswirtschaft und Statistik*, 107th year, no. 1, 1971.

Brunner, Karl. "A Diagrammatic Exposition of the Money Supply Process." *Schweizerische Zeitschrift für Volkswirtschaft und Statistik* (December 1973): 481–533.

Brunner, Karl. "Inflation, Money and the Role of Fiscal Arrangements: An Analytic Framework for the Inflation Problem." In *The New Inflation and Monetary Policy*. Edited by Mario Monti. London: Macmillan, 1976.

Brunner, Karl. "Understanding the Great Depression." In *The Great Depression Revisited*. Edited by Karl Brunner. Boston: Martinus Nijhoff, 1981a.

Brunner, Karl. "The Control of Monetary Aggregates." In *Controlling Monetary Aggregates, III*, pp. 1–65. Boston: Federal Reserve Bank of Boston, 1981b.

Brunner, Karl. "The Pragmatic and Intellectual Tradition of Monetary Policymaking." *Schriften des Vereins für Sozialpolitik* 138 (1983): 97–142.

Brunner, Karl, and Meckling, William H. "The Perception of Man and the Conception of Government." *Journal of Money, Credit, and Banking* 9 (February 1977): 70–85.

Brunner, Karl, and Meltzer, Allan H. "A Credit Market Theory of the Money Supply and an Explanation of Two Puzzles in U.S. Monetary Policy." In *Essays in Honor of Marco Fanno, II*, pp. 151–76. Edited by Tullio Bagiotti. Padua: Edizioni Cedam, 1966.

Brunner, Karl, and Meltzer, Allan H. "Liquidity Traps for Money, Bank Credit and Interest Rates." *Journal of Political Economy* 76 (January/February 1968): 1–37.

Brunner, Karl, and Meltzer, Allan H. "The Uses of Money: Money in the Theory of an Exchange Economy." *American Economic Review* 61 (December 1971): 784–805.

Brunner, Karl, and Meltzer, Allan H. "A Monetarist Framework for Aggregative Analysis." *Proceedings of First Konstanzer Seminar on Monetary Theory and Monetary Policy*. Supplement to *Kredit und Kapital* 1 (1972): 31–88.

Brunner, Karl, and Meltzer, Allan H. "An Aggregative Theory for a Closed Economy." In *Monetarism*. Edited by Jerome Stein. Amsterdam: North-Holland, 1976.

Brunner, Karl, and Meltzer, Allan H. "Strategies and Tactics for Monetary Control." *Carnegie-Rochester Conference Series* 18 (Spring 1983): 59–103.

Büttler, H. J.; Gorgerat, J. F.; Schiltknecht, H.; and Schiltknecht, K. "A Multiplier Model for Controlling the Money Stock." *Journal of Monetary Economics* 5 (July 1979): 327–42.

Cukierman, Alex, and Meltzer, Allan H. "A Positive Theory of Credibility and Monetary Inflation." Working Paper, Graduate School of Industrial Administration, Carnegie-Mellon University, 1983.

Friedman, Milton. "A Monetary and Fiscal Framework for Economic Stability." *American Economic Review* 38 (June 1948): 245–64.

Friedman, Milton. "The Effects of a Full-Employment Policy on Economic Stability." In *Essays in Positive Economics*, pp. 117–32. Chicago: University of Chicago Press, 1953.

Friedman, Milton, and Schwartz, Anna J. A. *Monetary History of the United States 1867–1960.* Princeton: Princeton University Press, 1963.

Jensen, Michael C., and Meckling, William H. "Rights and Production Functions: An Application to Labor-Managed Firms and Co-Determination." *Journal of Business* 52 (October 1979): 469–506.

Johannes, James, and Rasche, Robert. Position papers prepared for the Shadow Open Market Committee, 1980–82. (Available from the Graduate School of Management, University of Rochester.)

Johnson, Harry G. "The Keynesian Revolution and the Monetarist Counter-Revolution." *American Economic Association Papers and Proceedings* 61 (May 1971): 1–14.

Karnosky, Denis. "The Link Between Money and Prices: 1971–76. Federal Reserve Bank of St. Louis *Review* 58 (June 1976): 17–23.

Korteweg, Pieter, and van Loo, P. D. *The Market for Money and the Market for Credit: Analysis, Evidence and Implications for Dutch Monetary Policy.* Leiden: Martinus Nijhoff, 1977.

Lombra, Raymond, and Moran, Michael. "Policy Advice and Policymaking at the Federal Reserve." *Carnegie-Rochester Conference Series* 13 (Autumn 1980): 9–68.

Lucas, Robert E., and Sargent, Thomas J. *Rational Expectations and Econometric Practice.* Minneapolis: University of Minnesota Press, 1981.

Mascaro, Angelo, and Meltzer, Allan H. "Long and Short Term Interest Rates in a Risky World." *Journal of Monetary Economics* 12 (November 1983): 485–518.

Meltzer, Allan H. "Keynes's General Theory: A Different Perspective." *Journal of Economic Literature* 19 (March 1981): 34–64.

Mishkin, Frederic S. "The Real Interest Rate: An Empirical Investigation." *Carnegie-Rochester Conference Series* 15 (Autumn 1981): 151–200.

Nelson, Charles R., and Plosser, Charles I. "Trends and Random Walks in Macroeconomic Time Series: Some Evidence and Implications." *Journal of Monetary Economics* 10 (September 1982): 139–62.

Okun, Arthur M. *Equality and Efficiency: The Big Trade-Off.* Washington, D.C.: Brookings Institution, 1975.

Rasche, Robert, and Tatom, Jack. "The Effects of the New Energy Regime on Economic Capacity, Production and Prices." Federal Reserve Bank of St. Louis *Review* 59 (May 1977a): 2–12.

Rasche, Robert, and Tatom, Jack. "Energy Resources and Potential GNP." Federal Reserve Bank of St. Louis *Review* 59 (June 1977b): 10–23.

Schotter, Andrew. *The Economic Theory of Social Institutions.* London: Cambridge University Press, 1981.

Shiller, Robert J. "Can the Fed Control Real Interest Rates?" *Rational Expectations and Economic Policy*. Chicago: University of Chicago Press, 1980.

Tobin, James, "The Monetarist Counter-Revolution Today—An Appraisal." *Economic Journal* 91 (March 1981): 29–42.

Tobin, James, and Buiter, Willem. "Long-Run Effects of Fiscal and Monetary Policy on Aggregate Demand." In *Monetarism*. Jerome Stein, ed. Amsterdam: North-Holland, 1976.

Wallich, Henry. "The U.S. Economy Over the Next Five Years." A summary of his remarks presented at the annual meeting of the American Economic Association, December 1982. Mimeo.

9

MONETARY REFORM IN AN UNCERTAIN ENVIRONMENT*

Allan H. Meltzer

Introduction

The 20th century has produced a rich array of monetary experience. The experience can be organized in several different ways. One emphasizes the role of gold in international monetary arrangements. Early in the century, domestic monies of major trading countries were convertible into gold at a pre-established fixed price, and gold coins circulated. Currently, governments do not set the price of gold, and there is no formal requirement on governments to exchange gold for currency or currency for gold.[1] This is a relatively recent phenomenon, and there are some who prefer to return to a fixed, guaranteed price. A second method of organization focuses on the arrangements for exchanging a country's currency for other currencies and particularly on the choice between fixed and fluctuating exchange rates. Major trading countries now either permit exchange rates to be determined by market forces or adjust the rates frequently to reflect market forces. A third method of organizing experience focuses on the role of governments or central banks in the monetary system. Under either

---

*Reprinted from *Cato Journal* 3 (Spring 1983): 93–112. An earlier version of this paper was presented at the 1982 Berlin meeting of the Mont Pelerin Society.

The author is John M. Olin Professor of Political Economy and Public Policy at the Graduate School of Industrial Administration, Carnegie-Mellon University. Helpful comments were received from Karl Brunner, Carl Christ, Tim Congdon, Alex Cukierman, Milton Friedman, Alvin Marty, and Lawrence H. White.

[1]Some writers want to restrict the term "gold standard" to refer to a relation between the number of ounces (or grams) of gold and the unit of account, say one guinea is one ounce of gold. Here, the "guinea" is a unit of account, i.e., a convention for expressing values. The convention tells us nothing about money prices or about the relation of gold to money prices or the price level. For gold to affect the price level, there must be a connection between ounces of gold and money prices. This requires more than the choice of a unit of account. Fixing the price of gold by agreeing to buy and sell ounces of gold at a fixed price establishes a link and opens the possibility of stabilizing the price level by buying and selling gold. I see no point to "reform" of the unit of account. One unit, even an abstract unit, is as useful as any other.

a gold standard or a regime of fixed currency exchange rates, the government sets a price and agrees to buy and sell its money at that price. The decision to control the price or exchange rate leaves the determination of the quantity to market forces. A decision to control the quantity of money perforce requires that the prices of gold and other currencies be permitted to change.

Experience with the various monetary arrangements has served to heighten awareness of the disadvantages of each. The interwar gold standard transmitted the price deflation and contraction of the early 1930s, and contributed to the depth and extent of the period known as *the* depression. The postwar, international system, known as Bretton Woods, established fixed, but adjustable, exchange rates and, after more than a decade, increased welfare by establishing convertibility between major currencies. The price of gold was fixed, but gold had a minor role, and its role diminished as the system matured. The Bretton Woods system avoided deflation but transmitted inflation. When the system ended, major trading countries moved toward a loose system of domestic monetary control with fluctuating or adjustable exchange rates and preannounced targets for growth of one or more monetary aggregates.

Some main problems with the current arrangement are well known. Most countries have not avoided inflation; costs of disinflation have been higher than generally anticipated; and in many countries, monetary targets have not been achieved with enough regularity to make the announcements of planned money growth credible. Consequently, expectations about growth of monetary aggregates are volatile at times; there is widespread skepticism about the ability of central banks to provide noninflationary money growth and about the costs of doing so. During the early 1980s, interest rates (at all maturities) in the United States and many other countries were higher (after adjusting for inflation) and more volatile than in the previous 50 years or more. High and variable rates of interest and variable money growth increase uncertainty and contribute to the stagnation of the economies of major trading nations. The concurrent increase in the variability of interest rates and money under current arrangements suggests that the present system did not trade higher variability of interest rates for lower variability of money growth. This suggests, in turn, that the variability of either money or interest rates, or both, can be reduced by monetary reform.

Monetary management, at the discretion of central banks or governments, based on forecasts of future economic activity and inflation, has *not* produced stability. Experience has shown that economists' forecasts of short-term changes are less accurate, and government actions less stabilizing, than many economists and officials once believed. Research has shown that every policy is a choice of rule; the only purely discretionary policy is a purely random or a haphazard policy. Hence, the rational choice of policy is a choice between rules.

Policy rules may differ in a variety of ways, including complexity, formal statement, prescribed flexibility, responsiveness to relative and absolute changes in supply and demand for goods and services, and in the uncertainty that they engender about the future. The more frequent changes in the policy rule, the less certain is the actual or perceived adherence to the rule. The flexibility that permits government to change policy has a cost: Anticipations about the future conduct of policy are altered. The effect of uncertainty is an important, but often neglected, characteristic that affects the cost of following alternative rules in a world subject to unpredictable changes.

Types of Monetary Reform

Interest in monetary reform has been stimulated by the combination of research and experience. Three types of reform, each with many variants, are advocated. One proposes a return to some type of gold or commodity standard under which the central bank would be obligated to buy and sell gold, or some other commodity, or basket of commodities, at a preannounced price. The second, a monetary rule, keeps the growth rate of money on a prescribed path. The third proposal, associated with Friedrich Hayek and Ludwig von Mises, eliminates the government and the central bank from the monetary system. Proposals for competitive, unregulated banking—often called "free" banking—leave control of money growth to the decisions of the public. Wealth-maximizing bankers produce the quantity and type of money that the public demands.

The distinguishing feature of a gold or commodity standard is that the government or central bank makes an enduring commitment to control one set of prices and accept the monetary and economic consequences that are consistent with the controlled prices. Friedman (1951) has presented a thorough analysis of the benefits and costs of commodity reserve currencies under the assumption that the level of output is independent of the choice of policy. The assumption of independence is restrictive, however. The choice of a monetary system determines the types of risks and uncertainty that society bears, and uncertainty affects the size of the capital stock. Hence, the assumption that output or consumption is independent of the choice of monetary standard should be relaxed.

The most familiar version of a quantity rule—Milton Friedman's monetary rule—requires the central bank to keep a (broad or inclusive) measure of money growth at a rate equal to the long-term average rate of growth of real output. Several alternative rules do not require constant money growth; they provide for systematic, short-term changes in the growth rate of money. Some require the central bank to vary money growth in the direction opposite to the short-run changes in the current or recent average rate of inflation, or to the current or average rate of change of a basket of commodity prices. These rules are a type of commodity-price stabilization scheme, but they avoid the cost of buying, selling, and storing commodities. The government sells securities to reduce money growth when the prescribed index rises and buys securities to increase money growth when the prescribed index falls. Another type of monetary rule, proposed by Friedman (1948), requires a cyclically balanced budget, a fixed tax structure, and fixed rules for tax and transfer payments. Exchange rates fluctuate freely. The stock of money grows, on average, at the rate of growth of government spending. The latter is equal to the maintained (identical) average rates of growth of taxes and output, so the average rate of money growth is equal to the average rate of growth of output. The budget deficit and surplus fluctuate cyclically; this permits money growth to rise relative to trend during recessions and deflations, and to fall relative to trend during booms or in periods of inflation.

A credible monetary rule reduces uncertainty about money growth, but does not eliminate all short- or long-term changes in the rate of inflation. Fluctuations in output or the budget affect short-term inflation. Productivity shocks that change the growth of output must be followed by changes in the growth of money to avoid long-term inflation or deflation. Under a monetary rule, the risks borne by the public depend, therefore, on the type of monetary rule that is adopted and on the type of shocks that occur. Generally, permanent and transitory changes in the level and growth rate of output cannot be predicted in advance or instantly identified when they occur, so the rule cannot be adjusted until *after* the changes in the *growth rate* of output have been established.

Proposals for monetary reform usually assume that the public prefers a noninflationary rate of money growth. This may be true, but it has not been demonstrated. Nor has it been shown that the rate of inflation that maximizes wealth, or the utility of wealth and private consumption, is identically zero. More likely, the costs and net benefit of price stability depend on the choice of institutional arrangements (or policy rules) used to achieve stability. Institutional arrangements that reduce risks and uncertainty lower the cost of achieving any chosen rate of inflation or deflation, including zero.

I have chosen to avoid discussion of the optimal rate of inflation. A monetary rule is as capable of producing one average rate of money growth as another; for a monetary rule, the issue is of secondary importance. Proposals that leave the rate of money growth to the market cannot assure price stability. Money growth is endogenous and its average rate of change depends on costs of production, alternative uses of gold and other real factors. Those who favor a gold standard or "free banking" urge, not always explicitly, some alternative to a stable average price level or an optimal average rate of inflation as a means of maximizing welfare.

To avoid discussion of banks, banking, and financial arrangements, I use the term "money" to refer to base money—currency or note issues and bank reserves. If money is produced by a government monopolist, money means the monetary base—the monetary liabilities issued by the monopolist. Private production of money refers to the production of currency or notes, which may circulate or be held as a reserve by other banks. Currency may be gold, and notes may be claims to a fixed quantity of gold or commodities. None of the proposals require 100 percent reserve requirements to be effective, although the costs and benefits of each reform change with the set of arrangements, including reserve requirements, mandated or chosen. Further, I assume that there is no regulation of interest rates or portfolios and no relevant restriction of private choice. Private producers of money can, if they choose, compete with the government.

Supplementing the broad, economic implications of a monetary reform are the broader issues of political economy. The monetary reform that the voters in democratic countries prefer may differ from the reform that the market would choose. It seems best to put issues of social or political choice aside until we have a better idea about the way the various reforms are likely to work.

The perspective I choose is that of a consumer interested in maximizing the utility of wealth or consumption. He prefers lower to higher risk; he is risk averse. Monetary reforms that increase uncertainty are rejected in favor of reforms with lower uncertainty even if wealth is the same. I argue that risk and uncertainty affect the level of income and consumption: Lower risk and uncertainty are associated with a larger capital stock, higher income, and higher consumption. A monetary reform that reduces uncertainty is preferred for this reason.

Uncertainty, Risk, and Real Income

My definitions of risk and uncertainty follow the definitions used by Knight (1921) and Keynes (1921, 1936).[2] Risk refers to the "known" distribution of outcomes. These are of two kinds. People may know the probability of an event, for example, the toss of an unbiased coin, or they may classify events based on experience or subjective belief. Following Knight (1921, pp. 224–5), we may identify the first with mathematical probability and the second with empirical probability. Uncertainty refers to events for which the distribution of outcomes is unknown, and the basis for classification is tenuous. An example, used by Keynes (1937), is the probability that capitalism would survive until 1970. Wars, atomic explosions, and various political decisions affecting tax rates or regulation are best described as uncertain as to timing and often as to occurrence. There is no useful way to predict many events, or to classify the time of their occurrence into distributions, or to compute the expected time of occurrence.

Risk and uncertainty cannot be eliminated. The distributions of future economic outcomes cannot be given fixed means and constant variances. Changes in taste or technology or political changes induce permanent changes in the level or growth rate of prices and output that cannot be predicted in advance. Often, such changes cannot be identified as transitory or permanent changes, or classified as changes in level or growth rate until sometime after the changes occur. Recent events, including changes in the price of oil, in the relative size of government, or the permanence of the decline in world inflation and the stability of political regimes in the Middle East, are illustrative.

The classification of events as risky or uncertain is not fixed, and the cost of risk bearings is not constant. Costs can be reduced for an individual or society by developing market arrangements, by the choice of policy rules, and by the choice of asset portfolios.

The choice of policy rules affects the ability to classify events. A credible system of fixed exchange rates lowers risk and uncertainty about the exchange rate, but increases the risk and uncertainty about money growth. A credible monetary rule lowers the risk and uncertainty about future money growth, but increases the risk and uncertainty about future exchange rates and interest rates. Each of these

[2]Meltzer (1982) compares Knight and Keynes and distinguishes their view of expectations from current versions of rational expectations.

rules generates different expected responses of prices and output and different variability of prices and output.

Diversification, pooling, and hedging are examples of market arrangements that reduce risk and the cost of risk-bearing. The development of each of these arrangements depends on someone's ability to classify events into probability distributions and compute expected values. Costs of risk-bearing differ with the degree of risk, measured by the parameters describing the distribution of outcomes. Differences in the cost of risk-bearing are likely to be smaller than differences between the cost of bearing risk and the costs of uncertainty. The reason is that uncertain events cannot be classified, so costs cannot be reduced by market arrangements that convert risky outcomes into smaller and more certain costs.

Individuals can reduce the cost of uncertainty, under any set of rules, by holding relatively safe assets in place of risky assets. Countries with a history of political instability generally have less capital per man, and less durable capital, than countries with stable governments. In such countries, the marginal product of capital is often high, but the return to investment is uncertain. People shift wealth to assets with values that are less dependent on political decisions, including foreign assets and precious metals. The stock of domestic real capital falls until the after-tax, risk-adjusted real return compensates holders for bearing the additional uncertainty.

The costs of bearing avoidable uncertainty fall on present and future generations. Domestic and foreign lenders demand a premium to compensate for the additional uncertainty, so real rates of interest are higher than the rates in more certain environments. Real investment is lower; the capital stock is smaller. Real income and consumption remain below the level that could be achieved in a less uncertain environment.

Monetary reform cannot compensate for all shocks arising from political instability, uncertainty about tax and spending policies, or many other sources of uncertainty.[3] But differences in monetary arrangements dampen or augment particular shocks to a greater or lesser extent and change the ways in which the shock is felt. An example is the difference in the effect of an unanticipated change in the size of a fiscal deficit. A rule requiring *constant* money growth prevents the deficit from being financed by money creation. A mon-

[3]This is recognized in proposals for reform by, *inter alia*, Simons (1948), Friedman (1948), Brennan and Buchanan (1980). Recent work by Brunner and Meltzer (1972), Christ (1979), McCallum (1982), and many others shows that some combinations of fiscal and monetary policy are unstable.

etary rule that requires money growth to rise and fall in fixed relation to budget deficits and surpluses increases the money stock during recessions, when prices and output fall, and reduces the money stock when prices and output rise cyclically. Even if the two monetary rules are accompanied by the same restriction on the growth of government spending and the same tax arrangements, they differ in the degree to which they reduce uncertainty. One reason is that the fiscal and monetary effects of real shocks differ.

If all shocks are temporary (e.g., unanticipated cyclical changes in aggregate demand), the two monetary rules generate indistinguishable long-term outcomes but different short-term outcomes. With constant monetary growth, deficits are financed by selling bonds, and surpluses are financed by retiring bonds. Under the rule requiring counter-cyclical issues of money, an unanticipated change in money finances part of an unanticipated deficit. Money is more variable and debt is less variable under the counter-cyclical monetary rule; but there is no differential uncertainty about future budgets or money growth under the two rules. People planning future consumption anticipate the same future tax rates, size of government, and price level under either rule.

The key assumption, implicit in the previous paragraph, is that changes in aggregate demand are drawn from a distribution with fixed mean and constant variance. The assumption permits investors to forecast the growth of aggregate demand, deficits, money, and output for an indefinite period. There is risk of fluctuations, but there is no uncertainty about the long-run position.

Suppose that, in addition to transitory or cyclical shocks to aggregate demand, there are permanent and transitory shocks to output. Technical innovation, weather, political disturbances, tariffs, and cartels are examples. A century or more ago, plagues or diseases that killed a significant fraction of the labor force would have a prominent place in the list of output shocks. When there are persistent changes in the growth rate of output or the level of output, there is uncertainty about future prices and rates of price change. This uncertainty is reflected in interest rates, exchange rates, and, therefore, in portfolios.

Typically, the duration of a shock is not known at the time it occurs, so the duration of any shock may be uncertain at first. As time passes, information about the shock increases, and the shock can be classified as a permanent or transitory shock to output, or as a permanent shock to the growth rate of output.[4] Since the two monetary rules require

---

[4] A permanent shock to the level of output is a transitory shock to the growth rate of output.

different responses of debt and money to finance any budget deficit or surplus that occurs, there are differences in uncertainty about the size and duration of the budget deficit, and about the future stocks of money and debt that will follow the shock. This uncertainty also is reflected in future prices and interest rates.

To pursue the example one step further, suppose the shock to output is a permanent, negative shock to the level of output. Immediately after the shock, prices are higher and output is lower. Whether the budget is in deficit or surplus depends on the fiscal rule and the relative responses of prices and output. If taxes are indexed for price level changes, there is a budget deficit. If not, there may be a deficit or a surplus. The size of the deficit or surplus depends on the progressivity of the tax system. The rule requiring constant money growth prevents any change in money. The alternative monetary rule requires money to change with the deficit. The effects on prices and output differ during the transition and, depending on the fiscal rule, the size and persistence of future budget deficits differ. The rule providing for changes in money to finance a deficit can close the deficit by raising prices and tax revenues. The rule that maintains constant money growth may require an increase in tax rates or a reduction in expenditures as part of the transition to an equilibrium at a cyclically balanced budget.

In the presence of non-neutral shocks, like the shocks to output just discussed, the two monetary rules produce different outcomes and different types and degrees of uncertainty. The outcomes depend on the distribution of shocks, about which little is known currently, and on the fiscal rules that interact with the monetary rules. One or the other rule may generate greater uncertainty, a lower capital stock, and a lower level of output. I see no way to choose between the two monetary rules until more is known about the interaction with fiscal rules and real shocks.[5]

Price and Quantity Rules Compared

A rule setting a growth rate for the quantity of money has two advantages over a rule setting the exchange rate. First, a monetary rule is likely to generate less uncertainty and, thus, produce a higher level of output. Second, the resource costs of the monetary rule are lower, as Friedman (1951) explained in detail. Less real output has to be stored as a monetary reserve. I accept Friedman's arguments

---

[5]McCallum (1982), using an intertemporal model, finds that a rule for constant money growth and cyclically balanced budget is unstable. See also Blinder and Solow (1976) and Christ (1979).

for the case in which output is fixed, with the minor amendments noted below. This section emphasizes an issue that Friedman neglects, the effects of price and quantity rules on the uncertainty and risk that the economy bears.

A gold or commodity standard is extremely costly to operate unilaterally. All the real shocks and all the monetary shocks in the world that change the relative demand for the commodity that is used as money affect prices and output in the country that maintains the standard. For example, under a unilateral gold standard, whenever wars, revolutions, increases in inflation abroad, or other unanticipated events increase foreigners' demand for gold, the domestic stock of money falls and the home price level falls until the rise in the relative price of gold restores equilibrium in the gold market. The agreement to supply gold at a fixed price means that every unanticipated event that affects the gold market leaves its mark on real income and prices in the home country. The cost of providing the services is borne by the public in the home country. Income and prices are more variable; uncertainty is higher; and the capital stock, income, and wealth are lower. Hence, I assume that any gold, or commodity, standard is a multinational standard.

The price rule is assumed to be an international set of fixed exchange rates. Central banks and governments agree to buy and sell a specific commodity, gold, or a well-defined basket of commodities, at a fixed price. For the present, costs of maintaining the standard are ignored, and all money is full-bodied money subject to a 100 percent reserve requirement under either a price or a quantity rule.

The quantity, or monetary, rule is a unilateral rule set to keep the price level stable on average. Base money grows at a rate equal to the difference between the maintained rates of growth of real output and base velocity. The fiscal policies accompanying the monetary and exchange rate rules are designed to reduce the effects of fiscal disturbances to the minimum consistent with knowledge about the real and monetary shocks affecting the economy.[6]

A principal advantage of a monetary rule arises from the constancy of money growth. Constant money growth implies that there is no correlation between money growth and velocity growth, so the variance of nominal output growth equals the variance of velocity growth. The variance of velocity growth is, in this case, equal to the variance

---

[6]The price or exchange rate rule requires greater harmonization of fiscal rules and, therefore, increases opportunities for cheating. There are monitoring costs for the quantity rule, but such costs are relatively small if the rule requires constant growth of the monetary base.

of inflation, plus the variance of the growth rate of real output, plus or minus any effect of correlation (covariance) between inflation and real growth.[7]

Fixed exchange rates are inconsistent with stable growth of money; money growth is endogenous. The variance of the growth rate of nominal output in a fixed exchange rate regime is equal to the sum of the variance of money growth and velocity growth plus or minus the effect of interaction (covariance) between the growth rates of money and velocity. The latter can be positive or negative, depending on the type of shocks that occur, the frequency with which the various shocks occur, and the location at which they occur—at home or abroad. I see no way to decide in advance whether money growth and velocity growth are positively or negatively correlated. In fact, the two typically move together cyclically but not always secularly.

Either of two conditions is required for lower variability of nominal output or income growth under fixed exchange rates. The growth rate of velocity must be less variable by an amount that compensates for the variability of money growth and any positive correlation between variability of the growth of money and velocity. Or, a negative correlation between velocity growth and money growth must be large enough to compensate for the variance of money growth.[8] Neither condition is likely to be met, and the data below suggest neither was achieved in the late 19th or early 20th century.

The opposite is more likely to be true. A fixed exchange rate system raises, and a monetary rule lowers, the variability of velocity growth. The reason is that with fixed exchange rates, the rate of inflation is not constant from year to year or even from decade to decade. The expected rate of inflation can be zero, but there is nothing in the rules of the commodity or gold standard that makes this certain.

The expected rate of inflation affects the demand for money and velocity, and the variability of expected inflation affects the variability of velocity. The increase in the variability of velocity may be large or small, but the variability of expected inflation is larger under a fixed exchange rate system than under a monetary rule. This effect

---

[7]Let m, v, y, and p be the rates of change of money, velocity, real output, and prices, and let V be a variance and C a covariance. Then,
$$V(m) + V(v) + 2C(m, v) = V(y) + V(p) + 2C(y, p).$$
The monetary rule sets $V(m)$ to zero, so $C(v, m)$ is zero also. The average expected rate of price change is zero, but prices change, so $V(p)$ is not zero.

[8]Using the notation in note 7, the first condition states that $V(v)$ must be smaller under fixed exchange rates by more than $V(m) + 2C(m, v)$. The second condition restricts $C(m, v)$ to be negative and restricts $|C(m, v)| - V(m)$ in relation to the difference in $V(v)$ under the gold standard and the monetary rule.

is offset, at least in part, by the lower variability of exchange rates. Under a monetary rule, differences between expected and actual exchange rates affect interest rates, the demand for money, and velocity. This source of variability is dampened, however, by the operation of forward markets and the close relation between changes in spot and forward rates (see Mussa 1979).

Empirical data for the U.S. under the gold standard and during the recent period of fluctuating rates (without a monetary rule) show (1) weak positive correlation between the money growth and velocity growth under the gold standard and (2) higher variability of velocity growth under the gold standard. These data suggest that the variability of nominal output is higher under a gold standard.

Bernholz (1982, Tables 2 and 3) computed the variance of output growth and the average rate of growth of output for five countries under the gold standard to 1913 and during selected periods after 1913. The variability of real growth is 1.5 to 4.5 times higher under the gold standard than during the period 1951–79. The growth rate of output under fluctuating exchange rates from 1967–79 is higher than under the gold standard to 1913 in Germany, Italy, and France. For Britain and the U.S., Bernholz shows two measures of real growth under the gold standard, one for a shorter and one for a longer span. In both countries, growth for the longer period is higher, and for the shorter period is lower, than in the years of fluctuating exchange rates. Despite the oil shocks in 1974 and 1979, which lowered real income in the 1970s, these data suggest that there is (1) a negative relation between variability or uncertainty and the level of income; and (2) greater variability under a gold standard than under a regime of fluctuating exchange rates.

Additional evidence on the costs of a gold standard is the relative size of expansions and contractions in the U.S. economy. One of the most regular features of U.S. peacetime cycles is that, on average, there are four years between peaks and four years between troughs, according to the dating of peaks and troughs by the National Bureau. The averages differ little for 24 peacetime cycles, 10 peacetime cycles under the gold standard (1879–1919), and 5 peacetime cycles between 1945 and 1980. In contrast, there is a notable difference in the lengths of expansions and contractions. The gold standard cycles are evenly divided between months of contraction and months of expansion. Since 1945, peacetime expansions are one-third longer,[9] and peace-

---

[9]The longest expansion, 106 months, includes the Vietnam war, so it is not a peacetime expansion and is excluded.

time contractions are less than one-half their average length under the gold standard.

A study of annual velocity growth for 1869 to 1949 using a broad definition of money, and from 1915 to 1949 using a narrow definition of money, shows a weak contemporaneous positive relation between money growth and velocity growth (see Gould, Miller, Nelson, and Upton 1978). On average, changes in money growth were positively related to changes in velocity growth under the pre-World War I and interwar gold standard. A shift from the gold standard to fluctuating exchange rates and constant money growth would have eliminated the variability of income arising from the positive covariance and from the variability of money growth.

The rate of change of base velocity and monetary velocity was considerably more variable under the gold standard than under the Bretton Woods system, or in the recent period of fluctuating exchange rates. Calculations reported in Brunner and Meltzer (1982) show that the variance of the quarterly rate of growth of base velocity during the decade of the 1970s was about 2 percent at annual rates. This is less than half of the variance of base velocity under the gold standard and, as shown in Gould et al. (1978), a fraction of the variance of monetary velocity (M_2) for 1869–1949 or (M_1) for 1915–49.

Under a fixed exchange rate, the variability of money growth is higher; partly as a response to variable money growth, the variability of velocity growth appears to have been higher, by a large factor, during the years of the gold standard. The correlation between money growth and velocity growth further increased the variability of nominal output growth. The gold standard added to fluctuations in prices and output; uncertainty was greater and the demand for capital lower than would have been achieved under a rule requiring constant money growth. Consequently, real output was lower than would have been achieved with less variability.

Friedman (1951) discusses the resource costs of a commodity reserve currency and the relative advantages of several types of standard. He estimates the annual resource to be as much as half of the average growth rate of annual output, using data for the late 1940s and assuming that, on average, there is no inflation. A similar computation— using the current ratio of money to income in the U.S. as a reference— reduces the cost to about 16 percent of the average, annual growth rate of output. Unless there is a reason to anticipate a dramatic decline in average cash balances, the resource cost of a full commodity standard remains high.

Resource costs of an international standard are probably higher. The ratio of money to income in much of the world is above the U.S.

213

ratio, so a larger fraction of world commodity stocks would have to be held as monetary stocks, and a larger fraction of the growth rate of output would be added to the stocks on average. If gold and other metals are exhaustible resources, their prices rise over time relative to the prices of reproducible commodities. The rise in price encourages private holding of gold (or commodity money) instead of productive capital, but also lowers the resource cost of increasing monetary gold stocks.[10]

It is difficult to estimate the size of the price increase. We cannot separate, or hold constant, the policies of the principal governments that control most gold production so as to obtain an estimate of returns to scale in gold production. The crude data in Schwartz (1982) and Fellner (1981) do not show evidence of constant returns to scale in gold production. Fellner (1981) notes that the price elasticity of the supply of gold has been low, and possibly negative, during the past several decades.

A further complication in evaluating the costs of a gold standard arises from changes in the demand for industrial and commercial use. Growth of these demands absorbed much of the new production in recent years but, again, it is difficult to separate the effect of expected inflation on the demand for jewelry from other determinants of the demand for gold (see Schwartz 1982, pp. 176–8).

Friedman (1951, pp. 215–8) suggests that, in the past, the relatively high resource cost of holding gold as reserves encouraged a steady decline in the ratio of gold to circulating money. The introduction of paper money raises monitoring costs and increases uncertainty about convertibility and about the future price level. Uncertainty adds to the real costs of maintaining the system.

"Free" Competitive Banking

A gold standard or commodity money standard requires the government to control a price. A monetary rule gives the power to control money to a government monopolist but limits the monopolist's freedom to set a price or choose a quantity other than the prescribed quantity or growth rate. General economic reasoning does not support price control and does not support the grant of monopoly power, even limited power, except under a very limited set of circumstances.

---

[10]With constant returns, all of the additional gold is provided by new production and with totally elastic supply by a rise in the price of gold relative to commodities. Between these extremes the amount of additional resources used for gold production depends on the elasticity of supply.

Proposals for unregulated, competitive banking are attempts to avoid both price fixing and government monopoly.

The usual argument for fixing a price or granting a monopoly is that "free" competitive banking is too costly. There are three main reasons for the alleged excess social cost. One is the claim that costs of monitoring private producers are high. The second is the social cost of an epidemic of bank failures. The third is the risk of a change in relative prices or the risk of fraud or default.

The first cost arises because profit maximizing, "free" competitive bankers will reduce the reserve ratio to less than 100 percent. The opportunity to reduce the cost and the competitive price of the service arises because the marginal cost of resources used to produce paper money is less than the exchange value of the additional money. It costs no more to print a $10 bill than to print a $1 bill, but the former exchanges for 10 times as much as the latter. If all producers follow this strategy, prices rise and real value of the bills falls. If producers follow widely different strategies, some will fail. The community loses by bearing the additional uncertainty. The same quantity of real balances can be produced at lower resource cost and with lower default risk by a government monopolist that maintains a preannounced, constant rate of money growth.

The second, and possibly larger, cost of "free" competitive production of money arises from the absence of a central bank that acts as lender of last resort to the financial system. The existence of a lender of last resort reduces the uncertainty that the community bears and reduces the size of the optimal reserve held by banks. The reduction in uncertainty (and cost) can be achieved, without an off-setting cost, if the lender charges the borrower a penalty rate. The penalty rate assures that borrowers will choose to repay the loans promptly and borrow only when there are large, transitory changes in demand for currency or commodity money. A monopoly central bank, operating under a monetary rule, cannot fail. Again, the monopolist reduces risk and cost.

A central bank operating in a fractional reserve system issues default-free currency and can buy securities from the market when unanticipated shocks induce all private issuers to sell securities simultaneously. Experience in the 19th century, reported and analyzed in Bagehot's *Lombard Street*, shows the benefits of having a lender of last resort. The failure of the Federal Reserve to act as lender of last resort in the early 1930s, reported and analyzed in Friedman and Schwartz's *Monetary History*, shows the costs that society bears when the lender of last resort fails to carry out this responsibility.

Neither private insurance nor a commodity reserve is a perfect substitute for the lender of last resort. A private insurance company has no special advantage that permits it to sell securities when the banks that it insures are unable to do so. Holding reserves, in gold or commodities, is more costly than issuing currency that is free of default risk.

A government monopoly of the issue of base money rests on a real advantage of government as a debtor. Governments can tax to pay debts and never are forced to default on the (nominal) value of their domestic debts. This advantage permits the government to reduce the default risk on the nominal value of money to zero.

The government can reduce or even eliminate its advantage as lender of last resort by abusing the power to issue money. Some advocates of "free" banking believe this is a fatal flaw in proposals for a monetary rule. They claim, correctly, that there must be either some limitation on the issue of base money by the lender of last resort or some strict definition of the conditions under which the central bank can depart from the monetary rule.

The problem can be eliminated by defining precisely the conditions under which the central bank departs from the monetary rule. A proper definition eliminates ambiguity, for example, by specifying that the central bank must lend at a penalty rate (above the market rate) on specified collateral (eligible paper) such as Treasury bills or prime commercial paper. Banks that do not hold "eligible paper" should be permitted to fail. The purpose of the lender of last resort is not to prevent all failures; the purpose is to prevent the type of bank runs described by Bagehot (1873), Friedman and Schwartz (1963), and others.[11]

Discussions of competitive banking often point to the experience of the Scottish banks during the 18th and part of the 19th century (Vera Lutz 1936; Hayek 1978; and Pedro Schwartz 1982). The experience shows only that a private banking system can function for long periods of time without repeated failures. It does not show that a private banking system is efficient or that the risks borne by the Scottish community were reduced to a minimum. Further, the lessons to be learned from the Scottish experience are ambiguous. There

---

[11]If there is always a market for eligible paper at higher price (lower discount) than the central bank's penalty discount rate, the lender of last resort serves as a standby facility that reduces perceived risks at low cost. In this case, the monetary rule is never violated. Either the subjective (perceived) risk of bank runs, "panics" and temporary market failures would decline, eventually, or we would learn more about the optimal rule for contingencies and the conditions under which "panics" occur.

is reason to question whether the Scottish banks were fully independent of the Bank of England.[12]

If experience with competitive money does not reduce risk and
uncertainty to the minimum attainable, investment in real capital
and the level of output are lower than attainable. Greater uncertainty
induces banks and the public to hold more gold and commodity
money than they would choose to hold in a society with lower risk
of bank failure and lower uncertainty. Interest rates remain above
the marginal product of capital by a risk premium equal to the cost
of bearing uncertainty. People hold a smaller share of wealth in the
form of productive real capital, so output and consumption are lower.

Survival is not the proper standard of comparison. Economic history shows that many arrangements survived for long periods. Where
there are differences in the social costs of different monetary systems,
particularly in the relative costs of bearing uncertainty and the comparative resource costs of maintaining the systems, the best system
is the one that minimizes cost.

Nothing in this section should be read as opposition to private
money. Individuals or groups should be permitted to issue and use
privately produced money or monies, including foreign money and
specie, if they choose to do so. The objective of policy rules is to
reduce the uncertainty that the community must bear, not to prevent
voluntary risk taking.

Conclusion

The right to own gold is a valuable right. The fact that many people
choose to exercise the right is informative about the uncertainty or
risks that people perceive. They may fear inflation, or confiscation of
their assets, or some type of political restriction on property. They
may fear default on the note issue following a wave of bank failures.
Whatever the reason, ownership of gold or precious metals reduces
the uncertainty that individuals perceive and bear, but also reduces
the demand for productive assets and the capital stock. Society is
poorer because of the uncertainty that leads individuals to hold gold
instead of productive capital.

The choice of a monetary standard is a decision to reduce some
private risks by incurring costs that are borne by society as a whole.

[12]The Scottish experience is open to different interpretations. Tim Congdon points out
in correspondence that some earlier students of Scottish banking history recognized
that the Bank of England served as lender of last resort to the Scottish banks. In Congdon
(1981, n. 52), Congdon refers to Clapham's account of the failure of the Ayr Bank. His
letter provides additional references suggesting that the Bank of England was lender
of last resort to Scottish banks.

These costs include the resource cost of maintaining and operating the standard and the cost of bearing the risk that the standard imposes. The basis for rational economic choice between monetary standards, or the choice between "free" competitive banking and a central bank, is relative efficiency. The most efficient monetary arrangement minimizes the cost and maximizes the benefits to individuals subject to the standard.

The efficiency criterion is more difficult to apply to the choice of monetary standards than to many other choices. An international commodity standard requires a cartel arrangement to keep the commodity's price at a set level. A monetary rule that fixes the growth rate of money depends for its execution on a monopoly central bank. Economic efficiency is rarely compatible with either price-fixing or monopoly arangements. Yet, in the case of money, a monopoly central bank can be the most efficient method of producing money.

The principal reasons are that a monopoly central bank lowers the resource cost of the standard by substituting inconvertible paper money for commodity money, by reducing some monitoring or enforcement costs, and by lowering the levels of risk and uncertainty that society bears. On the other hand, the rule limiting the issue of inconvertible paper money requires monitoring to prevent inflation. And a fluctuating exchange rate introduces risks of exchange rate changes in place of the risk of price fluctuations inherent in a system of fixed exchange rates.

For a small country, the cost of exchange rate fluctuations often exceeds any gain from controlling the price level of domestic commodities. Such countries can fix their exchange rate by pegging to the currency of a larger country that chooses a monetary rule. They benefit from price stability elsewhere by paying the cost of maintaining a fixed exchange rate.

A "free" competitive banking system has higher resource cost, higher monitoring cost, and greater cost of uncertainty than a monetary rule that fixes the growth of inconvertible paper money. Competitive producers have an incentive to lower the ratio of commodity reserves to money so as to reduce the cost of producing money and the price of their services. The reduction in resource cost increases default risk. The absence of a lender of last resort increases the cost of maintaining "free" competitive banking. A competitive producer of money bears an avoidable risk. To survive, the producer must receive compensation. Interest rates are raised by the risk premium, so the capital stock is smaller and income is lower under competitive banking.

Friedman (1951) analyzed the resource cost of various commodity standards on the assumption that output is given. His analysis shows that the resource cost of producing money is higher for commodity money standards than under a properly specified rule for the production of inconvertible paper money.

The risks borne by a country on a unilateral or multinational commodity standard also appear to be larger. Money growth is endogenous and is more variable. Velocity growth and the growth of output are likely to be more variable also. Available data support this conclusion. The growth rates of output and velocity were more variable under the classical gold standard than during the period after World War II, or during recent years of fluctuating exchange rates. Real output rose more slowly in several countries during the gold standard than in the 1970s. Contractions were longer absolutely and relative to expansions. These findings are consistent with higher uncertainty and higher real rates of interest.

Monetary reform can be a means of increasing efficiency and lowering the uncertainty that society bears. If society adopts a rule for money growth that is properly specified, enforceable, and compatible with a fiscal rule, interest rates will be lower, capital stock larger, and output higher. A monetary rule without a fiscal rule cannot assure stability.

Democratic societies do not choose rules or establish institutions solely to achieve efficiency and lower risk. Often, the current generation of voters has other aims. Political economy or social choice may eventually explain why we do not have properly specified monetary and fiscal rules. Or, we may not have demonstrated the full range of benefits, or pointed out the welfare gains, from monetary and fiscal reform.

References

Bagehot, Walter. *Lombard Street.* New York: Scriber, Armstrong & Co., 1873.
Bernholz, Peter. "The Political Economy of Monetary Constitutions in Historical Perspective." Multilithed. Basle, 1982.
Blinder, Alan S., and Solow, Robert M. "Does Fiscal Policy Still Matter? A Reply." *Journal of Monetary Economics* 2 (November 1976): 501–10.
Brennan, Geoffrey, and Buchanan, James M. *The Power to Tax.* Cambridge: Cambridge University Press, 1980.
Brunner, Karl, and Meltzer, Allan H. "Money, Debt and Economic Activity." *Journal of Political Economy* 80 (September/October 1972): 591–677.
Brunner, Karl, and Meltzer, Allan H. "Strategies and Tactics for Monetary Control." *Carnegie-Rochester Conference Series* 18 (Spring 1983).
Christ, Carl F. "On Fiscal and Monetary Policies and the Government Budget Restraint." *American Economic Review* 69 (September 1979): 526–38.

Congdon, Tim. "Is the Provision of a Sound Currency a Necessary Function of the State?" Presented at the Conference on Liberty and Markets, Oxford, 1981.

Fellner, William. "Gold and the Uneasy Case for Responsibly Managed Fiat Money." In *Essays in Contemporary Economic Problems,* pp. 97–121. Edited by William Fellner. Washington, D.C.: American Enterprise Institute, 1981.

Friedman, Milton. "A Monetary and Fiscal Framework for Economic Stability." *American Economic Review* 38 (June 1948): 245–64. Reprinted in *Essays in Positive Economics,* pp. 133–56. Edited by Milton Friedman. Chicago: University of Chicago Press, 1953.

Friedman, Milton. "Commodity-Reserve Currency." *Journal of Political Economy* 59 (June 1951): 203–32. Reprinted in *Essays in Positive Economics,* pp. 204–50. Edited by Milton Friedman. Chicago: University of Chicago Press, 1953.

Gould, J. P.; Miller, M. H.; Nelson, C. R.; and Upton, C. W. "The Stochastic Properties of Velocity and the Quantity Theory of Money." *Journal of Monetary Economics* 4 (April 1978): 229–48.

Hayek, F. A. *The Denationalisation of Money.* 2d ed. London: Institute of Economic Affairs, 1978.

Keynes, John M. *A Treatise on Probability.* London: Macmillan, 1921.

Keynes, John M. *The General Theory of Employment, Interest and Money.* London: Macmillan, 1936.

Keynes, John M. "The General Theory of Employment." *Quarterly Journal of Economics* (February 1937): 209–23.

Knight, Frank H. *Risk, Uncertainty and Profit.* Boston: Houghton Mifflin, 1921. Reprinted, London School of Economics, 1933.

Lutz, Vera C. (Smith). *The Rationale of Central Banking.* London: King, 1936.

McCallum, Bennett T. "Are Bond-Financed Deficits Inflationary?" Multilithed. Pittsburgh: Carnegie-Mellon University, 1982.

Meltzer, Allan H. "Rational Expectations, Risk, Uncertainty and Market Responses." In *Crises in the Economic and Financial Structure,* pp. 3–22: Edited by Paul Wachtel. Lexington, Mass.: D.C. Heath, Lexington Books, Solomon Bros. Center Series, 1982.

Mussa, Michael. "Empirical Regularities in the Behavior of Exchange Rates and Theories of the Foreign Exchange Market." *Carnegie-Rochester Conference Series* 11 (1976): 9–58.

Schwartz, Anna J., ed. *Report of the Commission on the Role of Gold in the Domestic and International Monetary Systems.* Washington, D.C.: U.S. Treasury Dept., 1982.

Schwartz, Pedro C. "Central Bank Monopoly in the History of Economic Thought." Multilithed. Madrid: Complutense University of Madrid, 1982.

Simons, Henry C. *Economic Policy for a Free Society.* Chicago: University of Chicago Press, 1948.

COMMENT

FEDERAL RESERVE FALLACIES*
Robert L. Greenfield

Allan H. Meltzer numbers among the Federal Reserve's most inde-
fatigable critics. Indeed, it is to a significant extent the result of his
incisive exposure of the faulty conceptual foundations of U.S. monetary policy that regard for the Fed has waned dramatically. In amplifying the case for monetary reform, I shall argue that little has changed
since 1964, when Meltzer (1966, p. 91) wrote, "detailed study of the
Federal Reserve's procedures reveals that their knowledge of the
monetary process is woefully inadequate, unverified and incapable
of bearing the heavy burden placed upon it."

Monetary reformers must continue to make this point explicit.
Failure to do so risks inadvertently lending credibility to the Fed.
Even as trenchant a critic as Milton Friedman, himself a proponent
of a money stock growth rule and an economist hardly interested in
bolstering the Fed's image, may do just that when in a widely read
February 1, 1982, piece in the *Wall Street Journal* he writes, "the
real problem is not that the Fed does not know how to produce stabler
monetary growth, but that . . . the Open Market Investment Committee of the Fed [does] not regard it as important to do so."

Can the "know-how" to which Friedman refers legitimately be
ascribed to the Fed? In addressing this question, we must bear in
mind that *interpretation,* not bare fact, is the matter at issue. To
succeed, a monetary reform movement must make clear that the
disagreeable circumstances in which people live cannot be squared
with the Fed's interpretive account of its own activities. Though it
remains true, for reasons long ago recognized by Friedrich A. Hayek
(1945; 1948, passim; 1978), that even exemplary understanding of
economic theory cannot produce the utopian policy of which the
textbooks are enamored, deficient understanding on the part of policymakers can nonetheless wreak the sort of havoc we currently
witness. Ideas do indeed have consequences.

---

*Reprinted from *Cato Journal* 3 (Spring 1983): 113–20, with new title and revisions.
The author is Professor of Economics and Finance at Fairleigh Dickinson University.

Federal Reserve Fallacies

In an April 1981 debate sponsored by the *Journal of Money, Credit, and Banking* (Axilrod et al. 1982), Meltzer and Robert Rasche supported the proposition that "the Federal Reserve's procedures for controlling money should be replaced." Peter Sternlight, Manager of the Federal Reserve Open Market Account, and Stephen Axilrod, Federal Reserve Board Staff Director for Monetary and Financial Policy, stood for the negative. The transcript of the debate supports my contention that a concern for first principles is unlikely to be found among those who conduct monetary policy.

Axilrod (1982, p. 132) begins with the Fed's customary disclaimer, citation of the vagaries of money stock control:

> [T]he money supply varies substantially from the noise that comes through the fact that we have a trillion dollar economy. Money goes through banks continuously. Sometimes the treasurer of a corporation is late for work, and sometimes he takes the day off, or his assistant is sluggish. The money stays in the bank too long, then it gets quickly withdrawn. Substantial variation results.

Taken at face value, these remarks assert that the mere disbursement of money causes it to be extinguished. But surely this is not the case. When money is spent, it does not go out of existence. It merely passes from holder to holder. In the case of deposit money, the recipient of the expenditure gains possession of the bank liability lost by the individual writing the check, while the recipient's bank gains possession of the reserves, a Federal Reserve liability, lost by the bank on which the check is drawn.

To further emphasize the Fed's plight—and in terms whose sheer familiarity may be persuasive—Axilrod (1982, p. 133) argues that an otherwise advantageously used nonborrowed reserves target exposes the money stock to a pernicious variability that arises as a result of changes in the demand for money:

> If all of you have had money and banking courses, and I trust that you have had them, you know there are varying reserve requirements ... on various kinds of deposits. ... If the deposit mix changes so that a given level of reserves would produce less money than desired, borrowing (and total reserves) could expand under a nonborrowed reserves target to produce the desired amount of money. Thus a nonborrowed reserves target is advantageous when unexpected shifts are occurring on the supply-of-money side, in contrast to the demand side.

Axilrod apparently draws a distinction between Federal Reserve actions intended to maintain a given nominal stock of money and those resulting in an increased nominal money stock. Yet insofar as satisfying the demand for money to hold is concerned, it makes little difference whether, at a given price level, the nominal stock of money shrinks or the nominal demand for money rises. In both cases the real demand for money comes to exceed the real stock available to be held. In both cases that excess demand reveals itself as an excess supply of other things in general and thereby exerts downward pressure on the prices of those other things. In neither case does that excess demand *per se* summon forth additional nominal money balances.

Money's supply and demand "interact, then, not to determine the nominal quantity of money—that is determined on the supply side—but to determine the nominal flow of spending and the purchasing power of the monetary unit" (Yeager 1978, p. 6; also see Yeager 1968). (Shrinkage of the nominal money stock reflecting a reduced ratio of money to monetary base is a development on the supply side. Its control of the monetary base enables the Fed to mitigate the impact of any such development.) An excess demand for money, rather than impinging on the nominal stock of money itself, adapts the unchanged stock to the changed circumstances by increasing money's purchasing power. This distinction between the private sector's determination of the real (purchasing power) stock of money and the Fed's control of the nominal stock of money is the *sine qua non* of orthodox monetary theory. Axilrod (1982, p. 136), however, summarily dismisses this distinction, claiming, "[money-stock] control is not as 'simple' as that. . . . Because of the variations in money demand I noted earlier, money may grow *on its own* ten percent this month and zero percent next month " (emphasis added).

What I find distressing about this is not merely the fact that the Fed's Staff Director for Monetary and Financial Policy promotes such a fallacy. Worse yet, no one—not a member of the side for the affirmative, not a member of the Ohio State University audience—prevailed upon him and insisted that he explain just how he imagines demand to be an independent determinant of the nominal stock of money.

That he is not taken to task leaves Axilrod uninhibited in promoting these fallacious views. Indeed, in their "Federal Reserve Implementation of Monetary Policy: Analytical Foundations of the New Approach," a paper read at the 1980 American Economic Association meetings and printed in *Papers and Proceedings*, Axilrod and David Lindsey (1981, p. 246), Assistant Director, Federal Reserve Division of Research and Statistics, write, "under a reserve operating target . . . the money stock is determined by the interaction of supply and demand functions, with a short-term interest rate . . . serving as the endogenous price variable."

Here again arises the failure to distinguish between determination of the nominal and determination of the real stock of money. The confusion mounts, however, as a result of the authors' portrayal of the interest rate, the price of credit, as the asset price of money.

A September 1979 *Federal Reserve Bulletin* article entitled "The Role of Operating Guides in U.S. Monetary Policy: A Historical Review" further documents the Fed's reliance upon a supply-and-demand analysis of nominal money stock determination. Here, Governor Henry Wallich and his coauthor, Assistant to the Board Peter Keir, write (1979, p. 688):

> When incoming data show a sudden marked acceleration or slowing in money growth rates, the Committee must decide whether the change is a temporary aberration or a more fundamental change in money demands that stems from a basic adjustment in the performance of the economy. Since Committee actions affect the public's willingness to hold money with a lag through interest rates, attempts at fine tuning could produce perverse results.

Wallich and Keir couch their portrayal of money demand as an independent determinant of the nominal money stock in terms strongly reminiscent of doctrines once thought discredited by the famous mid-19th-century British monetary debates. In contending that a limited demand for money restrains attempts to issue money beyond the "needs of trade," writers on the Banking School side of those debates slighted the essential property of the medium of exchange. People need not be induced to invest in the routine medium of exchange. Rather than refuse payment of the ordinary sort, people accept money— even beyond their willingness to hold it—and change their own spending plans accordingly. An excess supply of money thus touches off a process whereby the demand for money falls passively into line as prices and incomes rise to the point at which all the newly created money winds up demanded in cash balances after all.

Like their Banking School predecessors, Wallich and Keir deny the possibility of money's being overissued. Their supply-and-demand account of nominal money stock determination requires them to regard any money in existence as money demanded in cash balances. It further mistakenly leads them to regard the significance of Federal Reserve open-market purchases as deriving not from the excess supply of money they initially produce, but from a supposed interest-rate-induced change in the quantity of money demanded. Such a view, however, leaves the paramount question unanswered: If not an excess supply of money, what for the past 30 years has driven prices steadily upward?

My review of the Fed's promotion of suspicious doctrine would remain incomplete were I to neglect the contributions of Federal Reserve Board Chairman Paul Volcker. Particularly noteworthy are the remarks he made in an interview that appears in the September 19, 1982, *New York Times Magazine*. In arguing for monetary reform, we cannot afford to let go unchallenged Chairman Volcker's disclaimers in the matter of the Fed's responsibility for the money stock's behavior.

Volcker (in Tobias 1982, p. 72) attempts to explain the precipitous money stock contraction that followed the March 1980 imposition of credit controls by noting:

> Anyhow, the economy had this abrupt fall, and the money supply fell very rapidly along with it. . . . Consumers suddenly thought they'd better not use their credit cards. . . . But they had bills to pay, and so they drew down their cash balances. So you had this wild decline in the money supply for six weeks or so.

The credit controls were lifted some five months later, at which time the money stock began to exhibit explosive growth. According to Volcker (in Tobias 1982, p. 72), the Fed's expectations that the money stock growth rate would fall were disappointed for the following reason:

> [T]he economy was picking up much faster than anybody realized. If it hadn't been the focus of so much attention, I don't think it would have made much difference, but everybody had come to look at the money-supply figures as the symbol of policy. And we were in the midst of an election campaign, so everybody could attribute political interpretations to everything that happened. That didn't help any.

These remarks resist classification under the heading of any *one* fallacy. They begin by echoing Axilrod's sentiments that the mere expenditure of money causes it to be extinguished. Needless to say, this is not the case. The expenditure of money, rather than causing it to vanish, simply results in a transfer of its ownership.

Mr. Volcker then proceeds to contend that the stock of money quite passively mimics movements in income. He should be reminded that a central bank loses control over the money stock as a result only of its own decision to forego monetary stability in favor of the pursuit of some other objective. Postponing the painful effects of reducing or even stabilizing the rate of inflation or attempting to peg an interest or exchange rate may indeed require a central bank to sacrifice its money stock control. Nevertheless, the decision to pursue such illusory objectives is one deliberately taken by that central bank or some higher authority.

Finally persuaded that unwarranted modesty was not the source of Volcker's insistence that the Fed brandishes much less influence than most people imagine, the interviewer, Andrew Tobias, undertakes some innovative theorizing of his own. He ventures: "when the stock market takes a frightening plunge, the money supply has in a sense plunged too. Stockholders feel poorer, can borrow less, spend less freely" (1982, p. 76). In response, Volcker advises caution, saying: "I wouldn't call it the money supply or even the credit supply, but I agree that it's a factor. The big engine for this kind of stuff has not been stocks recently but houses. Everybody began taking out their equity with second mortgages, convinced the equity was going to increase forever and ever" (in Tobias, p. 76).

Chairman Volcker certainly is aware that banks are constrained in terms of their ability to extend loans. An individual bank can lend out no more than it can afford to lose, namely, the amount of its excess reserves. It is the Fed's provision of base money that is the fundamental determinant of the nominal size of the money and banking system.

The Fed's campaign to discredit M1 as a gauge of monetary policy raises further questions concerning the authorities' understanding of banking theory. The pretext for this campaign is, of course, the alleged distortion of M1 resulting from the transfer of funds from maturing All Savers Certificates to demand deposits.

Now, examination of the definitions of the monetary aggregates may lead one, along with Volcker in an address delivered before the Business Council and printed in the October 12, 1982, *Wall Street Journal*, to conclude that such a movement of funds must increase M1. Demand deposits are included in M1, while All Savers Certificates are not; the definition is clear. (Or, as Volcker puts it, "Shifts . . . among All Savers Certificates, checking accounts, money-market certificates, money-market mutual funds and the new [money-market fund-type] account[s] would all leave M2 unaffected because they are all counted within that aggregate.") A remaining question, however, concerns the reserve requirement ramifications of such a movement of funds.

If Certificates had no reserve requirements attached to them, the contraction of a loaned-up banking system made necessary by the reserve deficiencies arising from the movement of funds from those Certificates to demand deposits would leave M1 unchanged. That Certificates did have reserve requirements attached to them—though smaller than those pertaining to demand deposits—suggests that the banking system contraction was not large enough to fully offset the initial movement of funds. (The Deregulation and Monetary Control Act of 1980 provides for the elimination of reserve requirements on personal time deposits. The Legal Department of the Federal Reserve Bank of New York informs me that the phase-down of these requirements was about 60 percent complete at the time the Certificates matured, leaving them at roughly 1.5 percent.) M1 did increase, but not to the extent indicated by an analysis that disregards the reserve requirement ramifications of the deposit mix change. Yet the November 5, 1982, *Merrill Lynch Weekly Credit Market Report* (p. 4), following Volcker's lead in ignoring these additional considerations, overstates the impact upon M1 and proceeds to assure its readers that "nondistorted M1," a new wrinkle, lies within the Fed's target range.

The Case for Monetary Reform

To those who manage the Federal Reserve System, the "know-how" that counts is that which enables them to grapple with exigencies arising from the need to ensure the System's surviving another day. The case for monetary reform, on the other hand, rests precisely on what Hayek (1941, pp. 407–10) reminds us "used to be considered the duty and privilege of the economist to study and emphasize the long-run effects which are apt to be hidden to the untrained eye and to leave the concern for the immediate effects to the practical man, who in any event would see only the latter and nothing else."

Notwithstanding the growing disenchantment with the Fed, the recent spate of articles purporting to explain what the Fed's short-run model *really* is attests to that institution's success in raising the often dangerously myopic view of the practical man to the dignity of science.

References

Axilrod, Stephen H. and Lindsey, David E. "Federal Reserve System Implementation of Monetary Policy: Analytical Foundations of the New Approach." *American Economic Review* 71 (May 1981): 246–52.

Axilrod, Stephen H. et al. "Is the Federal Reserve's Monetary Control Policy Misdirected?" *Journal of Money, Credit, and Banking* 14 (February 1982): 119–47.

Friedman, Milton. "The Federal Reserve and Monetary Instability." *Wall Street Journal*, 1 February 1982, p. 20.

Hayek, Friedrich A. *The Pure Theory of Capital*. London: Routledge & Kegan Paul, 1941. Cited section reprinted in his *A Tiger by the Tail*, p. 34. San Francisco: Cato Institute, 1979.

Hayek, Friedrich A. "The Use of Knowledge in Society." *American Economic Review* 35 (September 1945): 519–30. Reprinted in his *Individualism and Economic Order*, pp. 77–91. Chicago: University of Chicago Press, 1948.

Hayek, Friedrich A. "Competition as a Discovery Process." In *New Studies in Philosophy, Politics, Economics and the History of Ideas*, pp. 179–90. Chicago: University of Chicago Press, 1978.

Meltzer, Allan H. "The Federal Reserve System After Fifty Years." *Hearings of the Committee on Banking and Currency*. U.S. House of Representatives, Vol. 2, 1964, pp. 926–39. Reprinted in Richard A. Ward, *Monetary Theory and Policy*, pp. 90–97. Scranton: International Textbook Co., 1966.

Merrill Lynch Weekly Credit Market Report, 5 November 1982.

Tobias, Andrew. "A Talk with Paul Volcker." *New York Times Magazine*, 19 September 1982.

Volcker, Paul A. "Speech to the Business Council." *Wall Street Journal*, 12 October 1982, p. 30.

Wallich, Henry C., and Keir, Peter M. "The Role of Operating Guides in U.S. Monetary Policy: A Historical Review." *Federal Reserve Bulletin* 65 (September 1979): 679–91.

Yeager, Leland B. "Essential Properties of the Medium of Exchange." *Kyklos* 21 (1968): 45–69. Reprinted in *Readings in Monetary Theory*, pp. 37–60. Edited by Robert W. Clower. Baltimore: Penguin, 1969.

Yeager, Leland B. "What Are Banks?" *Atlantic Economic Journal* 6 (December 1978): 1–14.

10

A PROPOSAL TO CLARIFY THE FED'S POLICY MANDATE*
Robert P. Black

Importance of Evaluating Monetary Policy

Some people might wonder why the Federal Reserve's policy-making function would interest anyone at this particular point in history. After all, the general economic and financial picture at present is reasonably bright. Although the rate of real economic growth has slowed somewhat from the exceptionally robust pace of the first six quarters of the recovery, overall activity is still rising. Further, in the financial arena, interest rates have declined significantly in recent months, the nervousness that was so prevalent in banking and securities markets has diminished, and equity prices are at historically high levels. Finally, and perhaps most important from a longer run perspective, the inflation rate has remained low by the standards of recent years, to the surprise of some economists who had expected the rate to be moving back up by now. To be sure, the nation still faces a number of serious economic problems. But the most pressing difficulties would seem to lie in the areas of fiscal and trade policies rather than monetary policy per se.

There are at least some people, however, who believe that monetary policy is still an appropriate topic for discussion. Two reasons can be given for this continued interest. First, some economists believe that the dangers presented by the federal deficit have been exaggerated and that the more important near-term threat to the business expansion and future prosperity is the possibility of an excessively restrictive monetary policy. This concern that Fed policy might be too tight has diminished in recent months as interest rates have declined and growth in the money supply has resumed, but it

*Reprinted from *Cato Journal* 5 (Winter 1986): 787–95.

The author is President of the Federal Reserve Bank of Richmond. The views expressed here are his and not necessarily those of the Federal Reserve System. Comments regarding current economic conditions in the paper refer to early 1985, when the paper was prepared and delivered at the Cato Instutite's Third Annual Monetary Conference.

is likely to reemerge quickly if economic activity turns out to be weaker in the months ahead than is now anticipated.

Second—and in my personal view, more important—it is by no means clear that the longer run inflation problem has disappeared. For one thing, the recent inflation performance looks favorable only when compared to the exceptionally rapid increases in the price level in the late 1970s and early 1980s. In this regard, it is worth recalling that the inflation rate when the Nixon price control program was imposed in August 1971 was very nearly the same as it is today— about 4 percent. It is also worth remembering that an inflation rate of 4 percent leads to a doubling of the price level every 17.5 years.

If households and business firms could know for certain that inflation would remain at 4 percent indefinitely, maybe they could adjust to it and live with it. Even though longer run inflationary anticipations are probably lower now than they were a year ago, however, I do not sense any strong or widespread conviction that moderate inflation is here to stay. On the contrary, I think that many people are aware that measured inflation is currently being held down at least to some extent by the strength of the dollar in the foreign exchange markets and by the decline in oil prices. They realize that somewhere down the road the favorable effect of these conditions on the price level may disappear and that, if and when it does, the risk of another round of high inflation will increase.

It would seem then that inflation—despite a significant slowing— is still a serious problem in the sense that it could well reaccelerate in the future in an unpredictable and therefore highly disruptive manner. That possibility alone is enough to make an evaluation now of the strategy of monetary policy worthwhile. At the same time, the generally favorable immediate conditions I noted earlier may enable us to conduct this evaluation with a broader and longer run perspective than would be possible if current Fed policy were a pressing current political issue.

Ambiguous Nature of the Fed's Legislative Mandate

It is generally true that a clear and attainable objective is a necessary condition for the success of any policy strategy. As I have argued elsewhere, however, it is not at all obvious that Fed monetary policy has such an objective (Black 1984). This lack of an attainable objective is largely the result of the ambiguous nature of the Fed's legislative mandate. The most direct statement of the current mandate is contained in Section 2A of the Federal Reserve Act, as amended by the Humphrey-Hawkins Act of 1978. This provision states that Fed pol-

icy should promote maximum employment, stable prices, and moderate interest rates. These objectives are to be pursued "effectively."
Further, they are to be pursued with due attention to production,
investment, real income, productivity, and international trade and
payments, as well as employment and prices. No guidance is given
regarding the priorities of these various objectives or the time horizon
over which the Fed's success in achieving them is to be evaluated.

It should be obvious to anyone that a mandate which instructs the
Fed, in essence, to pursue all desirable economic objectives is no
basis for an effective strategy for monetary policy. Such a broad
mandate merely transfers all of the hard strategic choices regarding
priorities, time frames, and what is and what is not feasible to the
Fed, which is in no position to make them precisely because it has
no clear mandate. In short, the lack of specificity in the Fed's mandate
puts it in a Catch 22 position.

In practice, of course, policy choices have to be made, and they
are made. Because there is no operationally meaningful objective,
however, the choices are necessarily made in a highly discretionary
manner that gives substantial weight to current, very short-run economic and financial conditions. I use the word *necessarily* quite
deliberately. Because the Fed's current mandate includes so many
diverse objectives, it is constantly under pressure to correct whatever
economic problem is perceived to be most pressing at the moment,
whether it be high interest or exchange rates, unemployment, inflation, or something else. In this kind of situation, the Fed must have
the flexibility to react quickly and decisively to emerging economic
conditions and to particular economic and financial problems as they
arise. Viewed from this perspective, the frequent references of many
Fed officials to the need for discretion and judgment in conducting
monetary policy on a day-to-day basis are not difficult to understand.

I believe that a fairly convincing case can be made that any public
institution with as many diverse responsibilities as the Fed must
have some degree of freedom to deal with contingencies. But the
dangers associated with conducting monetary policy in a predominantly discretionary manner that focuses principally on the current
state of the economy are well known. First, monetary policy actions
affect the economy with long and variable lags. These lags, coupled
with the inability of economists to forecast future economic conditions with high confidence, present the risk that a highly discretionary policy will tend more to destabilize the economy than to stabilize
it. Second, a discretionary approach to policy fosters the notion that
the Fed is able to fine tune the economy satisfactorily even in the
absence of compelling evidence that such is the case. Finally—and

somewhat paradoxically—discretionary policy tends to subject the Fed to the political pressures of the day, an outcome that its framers were eager to avoid. Whenever special interest groups realize that the Fed conducts monetary policy in a discretionary manner, they typically increase the pressure they put on the Fed to pursue the particular goals they consider important.

For all of these reasons, it would seem to make sense to narrow the Fed's mandate in order to reduce its need to rely heavily on discretion in conducting policy. Such a narrowing would enable the Fed to develop a cohesive strategy with clear and feasible objectives and, in my opinion, would very likely improve the quality of monetary policy over time.

Narrowing the Fed's Mandate to Price Stability

If you have accepted my argument to this point, I would like to recommend a particular objective to be the preeminent and perhaps even the unique goal of monetary policy—price stability. By price stability I mean, of course, stability in the aggregate price level or, what amounts to the same thing, stability in the general purchasing power of money. I realize that this is not a new idea.[1] I also recognize that a detailed recommendation would have to specify very precisely the meaning of the word "stability." The general notion of price stability should be sufficiently concrete, however, to allow me to make my main points.

There are a number of good reasons for elevating price stability to a predominant position among the objectives of monetary policy. Let me focus just briefly on three that seem especially important to me.

First, price stability is a feasible objective for Fed policy. The close longer run correlation between the growth of monetary aggregates and the price level is one of the most firmly established empirical relationships in economics. It is true that institutional changes, technological advances, and other developments sometimes distort this relationship temporarily. But the technical ability of the Fed to stabilize the price level over a period of years through longer run control of the monetary aggregates is not seriously disputed. Since there is widespread agreement that price stability is a feasible goal for monetary policy, adopting it as the principal goal would almost certainly increase the credibility of Fed policy substantially.

Second, while there is general agreement that the Fed can achieve price stability through monetary policy, there is much less agreement

[1]See Fisher (1934) for an interesting account of earlier proposals.

regarding the Fed's ability to influence the other variables mentioned in its current mandate in a systematic and socially beneficial way— particularly real variables such as employment and production. Back in the 1960s, when the Phillips curve literature and the idea of a trade-off between inflation and employment were the intellectual basis for much macroeconomic policy, many economists believed that monetary policy could contribute to the close control of real variables. A major conclusion of monetary research in the 1970s and 1980s, however, is that efforts to manipulate real variables will be thwarted by changes in the rate of inflation expected by the public. For example, efforts to "stimulate" real activity by increasing the rate of growth of monetary aggregates will raise the rate of inflation anticipated by business firms and workers and result in an increase in nominal wages and prices. This result, of course, is just an elabo- ration of a central theme of classical monetary economics. In any case, it makes little sense in these circumstances to charge the Fed with active responsibility for the maintenance of high employment, even though high employment is obviously a desirable economic result. The most that can reasonably be expected of monetary policy in this area is the avoidance of monetary surprises that can cause painful and costly temporary variations in employment and output around their longer run trends.

The third reason I favor price stability as the principal objective for Fed policy cannot be stated and defended as rigorously as the two just noted, but I think it is an important reason nonetheless. Specifically, I think a convincing argument can be made that raising the priority of price stability would be consistent with the basic constitutional monetary powers granted to the government by the people.[2] The Constitution contains two monetary clauses: Article I, section 8, authorizes the federal government to coin money and regulate its value; Article I, section 10, forbids the states to coin money, issue bills of credit, or make anything other than gold and silver legal tender.

I do not believe there is any firm evidence that the framers of the Constitution intended the phrase ". . . regulate the value thereof . . ." in Article I, section 8, to require the federal government to vary the quantity of money with a view to fixing or otherwise stabilizing the price level. It is more likely that the term "value" was intended to refer to the value in terms of specie of the money the government

---

[2]The argument in this and the following paragraph was strongly influenced by the discussion of the monetary clauses of the Constitution in Hammond (1957, pp. 89–113).

was authorized to coin, since there can be little doubt that the Founding Fathers intended to establish and to insure the perpetuation of a bimetallic commodity standard. It seems clear, however, that the two clauses were intended among other things to preclude the issue of fiat money by either the states or the federal government. It is true that only the states were expressly forbidden to issue fiat money. But it was clearly understood at the time the Constitution was written that the federal government was to have only the powers expressly granted to it, while the states were to retain all powers not expressly denied to them. This intention to preclude fiat money was almost certainly motivated by the disastrous experience with the continental currency and can be correctly viewed as an implied intention to create a monetary system in which price stability would be an inherent characteristic. I do not believe that a comparable argument can be mustered for any of the other objectives cited in the Fed's present legislative mandate.

Much has happened to our monetary institutions since 1789. The apparent intention of the framers to prevent the issue of fiat money by the government did not succeed, and we now have in essence a fiat money system. Making price stability the preeminent objective of monetary policy within the framework of the present system, however, would foster what appears to have been a preeminent implicit monetary objective of the Founding Fathers.[3]

Monetary Targeting as the Appropriate Policy Strategy

Now that I have summarized the case for restricting the Fed's macroeconomic mandate to price stability, let me just touch briefly on the choice of a strategy to achieve this goal. As I see it, the choice of a strategy is secondary to the adoption of price stability as the primary objective of policy, but it is nonetheless an important issue.

Any number of strategies for achieving price stability are possible. Some have suggested returning to the gold standard or adopting some other commodity standard. Another possibility would be to adopt a rule under which the Fed would vary its policy instruments in some

---

[3]It should be noted here that an attempt to incorporate an explicit price stabilization mandate in the original Federal Reserve Act was defeated. Several further attempts in the 1920s also failed. In this period, however, the United States was still officially on the gold standard. Much of the opposition to these proposals seems to have resulted from the belief that the adoption of an explicit price stability objective would have amounted to a questionable substitution of Federal Reserve discretion for the automatic features of the gold standard. See Fisher (1934, pp. 148–85).

automatic or quasi-automatic way in reaction to deviations of the inflation rate, nominal GNP, or perhaps some other variable from a desired longer run path.

There is something to be said for each of these proposals in the light of recent experience, but each of them raises technical and in some cases political questions that would be difficult to resolve. With this in mind, it seems to me that the best approach at least for the time being would be to pursue price stability through a more determined application of the monetary targeting procedure we already have in place.

I am well aware of the questions that have been raised regarding the current procedure. On one side of the question, some economists believe that financial innovation and the deregulation of interest rates have reduced the predictability of the relationship between the growth of the monetary aggregates and the behavior of the price level and other economic variables. The disruptive initial impact of interest rate deregulation is now behind us, however, and it is not unreasonable to suppose, with most interest rate ceilings removed, that financial innovation will proceed at a slower and steadier pace in the years ahead. With this in mind, I think there is every reason to believe that a gradual reduction over time in the actual growth of the monetary aggregates would be sufficient to achieve price stability. My own feeling is that M1 would be the best aggregate for the Fed to focus on at present for a number of practical reasons. If conditions make it more practical to emphasize some other measure in the future, I would certainly support a change.

Other economists are skeptical of our current monetary targeting procedure for different reasons. In particular, these economists believe that certain features of the present procedure such as the use of single rather than multi-year targets and the allowance of so-called base drift significantly reduce the likelihood that the *actual* growth in the aggregates will in fact be reduced in the context of a basically discretionary approach to policy.[4] Such skepticism is not unreasonable in view of the experience with the present targeting procedure over the last decade. This simply underlines, however, my point that an unambiguous price stability mandate is essential to the success of *any* particular strategy for achieving it. Having said that, I do believe that the adoption of a multi-year target band, along the lines of the

---

[4]The term "base drift" refers to the present practice of using the *actual* rather than the target level of each monetary aggregate in the base year as the base for the target in the next year.

suggestion Poole made several years ago, would be a strong incremental improvement in the present procedure.[5]

Summary and Conclusion

The main points of this paper can be summarized as follows. First, although the general economic picture is brighter than usual at present, we still face a number of longer run problems. In particular, despite the sustained period of lower inflation in recent years, there is no basis for concluding that price stability has been permanently achieved. Therefore, a reevaluation of the strategy of monetary policy at this time is appropriate. Second, a case can be made that the most constructive change that could be brought about at present would be to narrow the Fed's mandate in order to specify the objective of policy in an operationally meaningful way. The present mandate essentially forces the Fed to follow a discretionary approach that, among other things, undermines the Fed's independence. Third, if a decision to narrow the Fed's mandate is made, strong consideration should be given to elevating price stability to a preeminent position among the objectives of Fed policy because price stability is a more feasible objective than others that might be considered, and raising it to a predominant position would be consistent with the intent of the authors of the monetary clauses of the Constitution. Finally, while a number of specific monetary strategies for pursuing price stability are possible, a more determined application of the present strategy of targeting monetary aggregates along with some incremental technical changes in the present targeting procedure should be sufficient to achieve the objective over time.

In conclusion, I hope some of my comments will help to promote a public dialogue on the Fed's mandate. Beginning such a dialogue at present would seem to be especially promising. The credibility of monetary policy is unusually high now. An effort to specify our objective more clearly would build on this base and help extend our improved performance. In addition, as I suggested at the outset, it would probably be more fruitful to tackle some of the longer term issues I have raised now when the economy is performing relatively well rather than later when the Fed may be under intense political pressure to deal with some pressing immediate problem.

References

Black, Robert P. "The Fed's Mandate: Help or Hindrance." Federal Reserve Bank of Richmond *Economic Review* 70 (July/August 1984): 3–7.

[5]See Poole (1976, pp. 247–59).

Fisher, Irving. *Stable Money: A History of the Movement.* New York: Adelphi Company, 1934.

Hammond, Bray. *Banks and Politics in America: From the Revolution to the Civil War.* Princeton, N.J.: Princeton University Press, 1957.

Poole, William. "Interpreting the Fed's Monetary Targets." *Brookings Papers on Economic Activity* 1 (1976): 247–59.

PART IV

MONETARY POLICY AND GOLD: THE CENTRAL ISSUES

11

GOLD STANDARDS: TRUE AND FALSE*
Joseph T. Salerno

The Basic Characteristics of a Genuine Gold Standard

Expressions of sympathy for gold as a potentially useful device for restraining the more flagrant excesses of the political control of money hardly constitute an endorsement of the overall traditional case for the gold standard. For implicit in the case for gold is a vision of an ideal monetary system in which *government is totally and permanently debarred from manipulating the supply of money*. Under the ideal hard-money regime, the composition, quantity, and value of the commodity used as money is determined exclusively by market forces. In fact, strictly speaking, the advocate of hard money does not favor a gold standard per se, but endorses whatever commodity is chosen by the market as the general medium of exchange. The hard-money program tends to be couched in terms of the gold standard because gold represents the money that emerged in the past from a natural selection process of the free market that spanned centuries.

With this caveat, I now turn to the characteristics of a "real" or "genuine" gold standard as this is construed within the context of the traditional, or hard-money, case for gold. The defining characteristic of such a monetary system has been incisively identified by Milton Friedman. In his words, "A real, honest-to-God gold standard . . . would be one in which gold was literally money, and money literally gold, under which transactions would literally be made in terms either of the yellow metal itself, or of pieces of paper that were 100-per cent warehouse certificates for gold."[1]

---

*Reprinted from *Cato Journal* 3 (Spring 1983): 239–67, with revisions.

The author is Associate Professor of Economics in the Lubin Graduate School of Business at Pace University.

[1]Friedman, "Has Gold Lost Its Monetary Role?" in *Milton Friedman in South Africa*, ed. M. Feldberg, K. Jowell, and S. Mulholland (Johannesburg: University of Cape Town Graduate School of Business and The Sunday Times, 1976), p. 34. (Friedman's address was given at the University of Cape Town, 2 April 1976.)

Thus, under a genuine gold standard, the monetary unit is, in fact as well as in law, a unit of weight of gold. This is the case whether the monetary unit bears the name of a standard unit of weight, such as a "gram" or "ounce," or whether it bears a special name, like "dollar" or "franc," that designates specifically a standard weight of the commodity used as money.

While it is true that certain types of government intervention in the monetary system are consistent with the basic criterion of a genuine gold standard, it is equally true that no particular government policy is essential to the operation of this monetary standard. Indeed, as Friedman notes, "If a domestic money consists of a commodity, a pure gold standard or cowrie bead standard, the principles of monetary policy are very simple. There aren't any. The commodity money takes care of itself."[2]

Under the quintessential hard-money regime, therefore, the money-supply process is totally privatized. The mining, minting, certification, and warehousing of the commodity money are undertaken by private firms competing for profits in an entirely unrestricted and unregulated market. The money supply consists of gold in various shapes and weight denominations and claims to gold, in the form of paper notes or checkable demand deposits, that are accepted in monetary transactions as a substitute for the physical commodity money. These money substitutes are literally warehouse receipts that are redeemable for gold on demand at the issuing institutions, which hold a specifically earmarked reserve of gold exactly equal in amount to their demand liabilities. Barring fraud or counterfeiting, the total supply of money in the economy is therefore always equal

[2]Friedman, "Monetary Policy: Theory and Practice," *Journal of Money, Credit, and Banking* 14 (February 1982): 99. For works detailing the nature and operation of a pure commodity money, see Murray N. Rothbard, "The Case for a 100 Per Cent Gold Dollar," in *In Search of a Monetary Constitution*, ed. Leland B. Yeager (Cambridge, Mass.: Harvard University Press, 1962), pp. 94–136; idem, *Man, Economy, and State: A Treatise on Economic Principles*, 2 vols. (Los Angeles: Nash Publishing, 1970) 2:661–764; idem, *What Has Government Done to Our Money?* (Novato, Calif.: Libertarian Publishers, 1978); Milton Friedman, "Real and Pseudo Gold Standards," in *Dollars and Deficits* (Englewood Cliffs, N.J.: Prentice-Hall, 1968), pp. 247–65; idem, *Essays in Positive Economics* (Chicago: The University of Chicago Press, 1970), pp. 206–10; idem, *A Program for Monetary Stability* (New York: Fordham University Press, 1959), pp. 4–9; idem, "Should There Be an Independent Monetary Authority," in *In Search of a Monetary Constitution*, pp. 220–24; Mark Skousen, *The 100 Percent Gold Standard: Economics of a Pure Money Commodity* (Lanham, Md.: University Press of America, 1980); and Joseph T. Salerno, "The 100 Percent Gold Standard: A Proposal for Monetary Reform," in *Supply-Side Economics: A Critical Appraisal*, ed. Richard H. Fink (Frederick, Md.: University Publications of America, 1982), pp. 458–74.

to the total weight of gold held in the money balances of the nonbank public and in the reserves of the banks.

The total supply of money in conjunction with the total demand of the public for money balances determines the value or purchasing power of money in terms of other goods and services on the market. Thus, for example, if the demand for money increases while the supply of money remains unchanged, the purchasing power of money rises. That is to say, the alternative quantities of goods and services for which a given unit of money, such as an ounce of gold, exchanges increase; or, obversely, the money prices of goods and services undergo a general fall. A rise in the purchasing power of money also results from a decrease in the supply of money in the face of an unchanged monetary demand. On the other hand, a decline in the demand for money or an augmentation of its supply, other things remaining equal, brings about a decrease in the purchasing power of the monetary unit manifested in a general rise of money prices in the economy.

Like the purchasing power of money, the quantity of money itself is governed purely by the market conditions affecting the overall demand for and supply of gold. These include the total demand for gold for monetary and nonmonetary uses and the monetary costs involved in producing gold. A change in either factor brings about a change in the quantity of money in the economy.

To see how this occurs, let us begin from a position of equilibrium in which the supply of and demand for money, and hence its purchasing power, are constant. In this situation, gold-mining firms maximize monetary profits by producing a quantity of gold per year just equal to the annual amount allocated to nonmonetary uses plus the amount used up or destroyed in monetary employment during the course of the year. In this equilibrium situation the net return to a unit of gold, say an ounce, employed in industrial production processes tends to be equal to an equivalent weight of monetary gold.

An improvement in the technology of mining gold or the discovery of new, more accessible sources of gold destroys this initial equilibrium by lowering the costs and thereby increasing the profitability of gold production, resulting in an increased annual output of gold. With an unchanged demand for money, the larger supply of the commodity money exerts an upward pressure on prices that reduces the purchasing power of money, as each gold ounce now purchases fewer goods and services on the market.

The general rise of prices in the economy includes the prices of goods in whose production gold enters as an input, such as jewelry, dental filling, and various electronic products. The result is that a unit of gold employed in industrial processes now yields a net return in terms of monetary gold that is greater than its own weight, and this encourages entrepreneurs to allocate additional quantities of the metal to the production of various consumer and capital goods. The resulting increase in the supplies of these gold products eventually drives their prices down and eliminates the discrepancy between the value of gold in monetary and nonmonetary uses. The absorption of part of the new gold in nonmonetary uses thus serves to temper the effect of the increased output of gold on the money supply. Nonetheless, in the new equilibrium, the supply of monetary gold will have risen, producing a general increase in prices or a reduction in the purchasing power of money.

In the opposite case, in which the costs of producing the monetary metal increase, due for instance to a depletion of the most accessible gold ore deposits, the result is a reduction in the annual rate of production of gold. In the long run, this reduction entails a contraction of the industrial uses of gold as well as a decline in the money supply and, hence, a general fall in prices or rise in the purchasing power of money.

While changes in the monetary costs of producing gold, therefore, do have an effect on the money supply, this effect tends to be minimal. The reason is that gold is an extremely scarce as well as a highly durable commodity, and its annual production tends to be a tiny proportion of the existing stock. As a result, even relatively large reductions or increases in the costs of producing gold will not cause great short-term fluctuations in the supply of money.

The quantity of money also responds to forces operating on the demand side. For instance, an increase in the demand for money, other things constant, effects a general lowering of prices in the economy, including lower prices for the resources employed in mining gold. Consequently, the production of gold is rendered more profitable relative to the production of other goods and services. Entrepreneurs respond by increasing the rate of production from currently operational mines, by reopening old mines whose continued operation had become unprofitable, and by initiating the exploitation of known but previously submarginal deposits of gold. They also increase investment in the search for new sources of gold and in the development of new and less costly methods of extraction. Furthermore, the higher monetary value of gold gives individuals an incentive to shift additional amounts of existing gold from industrial and consumption uses to monetary employments. Thus, an increase in the market demand for money, which is initially satisfied by an increase in the purchasing power of the monetary unit, calls forth a gradual expansion of the supply of money that tends, in the long run,

244

to offset the initial decline in prices and to restore the purchasing power of money.

Conversely, a fall in the demand for money causes a general rise in prices and, in the process, drives up the costs associated with mining gold. As higher costs reduce the profit margins of gold-mining firms, the production of the metal tends to fall off. Also, the general price rise in the economy spreads to all industrial inputs, including gold, and this stimulates a shift of some units of gold out of money balances and into industrial employments. The operation of these forces eventually results in a contraction of the supply of money that tends to reverse the initial rise of prices and reestablish the original purchasing power of the monetary unit.

The foregoing analysis of the factors governing the quantity and purchasing power of money under a pure commodity standard permits us to lay to rest two persistent and related objections to the gold standard.

The first criticism is that the supply of gold and, therefore, of money is determined "arbitrarily," since it depends on such fortuitous factors as discoveries of new mines and technological improvements in the methods of extraction. This is surely a curious, if not vacuous, use of the term "arbitrary" since the supplies of oil, copper, wheat, and, for that matter, of all goods produced on the market are influenced by changes in the availability of the natural resources required in their production as well as by advances in technology. Moreover, in the specific case of gold, purely fortuitous discoveries of new gold deposits and of improved methods of extraction have long ceased to have a significant effect on the annual output of gold. The regularization of gold production has resulted from the operation of the market itself. In a pathbreaking but unduly neglected article on "Causes of Changes in Gold Supply," Frank W. Paish observed:

> [T]he power of economic forces to accelerate or delay the exhaustion of existing deposits, and to promote or discourage the discovery of new ones, is now so great that changes in the output of gold are now much less 'accidental' and much more 'induced' than they were half a century ago. Today, indeed, there is no reason to assume that the output of gold is less sensitive to changes in costs than is the output of other commodities.[3]

The second charge frequently brought against the gold standard is that it cannot provide for the monetary needs of a growing economy. Increases in the supply of money, it is alleged, are necessary to

---

[3]Paish, *The Post-War Financial Problem and Other Essays* (London: Macmillan, 1950), p. 151.

245

finance the purchases of the increasing quantities of goods and services resulting from economic growth. The gold standard cannot be depended on to produce the required additions to the money supply at the right times or in the right proportions. The consequence of such monetary deficiency is a stunting of economic growth or possibly even a precipitous depression.

However plausible, this line of reasoning is untenable because it ignores the mechanism of demand and supply operative in a free market for money. The market ensures that *any* quantity of money is capable of performing all the work required of a medium of exchange by adjusting its purchasing power to the underlying conditions of demand and supply. The increasing stocks of goods sellers seek to exchange for money in a growing economy represent an overall increase in the demand for money. Thus, if the quantity of money remains unchanged in the face of a growth in real output, the result is a general bidding down of prices in the economy and a corresponding increase in the purchasing power of money. With each unit of money now capable of doing more work in exchange, the same quantity of money suffices to finance the increased volume of transactions.

But this is by no means the end of the process. The general decline in prices brought about by the increased demand for money directly stimulates growth in the money supply. On the one hand, it renders gold mining more profitable. On the other, it causes a fall in the value of gold in industrial uses. The result is a flow of additional gold into the money balances of the public from these two sources. This expansion of the money supply tends to mitigate the fall of prices in the economy. Under a genuine gold standard, then, the growth in real output tends to naturally call forth additions to the money supply.

Finally, let me turn my attention to an objection raised specifically against the 100 percent gold standard, usually by proponents of a gold-based private fractional reserve or "free" banking system. It is alleged by these critics that the 100 percent reserve requirement for banks represents an arbitrary interference with a truly free-market banking system, wherein considerations of profit and loss would dictate the fraction of its demand liabilities that a bank keeps on hand in gold.

The basic problem with this allegation is that it confuses two very different types of institutions. The first type, let us call it a "bank," operates directly on the money supply. The second, which I shall call a "money market mutual fund" for lack of a better term, influences the money supply only indirectly through its impact on monetary demand. Both of these institutions could and probably would exist as the product of purely private contractual arrangements consistent with a free-market monetary regime. It is the identification of the precise nature of these contractual arrangements that is the key issue here.

In the case of a bank, the 100 percent reserve requirement is not arbitrarily imposed from outside the market, but is dictated by the very nature of the bank's function as a money warehouse. Now, we may not wish to use the name "bank" to designate such an institution, but that is beside the point.

What is important is that if people generally perceived a need, for whatever reason, to store a portion of their money balances outside their own households or businesses, entrepreneurs would invest in the establishment of money warehouses on the free market. For a competitively determined price, such a firm would accept gold deposits and store them under conditions stipulated in the contractual agreement entered into with the depositors. This transaction is not a credit transaction. The depositors' gold is not *loaned* to the money warehouse to dispose of as it sees fit (for a stipulated period of time) but rather is *bailed* to it for the specific purpose of safekeeping. Under the terms of a bailment, the bailor surrenders physical possession of his property to the bailee for a stipulated purpose. Should the bailee use or dispose of the property for any but the specific purposes stipulated in the bailment contract, he would be violating the contract and committing fraud against the bailor.

Thus, a money warehouse operating on the free market is contractually obligated to always maintain in its vaults the entire amount of its depositors' gold. Loaning part of it out at interest to a third party obviously constitutes an infringement of its contractual agreements.

Now things do not change just because the warehouse receipts or money certifcates issued by the firm to its depositors, which entitle them to take physical possession of their gold as per terms of the contract, come to be used as money substitutes in exchange. Should the money warehouse print up and loan out additional quantities of (pseudo-) receipts and then honor them by paying out its depositors' gold, it would still be defrauding them even if it took due care to always maintain a reserve of gold more than adequate to meet all their calls for redemption. In the same way, a tailor would be defrauding a customer who left a tuxedo with him to be altered if he rented it out to a third party, even though the tailor took special precautions to insure the tuxedo's availability when the owner showed up with his claim check.

In short, under a free-market monetary regime, banks are required to hold a 100 percent gold reserve for their notes and demand deposits, precisely because these are the contractual terms on which such money substitutes are issued. In this respect, free-market banks are under the same legal obligations as armored car companies in today's economy. Money is bailed to the latter for the performance of the specific tasks of transportation and temporary storage. I doubt if anyone would seriously suggest that the legal requirement that these companies retain in their physical possession the full amount of money for which they have issued receipts constitutes an arbitrary intervention into the free market.

But there is a second type of nonbank institution that would very likely develop and flourish in an unrestricted market for monetary and financial services and that could have a significant, although indirect, effect on the supply of money. The prototype of this institution is the current money market mutual fund.

Unlike banks qua money warehouses, money market funds are not in the business of storing money. Their contractually specified function is to manage a short-term, fixed-income asset portfolio for their investors or shareholders. In effect, each shareholder has title not to a specific sum of money but to a pro rata share of the asset portfolio. Money market fund shares, therefore, are not ownership claims to money but to nonmonetary financial assets that are, for all intents and purposes, maturing daily. Checks written on money market funds are simply orders to the fund's managers to liquidate a specified portion of the investor's share of the portfolio and to pay a third party according to the terms of the contractual agreement between the fund's managers and shareholders.

Under a free-market monetary system, money market funds would not be legally obliged to maintain 100 percent gold reserves or any reserves at all because of the specific contractual arrangements under which they exist and operate. It may be the case, however, that some funds, possibly to appeal to the more risk-averse members of the public, offer investment portfolios containing a significant proportion of money or warehouse receipts for money. For example, a fund may feature a portfolio that is 20 percent invested in monetary gold. The managers of the fund would then be contractually obligated to always maintain 20 percent of the fund's assets in the form of gold. Whether or not one wishes to refer to such an institution as a "fractional-reserve" bank is not the crucial issue. The important thing for the advocate of a genuine, 100 percent gold standard is that this financial arrangement is, in fact, purely the product of a private contractual agreement and therefore consistent with a free market in money.

In the case of a money market fund whose assets are partially in the form of money, its shares represent ownership claims to money balances as well as to nonmonetary financial assets. The fund, in effect, is a hybrid institution operating partly as a money warehouse or bank. Its money assets should therefore be imputed on a pro rata basis to the money balances of its individual shareholders and the total counted in the aggregate money supply.

Not only are money market funds, of the pure or hybrid type, fully in accord with the principles of a genuine gold standard, but, in a denationalized monetary regime, it is not difficult to envision their shares becoming the predominant means of payment in the economy. This would bring about a precipitous fall in the demand for money, and hence for gold in monetary use, and the eventual reallocation of most of the monetary gold stock to nonmonetary employments. Taken to its extreme, this development would result in only a minute fraction of the existing gold stock remaining in monetary employment solely as a means for clearing balances between money market funds, whose shares are the only means of payment utilized by the general public.

While I would not expect this extreme scenario to play itself out, it illustrates how market forces might operate to reduce the much-lamented "resource cost" of a genuine gold standard. Only in this case, as opposed to that of a government-monopolized paper fiat currency, the cost saving is genuine, because it is produced by the voluntary choices of market participants.

The Gold Price Rule: A Pseudo Gold Standard

In sharp contrast to the proponents of a genuine gold standard, who seek to put an end to government monetary policy by completely denationalizing the money-supply process, it is the intent of the advocates of a gold price rule to integrate gold into existing fiat-money arrangements in such a way as to improve the conduct of government monetary policy.

For example, economist Alan Reynolds, a staunch supporter of a monetary policy based on a gold price rule, argues: "The purpose of the gold standard is to improve the efficiency and predictability of monetary policy by providing a flexible signal and mechanism for balancing the supply of money with the demand for money at stable prices."[4] Elsewhere Reynolds writes: "The central issue, however, is whether monetary policy is to be judged by clumsy tools, like MI, or by results. When sensitive prices [such as the price of gold] are

[4]*Testimony before the United States Gold Policy Commission,* Political and Economic Communications (Morristown, N.J.: Polyconomics, Inc., 1981), p. 15.

falling, money is too tight; when prices are rising, money is too loose."[5]

Two other prominent supporters of a gold price rule, Arthur Laffer and Charles Kadlec, state that "The purpose of a gold standard is not to turn every dollar bill into a warehouse receipt for an equivalent amount of gold, but to provide the central bank with an operating rule that will facilitate the maintenance of a stable price level."[6]

What is of overriding significance in the foregoing passages is the explicit or implicit characterization of the gold standard as a mechanism deliberately designed to implement specified policy goals, such as a stable price level, that are aimed at by the government money managers. For it is the underlying conception of the nature and role of money, which is implied in this portrayal of the gold standard, that ultimately and irreparably divides the modern from the traditional advocates of a gold-based monetary regime. I shall make this point in greater depth after I spell out why the gold price rule is not a genuine gold standard.

Friedman has aptly characterized a pseudo gold standard as "a system in which, instead of gold being money and thereby determining the policy of the country, gold was a commodity whose price was fixed by governments."[7] While Friedman is referring here to the international monetary system between 1934 and 1971, his characterization applies to the various proposals for a monetary regime based on a gold price rule. In fact, proponents of the gold price rule have themselves pointed to the Bretton Woods system as the historical embodiment of the essence of their proposal.[8]

Basically, under a gold price rule, the Fed is charged with fixing the dollar price of gold. However, gold itself is not money but the "external standard" whose price the Fed is to fix in terms of the existing fiat dollar. Nor is it necessary that the Fed itself directly buy and sell dollars for gold to maintain the fixed gold price. The "intervention asset," that is, the asset which the Fed trades on the market for gold, may just as well be U.S. government securities or foreign exchange or any commodity. All that is required of the Fed is that it sell some assets for dollars on the open market when the price of gold rises, thus deflating the supply of money and bringing the gold

[5]Reynolds, "The Monetary Debate: Stabilize Prices, Not Money," *Wall Street Journal* (29 June 1982): 26.

[6]Arthur B. Laffer and Charles W. Kadlec, "The Point of Linking the Dollar to Gold," *Wall Street Journal* (13 October 1981): 32.

[7]Friedman, "Has Gold Lost Its Monetary Role?" p. 36.

[8]See, for example, Robert A. Mundell, "Gold Would Serve into the 21st Century," *Wall Street Journal* (30 September 1981): 32.

price back to its "target" level. If the price of gold begins to fall, the Fed is to purchase gold or other assets on the market, creating an inflation of the supply of dollars that drives the price of gold back up to its target level.

By using the gold price as a proxy for the general price level, the advocates of a price-rule regime thus hope to stabilize the purchasing power of the fiat dollar. While some of its supporters have made vague references to the desirability of getting gold coin into circulation,[9] it is clear that the gold price rule is not meant to provide a genuine gold money.

In fact, gold itself need not play any role at all in the price-rule regime. As Arthur Laffer and Marc Miles point out, the external standard "could be a single commodity or a basket of commodities (a price index)."[10] Indeed, recently there have been calls for the Fed to institute a price rule targeting an index of spot commodity prices.[11]

Stripped of its gold-standard terminology, the price rule can be seen as a technique designed to guide the monetary authorities in managing the supply of fiat currency. It is thus very similar in nature, if not in technical detail, to the quantity rule advocated by the monetarists. This is clearly evident in Laffer and Miles' admission that "in an unchanging world where all information is freely available, there of course would be a 'quantity rule' which would correspond to a given 'price rule.' "[12]

What may be called "price-rule monetarism," then, is vulnerable to criticism on precisely the same grounds as the more conventional quantity-rule monetarism. The most serious criticism of both varieties of monetarism is that they fail to come to grips with the root cause of inflation, namely, the government monopoly of the supply of money. The built-in inflationary bias of the political process virtually guarantees that both quantity and price rule targets will be ignored or revised when they become inconvenient to the government money managers.

We may appeal to history for evidence regarding the success of the gold price rule in stanching the flow of government fiat currency. We need look no further than the late, unlamented Bretton Woods system (1946–71). Under this "fixed-exchange-rate" system, the U.S. mon-

---

[9]Mundell, "Gold Would Serve," p. 32; Arthur B. Laffer, *Reinstatement of the Dollar: The Blueprint* (Rolling Hills Estates, Calif.: A. B. Laffer Associates, 1980), p. 7.

[10]Arthur B. Laffer and Marc A. Miles, *International Economics in an Integrated World* (Oakland, N.J.: Scott, Foresman and Co., 1982), p. 399.

[11]See Reynolds, "The Monetary Debate," p. 26; and Laffer and Kadlec, "Has the Fed Already Put Itself on a Price Rule?" *Wall Street Journal* (28 October 1982): 30.

[12]Laffer and Miles, *International Economics*, p. 401.

etary authority followed a gold price rule, buying and selling gold at an officially fixed price of $35 per ounce. Foreign monetary authorities, on the other hand, pursued a dollar price rule, maintaining their respective national currencies convertible into dollars at a fixed price. According to Laffer and Miles, "as long as the rules of the system were being followed, the supplies of all currencies were constricted to a strict price relationship among one another and to gold."[13]

Unfortunately, "the rules of the system" were subjected to numerous and repeated violations and evasions, including frequent outright readjustment of the price rules, i.e., exchange-rate devaluations, when they became inconvenient restraints on the inflationary policies pursued by particular national governments. Needless to say, the Bretton Woods system did not prevent the development of a worldwide inflation which brought the system to its knees in 1968 and led to its final collapse in 1971.

Money: Policy Tool or Social Institution?

From this brief overview of the gold price rule, it is evident that its proponents accept the currently prevailing view of money as a "tool" of government policy. According to this view, the monetary system is or ought to be deliberately and rationally constructed so as to promote as efficiently as possible the attainment of the various macro-policy goals sought by government planners. These policy goals are formulated and ranked in accordance with criteria that are developed independently of, and often in conflict with, the valuations and choices of market participants as these are expressed in the pattern of prices and quantities that spontaneously emerge in the free-market economy. From this standpoint, the degree to which a particular monetary policy is judged to be "optimal" depends on the extent to which it succeeds in altering the spontaneous microeconomic processes of the economy to yield macro-statistical outcomes that are consistent with the planners' chosen policy goals.

Thus, those who defend the gold standard on the basis of its superiority or optimality as a technique of monetary policy differ little from the supporters of fiat money in their mode of argumentation. Both sides direct their arguments almost exclusively to the question of what means, that is, what monetary policy, is best suited to achieve certain identifiable and quantifiable macro-policy goals whose desirability—except for possible differences regarding weighting and statistical expression—is not subject to dispute.

---

[13]Ibid., p. 260.

The widely accepted goals that a successful monetary policy is supposed to achieve include: the maintenance of a stable value of the monetary unit or, more accurately, of constancy in some selected price index, e.g., the CPI, the GNP deflator, or an index of spot commodity prices; the mitigation of cyclical fluctuations via the stabilization of various statistical aggregates and averages, such as the unemployment rate, the GNP index, the index of industrial production, and others; the maintenance of a high rate of secular growth in real output, once more as gauged by the behavior of selected statistical indicators; and stability of "real" interest rates.

Whether or not free-market processes should be modified in the service of such extramarket, macro-policy goals by government manipulation of the supply of money—that is, whether or not government should conduct a monetary policy at all—is obviously never addressed by those who explicitly regard money as a political tool deliberately and specifically fashioned for such a use.

In sum, the arguments of the policy-oriented advocates of gold are founded upon a presumption regarding the phenomenon of money which they share in common with their anti-gold opponents and which is emphatically rejected by hard-money advocates. This presumption is that money is a mechanism consciously designed and constructed to serve certain known purposes. These purposes are those of a small group of individuals acting in concert, namely government planners, and are therefore limited in number, subject to a unitary and consistent ranking and capable of being readily communicated to those undertaking the design of the monetary system. Following Hayek, the attitude toward monetary institutions to which this presumption gives rise may be designated "constructivism."[14]

The constructivist approach to the nature and function of money is logically bound up with a particular view of the origin of money. According to this view, money originated in an extramarket social agreement or legal fiat as a useful convention consciously designed to overcome the perceived problems and inefficiencies of direct exchange.

It should be emphasized here that the basic point at issue between the monetary constructivists and those advocates of the gold standard

[14]For illuminating critiques of the constructivist approach to social phenomena, see Hayek, "Kinds of Rationalism," in idem, *Studies in Philosophy, Politics and Economics* (New York: Simon and Schuster, 1969), pp. 82–95; and idem, "The Errors of Constructivism," in idem, *New Studies in Philosophy, Politics, Economics and the History of Ideas* (Chicago: University of Chicago Press, 1978), pp. 3–22.

who adopt a Mengerian perspective[15] is not the normative one of whether money *ought* to be a tool of policy or an integral element of the market process but the existential one of whether money *is* one or the other. In affirming that money is in fact a market institution, hard-money advocates do not mean to deny that money can be subjected to political control, just as they would not wish to deny that market prices and interest rates can be controlled by the political authorities. Indeed, Menger himself pointed out that "legislative compulsion not infrequently encroaches upon this 'organic' developmental process [of money's emergence] and thus accelerates or modifies the results."[16] But this is precisely the crux of the hard-money, or traditional, case for gold.

In the same way that price controls alter the "quality" of the affected prices, government monetary policy impinges on the "quality" of the institution of money. From the standpoint of market participants, a price that is subject to change only by bureaucratic fiat ceases to function effectively in providing relatively quick and accurate information regarding changes in present and future economic conditions as well as the incentives needed to induce actions in accordance with this information. An element of discoordination is thereby introduced into the market economy, and its most obvious (but not only) manifestation is the failure of the plans of buyers and sellers to match, as reflected in surpluses or shortages of the good in question.

Now, it may well be that the state of affairs that develops under the stimulus of the price control is, at least temporarily, consistent with government policy goals, as was the case in the United States during the "gasoline shortages" of the 1970s. Nevertheless, in terms of its social coordinating function, as opposed to its function as a policy tool, it is also quite clear that the controlled price is qualitatively inferior when compared to its free market counterpart. Or, in other words, in attempting to deliberately transform a spontaneous market price into a tool for realizing their own extramarket objectives, government planners render it much less fit to serve the diverse and multitudinous ends pursued by market participants.

---

[15]Carl Menger demonstrated that money is an "organic" or "unintentionally created" social institution that is "the unintended result of innumerable efforts of economic subjects pursuing individual interests." Menger, *Problems of Economics and Sociology*, ed. Louis Schneider and trans. Francis J. Nock (Urbana, Ill.: University of Illinois Press, 1963), p. 158. For a detailed account of the Mengerian perspective on money, see Gerald P. O'Driscoll, Jr., "Money: Menger's Evolutionary Theory," *History of Political Economy* 18 (Winter 1986): 601–16.

[16]Menger, *Problems of Economics*, p. 157.

Analogously, when the political authorities arrogate to themselves a legal monopoly of issuing money, the character of the money-supply process undergoes a radical transformation. The government fiat-money managers are not in a position to receive the same information as free-market money suppliers pertaining to changes in the conditions affecting the demand for and production of the commodity money. Nor, as de facto monopolists, do they confront the incentives that would induce them to respond appropriately to such knowledge even if they could somehow miraculously obtain it. The upshot is that market participants receive an inferior quality, and inexorably inflated, medium of exchange that tends to greatly impair the coordination, and hence achievement, of their individual purposes. This is the case even if, in contradiction of the lessons of theory and history, we assume that government money managers foreswear inflation and succeed in achieving their announced macro-statistical policy objectives, such as a stable price level and "full employment." The reason is that money and monetary policy are not "neutral" to the constituent microeconomic processes and quantities of the overall economy. Manipulating the supply of money to insure a particular aggregate statistical outcome, therefore, inevitably has an impact on these processes and quantities, diverting resources from those uses that are in accordance with consumers' preferences.

COMMENT

IS GOLD THE ANSWER?*

David I. Meiselman

I agree with Professor Salerno that a 100 percent gold standard holds great appeal. Experience with government management of money has ranged from unsatisfactory to downright disastrous. This is especially true of the discretionary monetary policy under our current fiat, fractional reserve system.

The appeal of gold-linked money is based on several important factors. First, there is the possibility of a self-correcting adjustment mechanism and good stabilization properties under a 100 percent gold standard or under some other gold standard arrangement. A gold-linked system, even a 100 percent gold standard, may be better than some alternative arrangement, but gold does not, in principle, either create or lead to stable prices and a stable economy, nor have various gold arrangements in the past done so. Indeed, as the events of 1929 to 1933 in the United States and Great Britain clearly demonstrated, holding on to a fixed price of gold may lead to disaster.

Instability and banking collapse *outside* the United States, as well as deliberate undervaluing of the French franc in an attempt by France to attract gold from other countries, were major factors in the sharp decline in the U.S. gold stock in 1930 and 1931. Abiding by the gold standard rules, the Federal Reserve increased the discount rate and took other deflationary measures to protect the gold stock at a time when the U.S. economy was already experiencing deflation and severe economic contraction. To be sure, gold did stop leaving the country. Measured by that gold-standard criterion, Fed policies did work. However, the unfortunate side effect was the economic collapse that followed.

The experience of the 1930s illustrates how a country with a fixed exchange rate or a fixed price of gold cannot have an independent

---

*Reprinted from *Cato Journal* 3 (Spring 1983): 269–75, with new title and revisions.
The author is Professor of Economics and Director of the Graduate Economics Program in Northern Virginia, Virginia Polytechnic Institute and State University.

monetary policy, including one that would result in stable prices. It also illustrates that how a gold standard works in practice depends crucially on identifying and understanding the sources of a change in the demand for gold. Moreover, it raises serious questions about the stabilization properties of gold and illustrates the inability of any one country on the gold standard to protect or to insulate itself from severe foreign disturbances, especially under fixed exchange rates.

Most proponents of a gold-based or a gold-linked currency seem to assume that the United States government is the sole source of inflation and instability in an otherwise noninflationary and stable world. Were this so, unilateral adoption of a gold standard might make sense. But the United States is not the only country guilty of monetary mischief. We have difficulties enough with our own government. If the United States were to adopt a gold standard, how could we then get the rest of the world to behave itself?

Another appeal of gold-linked money is that the arrangement would somehow make it easier to know what money is. Clearly, the precise boundary line between money and nonmoney is sometimes inexact. The problem is not resolved, however, by stating that a unit of money is defined as some fixed weight of gold, as it was supposed to have been before 1933 when it was said to be about ½0th of an ounce of gold. To be sure, before 1933 the price of gold was $20.67 an ounce, so that one dollar was approximately ½0th of an ounce of gold. However, a system in which the unit of account is ½0th of an ounce of gold merely reflects the fact that the price of gold is pegged—by government price fixing and intervention—at $20 an ounce. Thus, the dollar as unit of account is ½0th of an ounce of gold merely because gold is $20 an ounce! If wheat is pegged at $5 a bushel, is money as the unit of account ⅕th of a bushel of wheat?

Government intervention and price fixing to peg the nominal value of a commodity do not make money or the unit of account "real," nor do they assure that the real (as opposed to the nominal) value of the price-fixed commodity will persist. To peg the nominal price of a commodity such as gold typically requires that the price-fixing scheme be financed by money issue when the pegged price is above the market price of the commodity. When the pegged price is below the market price, the commodity must be sold to the market and the money receipts from the sale are usually withdrawn from circulation, thereby decreasing the money stock. Moreover, when government purchases of gold or some other commodity cause an increase in the quantity of money, the resulting inflation increases the nominal prices of *other* goods, but not the nominal pegged price of gold. The converse is true when government sales of gold are required to keep the gold price from rising. This is why fixing the price of gold (or fixing exchange rates) precludes an independent monetary policy, including one that would otherwise result in stable prices or in damping fluctuations.

Price fixing only guarantees that the nominal price remains constant in terms of nominal dollars, at least until the government alters the pegged price. It does not follow that other prices (in terms of the fixed nominal priced commodity) will also remain stable or that some average of other nominal prices will remain stable. Perforce, there is no way that pegging the *nominal* price of one commodity can result in stable *real* values, including the real value of the price-fixed commodity.

We once (before 1933) maintained a fixed nominal price of gold. However, accounts were still kept in dollars, not units of ½₀th of an ounce of gold, even though they were made equivalent by government intervention in the gold market. When the price of gold went to $35 an ounce, did this mean that prices meaningfully increased 75 percent because the dollar was ⅟₃₅th of an ounce of gold? A dollar bought 75% less gold but not 75% less of the goods in the CPI basket.

Intervention to fix the price of gold would require Treasury purchases of gold whenever the free-market price of gold increased. Gold is now convertible into dollars, but not at a legally fixed price; there is a free market in gold. Convertibility is not the issue; price fixing is. Indeed, past concern for maintaining the fixed gold price was a major source of, and rationalization for a wide range of anti-competitive and costly interventions by the government.

Professor Salerno wrestles with the interesting questions of what the payments mechanism and the financial and banking system would be like under a 100 percent gold standard in which gold certificates had 100 percent gold reserves and banks were required to hold 100 percent gold reserves behind notes and deposits. Banks would be, at least initially, warehouses for gold, and bank notes and deposits would be like warehouse receipts for the gold.

Given the economic incentives in these arrangements, it is likely that the system would evolve into a fractional reserve system with gold as the reserves. Such a system would then have all of the inherent problems of economic and price instability that a fractional reserve system entails. And this would be especially true in the context, not of the closed economy model that Professor Salerno seems to adopt, but in the realistic context of an open economy where other countries are not necessarily on the same 100 percent or fractional gold standard and where there are constant economic, political, and military disturbances.[1]

In fact, I find the widespread implicit assumption of a closed economy among gold standard advocates one of the most serious flaws in their analyses. If an international gold standard is envisaged, we must face the problem of how to get the Russians, Italians, and Argentineans to join in making it a multilateral system. If the United States unilaterally adopts a fixed price of gold, I do not know of anything inherent in that act that would lead other countries to follow, especially countries not now linked to the dollar by fixed exchange rates.

Another flaw in the analysis is the implicit assumption that when the stock of gold, or money, changes, prices adjust quickly, costlessly, and uniformly, leaving both relative prices and real variables essentially unchanged *in the short run*. Price and wage rigidities are ignored as are uncertainty and the costs of adjustment. This hardly squares either with the evidence or with the analyses of the great Austrian economists whose authority Professor Salerno selectively envokes.

Fixing the nominal price of gold does not, cannot, and never has insured stable prices. The gold standard proposal confuses real and nominal prices. It also confuses the legally fixed nominal price of gold and the purchasing power of money. You cannot target a stable price level and a fixed nominal price of gold at the same time. Gold (and foreign exchange) price fixing constrains a country from inflating faster than an average of its trading partners but precludes pursuing better policies in inflating less.

The 100 percent gold standard is appealing because it would substitute a rule for discretion; the same is true for fixing the price of gold. The proponents of a gold standard and of a fixed nominal price of gold have an excellent point in proposing an explicit rule. The main problem of fixing the gold price is that *it is the wrong rule*—we can do better. If stable real value or stable purchasing power of money is what is meant by the quality of money, then a monetary rule that results in stable prices, rather than government price fixing in the gold market, is the rule that also insures the quality of money.

---

[1]See Milton Friedman, "Real and Psuedo Gold Standards," *Journal of Law and Economics* 4 (October 1961): 66–79; reprinted in his *Dollars and Deficits* (Englewood Cliffs, N.J.: Prentice-Hall, 1968), pp. 247–65.

12

A COMPENSATED DOLLAR: BETTER OR MORE LIKELY THAN GOLD?*

Phillip Cagan

Three Views on the Monetary System

In October 1980 a few members of Congress predisposed toward a gold standard attached a rider to a funding bill for the International Monetary Fund. The rider mandated a commission to make recommendations on the role of gold in the domestic and international monetary systems. The rider required that the commission be comprised of members of Congress, the government, and the public to represent a range of opinion. As appointed by the Secretary of the Treasury in the Reagan administration, few were supporters of gold. But the U.S. Gold Commission, as it came to be called, expressed such widely divergent views on the role or nonrole of gold that in the final *Report to the Congress of the Commission on the Role of Gold in the Domestic and International Monetary Systems* (1982) it agreed on essentially nothing.

The views expressed in the *Report*, both by the 17 members of the commission and the 70 witnesses whose individual presentations are summarized in an annex, can be classified fairly into three groups: (1) advocates of a partial or full restoration of the gold standard to achieve an "honest" currency; (2) monetarists who support a rigid or moderate form of monetary targeting to achieve price stability; and (3) those opposed to both of the preceding positions who believe that discretion in the conduct of monetary policy is essential to achieve general economic stability.

The *Report* gives the impression that the advocates of gold were pitted against the monetarists, with the proponents of discretion

---

*Partially extracted from Cagan (1982, 1984a, 1984b). Reprinted, with revisions, by permission of the American Enterprise Institute and North-Holland Publishing Co. The major part of this paper was originally presented at the Carnegie-Rochester Conference on Public Policy at the University of Rochester, April 15–16, 1983.

The author is Professor of Economics at Columbia University and a Visiting Scholar at the American Enterprise Institute.

calling for a plague on both those houses. The commission lost sight of a natural alliance between the advocates of gold and monetarism in opposition to discretion in the conduct of policy. Despite or perhaps because of the confrontational nature of the commission's deliberations, the *Report* partly skirts what I believe are the central issues concerning monetary policy and gold. Even though much has been written on these familiar issues, they are far from settled.

Advocates of a gold standard frequently speak reverently of an "honest currency" that has intrinsic value, such as gold, or is convertible into something else of value. Nothing enrages them more than a government that endows an inconvertible paper currency with the power of legal tender and then proceeds to overissue it, as has frequently happened, and allows it to depreciate. The economics literature calls this process "revenue from taxing money balances." Advocates of gold call it unauthorized government "theft" of private wealth.

Stripped of rhetoric, however, the position of the gold advocates is really a plea for a stable purchasing power of money, with as close a guarantee of stability as one can obtain in this uncertain world. There is no logical basis for their opposition to any monetary system that provides a reasonable promise of currency stability. Why then do advocates of gold regard monetarism, which shares the same goal, as inadequate?

As far as I can see, the opposition is not over principle but rather over technique. First, the advocates of gold do not believe that monetary targets without convertibility can ensure or achieve a stable value of the currency. One must admit that the history of inconvertible currencies does not lead an impartial observer away from that conclusion. This raises the commitment issue, which I discuss below. It might appear that advocates of gold could support inconvertibility if there were an ironclad commitment—say, a constitutional amendment—requiring a given rate of monetary growth. But they do not, because—and this is their second objection to monetarism—they do not believe that control over any prespecified definition of inconvertible money will work, essentially on the argument that monetary velocity is not predictable because of financial innovations and international influences. Few advocates of gold have spelled out this objection clearly (Reynolds 1982), but others—particularly the proponents of discretion—have done so extensively.

What about the opposition to gold? The performance of the gold standard can be evaluated by the economic conditions when it was in full force during the 19th century. Enemies of gold focus on periods when its adjustment mechanism required a decline in prices. They claim that the period of declining prices from 1879 to 1897 was dreadful, full of widespread misery and unrest in the United States. The proponents of gold largely ignore the state of the economy under the gold standard, apparently in the belief that "honest money" either outweighs or overcomes all obstacles.

How bad was the period of declining prices under the gold standard? Let us take a brief look at the evidence for the pre-World War I period.[1] Table 1 shows rates of growth of real income for the United States and the United Kingdom between midpoints of reference-cycle phases, which avoids the distortion of choosing a particularly good or bad year at the beginning or end of the period. For the United Kingdom the real growth rate was greater in the period of declining prices from the late 1870s to the mid–1890s than in the later period

---

TABLE 1

U. S. AND U. K. PRICE TRENDS AND OUTPUT GROWTH, 1870s TO WORLD WAR I

Country	Rate of Change Between Cycle Phases (Percent per Year)		
	Implicit Price Deflator	Real Income	Real Income per capita
United States			
Deflation of Prices[a]			
1873–78 contr. to			
1895–96 contr.	−1.5	3.6	1.4
1878–82 exp. to			
1895–96 contr.	−1.3	2.5	0.3
Inflation of Prices			
1895–96 contr. to			
1913–14 contr.	1.9	3.8	1.9
United Kingdom			
Deflation of Prices			
1874–79 contr. to			
1893–1902 exp.	−0.6	2.3	1.4
Inflation of Prices			
1893–1900 exp. to			
1913–14 contr.	0.8	1.6	0.8

[a]National Bureau of Economic Research reference cycles: contr. = contractions and exp. = expansions.

SOURCE: Friedman and Schwartz (1982, Tables 5.7 and 5.8).

---

[1]See also Bordo (1981) and Meltzer (1983).

of rising prices to World War I. For the United States the later period
of rising prices had a higher real growth rate, but not by much if the
mid–1870s rather than early 1880s (in which output was unusually
high relative to trend) are used as the base for the earlier period.
Deflation does not appear to have been a deterrent to output growth.

What about fluctuations in growth? From 1879 to 1897 under long-
run declining prices there were five business-cycle contractions in
the United States, and from 1897 to 1914 under long-run rising prices
there were also five business contractions. Table 2 presents a comparison of the two periods. The first five have a higher average amplitude of fluctuation that the second five do, but not by much. On the
other hand, the first period had proportionately fewer months of
contraction, a fact to set against its deeper contractions. Finally, the
unrest in the first compared with the second period reflects in part
the burden to borrowers of an unexpected decline rather than a rise
in prices. Borrowers (in this period mainly farmers) are politically
noisier than lenders, and perhaps it is wise for political stability to
"pay them off" with rising prices. But that would be an underhanded
argument to use against gold and not one that monetarists, who
espouse stable prices, would use.

It was not the departures from price stability under the gold standard that deserve criticism. Rates of price change that averaged less
than 2 percent per year can hardly be held up to scorn by anyone
who has lived through the 1970s. The main problem with the pre-
World War I period was the serious cyclical fluctuations in monetary
growth despite gold convertibility, with consequential fluctuations
in economic activity, which an emphasis on long-run price movements overlooks. The worst business cycles in that period had banking panics and sharp monetary contractions, in 1884, 1890, 1893,
1907, and 1914. The monetarists rightly claim that eradication of such

TABLE 2

COMPARISON OF U.S. BUSINESS CYCLES BETWEEN PRICE
DEFLATION 1879–1897 AND PRICE INFLATION 1897–1914

Period	Duration in Months (Percent of Total Period)		Average Change in Economic Activity (Percent)	
	Expansions	Contractions	Expansions	Contractions
1879–1897	123(56%)	96(44%)	21.7	−22.2
1897–1914	109(52%)	101(48%)	20.0	−18.7

SOURCE: Moore (1961, pp. 104, 671).

fluctuations would produce considerable improvement. Many informed advocates of a gold standard emphasize that fluctuations in monetary growth are a source of instability and therefore propose a return, not just to gold backing, but to a 100 percent gold standard. This would eliminate monetary fluctuations that arise from fractional reserve banking.

In the early part of this century one might have considered the abolition of fractional reserve banking in favor of a 100 percent gold standard, however politically impossible and academic, as not technically impossible. Today, with existing payments practices and those underway, these reforms are no longer reasonable. Consequently, the monetary authorities under a gold standard must be concerned with managing the money supply so as to maintain convertibility, which means keeping the ratio of the gold reserve to the money stock within appropriate minimum and maximum levels. As I have argued elsewhere (Cagan 1982), it would be highly *un*desirable to allow such a system to operate without management to keep the gold ratio within its allowed range, because losses of gold when the reserve ratio was at its minimum point would impose sharp contractionary pressures on the economy; and conversely large inflows above the maximum ratio would impose disruptive contractionary pressures on foreign currencies tied to gold. And whether desirable or not, gold flows *will* be moderated by management. The pre-World War I central banks managed the gold standard and frequently intervened to oppose gold flows. Such intervention after World War I was carried to the point of seriously impeding adjustments of the balance of payments.

The basic problem is that, when gold flows begin, it takes time to reverse them because of lags in monetary effects on the economic conditions that give rise to the flows. Consequently, the authorities have to act ahead of potential gold flows by guiding monetary and economic developments. That can be done by monetary targeting or by more discretionary methods, but it vitiates the automatic system which the gold advocates have in mind. To the monetarists, therefore, the gold standard is an incompletely specified system, and, if monetary targeting is adopted, gold convertibility is an undesirable constraint.

The advocates of discretion, unlike the monetarists, are natural enemies of gold (and monetarism, too). Although there can be and has been considerable discretion practiced by monetary authorities under the gold standard, full discretion calls for an inconvertible fiat currency with no monetary targets. The goals might include long-run price stability, but under discretion there is no procedure that

265

ensures that any particular goal will be achieved. Advocates of gold and monetarists differ over technique, but they are clearly at odds with the advocates of discretion over the commitment to price stability.

The attitude toward price stability has swung full circle since the 1930s. The Keynesian revolution in macroeconomics, with its support for full-employment policies and lessened concern with price stability, dominated thinking after World War II until the late 1960s. It gave way in the 1970s to the recognition that aggressive stimulation of economic activity to minimize unemployment was inflationary in the long run. Most compelling was the lesson that inflation, once unleashed, was extremely difficult to contain, much less reverse, and indeed tended to escalate. The experience since World War II suggested that price stability can only be achieved under monetary systems that have a procedure for guaranteeing it. No economic objective can ever be guaranteed completely, of course, but some procedures are more binding than others and therefore provide a better guarantee.

The costly effort to reduce the high inflation rates of the 1970s confirms that price stability remains a major objective of monetary policy in many countries, to be pursued and hopefully achieved in the years ahead.

Guaranteed Commitments to Price Stability

A properly conducted monetary policy can in principle stabilize the price level. But it requires some discretion to allow for changes in the relationship between the price level and the monetary base controlled by the monetary authorities. If the authorities have discretion, there is no guarantee of how they will act and no guarantee that price stability will be achieved. In short, a guaranteed commitment to price stability requires a workable rule that can be clearly specified. How is it to be formulated?

Hall (1983) has proposed a rule that, whenever a specified price index rises or falls, the Federal Reserve will raise or lower, respectively, the federal funds or Treasury bill rate by a certain amount, and continue such action in steps until the price index returns to its original level. This rule avoids the necessity of defining money but relies on the necessity of specifying monetary actions in terms of a nominal interest rate, which will presumably remain unambiguous. It might not work if the rate of inflation were to increase faster than the specified increases in the nominal interest rate. Aside from the effect of inflation on the nominal interest rate, moreover, the rule, though workable, would be highly inefficient. The effect of changes in interest rates on the price level takes a long time and is highly variable in magnitude. The proper change in the interest rate is not the same amount at all levels of the rate and under different economic conditions.

Friedman's (1960) proposal for a monetary target was to set old M2 on a 2 or 3 percent growth path, and the outcome, though perhaps not perfect price stability, seemed close enough. Many still find that proposal attractive, though until recently the new M1 was preferred.

Opponents of monetary targeting view it as too rigid and as inferior to operating procedures that take greater account of information on money market conditions and general economic activity. In this view monetary targeting is plagued by unpredictable changes in the demand for money balances, both in the short run of days and weeks and in seasonal and cyclical movements and trends. For cycles and trends, the problem is not only that the demand is affected by changes in interest rates, which can be allowed for at least in theory, but also that the quantity of money to be controlled cannot be sharply delineated. Consequently, the relation of any designated monetary aggregate to economic activity and prices is loose and changeable, subjecting monetary targeting to serious errors.

The essence of this criticism is that money is not an unambiguous concept. Defining it either as the means of payment or as a temporary store of purchasing power is insufficient to determine its precise boundaries. Monetarists counter that money can be empirically defined despite its theoretical ambiguity. Over the years new forms of money have been brought under the definition by successively expanding its coverage from gold coins and certificates to include first bank notes, then demand deposits, and recently other checkable deposits and close substitutes.

Critics of monetarism deny that such patchwork redefinitions of money have been adequate or can continue to be so. The criticism has intensified in recent years as financial developments have expanded the range of instruments as well as institutions that provide transaction services. Since depository institutions were the sole providers of transaction services in the past, the provision of such services by others is an innovation. Many other services of the new electronic transfer technology are in the offing. The businesses offering them may become quite varied. These financial developments are augmenting the traditional concept of money and, so long as they continue, diminish the relevance of past data in determining the boundaries of money.

Evidence of the importance of financial innovation was an unpredictable shift in the demand for money in the mid-1970s (Judd and

Scadding 1982) and the dramatic decline in M1 velocity growth in the 1980s. Recent financial developments may in large part be due to past failures to contain inflation, but they are not necessarily going to abate. Even if the trend of velocity henceforth remains constant, the potentiality of changes in the demand for money destroys the credibility and therefore acceptability of a rigid commitment to unchanging growth in a particular monetary aggregate. Some mechanism for adjusting the monetary target has to be in place or price stability cannot be guaranteed.

A rule could allow for the monetary authorities to make appropriate adjustments in the growth rate of the monetary aggregate or its definition whenever necessary. But that would be discretionary. For a nondiscretionary rule, adjustments of the monetary target for deviations of velocity from its assumed trend path could be made every quarter based automatically on the previous quarter (as was suggested by Bronfenbrenner 1961a, 1961b) or, to avoid being over responsive to transitory fluctuations in velocity, at the end of every business cycle based automatically on the previous full cycle (as was suggested by Fellner 1982). These adjustments could correct for any changes in the trend of velocity, but adjustments to make up for past errors in the assumed trend would take time and be painful. Since monetary authorities have shown an unwillingness to contract the economy to make up for past errors of the targets on the upside, it is unlikely that any such overshooting would be corrected, whether it required a discretionary or systematic adjustment of monetary targets for shifts in velocity. Most likely, therefore, there would be an inflationary bias.

The appeal of the gold standard is that it solves two of these problems. First, if control over the quantity of transactions balances becomes more difficult and discretionary monetary policy is unable to achieve reasonable stability of the price level, convertibility into gold can provide the needed control of the relevant monetary quantities for stabilizing the price level. Second, even if monetary policy continues to be capable of achieving stability of the price level, discretionary control may still fail to do so, as in the past, because of inadequate determination or inability to pursue policies that would be successful. Convertibility provides a mechanism for making a commitment to price stability.

I see no escape from the conclusion, inherent in the position of the advocates of gold, that only a convertible monetary system is sufficiently free of discretion to guarantee that it will achieve price stability.[2] The operation of any inconvertible monetary system intro-

---

[2]See also Greenfield and Yeager (1982) and Leijonhufvud (1984).

duces a discretion in management that cannot guarantee price stability despite the efficacy of its monetary controls. Of course, no system can guarantee that the system itself will not be tinkered with or abandoned. But if one is looking for some kind of long-lasting commitment of a constitutional nature, a convertible monetary system seems to be the only practical possibility.

At the same time I do not see the United States or any other major country formally adopting a convertible gold or commodity standard within the foreseeable future, simply because convertibility does constrain discretionary responses to short-run movements in prices and output. Reflecting the majority discretionist view, modern democracies are no longer willing to turn their economic fate over to a standard like gold mainly supplied from Russia and South Africa, and that's that. Moreover, should discretionary policies somehow succeed in keeping inflation within bounds, they will certainly not lose support. In the years ahead the United States might possess sufficient determination to maintain reasonable price stability.

On the other hand, perhaps not. What then? Let me consider the possibility that the economy will be subject to continuing unpredictable rates of inflation and conjecture about how the monetary system might or could evolve into a convertible monetary system, but without gold, which clarifies the essential characteristics of such systems.

An Alternative to Gold Convertibility

Compensated Private Dollars

If uncertainty over the real value of dollar assets in the long run is sufficiently great, and if the government does nothing to relieve the uncertainty, there will be a strong incentive for innovators to offer stability of value. This could be accomplished by offering a compensated account. How might this happen? Consider the opportunities of a major supplier of transactions accounts, such as Sears and Roebuck, which has announced plans to offer an array of mutual funds and investment accounts. It will in time very likely provide a variety of means along with other suppliers whereby holders can transfer deposits conveniently to designated third parties. This transfer could be accomplished at the sender's fund by selling some of its assets for a demand deposit in a commercial bank and wiring the deposit to the designated account of the third party, whereupon the deposit would be used to purchase assets for the third party's fund. (Conceivably, direct transfers of short-term assets such as Treasury bills could be worked out to simplify the process.) With a variety of such transactions accounts in existence, Sears could gain a competitive advantage by offering to compensate the accounts in some of its funds. Compensation would mean that the accounts would be converted into dollar demand deposits at a rate equal to the increase in a specified index of the general price level over the period since each account was acquired. A simple method would be to define the new Roe bucks as equal to $1 at the initial base point of time, and equal to $1 *times* the price index (set at unity at the base time) at the time of transfer. Since the dollar would remain the unit of account, this compensation is equivalent to indexing. If the indexing were done continuously by extrapolating movements in the price index in order to avoid discontinuous jumps, speculation to take advantage of the adjustments would not be profitable in real terms.

Such an account would offer stability of purchasing power. What are the requirements for offering a compensated account? Most of the assets of the fund would also have to be denominated in Roe bucks. This requires that the fund be built up by making loans in the same unit of account. If the rate of inflation were uncertain, many borrowers might be willing to contract in the compensated Roe bucks. The fund must also hold regular dollars to provide conversion on demand. The dollar reserves would be subject to uncertain depreciation or appreciation in purchasing power, of course, and Sears would therefore be subject to possible losses on the reserve as well as the risk of default on its other assets. However, if the reserve ratio were not too high, and if the dollar never depreciated at a rapid rate, the profit to Sears in providing a compensated transactions account could be attractive at sufficient volume. If attractive, competitors would follow suit, and most transactions balances might come to be held in such compensated accounts. The most financially secure firms would capture most of the business.

Under the hypothesized circumstances such a development would be superior to the alternative of a money that fluctuated in value. The government might encourage the complete development of such privately issued compensated money, once it seemed feasible, by offering insurance and by committing itself to a low constant rate of growth of the monetary base. This would help minimize the losses on the reserves held against the compensated accounts, and presents no problem since financial innovations do not affect the nature of the base. Such a precommitment of base growth eschewing discretion might be politically acceptable if the base had by then lost much of its influence over economic activity and the existence of compensated money made the long-run value of base money of little concern to any one.

The Roe bucks would provide a convertible money with a stable value. They would therefore offer all the advantages of a gold standard adjusted for drift in value without the necessity of a gold reserve or dependence on the vagaries of the world gold supply. The dollar monetary base into which it was convertible would be supplied, unlike the gold standard, by the U.S. government at a constant reliable growth rate. As a matter of fact, if most of the money supply privately held were compensated, the quantity of the monetary base could be fixed and never changed, without producing appreciation in the value of the privately issued money in circulation, or could be increased at a moderate rate to provide a source of revenue.

The evolution of such a monetary system is not entirely fanciful, since it does not require legislative enactments but only private incentives and government acquiescence. Private money that was compensated and convertible would be superior to a fiat monetary system that was unable to control inflation, and would have major advantages over a gold standard.

But a private money supply would also not be controllable by government monetary policies and would be largely determined by the demand for it. It would vary procyclically in the short run even if determined in the long run by its convertibility into the monetary base. Monetary studies have long documented the undesirable tendency of uncontrolled private issues to be procyclical, and the fact that they were compensated would not prevent this. The modern view of monetary policy is that procyclical variations are undesirable and should be opposed. Under a privately issued supply as envisioned here they would be *un*opposed, because the Federal Reserve would be committed to a constant growth of the monetary base and so could not vary its open market operations. In this case, therefore, a guarantee of stability in growth of the base rules out countercyclical policies.

Compensated Federal Dollars

Despite its procyclical fluctuations, such a private money supply would not clearly be worse than the inconvertible government money we have had. But it is likely to be politically vulnerable to government intervention. A simple form of intervention is nationalization. The federal government could issue compensated money that is convertible into federal funds and Federal Reserve Notes, the latter comprising the monetary base which is precommitted to a fixed rate of growth.[3] Let me discuss how such a monetary system might work and what advantages it could have.

[3]For a related scheme, see Vaubel (1977, pp. 451–52).

But, first, why would there be two kinds of government money? They would each serve separate functions. One provides convertibility into a money for which the supply is (promised to be) beyond the control of the government and preferably is absolutely predictable.[4] The second ensures a stable value via compensation. It is impractical to compensate an *in*convertible currency, since the compensation would have to be accomplished by paying dividends on holdings, whereas convertible money can be compensated simply by periodically changing the conversion rate. Compensating an inconvertible currency can also be dangerously inflationary, inasmuch as its issue can be inflated with little political opposition in efforts to stimulate economic activity, however slim the benefits.

How would the government compensate such a money issue which we may call federal dollars? In exactly the same way that it could adjust the dollar for drift in the value of gold (as proposed by Fisher 1920) when convertibility into gold is to be maintained, except that here convertibility would be into the monetary base. The conversion rate of exchange between base money and federal dollars would be periodically adjusted automatically according to changes in a price index so as to maintain the purchasing power of the federal dollars constant. Unlike the Roe bucks, the federal dollars, being the primary medium of exchange, *would undoubtedly become the unit of account,*[5] and therefore their compensation is not equivalent to indexing, which is not possible when prices are in the same unit. To be sure, in terms of long-run equilibrium real values, compensation and indexation are equivalent, but the essence of monetary systems is the dynamics of adjustments, and the two differ in their dynamics.[6] Compensation of federal dollars would work to offset changes in their value in terms of goods and services, not continuously as with indexing, but only after the resulting changes in their supply through conversions to

[4]The property of predictable supply differentiates this scheme from the Keynes Plan (1943), whose "bancor" was to be issued and controlled by an international clearing union.

[5]If base dollars were to remain the unit of account in which prices of most goods and services were expressed, on the other hand, the federal dollars could be continuously indexed as described above for Roe bucks. Speculation against the adjustments would not then be profitable, and conversion fees for exchanging the base and federal dollars could be zero.

[6]The choice of numeraire in a monetary system is of no importance so far as static equilibrium values are concerned, but it makes considerable difference for the dynamics of the system. When the value of the numeraire changes, the prices of all other goods and services must change, which does not occur smoothly or quickly and creates problems, whereas a medium of exchange whose own price can change relative to the numeraire has quite different dynamics.

and from the predetermined supply of base money affected the market prices of goods and services, as under a convertible gold standard. Because of the delayed change in market prices, however, speculation against adjustments in the exchange rate between base and federal dollars becomes profitable, and must be prevented by appropriate conversion fees.[7]

The compensated federal dollars would be separate accounts at the Federal Reserve. They would probably force off the market all private monies that were denominated differently. While private institutions could choose to denominate assets and liabilities in either of the two government monies, they would undoubtedly prefer the compensated federal dollars. Substitute transactions balances that implicitly offered compensation by being convertible into federal dollars would also continue to exist if not prohibited. If the real rate of interest were not too high, the demand for noninterest-bearing federal dollars would be far from zero because of their greater safety. Even if the base and not federal dollars were legal tender, most financial assets and transactions balances would be denominated in compensated federal dollars to be protected against changes in the value of the base money.

The amount of the monetary base in circulation would be predetermined and would be held as reserves by private sector institutions and the department of the Federal Reserve that issued the compensated federal dollars convertible into the base. A historical precedent (without compensation) is the currency and banking departments of the Bank of England under Peel's Act (Leijonhufvud 1984, p. 103). How much reserve this Federal Reserve department need hold could be specified or left open. Even without much of a reserve, base money to meet conversions could always be acquired from the private sector via open market sales of securities, and excesses released via purchases. Currency could be denominated in either base dollars or compensated federal dollars, but probably the latter to provide long-run constancy of its value and ease of exchange in the market (assuming federal dollars were the unit of account). While the government could be allowed to gain revenue from its issue of base money depending on the rate of growth specified, it could not gain from inflating the supply of compensated federal dollars, since convertibility means that the demand for them determines the supply outstanding and their real value cannot be depreciated.

A discretionary monetary policy could be conducted in compensated federal dollars with the traditional purposes of stabilizing eco-

---

[7]On avoiding speculation, see Fisher (1920) and Cagan (1982).

nomic activity and financial markets, but the policy would be constrained by the necessity of maintaining convertibility into the base. The constraint would be binding when, as a result of the relative overissue of federal dollars, the exchange rate prompted the conversion of federal dollars for base money. Or the overissue might initially show up only as a rise in commodity prices expressed in federal dollars. Then the rise in prices would trigger adjustments of the conversion rate to increase the number of base units per federal dollar, and this would reduce the growth of federal dollars. These adjustments would often not occur rapidly enough to prevent conversions, however. Supply shocks could also produce a rise in prices. Conversions could occur as well through balance-of-payments deficits if foreign exchange rates were fixed or through increased foreign demands for the base money as a key international currency. Conversions would produce a loss of base reserves, which would force a decline in growth or even contraction of federal dollars to reverse the market forces leading to conversions. Similarly, net conversions of base money for federal dollars would occur when the exchange rate of federal dollars for base money appreciated to the conversion point.

Since large conversions could occur due to foreign demands, it might be desirable to allow the suspension of convertibility under certain circumstances, such as wartime. Governments under the gold standard frequently suspended convertibility even without explicit authorization. An implicit or explicit authority to change the prespecified issue of base money would, however, compromise its basic purpose of providing a monetary standard like gold that was outside the control of government. Its rate of issue might be tied to economic growth, but not otherwise be changed except under explicitly prescribed conditions.

If the system worked properly, no one would have an incentive to use base money rather than compensated federal dollars, and most of the base money would end up in the reserve of the Federal Reserve department issuing federal dollars and perhaps in the reserves of foreign central banks. That would not matter. The management of federal dollars would always be conducted with the same objectives: the maintenance of convertibility which requires long-run stability of value after compensation, and short-run stability of economic activity to head off pressures affecting the general price level. The Federal Reserve would still face the problem of what to do about disturbances that cannot be anticipated. Given the inflexibility of prices and wages, monetary policy would have some leeway to pursue other objectives. Presumably excess reserves would be held to allow gradual adjustments; adjustments cannot be forever avoided, however, if a commitment to long-run price stability is going to be kept.

There may perhaps be a danger to the maintenance of convertibility, because the federal dollars would have no limitation on their issue except for the obligation to maintain their convertibility into the base, and, if they were overissued in an effort to stimulate economic activity, the requirement to maintain convertibility could break down or subject the economy to sharp contractions of the outstanding federal dollars. Wise management of the federal dollars would therefore be important, as it has always been for monetary policy even under the gold standard. No system is foolproof.

Such a monetary system would be too confining for advocates of discretion in monetary policy. But the system has something to satisfy almost everyone else. Although the advocates of gold would not have their gold standard, they would have convertibility into the monetary base whose supply was prespecified. With such an alternative to gold available (as well as a compensated money), gold might finally become a relic. Although I hesitate to promise this outcome, one could no longer consider gold-mining stocks a prudent investment. The monetarists would have a constant rate of growth of the monetary base, and could argue with the discretionists over the proper control of the compensated federal dollars. And the public would have available compensated and convertible federal money protected from potential inflation and thus protected from the errors of central bankers and their economic advisers. At the same time the government would have no incentive to depreciate the value of money.

Such a monetary system is too radical and bizarre to be established by law. It would have to establish itself. This could happen, though the absence of historical precedents is negative. Yet if we ever reached the point where compensated Roe bucks were introduced because of uncertainty over the future value of the dollar, the logical next step would be for the government to provide similar compensated money in order to gain control over unstable issues of private money.

Overview and Conclusion

The period since World War II, and the 1970s in particular, has made it more doubtful than ever that monetary management can achieve long-run price stability. The rise of monetarism, and in particular monetary targeting, is largely due to the persistence of inflation which no one professes to want. The present policy battlelines are extremely unstable: the new financial developments strike a blow at discretion as well as monetarism by increasing the difficulties of conducting monetary policy. To achieve long-run price stability, monetary targeting requires some discretion to make adjustments, except perhaps for the Fellner (1982) rule. Under full discretionary management the long-run price level is subject to no bounds and to considerable uncertainty.

It is hard to see how much uncertainty can ever be eliminated or even substantially reduced except by some constitutional-type of commitment to a stable value of money. Hence convertible monetary systems, which were not thought important in the original "rules versus discretion" debate, have come to be taken seriously in discussions at the theoretical level, though not yet widely as an alternative to be adopted. A commitment to price stability can be met by a monetary system that satisfies two conditions: (1) convertibility into a money whose supply is prespecified and not subject to discretion and (2) adjustments for drift in the long-run value of the circulating money. (It is also politically imperative to avoid a dependence on Russian and South African gold supplies or, for that matter, any unpredictable supply.)

The nature of convertible monetary systems was illustrated here by one that meets these conditions and could evolve out of present problems of discretionary management: compensated federal dollars that are convertible into the monetary base, which in turn has a fixed rate of growth. The growth of the base can be fixed by a constitutional amendment without ambiguity, because its nature and supply are not affected by financial innovations. It will drift in value, however, and so the money in circulation needs to be adjusted to maintain a stable value. Convertibility between the two makes the adjustment feasible. The adjusted money would not be subject to any supply constraints other than convertibility and so would allow any degree of discretionary monetary policy consistent with the maintenance of convertibility. The public would be protected against an inflationary overissue by convertibility and against drift in value by adjustment. The adjustment and convertibility would discourage the government from overexpansion. The issue over convertibility does not logically concern the unpredictability of gold supplies, therefore, but rather the constraint it imposes on the discretionary management of money.

It is the commitment to price stability that the gold standard symbolizes. If a nation can make the commitment, it does not need the gold standard. Without the commitment, a standard is irrelevant.

References

Bronfenbrenner, Martin. "Statistical Tests of Rival Monetary Rules." *Journal of Political Economy* 69 (February 1961a): 1–14.

Bronfenbrenner, Martin. "Statistical Tests of Rival Monetary Rules: Quarterly Data Supplement." *Journal of Political Economy* 69 (December 1961b): 621–25.

Bordo, Michael D. "The Classical Gold Standard: Some Lessons for Today." Federal Reserve Bank of St. Louis *Review* 63 (May 1981): 2–17.

Cagan, Phillip. *Current Problems of Monetary Policy, Would the Gold Standard Help?* Washington, D.C.: American Enterprise Institute, 1982.

Cagan, Phillip. "The Report of the Gold Commission (1982)." *Carnegie-Rochester Conference Series on Public Policy* 20 (1984a): 247–68.

Cagan, Phillip. *The Uncertain Future of Monetary Policy.* Sixth Henry Thornton Lecture. London: Centre for Banking and International Finance, The City University, 1984b.

Fellner, William. "Criteria for Useful Targeting." *Journal of Money, Credit, and Banking* 14, part 2 (November 1982): 641–60.

Fisher, Irving. *Stabilizing the Dollar.* New York: Macmillan, 1920.

Friedman, Milton. *A Program for Monetary Stability.* New York: Fordham University Press, 1960.

Friedman, Milton, and Schwartz, Anna J. *Monetary Trends in the United States and the United Kingdom.* Chicago: University of Chicago Press, 1982.

Greenfield, Robert L., and Yeager, Leland B. "A Laissez-Faire Approach to Monetary Stability." *Journal of Money, Credit and Banking* 15 (August 1982): 11–16.

Hall, Robert E. "Explorations in the Gold Standard and Related Policies for Stabilizing the Dollar." In *Inflation: Causes and Effects.* Edited by Robert E. Hall. Chicago: University of Chicago Press for the National Bureau of Economic Research, 1983.

Judd, John P., and Scadding, John L. "The Search for a Stable Money Demand Function: A Survey of the Post-1973 Literature." *Journal of Economic Literature* 20 (September 1982): 993–1023.

[Keynes Plan 1943.] "Proposals by British Experts for an International Clearing Union." In *Proceedings and Documents of the United Nations Monetary and Financial Conference,* vol. 2, pp. 1548–73. Washington, D.C.: Government Printing Office, 1948.

Leijonhufvud, Axel. "Constitutional Constraints on the Monetary Powers of Government." In *Constitutional Economics,* pp. 95–107. Edited by Richard B. McKenzie. Lexington, Mass.: Lexington Books, D.C. Heath and Co., 1984; reprinted (with revisions) in this volume.

Meltzer, Allan H. "Monetary Reform in an Uncertain Environment." *Cato Journal* 3 (Spring 1983): 93–112; reprinted in this volume.

Moore, Geoffrey H., ed. *Business Cycle Indicators,* vol. 1. Princeton, N.J.: Princeton University Press for National Bureau of Economic Research, 1961.

Reynolds, Alan. "The Trouble with Monetarism." *Policy Review* 21 (Summer 1982): 19–42.

U.S. Gold Commission. *Report to the Congress of the Commission on the Role of Gold in the Domestic and International Monetary Systems.* 2 vols. Washington, D.C.: Government Printing Office, March 1982.

Vaubel, Roland. "Free Currency Competition." *Weltwirtschaftliches Archiv* 113, no. 3 (1977): 435–61.

PART V

THE DENATIONALIZATION OF MONEY

13

COMPETING CURRENCIES: THE CASE FOR FREE ENTRY*

Roland Vaubel

Barriers to Currency Competition

Currency competition for the established national central banks can come from foreign central banks or from private money suppliers (at home or abroad). At present, currency competition from both sources is severely restricted in many countries.

Currency competition from *foreign central banks* can be restricted in several ways:

- The currency issued by the national central bank can be prescribed as a private unit of account;[1]
- Contracts in foreign currencies can be prohibited by law or discouraged through discriminatory contract enforcement in the courts;[2]
- Governments can restrict or discourage the holding of foreign currencies by residents (or the holding of the domestic currency by foreigners) and thereby interfere with the choice of means of payments;
- Governments can refuse to accept any other currency than the one issued by their central bank.

Currency competition from *private money suppliers* is not admitted in any industrial country, but there have been many instances of such competition in monetary history (see Vaubel 1978a, pp. 387–400). To the extent that money may be issued by private enterprises

---

*Reprinted from *Cato Journal* 5 (Winter 1986): 927–42, with new title and revisions. This paper is a synthesis of Vaubel (1976, 1977, 1978a, 1978b, 1980, 1982a, 1982b, 1983, 1984).

The author is Professor of Economics at the University of Mannheim.

[1]For instance, the national currency is prescribed for the denomination of company capital in W. Germany, France, United Kingdom and for all obligations which enter the land register (W. Germany, France) or which have to be notarized (Belgium, France).

[2]In the United Kingdom, for example, the courts do not award foreign currency claims if the contract has been concluded between residents or in a "third" currency.

at all, it must usually be denominated in the currency issued by the central bank. Moreover, with minor exceptions, private enterprises are not permitted to issue currency (notes and coins). Their supply of deposits is subject to reserve requirements and many other regulations.

The existence of these barriers to entry raises three questions: (1) What welfare-theoretic grounds are there to justify restrictions of currency competition from foreign central banks? (2) If there is a case for free currency competition from foreign central banks, why doesn't this case extend to private banks as well? (3) If private banks should be free to supply currencies of their own, why should the government (its central bank) supply money, or a monetary unit of account, at all? These questions are the topics of the following three sections.

The Case for Free Currency Competition among Central Banks

The standard argument against barriers to entry is that they narrow the consumers' freedom of choice and that they raise the price, and reduce the supply and the quality, of the product in question. Prima facie, an increase in "price" and decrease of supply may seem to be desirable in the case of money. Do not a smaller supply and a higher "price" of money imply less inflation? No, because the argument confuses the price of acquiring money (the inverse of the price level) with the price (opportunity cost) of holding money[3] and overlooks the fact that the holding demand for money is a demand for real balances. Since money is an asset to be held, demand for it depends on the price of holding it. The yield forgone by holding a money that bears no interest or is subject to non-interest bearing reserve requirements, is larger, the higher the expected inflation rate. An inflation-prone central bank loses real money demand to less inflation-prone foreign central banks.[4] In this way, it loses both revenue and its power to affect the national economy through monetary policy. Thus, the removal of barriers to entry encourages less inflationary monetary policies. In real terms, the standard case against barriers to entry applies to the product money as well: the removal of barriers raises

---

[3]Harry Johnson (1969) has pointed out the same confusion in the work of Pesek and Saving (1967).

[4]In the absence of a forced or legal disequilibrium exchange rate, the less inflationary money prevails ultimately not only as a store of value but also as a means of payment. "Gresham's Law" operates only under very specific conditions created by government interventions (Vaubel 1978a, pp. 82–89).

the *real* quantity of money and reduces the relative price of *holding* it.

If the standard case for competition applies, it implies not only removal of barriers to entry but also prevention of collusion among the public producers of money. Collusion is the international coordination of monetary policies.[5] In the extreme case, it takes the form of fixed exchange rates, an international holding-price cartel among money producers.[6]

Competition among central banks reduces inflation in at least three ways:

1. *"Exit"*[7]—The world demand for money shifts from the currencies that are expected to depreciate and to be risky to currencies that are expected to appreciate and to be more stable.

2. *"Voice"*[7]—Even if exit does not help, public opinion in the more inflation-ridden countries is impressed by the example of the less inflation-ridden countries. It makes the government (the central bank) responsible for its inferior performance. In politics, too, competition works as a mechanism of discovery and imitation.

3. *Acceleration Effect*—Even in the absence of exit and voice, an inflationary monetary impulse in one country affects the price level faster than a simultaneous monetary expansion of equal size that is common to all, or several, countries. This is because the uncoordinated national monetary impulse affects the exchange rate, and to that extent the price level, almost immediately. By rendering the causal connection between money supply and price level more transparent, international currency competition reduces the likelihood of inflationary monetary policies.

In spite of these beneficial effects, free entry and, more generally, international currency competition are not usually advocated by national central banks, not even by the competitive ones. The Bundesbank, for example, launched a campaign in 1979 to convince the German public and foreign monetary authorities that everything had to be done to prevent the mark from taking over a larger part of the

[5]For a critical analysis of the welfare-theoretic arguments in favor of monetary-policy coordination see Vaubel (1983). Vaubel (1978b) shows that, in 1969–77, the average rate of European monetary expansion has always been negatively correlated with the dispersion of national rates of monetary expansion in the seven main countries.

[6]For a more detailed exposition see Vaubel (1978a, pp. 33f.). De Grauwe (1985) shows that, in 1979–84 the (full) members of the European Monetary System reduced their inflation less than the other major OECD countries on a weighted average.

[7]This is the terminology of Hirschman (1970).

dollar's position as an international currency, especially as an official reserve currency.[8]

Typically, central bankers object to international currency competition on the grounds that it renders national monetary management more difficult and risky, and it destabilizes exchange rates and the whole international monetary system.

It is true that a spatial money monopolist enjoys a quieter life than a competitive producer who must take into account not only the changes in total money demand but also changes in its composition. If the demand for money shifts among currencies, a simple x percent rule for monetary expansion is not likely to be adequate. The forward premium and a world portfolio growth variable will have to be included in the money demand function[9] (or the monetary target has to be formulated for the "world" money supply or some proxy thereof).[10] Each central bank has to allow for the money supply decisions of other central banks.

Is international currency competition undesirable from an international point of view? It disciplines those who try to supply their product at too high a price. For instance, if international shifts in the demand for money have been responsible for the dollar's and sterling's weakness in the seventies and for the weakness of the French franc in the early eighties, they have played a crucial role in bringing about a correction. International shifts in the demand for money are not the cause of monetary instability but its consequence and symptom. They are part of the corrective feedback mechanism. They impose a constraint which, in open economies, is more likely to be admitted than a constitutional money supply rule.

Why do even central banks that would be competitive object to international currency competition? It is tempting to adopt a public-economics approach: the benefits of currency competition accrue to private money holders and users (lower inflation tax and inflation risk) and to domestic taxpayers (larger external seigniorage), but the cost, the greater difficulty of determining the optimal rate of monetary expansion, has to be borne by the central bankers. After all, bureaucrats tend to be held responsible for the errors they commit rather than for the opportunities they miss.

---

[8]Deutsche Bundesbank, "The Deutsche Mark as an International Investment Currency," *Monthly Report*, November 1979, p. 33. For a detailed critique see Vaubel (1982a). In a more recent article under the same title, the Bundesbank calls foreign holdings of DM assets "neither too large nor too small" (*Monthly Report*, January 1983, p. 13 of the German edition).

[9]For a theoretical and econometric implementation see Vaubel (1980).

[10]See the proposal by McKinnon (1983).

In the theoretical literature (notably Kareken and Wallace 1981), we find the objection that competition among central banks (outside monies) renders the equilibrium exchange rate(s) indeterminate because all, and only those, exchange rates which promise to be constant, are compatible with a rational expectations equilibrium. This objection is misleading because it assumes that monies are only stores of value and that they can be perfect substitutes. First of all, different groups of people who consume different baskets of commodities prefer different standards of value: since money serves as a standard of value, they would prefer different monies—i.e., monies that are stable in terms of different commodity baskets. Moreover, if for this reason (or owing to past government intervention) different monies coexist, currency transaction costs will reinforce the tendency toward the formation of (overlapping) payments circuits or currency domains. Thus, if money is also viewed as a standard of value and means of payment, two competing monies will hardly ever be perfect substitutes. The Kareken-Wallace view is not relevant to this world.[11]

Currency Competition from Private Suppliers: The Case for Free Entry

If free currency competition between the central banks of different countries has the salutary effect of reducing rates of inflation below the monopolistic rates, it is difficult to see why the case for a competitive supply of money should not also extend to competition from private banks of issue. From a present-day perspective, the suggestion of an unrestricted competitive supply of (distinguishable)[12] private high-powered money must be regarded as truly (counter-)revolutionary, and even Hayek needed more than half a year to proceed, in 1976, from the demand for "free choice in currency" to the case for the "denationalization of money."

Several justifications have been given for the prohibition of currency competition from private suppliers:

1. Profit-maximizing private issuers would increase the supply of their money until its price equals the marginal cost of producing it, namely zero; the result would be hyperinflation.[13]

---

[11]Haberler (1980, p. 44) writes about the Kareken-Wallace view (in paraphrasing Keynes): "it is an extraordinary example of how remorseless logicians can end up in Bedlam, if they get hold of the wrong assumptions."

[12]See Klein (1974).

[13]See Lutz (1936, pp. 4f.); Friedman (1959a, p. 7; 1969, p. 39); Pesek and Saving (1967, p. 129); Johnson (1968, p. 976); Meltzer (1969, p. 35); and Gehrig (1978, p. 454). This view has been criticized by Klein (1974, pp. 428–31); Vaubel (1977, pp. 449–52); and Girton and Roper (1981, pp. 21–24).

2. Private competitive supply of money renders the price level indeterminate.[14]
3. The private banking system is inherently unstable.
4. Monopolistic production of money by the state is an efficient way of raising government revenue.
5. The supply of money is a natural monopoly because of economies of scale in production or use.
6. Money exerts positive external effects; money, or the currency unit, may even be a public good.

The first argument repeats the confusion noted above: it mistakes the price of acquiring money for the price (opportunity cost) of holding money. What private profit maximization reduces to almost zero is not the value of money but the opportunity cost of holding it.

Some authors have objected that private suppliers of money may choose to maximize their short-run profits rather than their long-run profits, thus opting for hyperinflation at the time of their greatest success, when the present value of their confidence capital is at its maximum. Klein (1974, p. 449) and Tullock (1975, pp. 496f.) have replied that private enterprises tend to have a longer planning horizon than democratically elected governments and their central banks. However, this answer implies that central banks act as profit maximizers as well—in some cases a debatable assumption. The answer is rather that, if there is a danger of "profit snatching," money holders will prefer currencies that offer value guarantees. This point will be further developed in the concluding section. It implies that private money is likely to be inside money. The first objection can only apply to outside money.

The second argument is correct in pointing out that the price level is indeterminate—indeed, under any system of money production, for the initial supply of nominal balances is an arbitrarily chosen number. To serve as an objection to private currency competition, the argument would have to show that the rate of change of the price level is indeterminate as well under such a system.

The third argument may justify money production by governments, but it does not justify barriers to entry. Whether claims on the private banking system are excessively risky is a question which each money holder can be left to decide on his own depending on his individual degree of risk aversion.

Fourth, even if a system of optimal taxation requires a tax on money balances in addition to the wealth tax, what reason is there to assume

---

[14]Gurley and Shaw (1960, pp. 255ff.); Patinkin (1961, p. 116); and McKinnon (1969, p. 316).

that the collection of government seigniorage is more efficient than the taxation of private money creation or of private money holdings?

Fifth, if money is a natural monopoly good, the central bank does not need a legal monopoly (although it may have to be subsidized).[15] Since we do not even know whether money is a natural monopoly good and what its optimal characteristics are (for instance, whether it should be of stable or increasing purchasing power), barriers to competition from private issuers prevent us from finding out; the mechanism of discovery is blocked. A governmental producer of money is not an efficient natural monopolist unless he can prevail in conditions of free entry and without discrimination.[16] Historically, the major central banks have not acquired their national monopoly position in this way.[17]

Finally, if money exerts positive external effects or is even a public good, there may be a case for subsidization, or even for governmental production, of money, but not for barriers to entry. The private supply of money would be too small, not too large.

Should Governments Supply Money?

The previous section has shown that governmental production of money may be justified, if (i) the private banking system is inherently unstable, and/or if money is (ii) a natural monopoly good or (iii) a public good. Whether arguments (i) and (ii) apply is an empirical question which cannot be answered as long as free currency competition from private issuers is not permitted.[18] Monetary history does not provide a clear answer (Vaubel 1978a, pp. 387–401). Whether

[15]Subsidies may be justified even if marginal cost pricing is not the aim (because the additional taxation required would create excessive distortions elsewhere in the economy). They may be justified if the natural monopolist has passed the point of minimum average cost; for in this exceptional case, which Sharkey (1982, ch. 5) has emphasized, an efficient natural monopolist may be unable to produce the optimal quantity of output and to sustain himself against less efficient competitors if the government does not pay him a subsidy (which it should offer to all producers who supply at least as much output). Under Sharkey's assumptions, the subsidy must be sufficient to keep the net-of-subsidy average cost of the most efficient supplier of optimal output at the minimum average cost attainable for any smaller quantity of output.

[16]Nondiscrimination also implies that the government is willing to accept or pay any currency preferred by its private counterpart. Otherwise, a superior private money may not prevail in the market, merely because the government uses only its own money.

[17]The Bank of England, for example, was granted its monopoly not because it was gaining ground in the market but because it was losing out to the other joint-stock issuing banks which had emerged after the Bank's joint-stock monopoly had been abolished in 1826 (for details see Vaubel 1978a, p. 389).

[18]See Vaubel (1984) for an econometric test of the natural monopoly hypothesis and for a list of previous studies of this issue. The results are not conclusive.

money is a public good, as has often been claimed, is largely a matter of definition and needs to be clarified.[19] There is no generally accepted definition of a public good. However, most authors seem to consider nonrivalness a necessary and sufficient condition.[20] Others regard nonexcludability as an alternative sufficient condition.[21] A few treat the term public good as synonymous with positive consumption externality.[22]

In this paper we shall retain the benefit of being able to distinguish between the general concept of consumption externality and the polar case of a (pure) public good which, in terms of production units, is equally available to all members of the group in a quantity or quality that is independent of the size of the group (nonrivalness).[23] We shall call a free good a good for which exclusion is not profitable (nonexcludability). The question of whether there are also more limited Pareto-relevant consumption externalities will not be pursued here because they would merely justify subsidies to money holders and users.[24]

One group of authors ascribe a public good nature to money because "any one agent, holding cash balances of a given average size, is less likely to incur the costs of temporarily running out of cash, the larger are the average balances of those with whom he trades."[25] However, money balances do not satisfy the nonrivalness criterion (nor the nonexcludability criterion): as long as one person holds a unit of money and benefits from its "liquidity services," nobody else can own it and benefit from it. If he gives it away, he increases his own risk of temporarily running out of cash. Therefore, he will ask for a quid pro quo—a good, service, or some other asset.

For the same reason, it is not true that "the provision of a convertible currency is an international 'public good'" because "a convertible currency can be held and used by foreigners" (McKinnon 1979, p. 3) or that "the dollar is an 'international public good'" because "the United States provides the world's reserve currency" (Schmidt 1979, p. 143). Otherwise, any exportable good or asset which happens

---

[19]The remainder of this section is adapted from Vaubel (1984).
[20]The seminal modern contribution is Samuelson (1954).
[21]See notably Musgrave (1959, p. 9).
[22]Samuelson (1969).
[23]This is essentially Buchanan's definition (1968, p. 54).
[24]See Vaubel (1984, pp. 32–45) for a discussion of confidence externalities, price level externalities, and transaction cost externalities. The analysis shows that there may, but need not, be Pareto-relevant externalities in the demand and supply of money.
[25]Laidler (1977, pp. 321f.). A similar view seems to be taken by Kolm (1972, 1977) and Mundell (Claassen and Salin 1972, p. 97).

to be supplied by a government would be an international public good.

Kindleberger refers to "the public good provided by money as a unit of account" (1972, p. 434) and "standard of measurement" (1983, p. 383) and applies the term public good to "money"(1978a, pp. 9–10), "international money" (1976, p. 61; 1978b, p. 286), "an international unit of account," and "international monetary stability" (1972, p. 435). International monetary stability in the sense of stability of purchasing power or exchange rate stability is not a good but a quality characteristic of the product money. Quality characteristics, it is true, meet the nonrivalness test: enjoyment by one does not detract from enjoyment by others (nor can they be excluded from them) provided they have bought the good itself. However, this applies to the quality characteristics of all goods. If the publicness of its characteristics made a good a public good, all goods that are sold to more than one person would be public goods.

It might be argued that the benefits of a unit of account (and a price index) can be enjoyed by a person independently of whether he holds and uses the money which it denominates (Yeager 1983, p. 321). More specifically, a person or organization, by adopting a certain unit of account (and by publishing a price index for it), may convey information, a public good, to all others. This would imply that government should suggest a unit of account and publish a price index for it, but not that it should supply money, let alone the only (base) money[26] or monetary unit.

Brunner and Meltzer (1964, 1971) have emphasized that money itself is a substitute for information because it also reduces transaction costs, and because transaction costs can largely be reduced to the costs of information about possible transaction chains, asset properties and exchange ratios between assets. Since money is a substitute for information and since information is a public good, Hamada (1979, p. 7) and Fratianni (1982, p. 437) conclude, there is a "public good nature of money." However, to show that X is a substitute for a public good is not sufficient to prove that X is a public good. A fence, a dog, and an alarm system are all to some extent substitutes for police protection but they are not public goods. What has to be shown is not that money is a substitute for information but that it provides the public good of information.

Several authors have argued that "public consensus" or "social agreement" on a common money is a way of creating generally useful

---

[26]This conclusion is in fact reached by Engels (1981, pp. 10f.); Hall (1981, p. 21); and Yeager (1983, pp. 324f.).

knowledge and is thus a public good.[27] The knowledge in question is the predictability of individual behavior. What becomes predictable is not only the money which each individual accepts but also that each individual in the country accepts the same money.

Public decisions by definition meet the nonrivalness test. However, not all public decisions are public goods—they can be public bads (Tullock 1971). Since the aim of securing predictability of individual trading behavior, if taken to the extreme, may serve to justify the most far-reaching central planning by an omnipotent government (Hirshleifer 1973, p. 132), the mere fact that a certain act of government generates knowledge is not a sufficient justification. It has to be shown that the knowledge in question is worth its cost and that it is provided more efficiently by the government than by a competitive private sector. Both contentions are controversial.

The only operational proof that a common money is more efficient than currency competition and that the government is the most efficient provider of the common money would be to permit free currency competition. Whether the imposition of a common money or monetary unit is a public good or a public bad depends on whether money is a natural monopoly good or not. Hence, there is no independent public good justification for the government's money monopoly. The public good argument is redundant.[28]

Forecasting Monetary Arrangements under Free Currency Competition

If currency competition is to serve as a mechanism of discovery, government must not prescribe the characteristics of the privately issued currencies nor the organization of the private issuing institutions. Contrary to some proposals,[29] for example, it must not prescribe the monetary unit of account nor the types of assets that may be held by the issuing institutions.

[27]Hamada (1977, p. 16); Frenkel (1975, p. 217); Tullock (1976, p. 524); Tobin (1980, pp. 86–87); and, with respect to the unit of account, Hall (1983, p. 34); and Stockman (1983, p. 52).

[28]Currency competition might even be desirable if the process were known to converge to the government's money; for the government may not know in advance what type of money to converge to: "The monopoly of government of issuing money . . . has . . . deprived us of the only process by which we can find out what would be good money" (Hayek 1979, p. 5).

[29]Engels (1981) suggests that the government "has the task of defining the monetary unit . . . in terms of the market valuation of real assets . . . and of securing the solvency of issuing banks" (pp. 9f.). Hall (1983) believes that private money must be denominated in an interest-bearing reserve certificate which is issued by the government and is indexed to the price level. See Vaubel (1982b) for a critical review of Engels.

Refusal to prescribe specific arrangements does not prevent us from trying to forecast monetary arrangements under free currency competition; even Hayek (1978, pp. 70ff., 122ff.) has done so. Hayek believes that private money would be stable in terms of "the prices of widely traded products such as raw materials, agricultural food stuffs and certain standardised semi-finished industrial products" (p. 71) and that "competition might lead to the extensive use of the same commodity base by a large number of issue banks" (p. 123). Vaubel (1977) has suggested that "value guarantees . . . are likely to be a necessary condition for acceptance of a competing money" and that "in the presence of unpredictable fluctuations in the determinants of the demand for money, value guarantees can only be maintained with precision and instantaneously, if they can be validated through exchange rate adjustment vis-à-vis another currency for which a price index is calculated" (p. 451).[30] He believes that this reference currency, which cannot also be indexed (owing to the n-th currency problem), would be the outside money supplied by the government.

Another group of authors argues that the optimal money would appreciate relative to goods. Not all of them claim that the money which they regard as most efficient would also be most attractive to money users and prevail in the market, but this possibility should be considered. One variant is the so-called theory of the optimum quantity of money expounded by Friedman (1969), Johnson (1968), Samuelson (1963, 1969), and others; as Mussa (1977) has emphasized and criticized, it views money only as a store of value and ignores its standard of value function. According to another variant, which is due to Alchian and Klein (1973), the optimal monetary unit is stable in terms of a price index of all assets because the money cost of a given level of lifetime consumption utility ought to be held constant. Engels (1981) has recommended a real asset or pure equity standard because it would stabilize Tobin's q and thereby the business cycle. Engels suggests that such a unit would minimize the monetary risk for borrowers who invest in capital goods. However, the same is not likely to be true for all other debtors nor for all creditors. Bilson (1981) wants to transform money into an equity claim on a portfolio of real and nominal assets in order to render movements in the unanticipated rate of inflation countercyclical. A system of competing, private mutual fund monies is also envisioned by Fama (1982) and Greenfield and Yeager (1983). White (1984) predicts that they

---

[30]This is also Hayek's most recent forecast and practical proposal (1986).

would not displace the government's outside money as a general medium of exchange.

Whether privately issued money would appreciate relative to, or be stable in terms of, some composite of goods, cannot be predicted with certainty. However, experience with hyperinflation shows that the value of alternative monies, some of them private monies, tends to be linked to the price of one or more commodities. At times, for example in Germany in 1922–23, several commodity standards were used side by side. Chen (1975) reports a case in which this occurred over two centuries. Whether convergence toward a common standard of value and money is efficient and occurs depends on how similar the purchase and sale plans of different market agents are and how variable they expect the relative prices among commodities to be.[31]

What assets are private issuing institutions likely to hold if they are not restricted by government? They would minimize their balance sheet risk by having their assets and their money denominated in the same unit of account. The intermediation risk is zero in the case of equity or mutual-fund money. It is also zero in the case of commodity reserve money, however at the price of a zero real rate of return. The issuer of a money whose value is linked to a commodity price index can earn a positive real rate of return without incurring a monetary intermediation risk, if his assets are indexed as well; but he (and his creditors) cannot avoid a real intermediation risk. Thus, under free currency competition—even more than now—the composition of banks' assets will depend on the risk-yield preference trade-off of money users. Their degree of risk aversion is likely to differ, and it may vary over time. It cannot be reliably predicted— not even by governments.

References

Alchian, Armen A., and Klein, Benjamin. "On a Correct Measure of Inflation. *Journal of Money, Credit and Banking* 5, no. 1 (1973): 173–91.

Bilson, John F. O. *A Proposal for Monetary Reform.* Manuscript, University of Chicago, September 1981.

Brunner, Karl, and Meltzer, Allan H. "Some Further Investigations of Demand and Supply Functions for Money." *Journal of Finance* 19, no. 2 (1964): 240–83.

Brunner, Karl, and Meltzer, Allan H. "The Uses of Money: Money in the Theory of an Exchange Economy." *American Economic Review* 61, no. 5 (1971): 784–805.

Buchanan, James M. *The Demand and Supply of Public Goods.* Chicago: Rand McNally, 1968.

[31]See Vaubel (1978a, 1982b).

Chen, Chau-Nan. "Flexible Bimetallic Exchange Rates in China, 1650–1850: A Historical Example of Optimum Currency Areas." *Journal of Money, Credit and Banking* 7, no. 2 (1975): 359–76.

Claassen, Emil M., and Salin, Pascal, eds. *Stabilization Policies in Interdependent Economies.* Amsterdam: North-Holland, 1972.

Engels, Wolfram. *The Optimal Monetary Unit.* Frankfurt Main: Campus, 1981.

Fama, Eugene F. *Fiduciary Currency and Commodity Standards.* Manuscript, University of Chicago, January 1982.

Fratianni, Michele. "The Dollar and the ECU." In *The International Monetary System: A Time of Turbulence,* pp. 430–53. Edited by Jacob S. Dreyer, Gottfried Haberler, and Thomas D. Willett. Washington, D.C.: American Enterprise Institute, 1982.

Frenkel, Jacob A. "Reflections on European Monetary Integration." *Weltwirtschaftliches Archiv* 111, no. 2 (1975): 216–21.

Friedman, Milton. *A Program for Monetary Stability.* New York: Fordham University Press, 1959a.

Friedman, Milton. "The Demand for Money: Some Theoretical and Empirical Results." *Journal of Political Economy* 67, no. 4 (1959b): 327–51.

Friedman, Milton. *The Optimum Quantity of Money and Other Essays.* Chicago: Aldine, 1969.

Friedman, Milton. *Monetary System for a Free Society.* Manuscript, Hoover Institution, Stanford, Calif., November 1981.

Gehrig, Bruno. "Brauchen wir monopolistische Zentralbanken?" *Wirtschaft und Recht* 30, no. 4 (1978): 452–64.

Girton, Lance, and Roper, Don. "Theory and Implications of Currency Substitution." *Journal of Money, Credit and Banking* 13, no. 1 (1981): 12–30.

Grauwe, Paul de. "Should the U.K. Join the European Monetary System?" Treasury and Civil Service Committee, Subcommittee *Report on the European Monetary System,* London 1985, Annex.

Greenfield, Robert L., and Yeager, Leland B. "A Laissez Faire Approach to Monetary Stability." *Journal of Money, Credit and Banking* 15, no. 3 (1983): 302–15.

Gurley, John G., and Shaw, Edward S. *Money in a Theory of Finance.* Washington, D.C.: Brookings Institution, 1960.

Haberler, Gottfried. "Flexible Exchange-Rate Theories and Controversies Once Again." In *Flexible Exchange Rates and the Balance of Payments: Essays in Memory of Egon Sohmen,* pp. 29–48. Edited by John S. Chipman and Charles P. Kindleberger. Amsterdam: North-Holland, 1980.

Hall, Robert E. *The Role of Government in Stabilizing Prices and Regulating Money.* Manuscript, Stanford University, January 1981.

Hall, Robert E. "Optimal Fiduciary Monetary Systems." *Journal of Monetary Economics* 12, no. 3 (1983): 33–50.

Hamada, Koichi. "On the Political Economy of Monetary Integration: A Public Economics Approach." In *The Political Economy of Monetary Reform,* pp. 13–31. Edited by Robert Z. Aliber. London: Macmillan, 1977.

Hamada, Koichi. *On the Coordination of Monetary Policies in a Monetary Union.* Paper presented at the conference on "New Economic Approaches to the Study of International Integration," Florence, May/June 1979.

Hayek, Friedrich A. *Denationalisation of Money.* Hobart Paper Special, 70. London: Institute of Economic Affairs, 1976; 1978.

Hayek, Friedrich A. "Toward a Free Market Monetary System." *Journal of Libertarian Studies* 3, no. 1 (1979): 1–8; reprinted (with revisions) in this volume.

Hayek, Friedrich A. "Market Standards for Money." *Economic Affairs* 6, no. 4 (1986): 8–10.

Hirschman, Albert O. *Exit, Voice, and Loyalty.* Cambridge, Mass.: Harvard University Press, 1970.

Hirshleifer, Jack. "Exchange Theory: The Missing Chapter." *Western Economic Journal* 11, no. 2 (1973): 129–46.

Johnson, Harry G. "Problems of Efficiency in Monetary Management." *Journal of Political Economy* 76, no. 5 (1968): 971–90.

Johnson, Harry G. "Pesek and Saving's Theory of Money and Wealth." *Journal of Money, Credit and Banking* 1, no. 3 (1969): pp. 535–37.

Kareken, John, and Wallace, Neil. "On the Indeterminacy of Equilibrium Exchange Rates." *Quarterly Journal of Economics* 96 (1981): 202–22.

Kindleberger, Charles P. "The Benefits of International Money." *Journal of International Economics* 2, no. 3 (1972): 425–42.

Kindleberger, Charles P. "Lessons from Floating Exchange Rates. In *Institutional Arrangements and the Inflation Problem*, pp. 51–77. Edited by Karl Brunner and Allan H. Meltzer. Amsterdam: North-Holland, 1976.

Kindleberger, Charles P. *Manias, Panics and Crashes.* New York: Basic Books, 1978a.

Kindleberger, Charles P. "Dominance and Leadership in the International Economy: Exploitation, Public Goods, and Free Rides." In *Hommage a Francois Perroux.* pp. 283–91. Grenoble, 1978b.

Kindleberger, Charles P. "Standards as Public, Collective and Private Goods." *Kyklos* 36, no. 3 (1983): 377–96.

Klein, Benjamin. "The Competitive Supply of Money." *Journal of Money, Credit and Banking* 6, no. 4 (1974): 423–53.

Kolm, Serge-Christophe. "External Liquidity—A Study in Monetary Welfare Economics." In *Mathematical Methods in Investment and Finance*, pp. 190–206. Edited by Giorgio P. Szegö and Karl Shell. Amsterdam: North-Holland, 1972.

Kolm, Serge-Christophe "Fondements de l'économie monetaire normative: seigneurage, liquidité externe, impossibilité de remunérer les espèces." *Revue Economique* 28, no. 1 (1977): 1–35.

Laidler, David E. W. "The Welfare Costs of Inflation in Neoclassical Theory—Some Unsettled Problems." In *Inflation Theory and Anti-Inflation Policy*, pp. 314–328. Edited by Erik Lundberg. London: Macmillan, 1977.

Lutz, Friedrich A. *Das Grundproblem der Geldverfassung.* Berlin, 1936.

McKinnon, Ronald I. *Private and Official International Money: The Case for the Dollar.* Essays in International Finance, Princeton, 1969.

McKinnon, Ronald I. *Money in International Exchange.* New York: Oxford University Press, 1979.

McKinnon, Ronald I. *A New International Standard for Monetary Stabilization.* Washington, D.C.: Institute for International Economics, 1983.

Meltzer, Allan H. "Money, Intermediation and Growth." *Journal of Economic Literature* 7, no. 1 (1969): 27–56.

Mussa, Michael. "The Welfare Cost of Inflation and the Role of Money as a Unit of Account." *Journal of Money, Credit and Banking* 9, no. 2 (1977): 276–86.

Musgrave, Richard A. *The Theory of Public Finance.* New York: McGraw-Hill, 1959.

Patinkin, Don. "Financial Intermediaries and the Logical Structure of Monetary Theory." *American Economic Review* 51, no. 1 (1961): 95–116.

Pesek, Boris P., and Saving, Thomas R. *Money, Wealth and Economic Theory.* New York: Macmillan, 1967.

Samuelson, Paul A. "The Pure Theory of Public Expenditure." *Review of Economics and Statistics* 35, no. 4 (1954): 387–89.

Samuelson, Paul A. "D. H. Robertson (1890–1963)." *Quarterly Journal of Economics* 77, no. 4 (1963): 517–36.

Samuelson, Paul A. "Pure Theory of Public Expenditures and Taxation." In *Public Economics*, pp. 98–123. Edited by Julius Margolis and Henri Guitton. London: Macmillan, 1969.

Schmidt, Wilson E. *The U.S. Balance of Payments and the Sinking Dollar.* New York: New York University Press, 1979.

Sharkey, William W. *The Theory of Natural Monopoly.* Cambridge: Cambridge University Press, 1982.

Stockman, Alan C. "Comments on R. E. Hall's Paper." *Journal of Monetary Economics* 12, no. 1 (1983): 51–54.

Tobin, James. "Discussion." In *Models of Monetary Economies*, pp. 83–90. Edited by John H. Kareken and Neil Wallace. Minneapolis: Federal Reserve Bank of Minneapolis, 1980.

Tullock, Gordon. "Public Decisions as Public Goods." *Journal of Political Economy* 79, no. 4 (1971): 913–18.

Tullock, Gordon. "Competing Monies." *Journal of Money, Credit and Banking* 7, no. 4 (1975): 491–97.

Tullock, Gordon. "Competing Monies: A Reply." *Journal of Money, Credit and Banking* 8, no. 4 (1976): 521–25.

Vaubel, Roland. "Freier Wettbewerb zwischen Währungen?" *Wirtschaftsdienst* (Hamburg) 56, no. 8 (1976): 422–28.

Vaubel, Roland. "Free Currency Competition." *Weltwirtschaftliches Archiv* 113, no. 3 (1977): 435–61.

Vaubel, Roland. *Strategies for Currency Unification: The Economics of Currency Competition and the Case for a European Parallel Currency.* Tübingen: Mohr, 1978a.

Vaubel, Roland. "The Money Supply in Europe: Why EMS May Make Inflation Worse." *Euromoney* (December 1978b): 139–42.

Vaubel, Roland. "International Shifts in the Demand for Money, Their Effects on Exchange Rates and Price Levels, and Their Implications for the Preannouncement of Monetary Expansion." *Weltwirtschaftliches Archiv* 116, no. 1 (1980): 1–44.

Vaubel, Roland. "West Germany's and Switzerland's Experience with Exchange-Rate Flexibility." In *The International Monetary System: A Time of Turbulence*, pp. 180–222. Edited by Jacob S. Dreyer, Gottfried

Haberler, and Thomas D. Willett. Washington, D.C.: American Enterprise Institute, 1982a.

Vaubel, Roland. "Private Geldproduktion und Optimale Währungseinheit" (Review of *The Optimal Monetary Unit* by Wolfram Engels). *Weltwirtschaftliches Archiv* (1982b): 581–85.

Vaubel, Roland. "Coordination or Competition among National Macroeconomic Policies?" In *Reflections on a Troubled World Economy: Essays in Honour of Herbert Giersch*, pp. 3–28. Edited by F. Machlup, G. Fels, and H. Müller-Groeling. London: Macmillan, 1983.

Vaubel, Roland. "The Government's Money Monopoly: Externalities or Natural Monopoly?" *Kyklos* 37, no. 1 (1984): 27–58.

White, Lawrence H. "Competitive Payments Systems and the Unit of Account." *American Economic Review* 74, no. 4 (1984): 699–712.

Yeager, Leland B. "Stable Money and Free-Market Currencies." *Cato Journal* 3, no. 1 (1983): 305–26; reprinted (with revisions) in this volume.

14

STABLE MONEY AND FREE-MARKET CURRENCIES*
Leland B. Yeager

This paper tries to illuminate certain properties of actual monetary systems by contrasting them with imaginary systems. Even if none of the proposed reforms ever is adopted, examining how they might work may promote progress in monetary theory.

Our Preposterous Dollar

On reflection, our existing monetary system must seem preposterous. It is not difficult to understand how individually plausible steps over years and centuries have brought us to where we now are, but the cumulative result remains preposterous nevertheless. Our unit of account—our pervasively used measure of value, analogous to units of weight and length—is whatever value supply and demand fleetingly accord to the dollar of fiat money.

If balance between demand for and supply of this fiat medium of exchange is not maintained by clever manipulation of its nominal quantity at a stable equilibrium value of the money unit, then any correction of this supply-and-demand imbalance must occur through growth or shrinkage of the unit itself. Money's purchasing power—the general price level—must change. This change does not occur swiftly and smoothly. Money's value must change, when it does, through a long drawn-out, roundabout process involving millions of separately determined, though interdependent, prices and wage rates. Meanwhile, until the monetary disequilibrium has been finally corrected in this circuitous way, we suffer the pains of an excess demand for or excess supply of money.

Fundamentally, behind the veil of money, people specialize in producing particular goods (and services) to exchange them for the specialized outputs of other people. Since supply of goods constitutes

---

*Reprinted from *Cato Journal* 3 (Spring 1983): 305–26, with revisions.

The author is Ludwig von Mises Distinguished Professor of Economics at Auburn University.

demand for goods in that sense, any problem of apparent deficiency of aggregate demand traces to impediments to exchange, which discourage producing goods to be exchanged. Probably the most serious impediment—to judge from all the evidence supporting the "monetarist" theory of business fluctuations—hinges on the fact that goods exchange for each other not directly but through the intermediary of money (or of claims to be settled in money). Trouble occurs when a discrepancy develops between actual and desired holdings of money at the prevailing price level. Such a discrepancy can develop when the actual growth of the money supply falls short of the long-run trend or, more simply, when money actually shrinks. People and organizations try to conserve or replenish their deficient money holdings by exhibiting reduced eagerness to buy and increased eagerness to sell goods and services and securities. Since transactions are voluntary, the shorter of the demand side and the supply side sets the actual volume of transactions on each particular market. Production cutbacks in response to reduced sales in some sectors of the economy spell reduced real buying power for the outputs of other sectors. Elements of price and wage stickiness, though utterly rational from the individual points of view of the decision-makers involved, do keep downward price and wage adjustments from absorbing the full impact of the reduced willingness to spend associated with efforts to build or maintain cash balances. The rot snowballs, especially if people react to deteriorating business and growing uncertainty by trying to increase their money holdings relative to income and expenditure. In depression or recession, what would be an excess demand for money at full employment is being suppressed by people's being too poor to "afford" more than their actual money holdings. Relief of this (suppressed) excess demand for money somehow or other—perhaps by an increase in the nominal supply, perhaps through price and wage reductions that create the additional real money balances demanded at full employment—would bring recovery. An excess supply of money, at the other extreme, brings price inflation.

This theory of monetary disequilibrium can be extended to deal with stagflation and with the adverse side effects of anti-inflationary monetary policies by working out a close analogy between the stickiness of a price and wage *level* and the momentum of an entrenched upward *trend*. General interdependence or input-output-type interdependence helps account for this momentum. Not all cost pass-throughs can occur instantly. (But this does not mean that inflation is a cost-push phenomenon.) The momentum of price and cost increases makes it possible for excessive growth of the money supply in the past to produce a situation in which, once nominal money growth has been stopped or slowed (or even only its acceleration reduced), the money supply in purchasing-power terms is currently insufficient for a full-employment volume of economic activity.

The point relevant to what concerns us here is that imbalance between the actual quantity of money and the total of desired cash balances cannot readily be forestalled or corrected through adjustment of the price of money on the market for money because money, in contrast with all other things, does not have a single price and single market of its own. Monetary imbalance has to be corrected through the roundabout and sluggish process of adjusting the prices of a great many individual goods and services (and securities). Because prices do not immediately absorb the full impact of the supply and demand imbalances for individual goods and services that are the counterpart of an overall monetary imbalance, quantities traded and produced are affected also. Thus, the deflationary process associated with an excess demand for money, in particular, can be painful.

Yet even if, and perhaps especially if—contrary to reality—the purchasing power of the money unit were sufficiently flexible to forestall imbalance between money's supply and demand and if potential imbalances kept calling this flexibility into play, the resulting instability of the unit of account would impair coordination. Capricious redistributions between debtors and creditors and the further-reaching effects of changed real debt burdens are not the whole story by far. More than the meeting of minds between prospective debtors and creditors is impaired; for the unit of account is used pervasively in expressing bids and offers and the terms of transactions, in assessing costs and benefits, and in business and personal planning. Not merely coordination but, more broadly, economic calculation is at stake.

Consider how difficult constructing a house would be (ordering and fitting together the components, appliances, and all the rest) if the unit of length, the meter or the foot, kept changing and accordingly were perceived by different persons to have different sizes. Consider how preposterous it would be for the length of the meter to fluctuate according to supply and demand in the market for meter-sticks. Yet our dollar suffers from a comparable absurdity—or a worse one, in view of the associated macroeconomic disorders.

The remedy is to be sought in somehow arranging for the quantity of money always to match the demand for it at a stable value of the unit. Alternatively, the value of the unit must be stabilized and the quantity of the medium of exchange made appropriately responsive to the demand for it through decoupling the unit of account and the medium of exchange from each other.

Reformed Government Money

I shall say only a little about remedies within the realm of government money and nothing about a governmental gold standard, as these topics are covered elsewhere in this volume. Further, such a standard is very likely to be a mere pseudo gold standard rather than a real one (to make Milton Friedman's important distinction).[1] Anyone serious about the gold standard should favor leaving it to private enterprise, protected against governmental ruination. (I'll say a little about this later on.)

I used to favor the familiar monetarist quantity rule, but lately doubts have been plaguing me. Recent and ongoing financial innovations (money-market funds, sweep accounts, overnight RPs, overnight Eurodollars, highly marketable credit instruments, cash management devices, and all the rest) are rendering the very concept of money hopelessly fuzzy and the velocity of whatever constitutes money hopelessly unstable and unpredictable. So, anyway, goes a view that I cannot confidently dismiss.

If this view should be or should become correct, the monetarist rule would have become inapplicable precisely because of failure to adopt it unequivocally, credibly, and in due time. The troublesome financial innovations represent attempts to wriggle around interest ceilings and reserve requirements made particularly costly by inflation-boosted nominal interest rates, the inflation tracing in turn to a disregard of monetarist advice. Rejection of a prescribed treatment may allow a disease to develop to a stage at which the original prescription would no longer work and at which some quite different treatment becomes necessary. This does not mean that the doctors who made the original prescription—here, the monetarists—have anything to apologize for.

Anyway, the old proposal for targeting monetary policy on a broad price index deserves a fresh look. Underlying this proposal is the idea that incipient monetary disequilibrium would tend to show itself in prices. Movements away from a previously stable price level are symptoms of excess demand for or excess supply of money, either of which, but especially the former, impinges on real activity as well as on prices. Monetary policy aimed at price-level stability would coincide with resisting unemployment due to general deficiency of spending while not creating too much new money in a doomed attempt to cure unemployment of some other kind. This idea is not

---

[1]Milton Friedman, "Real and Pseudo Gold Standards," *Journal of Law and Economics* 4 (October 1961), reprinted in his *Dollars and Deficits* (Englewood Cliffs, N.J.: Prentice-Hall, 1968), pp. 247–65.

crucially dependent on any particular definition or measure of money, since imbalances between its supply and demand, and not those quantities separately, are what are to be detected and corrected.

The standard objection stresses time lags between the need for and the taking of corrective policy actions and then lags between the actions and their results. A price index, like individual prices, responds sluggishly. Because of these lags, results might run in the wrong direction by the time they appeared. This difficulty would bedevil a sharply shifting policy, however, more than a steady and consistent one. Ways might be found, furthermore, to mitigate the problem of lags, perhaps through attention to particularly sensitive commodity prices and to futures prices.

Indexing and Basket Currencies

Even so, proposals for nongovernmental remedies intrigue me more. First I shall consider some proposed remedies that, while not free of government involvement, do or could have private aspects.

Proposals for a stable unit of account come to the fore in times of severe inflation.[2] Under widespread indexing, the dollar of base-year

[2]And not only then; some were published during the 19th century when price levels were trending downward. After mentioning earlier proposals by Joseph Lowe and G. Poulett Scrope, W. Stanley Jevons recommended "a tabular or average standard of value," to be based on an index number. *Money and the Mechanism of Exchange* (New York: Appleton, 1875), chap. 25. Alfred Marshall recommended expressing debts and the interest on them, pensions, taxes, salaries, and wages in units of the purchasing power possessed by one pound sterling at, say, the beginning of 1887; eventually "the currency would . . . be restricted to the functions for which it is well fitted, of measuring and settling transactions that are completed shortly after they are begun." "Remedies for Fluctuations of General Prices," *Contemporary Review* (1887), reprinted in *Memorials of Alfred Marshall* (1925), pp. 197–99, and extracted in Milton Friedman, *Monetary Correction* (London: Institute of Economic Affairs, 1974), pp. 36–38. Friedman's booklet, pp. 39–45, also contains Brian Griffiths, "English Classical Political Economy and the Debate on Indexation." Walter Bagehot criticized Jevons' proposal in "A New Standard of Value," *The Economist*, November 20, 1875, reprinted in *Economic Journal* 2 (September 1892): 472–77. Aneurin Williams, anticipating Irving Fisher's proposal of three decades later for a "compensated dollar" (*Stabilizing the Dollar*, New York: Macmillan, 1920), proposed adjusting the gold content of the pound sterling in line with changes in the purchasing power of gold so as to keep the purchasing power of sterling constant. "A 'Fixed Value of Bullion' Standard—A Proposal for Preventing General Fluctuations of Trade," *Economic Journal* 2 (June 1892): 280–89. Robert Giffen criticized Williams' proposal in "Fancy Monetary Standards," *Economic Journal* 2 (September 1892): 463–71.

In recent years, though perhaps not still today, the most prominent advocate of indexing has been Milton Friedman. (See his *Monetary Correction*, as well as his "Using Escalators to Help Fight Inflation," *Fortune* 90 (July 1974): 94–97, 174, 176.) Friedman's chief argument appears to be that indexing would help break the sheer momentum of wage increases and would thereby lessen the unemployment associated purchasing power—we might call it the "constant"[3]—would be the unit of account, while the ordinary dollar in which demand deposits and currency are denominated remained the medium of exchange.[4]

Separate proposals by Jacques Riboud and by nine prominent European economists may be understood as variants of the proposal for a unit of base-year purchasing power.[5] The "Eurostable" or "Europa," as the new unit would be called under the respective proposals, would initially be defined as a composite of specified amounts of each of several national currencies. For convenience in arithmetic, we might think of the initial definition of *one hundred* Eurostables as *g* German marks plus *f* French francs plus *i* Italian lire plus *u* US dollars, and so on. We may think of 100 Eurostables as the total value of several little piles on a table, each of a specific national currency. Now, as national price levels rise (or fall) over time, the amount of currency in each pile is increased (or reduced) in proportion to its country's price index. The nominal amount of currency in each pile varies to keep its purchasing power unchanged;

---

with a program of slowing down monetary expansion and eventually returning to price-level stability. Trying to appraise that particular argument would be rather aside from the main topics of this paper.

[3]The name comes from Ralph Borsodi's proposal for a unit of steady purchasing power whose nominal dollar value would rise in step with the Consumer Price Index. Actually, Borsodi envisaged not just a mere unit of account but also a medium of exchange denominated in constants. The question arises, however, of whether such a system of indexing does not presuppose the continued existence of ordinary dollar prices and dollars in circulation. Such questions are considered later in this paper.

Anyway, a small-scale trial of Borsodi's proposal was begun in June 1972 in Exeter, New Hampshire, where two banks made available checking accounts and even currency denominated in constants. The experiment was discontinued in January 1974, supposedly because of the elderly Mr. Borsodi's physical weakness, because of doubts about legality, and because earnings on the assets (mainly Treasury securities) matching the constant liabilities did not fully cover expenses plus the indexed growth in the dollar value of the liabilities. See "Paying with Constants Instead of Dollars," *Business Week*, May 4, 1974, p. 29.

[4]If only bonds and other long-term contracts were denominated in "constants," then the base-year dollar would be serving not only as the standard of deferred payments but not as the general unit of account. The old textbook distinction between those two functions is perhaps not empty after all. (Alfred Marshall evidently had it in mind; see note 2.) Perhaps we should retain the distinction, especially if the idea of universal use of an index-defined stable unit of account turns out to be self-contradictory.

[5]Jacques Ribound, *Une Monnaie pour l'Europe: L'Eurostable* (Paris: Editions de la R.P.P., 1975), and *Eurostable*, Bulletin du Centre Jouffroy pour la Réflexion Monétaire, March–April 1977; Giorgio Basevi, Michele Fratianni, Herbert Giersch, Pieter Korteweg, David O'Mahony, Michael Parkin, Theo Peeters, Pascal Salin, and Niels Thygesen, "The All Saints' Day Manifesto for European Monetary Union," *The Economist*, November 1, 1975, reprinted in Michele Fratianni and Theo Peeters, eds., *One Money for Europe* (London: Macmillan, 1978), pp. 37–43. My present purposes do not require sharply distinguishing the features of these different proposals.

so the combined purchasing power of all the piles on the table remains constant also. Adjustments of this kind would be carried out at least as frequently as every month. Riboud envisages daily adjustments calculated with projections of the national price indexes and with whatever minor corrections proved necessary being made as the latest figure for each index became available. Constancy of the purchasing power of the Eurostable is defined with reference not to a single national price index only but to several specified indexes. In effect, the constant purchasing power of the Eurostable is the aggregate of the purchasing powers possessed by specified amounts of marks, francs, lire, dollars, and so forth *in the base month.*[6]

With details depending on the particular scheme in question, central banks or commercial banks would accept deposits and grant loans denominated in Eurostables or Europas. To be safe in incurring deposit obligations denominated in purchasing-power units and thus perhaps having to be honored in greatly increased nominal amounts of national currency, banks would have to hold assets similarly denominated. The question arises whether borrowers would be willing to incur debts perhaps repayable in unpredictably swollen nominal amounts of national currency. What would induce borrowers to incur such debts unless they could already count on receiving their incomes in such units? Especially low interest rates might constitute the inducement, but the low rates would be a disadvantage from the bankers' point of view.

---

[6]It seems to me that the following formulas would apply to the Eurostable system. The value of 1 Eurostable (or perhaps of 100 Eurostables, as suggested in the text) = $\sum_{i=1}^{n} u_i P_i$, where u_i = number of units of the ith country's currency in the base-period basket and P_i is the ith country's price index on the basis of its base-period figure being 1. The number of countries, currencies, and indexes involved is n. To consider exchange rates, let r_{jE} = number of units of currency j worth 1 Eurostable. (Currency j is a particular one of the currencies indicated by subscript i.) Let r_{ji} = number of units of currency j worth 1 unit of currency i; u_i and P_i have the meanings already indicated. Then

$$r_{jE} = \sum_{i=1}^{n} u_i P_i r_{ji}$$

The Eurostable or Europa is quite different from the Special Drawing Right of the International Monetary Fund and the Eurco and other composite units described in Joseph Aschheim and Y. S. Park, *Artificial Currency Units: The Formation of Functional Currency Areas*, Princeton Essays in International Finance, No. 114, April 1976. These artificial units are defined as baskets containing *fixed* nominal amounts of national currencies; instead of having fixed purchasing power, they lose it along with the national currencies composing their baskets.

We shall set aside the point that the two proposals mentioned, but the Europa scheme more so than the Eurostable scheme, envision that the new stable unit would serve not only as a standard of deferred payments and unit of account but also, increasingly, as a medium of exchange. Our concern here is just with how a separation of functions would work.

Separation of Functions and Its Theoretical Appeal

History can give us little direct help toward answering this question. Separation is, to be sure, far from unprecedented. In Germany during the hyperinflation after World War I, some bonds were denominated and some prices calculated in centners of rye, Swiss francs, or grams of gold. In ancient times and in the Middle Ages, the money circulating in commercial centers was a hodgepodge of variously denominated coins from both local and far-away mints;[7] so the unit of account and medium of exchange could not have been unified. Even in the United States, until beyond the middle of the 19th century, foreign as well as American coins were in use; and the notes of the shakier or less well-known state-chartered banks circulated at various discounts. But though examples of separation of functions, these were not cases of a single unit of account, distinct from the circulating medium, being in *general* use. Clearly they provide no example of a unit of account defined so as to have a stable purchasing power. The medieval "ghost moneys" described by Cipolla[8] were not such units, either; instead, they appear to have been multiples or fractions of some currently or formerly circulating coin used for convenience in arithmetic and accounting before the days of calculators.

What concerns us here is a different state of affairs; namely, how things would work with something like the Eurostable or Europa in general use as the unit of account and distinct from the medium of exchange. We may as well analyze the simplest case, in which the "basket" defining the unit contains just one national currency, whose nominal quantity would be periodically adjusted upward in proportion to a single index of prices quoted in terms of the circulating

[7]Heinrich Rittershausen, *Bankpolitik* (Frankfurt: Knapp, 1956), esp. pp. 58–60; Carlo M. Cipolla, *Money, Prices, and Civilization in the Mediterranean World, Fifth to Seventeenth Century* (Princeton, N.J.: Princeton University Press, 1956).
[8]Cipolla, chap. 4.

currency. The dollar of base-year purchasing power, Borsodi's "constant," would then be the unit of account. (The Eurostable/Europa scheme is essentially the same except in defining a stable unit with reference to several price indexes instead of only one.)

The idea of separating the unit of account and medium of exchange has appeal as conceivably a way not only of achieving a stable measuring rod for economic coordination and economic calculation but also of avoiding the macroeconomic disorders mentioned earlier by giving the medium of exchange a flexible, market-clearing price of its own.

The separation of functions might also, for good or ill, help wear down money illusion and inflation illusion. Money illusion, in the old sense of the term, is the tacit assumption that a dollar is a dollar, that money is a stable measure of value, and that changes in the general price level reflect disorders from the side of goods rather than from the side of money. What might be called inflation illusion is the related perception of inflation as a sort of plague affecting wages and prices rather than as the specifically monetary disorder that it really is. These illusions are supported by money's lack of any specific market (other than the foreign-exchange market, anyway) on which it is straightforwardly quoted and can be seen to be deteriorating. Money is quoted on millions of different markets in millions of different ways; but this very multiplicity of markets and of prices, many of which would be changing anyway even apart from any monetary disorder, obstructs any simple view of what is happening to money itself.

Things might be different if a Eurostable or some other index-defined constant existed against which national currencies were quoted every day. Such quotations would be the result of calculations, however, rather than of a direct market process; ordinary money still would not have an actual market specifically its own.

Difficulties with a Constant Unit and Indexing

We still are left wondering whether general cost accounting, pricing, and contracting in terms of Eurostables or constants, while ordinary money continued to serve as the medium of exchange, could help overcome the macroeconomic difficulties associated with money as we have known it.

Before facing more fundamental questions, let us, for completeness, recognize a couple of minor difficulties. A scheme involving use of a price index might create temptations to rig the index. Secondly, how would the use of stable units of accounts get launched?

What would induce borrowers to incur debts in such units? If people are going to undertake commitments to make future payments or repayments denominated in a stable unit, they will want to count on receiving income denominated in the same unit. They want to be obligated to pay the sort of money they expect to receive—except insofar as they are persuaded to gamble on doing otherwise, perhaps by an interest rate lower than on ordinary loans.

Here is a chicken-and-egg or Alphonse-and-Gaston problem. The more payments people are already scheduled to receive in a particular money, the more readily will they take on commitments to make payments in the same money. The spread of a practice facilitates its further spread,[9] but its not yet having gotten a good start hampers its ever getting started. Being one of the early users of a new unit would confer benefits on latecomers, if the reform could succeed, for which the early users could not collect compensation. They thus have inadequate incentives to provide what would be in part a public good.

A more fundamental difficulty is illuminated by supposing, or trying to suppose, that the practice has become quite general of not only expressing debts and other contracts but also pricing goods and services in constants. Prices in ordinary dollars, supposedly continuing to serve as the medium of exchange, are translated from the prices set in constants according to the current level of the price index whose "basket" of goods and services defines the constant. That is to say, if the current month's index of prices in ordinary dollars happens to stand 7 (say) times as high as the index in the base period—if the standard basket costs 7 times as many dollars as it did in the base period when, by definition, the dollar and the constant were equal in purchasing power—then the current exchange rate is 7 dollars per constant, and multiplication by 7 translates prices set in constants into current dollar prices.

But isn't there a contradiction here? If dollar prices are determined by applying the price index to translate prices set in constants, what is the meaning of the dollar price index? It expresses the average level of dollar prices calculated by means of the index itself (or by means of its latest published value, which may express the level of prices a few weeks earlier). In short, the dollar price level is the

---

[9]With money as with language, acceptability enhances acceptability. "The use of a particular language or a particular money by one individual increases its value to other actual or potential users. Increasing returns to scale, in this sense, limits the number of languages or moneys in a society and indeed explains the tendency for one basic language or money to monopolize the field." James Tobin, "Discussion," in *Models of Monetary Economies*, ed. John H. Kareken and Neil Wallace (Minneapolis: Federal Reserve Bank of Minneapolis, 1980), pp. 86–87.

arithmetical consequence of itself or of its own recent value. A rise in the index arithmetically raises its component prices and thus itself, and so on. The level of dollar prices is adrift, giving itself further momentum as it moves. It would be, anyway, unless a restricted quantity of medium-of-exchange dollars somehow provided it with an anchor after all. We shall return to this question, or the closely related question, of the real quantity of the medium of exchange.

Meanwhile, there does seem to be an internal contradiction in the very notion of all-around indexing, that is, of all-around price-setting in a constant unit related to the ordinary medium of exchange by calculations with a price index. If indexing comes to be employed not only in long-term contracts but also in general pricing, then it kills off the market-determined prices necessary for the construction of meaningful indexes. Employed beyond a certain degree, it destroys itself. This degree is analogous, in a way, to the critical mass of fissionable uranium or plutonium. To avoid the contradiction, indexing must not be employed quite generally, but only to provide a stable standard of deferred payments. Indexing is parasitical on its *not* being applied in setting most (or many) prices. It presupposes that most of the prices entering into the calculation of the index are determined by market forces—by people's bids and offers—directly in terms of the medium of exchange.

Yet the very meaning of generally setting prices in index-defined constants—which is what we have been trying to imagine—precludes people's continuing to express their bid and ask prices only in medium-of-exchange dollars without reference to their exchange rate against constants. Does this imply, then, that people would be negotiating prices in constants? That, too, is bedeviled with contradictions. Pricing and costing and bargaining in terms of constants would seem to be trying or threatening to change a historical datum, the constant itself, that is, the purchasing power that the dollar had in the base year.

All-around indexing, or pricing in constants, runs counter to free-market pricing in another way. It would replace current supply-and-demand determination of individual prices with *calculations,* calculations presumably applied to a pattern of prices established some time in the past. Unless somehow modified, it would freeze relative prices and remove them from the influence of up-to-date market conditions.

A further difficulty arises when people are trying to build up or run down their holdings of the medium of exchange. If the level of prices translated into medium-of-exchange dollars is adrift as a consequence of all-around indexing, as noted above, and if the quantity of medium of exchange is exogenously determined, then no process would seem to be at work tending to equate the actual and desired quantities of it. The exchange rate between dollars and constants, being a calculated number, is hardly something directly determined on the market by an equilibrating process.

Suppose that at its current purchasing power (however determined), people want to hold more of the medium of exchange than actually exists. How do they go about building up their holdings? They might start by bidding and asking lower prices for goods and services than translation from constants (calculations with the price index) would indicate. That would be a departure from the hypothesized all-around indexing. They might bid and ask lower prices in constants, thereby tending to alter the purchasing power of the constant. But since the constant is defined as a dollar of base-year purchasing power, changing its purchasing power means changing a historical datum—a contradiction in terms. Neither approach is compatible with what we are trying to conceive of—general pricing in terms of constants.

A conceivable alternative is that people, in trying to build up their cash balances, would not alter the prices they bid and asked but would simply hold back from buying things. (Their increased eagerness to sell things, not expressed in reduced selling prices, would have little operational meaning.) The outcome would be a recession in real economic activity of such degree that people no longer, after all, felt able to "afford" holding more than the actual quantity of medium of exchange. In that case, the joint existence of the constant and the medium-of-exchange dollar and the index-calculated exchange rate between them, far from providing a mechanism for painlessly ensuring monetary equilibrium, would pose an obstacle by making prices more nearly rigid or, perhaps more exactly, by making prices more nearly the arbitrary result of arithmetical calculations.

None of the ideas reviewed so far, then, would give the medium of exchange a price of its own determined on a market of its own in such a way as to keep its supply and demand painlessly in equilibrium. Widespread indexing as a stage of transition to something else might be conceivable, but the idea of universal indexing permanently associated with an ordinary medium of exchange verges on nonsense.

A more ambitious reform scheme might go beyond introducing a unit of account distinct from the medium of exchange. It might introduce demand deposits and even currency denominated in constants. Their issuers would presumably stand ready to redeem them in equivalent amounts of the ordinary medium of exchange, equivalences being calculated with a price index. There is no obvious reason why the market exchange rate between the two media of exchange should diverge significantly from the calculated rate; arbitrage should prevent that. If deposits and currency denominated in constants should totally displace the ordinary medium of exchange, the question would arise of what would be left for them to be redeemable in. Issuers might conceivably promise to add to everyone's holdings of these new media of exchange in proportion to the rise in the price index. But then the nominal money supply and the price level would be indeterminate (as in a monetary system managed fully in accordance with the fallacious real-bills doctrine); increases in each would call for increases in the other, indefinitely.[10]

Separate But Actual Units

Now that we have abandoned the idea of a generally employed abstract stable unit with a price-index-calculated exchange rate against ordinary money, let us suppose that the separate and stable—but now only relatively stable—unit of account actually exists as a commodity, say gold, or as a foreign currency.[11] Suppose that Americans came to use German marks or grams of gold as units of account while still making and receiving payments in ordinary dollars. (Offhand, no fundamental difference is apparent between using the mark and using gold as the other unit alongside the dollar, but this question may require further thought.) One difference from all-around indexing and similar schemes is that a currently market-determined exchange rate, and not just a calculated translation rate, does exist between the parallel unit and the domestically circulating dollar. Does this exchange rate and the market on which it is determined serve as a price and market "of its own" for the domestic medium of exchange in such a way as to solve or mitigate the macroeconomic problems previously reviewed?

Suppose, for definiteness, that Americans undergo a change in tastes and desire increased *real* holdings of dollar cash balances. Under ordinary circumstances with the nominal supply of dollars unchanged, a deflationary process sets in that cuts production and employment as well as prices. Under the separation of functions, however, the dollar appreciates against the mark or gold, meaning that the total quantity of the medium of exchange grows in terms of

[10]Cf. William Baumol, "The Escalated Economy and the Stimulating Effects of Inflation," *Rivista Internazionale di Scienze Economiche e Commerciali* 12 (February 1965): 103–14.

[11]As Heinrich Rittershausen says, a separation between the functions of money does occur on the international scene. *Bankpolitik*, pp. 61–62, 67–69.

the unit of account. (Alternatively, though perhaps less plausibly, the level of U.S. prices expressed in the marks or gold falls directly. In either case, the dollar money supply gains in purchasing power over goods and services.) The separation of the unit of account and medium of exchange, with translation between them at a flexible, market-determined price, does appear to be a way of avoiding or relatively painlessly correcting a monetary disequilibrium. But this conclusion requires further pondering.

We must ask, also, whether such a split system would be durable. Would it come into use in the first place if the general purchasing power of the mark or gold were only slightly less unstable than that of the dollar? And if the dollar were much more unstable, would it nevertheless persist in use as the medium of exchange? Since unification of money's functions is a convenience for its users, the mark or gold might then well displace the dollar as the medium of exchange also.

Durable or not, the system just mentioned is worth considering, for F. A. Hayek recognizes something similar as a preliminary step to the ultimate reform that he recommends (which is discussed below). Hayek would permit people in each country to use foreign currencies as units of account and media of exchange; these would be free to compete with the national currency.

Private Money

Realistically, private money must mean money that is *predominantly* so. The government would still be involved—in repressing force and fraud and in enforcing contracts. (I cannot go all the way with libertarians of the anarchist wing.)

As a libertarian, I favor allowing free banking—the competitive private issue of notes and deposits redeemable, presumably, in gold. Notes and deposits would be backed by merely fractional reserves, for efforts to enforce 100 percent banking in the face of contrary incentives and private ingenuity would require unacceptably extreme government interference.

For people serious about a gold standard, the monetary unit should be a physical quantity of gold, such as the gram or milligram, and not some abstract unit whose definition in terms of gold is subject to change. Yet I have doubts about whether such a system could catch on. How would the voluntary use of gold units catch on? If bankers are to issue note and deposit liabilities denominated in gold, they will want to hold assets—loans and investments—also denominated in gold. The problem of motivating people to go first in using new

310

units, already noted in connection with index-defined units, arises here too.

Furthermore, a gold monetary unit is preposterous in the same way as a fiat unit, although in lesser degree. The unit of value still lacks objectivity and dependability. Its size (purchasing power) depends on interaction between supply of and demand for an industrially rather unimportant substance being supplied and demanded predominantly for monetary purposes (that is, in association with the demand for money more broadly defined). The real size of a gold unit, as of a fiat unit, is changeable and undependable. Imbalance between the demand for and supply of monetary gold, like such imbalance for government-issued fiat base money, touches off a roundabout and sluggish process of adjustment in the unit's real value, a process with painful macroeconomic side effects. Furthermore, lapses of confidence in banks operating with fractional reserves could touch off a self-aggravating scramble for the gold on which the system is based.

Better alternatives are available. The government cannot avoid giving some encouragement to one or another system of private money. It is bound to do so by the manner in which it disengages itself from the present government-dominated monetary system. Therefore, the advantages and disadvantages of the different private systems are bound to be a topic of policy discussion. To say "let the market decide" is no adequate answer.

F. A. Hayek would authorize the issue of competing private fiat moneys. He has set forth the advantages of his proposal in some detail and has also tried to foresee and deal with difficulties.[12] My concern with his scheme is to ask the sorts of questions raised about indexing and other schemes already reviewed. What would determine the value of each money unit? How would price levels and the exchange rates among the different private currencies be determined? Would money acquire a price and market of its own in such a sense that the supply of and demand for each money would be equilibrated relatively painlessly?

---

[12]Hayek describes his proposal in *Choice in Currency*, Occasional Paper 48 (London: Institute of Economic Affairs, 1976), and *Denationalisation of Money*, Hobart Paper Special 70, 2d ed. (London: Institute of Economic Affairs, 1978). Cf. Thomas Saving, "Competitive Money Production and Price Level Determinancy" [*sic*], *Southern Economic Journal* 43 (October 1976): 987–94; Benjamin Klein, "The Competitive Supply of Money," *Journal of Money, Credit, and Banking* 4 (November 1975); Gordon Tullock, "Competing Moneys," *Journal of Money, Credit, and Banking* 7 (November 1976); Benjamin Klein, "Competing Moneys: Comment," *Journal of Money, Credit, and Banking* 7 (November 1976).

Under Hayek's scheme, each issuer would have his own unit (ducat, crown, florin, or whatever; the proposal does *not* envisage rival currencies all denominated in the same unit, such as a quantity of gold, although gold-dominated currencies could figure among the competing units). The different units would be free to fluctuate against each other. The value of each unit would not be a matter of sheer definition (as would be true of an index-defined abstract unit) but would depend on supply and demand. Each money would exist in some definite quantity. Each issuer would supposedly have an incentive to restrain his issues so as to keep the purchasing power of his unit stable, thereby attracting more and more holders. (Rather than go further and try to engineer an actual deflation of prices in terms of his money, he would presumably pay explicit interest on holdings.) The larger the real volume of his currency people would willingly hold, the larger the volume of loans the issuer could have outstanding and earning interest. Success in restraining his issue to the volume demanded at a stable value of his unit would itself strengthen that demand, which he could then profitably meet. Virtue would bring its own reward. Conceivably a single money might become the dominant or the only one used in a given territory. Its issuer would remain disciplined, though, by potential competition.

Under Hayek's scheme, separation of functions in one sense is lost—separation between the unit of account and medium of exchange—but separation is gained among the different monetary units, each of which would perform both functions.

If people wanted to acquire additional holdings of particular Hayek currencies, these would begin rising in value on the inter-currency exchange market and probably in purchasing power over goods and services also, leading their issuers to expand their amounts. If people wanted to reduce their holdings of particular currencies, they would fall in exchange value and probably in purchasing power, prodding their issuers, anxious to preserve their reputations, to try to reduce their outstanding issues, in the first instance by repurchasing them with reserves of other currencies. Through exchange-rate, purchasing-power, and quantity changes, then, and notably through quantity responses, equilibrium between desired and actual amounts of particular currencies would be maintained or restored.

But what happens if people desire to build up their real holdings of all currencies, or desire to build up the total real purchasing power that they hold in currencies in general? This desire might strike some currencies earlier or in greater degree, so that the same changes and incentives as mentioned above would occur. But suppose, instead, that the real demand for currency holdings increased uniformly.

Well, currencies would tend to gain in purchasing power (approximately uniformly, with exchange rates approximately unchanged). This would motivate their issuers to expand their circulations. However, the purchasing power signals would appear more slowly and more sluggishly than the exchange-rate signals would appear in the alternative case of only some currencies being directly affected.

But this may be a point in favor of the scheme: In practice, changes in the real demands for holdings of various currencies will not occur uniformly, and exchange rates will change, motivating changes in the issues most affected. In other words, just as nowadays, there will be no single market on which and single price at which currencies in general exchange against other things. However, people will no longer be dealing with money in general. Each currency will have a market and price of its own—the exchange market and its exchange rate.

In considering stable units of account or gold units serving in parallel with ordinary money as the medium of exchange, we noted the difficulty of getting such a system launched. People would have weak incentives to supply the public good of being its early users. The same would be true of trying to launch Hayek's system.

Another public-good aspect of a prudently managed currency is that, once well launched, it provides even people who do not hold it and do not make and receive payments in it with a stable unit of account in which they might conduct their calculations and express their claims and debts. Because of the free availability of his money as a unit of accounting and calculation even to parties who held little or none of it, a well-behaved issuer could not collect compensation for all the advantages he was conferring on the public in general. The social benefits of his maintaining a stable money would not come fully to his attention. The standard argument seems relevant that the purely private provision of public goods falls short of the optimum, plausibly defined.[13]

These points about public goods and externalities suggest that private-enterprise money would be at a disadvantage relative to government money. While the government incurs the costs of running

[13]Referring more to money in general than to specific currencies, Herbert Grubel notes that money saves resources otherwise consumed in accomplishing barter transactions, and it promotes productivity by encouraging specialization. Most of these benefits accrue to society as externalities. Herbert G. Grubel, *International Economics* (Homewood, Ill.: Irwin, 1977), p. 449.

For further distinction between the public and the private benefits of money, see J. R. Hicks, "The Two Triads," in his *Critical Essays in Monetary Theory* (Oxford: Clarendon Press, 1967), pp. 1–60.

a monetary system, it also more or less covers them from the seigniorage yielded by its quasi-monopoly position. These considerations may not be quantitatively important. (All sorts of private activities generate positive externalities without themselves being made unprofitable—for example, the benefits that relatively lazy shoppers get from the careful shopping of others, or free rides obtained on the information generated or publicized by organized markets.) Still, monetary reformers should face these points.

In a different respect, switching to a new currency creates a public *bad* if it shrinks demand for holdings of the old one, whose value consequently zigzags downward more sharply than otherwise. This problem of currency substitution might plague a system of competing private currencies even if it could somehow be successfully launched. According to the scheme's very logic, holders of the different currencies, as well as the financial press, would be alert to signs of unsound management and incipient depreciation of any one of them. Its holders would dump it and fly into others. Responses of this sort would destabilize the exchange rates between the different currencies, upsetting transactions and calculations. Like bank runs in the days before deposit insurance, such runs from one currency to another would be harmful from an overall point of view, though resulting from individuals' efforts to protect themselves.[14] (To recognize these disruptively sensitive responses is not to deny, however, that current and expected future purchasing-power parties would no doubt be the main systematic determinants of exchange rates.)

A possible variant of Hayek's schemes comes to mind. According to the original proposal, private issuers would strive to keep their moneys stable in value by suitable regulation of their quantities but would not keep them redeemable in anything in particular. (To get their moneys launched in the first place, issuers might promise to redeem them in definite amounts of government money; but as inflation continued to eat away the value of government money, redeem-

---

[14]For a description of this possible problem, though not for its relation to Hayek's proposal specifically, see Marc A. Miles, "Currency Substitution, Flexible Exchange Rates, and Monetary Independence," *American Economic Review* 68 (June 1978): 428–36.

The problem of instability from currency substitution seems more likely to characterize rival currencies competing even within countries than ordinary national currencies floating against each other on the foreign-exchange market. As long as one's fellow countrymen are still quite generally using the national currency, it is awkward and expensive for an individual or firm to try to initiate the shift to some other country's currency as its routine unit of account and medium of exchange even in domestic transactions. With money as with language, inertia tends to perpetuate an entrenched use.

ability in it would become more and more a dead letter.) Now, issuers might find it to their competitive advantage (or might conceivably be required) to promise redemption of their currencies on demand in gold (or in some other one or more commodities or even securities). The quantity of gold (or other redemption medium) per currency unit would not be physically fixed, however, but would be whatever quantity had a fixed purchasing power over the goods and services composing a specified bundle. That amount of gold would be recalculated each month (or day) from the open-market price of gold and from the prices of the various goods in the bundle. Issuers might also undertake to issue their currencies in exchange for the calculated amounts of gold, perhaps instituting a slight spread between their selling and buying prices of gold to cover expenses. Convertibility of this sort would give additional operationality to the expectation that issuers would strive to keep their money units stable in purchasing power; they would now be required to *do something* at the initiative of the money-holders.[15] Furthermore, if the different issuers kept recalculating the constant-purchasing-power amounts of gold in which their currencies were redeemable with reference to a common basket of goods and services, then an inconvenience of Hayek's system—that of a multiplicity of units of account, analogous to multiple systems of weights and measures—would be avoided. The operating properties of this variant system, however, remain to be explored.

A Single Stable Unit Distinct from the Medium of Exchange

By saving until now the reform that I currently prefer, I have avoided letting it monopolize the paper. Robert Greenfield and I have described it in detail elsewhere, provisionally calling it the "BFH system."[16] Like the reform proposed by Hayek, it would almost completely depoliticize money and banking. By the manner of its withdrawal from its current domination of our current system, the government would give a noncoercive nudge in favor of the new system. It would help launch a stable unit of account free of the absurdity of being the supply-and-demand-determined value of the

---

[15]This idea draws some inspiration from Aneurin Williams' and Irving Fisher's proposals, cited in note 2, for what Fisher called a "compensated dollar" and from Willford I. King, *The Keys to Prosperity* (New York: distributed by the Committee for Constitutional Government, 1948), pp. 209–10.

[16]Robert L. Greenfield and Leland B. Yeager, "A Laissez-Faire Approach to Monetary Stability," *Journal of Money, Credit, and Banking* 15 (August 1983): 302–15, where writings of Fischer Black, Eugene Fama, and Robert Hall are given credit for some component ideas.

unit of the medium of exchange. The government would define the new unit, just as it defines units of weights and measures. The definition would run in terms of a bundle of commodities so comprehensive that the unit's value would remain nearly stable against goods and services in general. The government would conduct its own accounting and transactions in the new unit. Thanks to this governmental nudge, the public-goods or who-goes-first problem of getting a new unit adopted would largely be sidestepped. The government would be barred from issuing money. Private enterprise, probably in the form of institutions combining the features of today's banks, money-market mutual funds, and stock mutual funds, would offer convenient media of exchange. Separation of a unit of account of defined purchasing power from the medium—or rather media—of exchange, whose quantity would be appropriately determined largely on the demand side, would go far toward avoiding macroeconomic disorders and facilitating stable prosperity. Lacking any base money, whether gold or government-issued money, on which ordinary money would be pyramided on a fractional-reserve basis, the BFH system would not share the precariousness and vulnerability of ordinary monetary systems.

Although I do not have the space for a full description of the BFH system and do not want to repeat myself by providing one here, I would like to forestall a few misconceptions that, as experience shows, are likely to arise. The BFH system is not a variant of the often proposed composite-commodity or commodity-reserve system of government money. It is not a variant of the tabular standard (widespread indexing). The definition of its unit of account does not require "implementation" through convertibility of any familiar sort, any more than does maintenance of the defined length of the meter. (Of course, ordinary business practice would force people to make and receive payments for current purchases and sales of goods and services and in settlement of debts in property actually worth the specified number of units of account. Banks would similarly have to settle net balances due on bank notes and checks sent through their clearinghouses.)

Under the BFH system, people would probably make payments by writing checks—checks denominated in the defined unit of account—on deposits and on holdings of shares of stock in institutions combining the features of mutual funds and banks. (These shares would have market-determined flexible prices.) These practices would not entail the textbook inconveniences of barter. The advantages of having a single definite unit of account and convenient methods of payment would be retained and enhanced. The absurdities of linking the unit of account and medium of exchange in the manner now familiar to us would be avoided. (By contrast with the situation in which both paper dollars and gold, say, were temporarily serving as both unit of account and medium of exchange, the conditions promoting convergence onto a single money serving both functions would be absent.)

Unlike the monetarism we are familiar with, which requires an accurate adjustment of the quantity of money to the demand for it and must therefore be suspicious of innovations that alter the supply-demand relation and even blur the concept of money, the BFH system can positively welcome deregulation and financial innovation. The government can take just as much a laissez-faire stance toward the financial system, once it has offered and promoted a particular definition of the unit of account, as it can take toward ordinary businesses that happen to employ a defined unit of length in their operations.

Concluding Remarks

It is easy to say that the best reform of all would institute a single worldwide money of assuredly constant purchasing power serving all four of money's traditionally listed functions. But recommending such a money would be empty unless we could specify how to achieve and maintain it. A monetary system is a set of institutions, sustained by laws, not a laundry list of desirable features. An abstract wish for ideal results does not itself chart a way out of present-day disorders.

It is easy, also, to point to complications and costs and nuisances associated with Hayek's and other reform schemes. In part, these would be open manifestations of complexities already existing but hidden in governmental monetary systems uniting the several functions of money (for example, distortions of information through inflation). These complications are different in detail under each scheme from what they are under unified government moneys. There is much to be said for having the complexities and costs evident, rather than keeping them as hard to perceive and cope with as they are nowadays.

With government no longer obscuring the relevant costs and benefits and no longer impeding financial innovation in efforts to shore up its own preposterous monetary system, we could expect private ingenuity to develop a monetary system—or a system transcending money—with features perhaps even more attractive than any we can now imagine.

317

15

MONEY, DEREGULATION, AND THE BUSINESS CYCLE*
Gerald P. O'Driscoll, Jr.

In this article, I examine the burgeoning literature on the behavior of unregulated banking systems. The analysis of banking and money has been dubbed the "legal restrictions theory." Many of the theory's conclusions are startling, as, for example, the proposition that it is unnecessary to control the quantity of depository liabilities in a competitive banking system.[1] Similarly, the theory's mode of analysis is unconventional; for example, its benchmark for examining the nature of banking services is a nonmonetary economy. It is precisely its unconventional analysis and startling conclusions, however, that make the legal restrictions theory both stimulating and worth further consideration.

In what follows, I first explicate the new view on banking and consider implications of that view for controlling economic fluctuations. I then present a critique and, finally, I suggest how some of the valuable insights of the legal restrictions theory might be integrated with important tenets of more traditional approaches to money and banking.[2]

The Legal Restrictions Theory of Money

The legal restrictions theory examines the seeming paradox that individuals simultaneously hold government currency and govern-

---

*Reprinted from *Cato Journal*, 6 (Fall 1986): 587–605.

The author is Senior Economist and Policy Advisor at the Federal Reserve Bank of Dallas. The views expressed in this paper are the author's and should not be construed as representing the official position of any part of the Federal Reserve System. The author wishes to thank Bennett McCallum, Neil Wallace, Dale Osborne, James E. Pearce, and Lawrence H. White for their helpful comments.

[1]This conclusion is, however, one that the legal restrictions theory shares with modern advocates of free banking. The reasoning of the two theories is quite different, however. For a cogent exposition of the free banking position, see White (1984a).

[2]Although I refer to the legal restrictions theory as the "new view," Cowen and Kroszner (1985) argue that it is anything but new. They contend that it has a long history, which begins in the 18th century. Although not entirely unrelated, the "new view" referred to herein is not Tobin's "new view" of the 1960s.

ment bonds. The currency is noninterest bearing, while government bonds bear interest. The paradoxical aspect of this behavior derives from the fact that both obligations are default-free liabilities of the same issuer. Assuming rational behavior by transactors, we would expect the interest-bearing securities to dominate currency. Accordingly, Neil Wallace (1983, p. 1) investigates the features of interest-bearing government securities "that prevent them from playing the same role in transactions as Federal Reserve notes. For if they could play that role, then it is hard to see why anyone would hold non-interest-bearing currency instead of the interest-bearing securities." The new view identifies legal restrictions as the source of the simultaneous demand for both currency and bonds and contrasts the current environment with an unregulated or laissez-faire system. Wallace (1983, p. 4) states the view forcefully and concisely:

> Laissez-faire means the absence of legal restrictions that tend, among other things, to enhance the demand for a government's currency. Thus, the imposition of laissez-faire would almost certainly reduce the demand for government currency. It could even reduce it to zero. A zero demand for a government's currency should be interpreted as the abandonment of one monetary unit in favor of another— for example, the abandonment of the dollar in favor of one ounce of gold. Thus, my prediction of the effects of imposing laissez-faire takes the form of an either/or statement: either nominal interest rates go to zero or existing government currency becomes worthless.

Wallace (1983, p. 1) identifies two conditions, the presence of one of which is *necessary* in order that government bonds not be substitutable for currency.[3] Either the bond must be nonnegotiable (as is true of U.S. savings bonds) or not issued in small denominations (as is true of Treasury bills). As Wallace (1983, pp. 2–3) further observes, neither of these two restrictions by themselves could prevent arbitrage by financial intermediaries. These intermediaries could purchase large denomination, negotiable bonds (that is, Treasury bills in multiples of $10,000) and issue bearer notes in small denominations. By matching maturities of these notes and those of the Treasury bills, the intermediary would be perfectly hedged. Since its assets are default-free by assumption, its bearer notes would also be default-free (fraud aside). Wallace thus identifies the crucial legal restriction that is *sufficient* for the coexistence of currency and bonds: government is a monopolistic provider of currency.

Absent legal restrictions, arbitrage would drive down the yield differential between bonds and currency to the costs of intermedi-

---

[3]A "bond" refers to a dated interest-bearing obligation, while "currency" refers to a noninterest-bearing note callable on demand.

ating between them. Wallace (1983, pp. 3–4) estimates that these might be less than 1 percent. If, as an approximation, one ignores the cost then either interest rates on bonds should be driven to zero or currency should disappear.

Another way of stating the conclusion is that money would not exist as a distinct financial asset. This restatement brings into sharper relief the clear connection between Wallace's statement of the legal restrictions theory and Fischer Black's (1970) analysis of how an unregulated financial system would operate.[4] Black assumes that depository institutions have complete freedom to create liabilities and to purchase financial assets as they see fit. Banks derive their income from the spread between their borrowing costs—chiefly interest on deposit liabilities—and their revenue, chiefly interest on loans. Black envisions that loans will take the form of negative bank balances, or, in other words, overdrafts on deposit accounts. Indeed, his description of the hypothetical system of positive and negative bank balances reads like a virtual foretelling of the modern cash management account at brokerage houses (Black 1970, pp. 10–11).

Black presents an evolutionary model of financial innovation, which begins with commodity money and ends in a moneyless world. Early in the evolutionary process real goods, as well as the commodity money, become priced in terms of an abstract unit of account. Black hypothesizes, however, that the means of payment will likely be a portfolio of common stocks. He thereby invokes an assumption that characterizes subsequent presentations of the new view: the separation of the means of payment and the unit of account.

Black (1970, p. 9) is also responsible for first articulating another characteristic proposition of the legal restrictions theory: in a deregulated financial environment, "it would not be possible to give any reasonable definition of the quantity of money. The payments mechanism in such a world would be very efficient, but money in the usual sense would not exist." In other words, having merged money and other financial assets, Black cannot readily quantify the former separately.

Wallace (1983, p. 4) takes a different tack and analyzes open-market purchases and sales of Treasury bills by a central bank in a laissez-faire regime. He assumes that there is a constant cost technology for producing currency, which is shared by private and government

---

[4]Wallace (1983, p.1, n.2) refers the reader to Fama (1980) and Hall (1982) "for other discussions of the legal restrictions theory." He also cites six other articles as applications of the theory, but does not refer to Black (Wallace 1983, p. 3). Black is clearly the intellectual predecessor, however, of Fama, Hall, and Wallace. The following discussion of Black's views draws from O'Driscoll (1985a, pp. 6–7).

intermediaries (a situation of "technological symmetry"). In other words, government and private notes are perfect substitutes produced under identical cost conditions. In Wallace's example there is a given private sector demand for currency. Thus, an expansion in the production of one type of currency results in the contraction of other types. An open market purchase of bills by the central banks constitutes just such a change. As the central bank increases its assets (Treasury bills), it will issue more liabilities (including currency). Since individuals now hold central bank currency, they will curtail their demand for commercial bank currency. In the process, resources are reallocated from private to public sector producers of currency. Wallace (1983, pp. 4–5) concludes that in a laissez-faire system there are no macroeconomic effects of banks issuing their own liabilities to purchase financial assets.[5] This conclusion, which holds for central banks and private issuers alike, is in startling contrast to conventional wisdom and constitutes the most important policy conclusion of the legal restrictions theory. That contention will be the focus of most of the rest of this article.

Economists have traditionally modeled banks as creators of money. Certain liabilities of private banks are added to those of central banks with the resulting magnitude constituting the money stock. The money-creation function is the benchmark for analyzing banks; of course, in creating money banks are also providing the payments services on which legal restriction theorists concentrate. In this view, however, banks as creators of a distinctive financial asset, money, are peculiar to a regime of legal restrictions. Consequently, conventional monetary theories are applicable only to a specific set of institutions. The legal restrictions theory lays claim to being a more general theory of financial intermediation. Moreover, by abstracting from banks' role as creators of money in a regulated system, legal restriction theorists feel that they better understand the nature of banking services. Or, as Eugene Fama (1980, p. 42) phrases it, "the banking system is best understood without the mischief introduced by the concept of money." Legal restriction theorists focus instead on the accounting and portfolio management services provided by banks.

It is now possible to restate the legal restrictions theory as a set of five interrelated propositions:[6]

---

[5]Wallace invokes the Modigliani-Miller theorem to justify the conclusion that central bank intermediation has no macroeconomic consequences. On this point, see also Fama (1980, pp. 45–47).

[6]Cowen and Kroszner (1985, pp. 2–4) adduce seven propositions characterizing the theory.

1. Money would not exist as a distinctive financial asset in the absence of legal restrictions;
2. The unit of account is separable from the means of payment;
3. Conventional monetary theories are applicable only to a specific set of financial institutions;
4. In a laissez-faire system, the provision of payment services by banks would have no special effects on prices or macroeconomic activity;
5. The provision of payment services—not the production of money—is the benchmark for analyzing banks.

The next section focuses on proposition four of the legal restrictions theory, namely, that a laissez-faire system would be insulated from economic fluctuations caused by monetary shocks.

Economic Fluctuations

Some writers have suggested that the problem of economic fluctuations would be attenuated if not eliminated in an unregulated banking system. Robert Greenfield and Leland Yeager (1983, p. 304) contend that such a system "offers much less scope than an ordinary monetary system for destructive monetary disequilibrium." They also suggest that runs on banks "would be less catastrophic under [this] system," essentially because banks would exchange liabilities under a floating rather than a fixed-rate domestic exchange system.

Fama (1980, p. 40) offers the most explicit underpinning for the position that economic fluctuations result from regulations compelling banks to play a special role "in the process by which a pure nominal commodity or unit of account is made to play the role of numeraire in a real world monetary system."[7] The core of Fama's argument is as follows. First, if there is competition, then there are actual or potential substitutes for the portfolios offered by any bank. Second, to attract depositors, banks must hold portfolios against which depositors are willing to hold claims. Third, competition insures that depositors are paid a return equaling that earned on the bank's portfolio less a management fee. Given that they are pure profit maximizers, the last assumption renders banks indifferent to the composition of their own portfolios. Instead, banks adjust their portfolios to the depositors' tastes and productive opportunities available (Fama 1980, pp. 45–46). In this sense, then, banks are passive agents, whose portfolios are determined by the nonfinancial sector.

[7]Yeager and Greenfield (1983) offer their own analysis of the problem, which I examine below.

If Fama's argument is correct, then banks are passive in another important sense: they exert no independent force on prices or real activity. The quantity and composition of their assets and liabilities are entirely demand determined. If one bank were autonomously to change its assets and liabilities, competition would insure offsetting changes by other banking firms. In the aggregate, banks would thus play no causal role in the determination of equilibrium price and quantity vectors. This conclusion is a neutrality finding writ large (Fama 1980, pp. 45–46).

In Fama's analysis, a real good functions as the *numéraire*. There is no price level as such to be determined, but only an equilibrium relative-price vector. What would be the question of price-level determination reduces to the issue of the stability of equilibrium in a barter, general equilibrium system (Fama 1980, p. 44). Consequently, macroeconomic phenomena constituted by or attendant upon price-level fluctuations are absent by assumption in the competitive banking environment postulated by Black, Fama, and Wallace.

In Fama (1980), the assumption of a nonmonetary economy is a modeling strategy to isolate the essential functions of a competitive bank. By contrast, Greenfield and Yeager (1983) view the abolition of money as an essential feature of a reform (one hesitates to say "monetary reform") that they propose. In the process, however, they appear to have confused an assumption with a substantive proof.

Greenfield and Yeager rely on the analysis of monetary disequilibrium presented in Yeager (1968). Money is unique in having no market of its own. Accordingly, an excess demand for money must be worked off in all other markets. Sticky prices result in quantity responses and pervasive real effects of the initial excess demand for money (cf. Greenfield and Yeager 1983, p. 309). In their analysis, Greenfield and Yeager (p. 310) identify the inelasticity of the supply of money as the necessary condition for macroeconomic disequilibrium to develop out of an excess demand for money (cf. Keynes 1964, pp. 234–36). The superiority of the proposed system, they assert, devolves around the demand determination of the means of payment.

Greenfield and Yeager seem to have confused themselves, if not their readers, with their argument about the demand determination of the means of payment. They point out that their "system would get rid of any distinct money existing in a definite quantity. . . . A wrong quantity of money could no longer cause problems because money would not exist" (p. 305). Simply put, there is no monetary disequilibrium in their system because there is no money (cf. Greenfield and Yeager, p. 303). The argument about the demand determination of the means of payment, which appears to be a substantive proof, really reduces to a crude approximation of the kind of stability analysis suggested by Fama. As will be seen, however, the Greenfield-Yeager system is still susceptible to economic disorders similar in effect to that of monetary disequilibrium.

At this point, we need to focus on a more basic question, namely: can market prices be determined in the Greenfield-Yeager system? This is the operative question because, as Greenfield and Yeager (p. 307) clearly state, they are proposing a barter system:

> With no money quantitatively existing, people make payments by transferring other property. To buy a bicycle priced at 100 value units or pay a debt of 100 units, one transfers property having that total value. Although the . . . system is barter in that sense, it is not *crude* barter. People need not haggle over the particular goods to be accepted in each transaction. The profit motive will surely lead competing private firms to offer convenient methods of payment.

First, it must be noted that there is no accepted sense in which the term "barter" is used other than to cover situations in which goods trade directly for goods.[8] Second, I know of no theory of "sophisticated" barter; Greenfield and Yeager do not present a theory of sophisticated barter but depend on the (nonexistent) theory of how such a world operates. One must conclude that they are talking of barter, pure and simple.

It might well be appropriate to reconsider the standard analysis of barter. Absent a new theory of barter, however, one must be pessimistic concerning the workableness of the Greenfield-Yeager system, which would appear to suffer from all the textbook problems of barter. Although Yeager and Greenfield (p. 303) really only assert the contrary, their claim is worth analyzing. They admit that the "system would indeed lack money as we know it," but they state that "it would not entail the textbook inconveniences of barter. The advantages of having a definite unit of account and convenient methods of payment would be retained and enhanced." The implicit argument is that it is capitalism's accounting system, not its payments system comprising a physical medium of exchange, which overcomes the calculational difficulties of barter.

A key element in the Greenfield-Yeager proposal is the government's defining a unit of value, which would then form a basis of a

---

[8]See Clower (1969, pp. 202–11). Clower (pp. 207–08) states the following as "the central theme of the theory of a money economy": "*Money buys goods and goods buy money; but goods do not buy goods.*" By contrast, in Greenfield and Yeager (1983), goods buy goods.

social accounting system.[9] Rather than choosing a single good (as in Fama's analysis) or securities (as in Black's model), Greenfield and Yeager (p. 305) suggest a composite bundle of commodities.[10]

> The prices of the individual commodities would not be fixed and would remain free to vary in relation to one another. Only the bundle as a whole would, by definition, have the fixed price of 1 unit. . . . The bundle would be composed of precisely gradable, competitively traded, and industrially important commodities, and in amounts corresponding to their relative importance. Many would be the materials used in the production of a wide range of goods so that the bundle as the value unit would come close to stabilizing the general level of prices expressed in that unit.

Greenfield and Yeager (pp. 303, 306) emphasize the differences between their proposal and those for a composite-commodity or commodity-reserve monetary system. No reserves of the composite bundle would be maintained by any agency or private entity. There is no convertibility but only a defined unit of value. The latter distinction is important to the authors as well as to the reader assessing their proposal.

There is a striking similarity between the logic of the trading process in the Greenfield-Yeager proposal and that in early Marxist schemes for allocating and distributing goods. It is instructive to draw the parallels, since doing so helps isolate a critical flaw in their proposal.

Marx's overriding economic goal was to replace capitalism's "anarchic" system of production with a system of conscious social control of the means of production (Lavoie 1985). Marx wanted to avoid any reliance on market prices in allocating resources and distributing goods. He suggested using labor time as a measure of the cost (value) of each commodity and actually exchanging goods according to their embodied labor time. Compare again Greenfield and Yeager (p. 307), who observe that "to buy a bicycle priced at 100 value units or pay a debt of 100 units, one transfers property having that total value."

Using labor time as a mechanism for allocating resources founders on the problem of labor's heterogeneity and nonuniformity. Marx

---

[9]Government plays an ironic role in many of the laissez-faire models of the payments mechanism. In Greenfield and Yeager (1983), government defines the unit of value. In Wallace (1983), government imposes laissez-faire. In Hall (1982a), government replaces the existing monetary standard by fiat and engages in interest-rate targeting. The use of "laissez-faire" in this class of models appears to be a neologism.

[10]Greenfield and Yeager (1983, p. 305) cite Hall's suggestion of a bundle of 50 kilograms of ammonium nitrate plus 40 kilograms of copper plus 35 kilograms of aluminum plus 80 square meters of plywood (of specified grade), but indicate a preference for an even more encompassing composite bundle.

tried to reduce heterogeneous, skilled labor to homogeneous, unskilled labor time. He did not, however, solve the valuation problem. A competitive market evaluates different types of labor but Marx wanted to eschew the use of anarchic market values. This left him with the analytically insoluble problem of evaluating heterogeneous labor without an evaluation mechanism (Lavoie 1985, pp. 67–74). Greenfield and Yeager face the even more complex problem of homogenizing the heterogeneous commodities of their composite *numéraire*. They (pp. 313–14) mention but do not solve the calculational problem:[11]

> Suppose that the . . . bundle were defined as 1 apple + 1 banana + 1 cherry. Prices are to be paid and debts settled in bundles-worths of convenient payment property. Now apples are struck by a fungus. What market forces arise to accomplish the appropriate changes in relative prices while still enforcing the unit's definition?

Greenfield and Yeager (pp. 313–14) are, as it were, hoisted on their own *pétard*. They themselves note that if a fungus attacks apples, the bundle becomes relatively scarcer; deflationary pressure is exerted on other commodities. But this is the very evil from which their nonmonetary exchange system was to deliver us. They note that bananas and cherries are among the commodities whose relative price will fall. The need for an adjustment of the prices of other commodities within the bundle adds to the adjustment problem rather than (partially) offsetting it. In general, there will be more not fewer price changes necessary because there are two additional composite goods whose prices have changed.

In taking account of the effects of the fungus attack, Greenfield and Yeager (p. 314) suggest widening the definition of the bundle. Indeed, they indicate that the wider the definition, the better the results. Consider, however, what would occur if the suggestion were carried to its logical extreme. Every trade would constitute an exchange against a representative bundle of all commodities. Using a conventional medium of exchange ("money," as we now know it) avoids having to calculate n-1 relative prices in making individual exchanges. The method of payment in the Greenfield-Yeager system would require just this exercise for each and every transaction. Their system would accordingly involve the calculational chaos of barter.

To give some historical-institutional relevance to the argument, the authors observe that changes in the relative scarcity of gold under

[11]Greenfield and Yeager (1983, p. 313) also invite misunderstanding by such phrases as "enforcing the unit's definition." They have assured us that the "unit of account does not require 'implementation' through convertibility of any familiar sort, anymore than does maintenance of the defined length of the meter" (p. 303). What, then, is to be enforced?

a gold standard produces familiar macroeconomic consequences. They suggest not a bimetallic but a trimetallic system as an improvement, ignoring the additional problems introduced by the possibility of relative price changes between goods in the composite bundle. I am not arguing, of course, that their system would be similar in all respects to a bimetallic or trimetallic system, but am only suggesting that it would involve the problems raised here.[12]

The analytical problem being discussed is inherent in any scheme to stabilize a price level or other constructed average price. The appeal of stabilizing a price level or subset of prices is that doing so will somehow minimize or diminish the number of relative price changes necessary in a market economy (cf. Friedman 1969, p. 106). To my knowledge no one has ever demonstrated this rigorously; Greenfield and Yeager certainly do not do so (cf. O'Driscoll 1986b). They in fact have done us the service of inadvertently showing why stabilizing a price or subset of prices would not necessarily diminish the costly market adjustments necessary in a monetary economy. Greenfield and Yeager have surely failed, however, to demonstrate their main practical point, that economic fluctuations would be eliminated in a nonmonetary system.

Whether economic fluctuations would occur in an economy with unregulated banks remains an open question. Resolution of the question would require both a fuller development of the legal restrictions theory and careful specification of the sources of cyclical disturbances. Models of the business cycle increasingly identify real factors as the cause of fluctuations. If these models are correct, then it is unclear what effect monetary deregulation would have on the timing, amplitude, or frequency of cyclical fluctuations.

Suppose, however, that economic fluctuations are caused only by monetary shocks. It would still be unclear whether we could be confident that an unrestricted banking system would eliminate these fluctuations. The uncertainty devolves on the issue of bank reserves and interbank deposits. The literature on the legal restrictions theory has little to say about settlement practices for banks (financial intermediaries) in a deregulated environment. Yet the issue is crucial, since two banks can only settle their liabilities by transferring a third asset, which is the liability of neither bank.[13] To facilitate settlement, banks may hold interbank deposits. More generally, however, banks

[12]Actually, as White pointed out to me, the Greenfield-Yeager proposal is more similar to Marshall's symmetalist proposal. See Marshall (1965, pp. 64–67).
[13]O'Driscoll (1985a, pp. 7–9) examines the issue in more detail; cf. Osborne (1985b, pp. 18–23).

will hold reserves of some asset acceptable to all as final settlement. Today, base money (deposits at Federal Reserve banks plus currency) constitutes the reserve asset. Even absent legal restrictions, there would be a finite demand for a reserve asset; again, the source of the demand would derive from the requirements of the interbank clearing process.[14]

Indeed, these considerations lead Dale Osborne (1985b) to conclude that banks would hold reserves even in a laissez-faire payments system. The optimal reserve ratio would be much closer to zero, however, than to one, which exposes the system to the periodic crises inherent in a fractional-reserve banking system. Osborne (1985b, pp. 22–23) concludes:

> It is hard to imagine that such a system could produce most of the uncertainties and absurdities that drive observers of our present system to despair. . . . But the speculations do not suggest that it would be free of monetary disturbances. The bankers of a free system would choose their reserve ratios as profit dictates. The optimal reserve ratio would be less than one. There would be furtive abundance, and it would vanish at the gusts of discredit that would blow among a free people as among others, even if less often.

Barren Money

In this section, I concentrate on the assumptions of the legal restrictions theory. John Bryant and Neil Wallace (1980, p. 1) provide the most explicit statement of the underlying assumptions:

1. Assets are valued only in terms of their payoff distributions.
2. Anticipated payoff distributions are the same as actual payoff distributions.
3. Under laissez-faire, no transaction costs inhibit the operation of markets and, in particular, the law of one price.

Taken together, these assumptions preclude any nonpecuniary yield from holding money.[15] Since currency yields no explicit return, there is no reason for rational economic agents to demand the asset. Any neoclassical economist worth his salt should be unsatisfied with this situation and quickly strive to identify the intervention generating this otherwise odd situation. In terms of their own assumptions, Bryant and Wallace have done a good job of modeling the problem,

[14] Recent historiography on the clearinghouse function in a free banking system includes Gorton (1985) and Timberlake (1984). White (1984a, pp. 1–22) presents a model of free banking in which banks demand reserves.

[15] Cf. White (1986, p. 5). The first assumption explicitly precludes a nonpecuniary yield on money. But the second and third assumptions separately exclude the possibility, since they eliminate the reason for money's yield.

but the assumptions underlying the legal restrictions theory should not go unchallenged.

The denial of a nonpecuniary yield to money is really another way of stating the old view that money is "barren." In an undeservedly neglected essay, W. H. Hutt (1956) surveyed the history of monetary economics and could find only one orthodox monetary theorist (Greidanus) who was not, to one degree or another, under the sway of the doctrine that money is barren. Though many economists have had all the elements of a correct theory—clearly perceiving that money provides conveniences, services, and cost savings—virtually all continued to assume explicitly that money's yield is, in Keynes's words, "*nil*" (Keynes 1936, p. 226).

The view that money yields no return is as old as Aristotle. It entered modern economics through the schoolmen, thence via John Locke and Adam Smith. Not surprisingly, Hutt traces the idea through the classical economists. What is surprising, however, are the illustrious neoclassical economists who have echoed the point down to the present. Whereas Locke said that "money is a barren thing" (Hutt 1956, p. 199), Böhm-Bawerk assured us that "money is by nature incapable of bearing fruit" (p. 203), and Wicksell described money as "sterile" (p. 204).

Perhaps the most puzzling of all is Keynes. His statement denying that money has a yield is the more remarkable, since it appears in the section of the *General Theory* in which he analyzes the liquidity premium on money. If we take him literally, then economic agents exhibit a preference for an asset with no yield.[16]

The confusion is even clearer in Marshall than in Keynes. Alfred Marshall (1965, pp. 38–39) explicitly recognized that some capital assets yield an implicit or nonpecuniary return but denied that money is one of these assets:

> Currency held in hand yields no income: therefore, everyone balances (more or less automatically and instinctively) the benefits, which he would get by enlarging his stock of currency in hand, against those which he would get by investing some of it either in a commodity—say a coat or piano—from which he would derive a direct benefit; or in some business plant or stock exchange security, which would yield him a money income.

[16]Keynes's point was precisely that money yields a nonpecuniary yield. That he felt compelled to say that money's yield is "*nil*" indicates, however, that the old view of barren money still held sway over him even as he was engaged in trying to overturn it. As Keynes said in the Preface to the *General Theory*, "the difficulty lies, not in the new ideas, but in escaping from the old ones, which, ramify, for those brought up as most of us have been, into every corner of our minds."

Likewise, Marshall (1965, p. 45) averred that holding resources in the form of noninterest-bearing money "locks up in a barren form resources that might yield an income of gratification if invested, say, in extra furniture; or a money income, if invested in extra machinery or cattle." So, in modern terms, Marshall recognized that assets can yield a money income, output that can be sold for money, an income in kind that may lead to a capital gain, or a nonpecuniary yield. Though money has benefits, Marshall felt constrained to repeat that money, nonetheless, has no yield of its own. Even when great minds like Marshall had all the elements of a theory of money as an asset with nonpecuniary yield, the dead hand of the past reached out and prevented them from forming the elements into a coherent whole.

Marshall was quite modern in noting that the yield on an asset can be either nonpecuniary or pecuniary. He simply denied that money has a yield of either kind. I submit that modern treatments of the demand for money make essentially the same mistake. The modern literature is quite clear in treating forgone interest as the cost of holding money, but is more ambiguous by far on the benefits derived from cash holdings. Following William Baumol, one tradition focuses on brokerage costs of moving in and out of interest-bearing assets. This explanation rings hollow as we return to a financial system with sophisticated financial instruments and cash management techniques. Following James Tobin, a second tradition focuses on liquidity preference as behavior toward risk. The latter approach perhaps adheres more closely to Keynes, but, in so doing, perpetuates his error on the yield from holding money.

Hutt contends that modern monetary theory incorporates an 18th-century view, which treats productivity in entirely physical terms: an asset is productive if it yields a return in kind, that is, if it bears fruit. If it yields no fruit, the asset is barren. Since money traditionally yielded no interest, 18th-century economists viewed it as barren. Modern capital theory has generally moved beyond that view by accepting that assets can yield an implicit return. This insight explains, for example, the holding of so-called idle land.[17]

When it comes to "idle balances," however, the 18th-century view holds sway. As suggested above, the neoclassical spirit is restive when confronted with a demand for an asset apparently having no yield. The restive spirit has yielded the legal restrictions theory. Indeed, so long as economists adhere to the 18th-century view on

---

[17]And it can serve to explain the holding of idle resources generally. For an insightful analysis along these lines, see Hutt (1939).

money, the legal restrictions theory may be the only consistent resolution of the conundrum.

Money yields a nonpecuniary return, just as does furniture, paintings, or wine collections. In deciding whether to hold more or less money, an individual compares, at the margin, the advantages of holding the money balances with the advantages of holding other assets. In doing this, the individual is comparing different expected yields; he is not comparing an asset yielding a return with one yielding no return. The latter would, indeed, be a paradoxical situation.

Once we accept that money yields a nonpecuniary return, the paradox identified by the legal restrictions theory is seen to be apparent rather than real. In other words, the paradox is resolved by denying the thesis. Along the way, we also manage to jettison a good deal of philosophical baggage that we can do well without.[18]

What I am identifying is a property of money that is the property neither of legal restrictions nor of historical accident, but which reflects a preference exhibited by individuals over time and in radically different trading environments. The peculiar property or characteristic is money's liquidity. J. R. Hicks (1974, pp. 38–39) has succinctly characterized the demand for liquidity as a desire for flexibility: "Liquidity is not a property of a single choice; it is a matter of a sequence of choices, a related sequence. It is concerned with the passage from the known to the unknown—with the knowledge that if we wait we can have more knowledge." In contrast, Hicks (1974, pp. 43–44) points out that "by holding the imperfectly liquid asset the holder has narrowed the trend of opportunities which may be open to him. . . . He has 'locked himself in.' " Hicks clearly links the demand for money (and other liquid assets) to uncertainty. In this sense, money can only be analyzed with a theory incorporating uncertainty.[19]

---

[18]One also avoids having to adopt the troublesome modeling strategy adopted in Bryant and Wallace (1980). Bryant and Wallace (1980, p. 6) defend the strategy by arguing that "the reader is not giving up much by entertaining [the three] postulates as a potential basis for a theory of financial systems. By not giving up much, we mean that existing alternative models of financial systems have taught us very little." I am inclined to agree that we would not be giving up much by jettisoning the macroeconomic models examined by Bryant and Wallace (1980, pp. 6–10). O'Driscoll (1985b) discusses the origins of the tradition presented here. Also, see O'Driscoll and Rizzo (1985, pp. 191–98).

[19]The latter point is scarcely original. If accepted, however, it precludes the strategy adopted by Bryant and Wallace (1980). O'Driscoll and Rizzo (1985) argue that uncertainty is the source of many economic processes and institutions, which can be analyzed only by incorporating uncertainty. Money is, in fact, one of the best examples of a market institution that would not exist in a world with perfect foresight and no trans-

Money is not merely highly liquid, but that asset which is perfectly liquid (see O'Driscoll 1985a, p. 11). It trades in every market and need never be sold at a discount.[20] Even highly liquid, nonmonetary assets are subject to the risk of price fluctuations. People are therefore willing to forgo substantial pecuniary returns in order to hold money balances yielding a nonpecuniary return. In highly regulated and substantially unregulated monetary systems alike, individuals have demanded absolutely liquid assets.

The previous analysis addresss the demand for liquidity. The legal restriction theorists may be interpreted as emphasizing a supply issue: why cannot intermediaries purchase interest-bearing assets and issue circulating notes ("currency") backed by these assets? It is certainly true that the willingness of people to forgo a pecuniary return does not imply that they need to do so. As Bryant and Wallace (1980, p. 11) insist, we must investigate the "transaction technology" in a modern economy. Bryant and Wallace (1980, pp. 14–15) and Wallace (1983, p. 3) estimate the costs of intermediating by observing the spread between the rates of return earned and paid by mutual funds. Wallace (1983, pp. 3–4) asserts that "there is no reason to expect that the cost of intermediating securities like Treasury bills into bearer notes would be much different from the cost of operating these intermediaries."

Observation suggests, however, that there is good reason to suppose a great deal of difference between the costs of supplying low-turnover deposits (money market mutual fund shares) and high-turnover currency. White (1986) examines the transaction cost structure and concludes that the intermediation costs for currency are of an entirely different order of magnitude than for deposits. He offers three types of evidence: historical evidence on currency issues in the Scottish free banking system; evidence about current practice with respect to traveler's checks; and a "back-of-the-envelope" calculation.

With respect to the first type of evidence, White (1986, p. 3) observes that "the legal restrictions theory provides us with a clear and falsifiable prediction: non-interest-yielding currency should not coexist with positive-interest-yielding securities in the absence of legal restrictions against the sort of intermediation that could produce

---

action costs. At this level of generality, Bryant and Wallace (1980) had their chief result as soon as they wrote down their assumptions. The analysis of liquidity draws on O'Driscoll (1985a, p. 11).

[20]This characterization takes not names but properties seriously (see Bryant and Wallace 1980, pp. 8–9). Choosing the empirical counterpart of the theoretical construct is not an easy task, as Osborne (1984 and 1985a) demonstrates.

interest-yielding bearer bonds backed by those same securities." In the free banking era (before 1844) Scottish banks had complete freedom to pay interest on bank notes and the banking environment was competitive. Yet noninterest-bearing currency flourished, falsifying the prediction of the legal restrictions theory.

Second, White (1986, pp. 4–5) notes the nonpayment of interest on traveler's checks today. Moreover, it would surely be computationally easier to pay interest on traveler's checks than on currency. Like deposits and unlike currency, traveler's checks are returned to their issuer after once being spent. There appear to be no restrictions on paying interest on traveler's checks.

White's third piece of evidence is perhaps the most interesting. He adduces arguments why interest-bearing currency would inherently be more costly to transact with than noninterest-bearing currency. He then makes a reasonable calculation of the costs of collecting the interest accrued on a note and concludes that it would be prohibitive (White 1986, pp. 6–10).

In substance, White's analysis parallels that offered in Fama (1983) on the question of interest-bearing currency. White's historical presentation and institutional analysis are more developed and specific than Fama's. Nonetheless, White's reasoning clearly supports the major conclusion reached in Fama (1983, p. 14): "Indeed, what is striking about currency history is that it seems impossible to find instances of a currency that survives as a generally accepted medium of exchange which is not denominated in fixed quantities of a unit of account and does not trade at face value."

Both theoretical arguments and observational evidence suggest that there was never a paradox to explain. It is certainly true that the existing financial system is replete with regulations. Some of these regulations would even serve to restrain an issuer from circulating interest-bearing currency if he wanted to do so. The evidence indicates, however, that the restraints are irrelevant. Interest-bearing currency would not plausibly evolve with reasonable assumptions made about costs and benefits. It has not existed when banks were free to issue it; it will probably not exist when banks are free to issue it again in the future.

Conclusion

White's analysis addressed the supply-side or cost considerations adduced by Bryant and Wallace. At least for argument's sake, the analysis accepts the plausibility of an interest-yielding currency. At minimum, however, the interest earned on money must always be *less* than that earned on nonmoney assets. For if money were to yield both a nonpecuniary return of liquidity services and an explicit market rate of interest, the return on holding money would be supranormal. Osborne (1984 and 1985a) argued that base money alone corresponds to the money of economic theory. It would be plausible to suppose then that currency would be the most liquid transactions money. Its lack of an explicit yield scarcely seems troublesome in that light.

One can, of course, deny, as Bryant and Wallace (1980) did, that there is a distinctive asset called money. In their case, the denial really is an implication of a methodological argument about the form that economic reasoning ought to take. It clearly is beyond the scope of this article to deal directly with that debate (but see O'Driscoll and Rizzo 1985). It would be unfortunate, however, if the debate over banking deregulation became entangled in a modern *methodenstreit*. More concretely, commitment to (or against) banking deregulation does not presume commitment to the equilibrium theorizing advocated by the legal restriction theorists. Indeed, historically, unregulated banking has borne little resemblance to the hypothetical "laissez-faire" systems postulated in various models derived from the legal restrictions theory. In that sense, the theory is a detour in the debate over banking deregulation.

From a different perspective, however, the legal restrictions theory has done a great service by challenging economists to rethink their commitment to monetary regulation. Wallace (1983, p. 6) correctly identifies that, on conventional grounds, the one remaining justification for legal restrictions on money is revenue collection. If economists pursue the suggestion of modeling legal restrictions on money as a species of *fiscal* policy, then the legal restriction theorists will have made a lasting contribution.

References

Black, Fischer. "Banking and Interest Rates in a World Without Money." *Journal of Bank Research* 1 (Autumn 1970): 9–20.

Bryant, John, and Wallace, Neil. "The Inefficiency of Interest-Bearing National Debt." *Journal of Political Economy* 87 (April 1979): 365–81.

Bryant, John, and Wallace, Neil. "A Suggestion for Further Simplifying the Theory of Money." Minneapolis, 1980. Photocopy.

Clower, Robert W., ed. *Monetary Theory: Selected Readings*. Baltimore: Penguin, 1969.

Cowen, Tyler, and Kroszner, Randall. "The Development of the 'New Monetary Economics.'" Cambridge, Mass., 1985. Photocopy.

Fama, Eugene. "Banking in the Theory of Finance."*Journal of Monetary Economics* 6 (January 1980): 39–57.

Fama, Eugene. "Financial Intermediation and Price Level Control." *Journal of Monetary Economics* 12 (1983): 7–28.

Friedman, Milton. *The Optimum Quantity of Money*. Chicago: Aldine, 1969.

Gorton, Gary. "Clearinghouses and the Origin of Central Banking in the United States." *Journal of Economic History* 45 (June 1985): 277–83.

Greenfield, Robert L., and Yeager, Leland B. "A Laissez-Faire Approach to Monetary Stability." *Journal of Money, Credit and Banking* 15 (August 1983): 302–15.

Hall, Robert E. "Explorations in the Gold Standard and Related Policies for Stabilizing the Dollar." In *Inflation: Causes and Effects*, pp. 111–22. Edited by R. E. Hall. Chicago: University of Chicago Press, 1982a.

Hall, Robert E. "Monetary Trends in the United States and the United Kingdom: A Review from the Perspective of New Developments in Monetary Economics." *Journal of Economic Literature* 20 (December 1982b): 1552–56.

Hicks, J. R. *The Crisis in Keynesian Economics*. New York: Basic Books, 1974.

Hutt, W. H. *The Theory of Idle Resources*. London: Jonathan Cape, 1939.

Hutt, W. H. "The Yield from Money Held." In *On Freedom and Free Enterprise: Essays in Honor of Ludwig von Mises*, pp. 196–223. Edited by Mary Sennholz. Princeton: D. Van Nostrand, 1956.

Keynes, John Maynard. 1936. *The General Theory of Employment, Interest, and Money*. New York: Harcourt, Brace & World, Harbinger Books, 1964.

Klein, Benjamin. "The Competitive Supply of Money." *Journal of Money, Credit, and Banking* 6 (November 1974): 423–53.

Lavoie, Don. *Rivalry and Central Planning. The Socialist Calculation Debate Reconsidered*. Cambridge: Cambridge University Press, 1985.

Marshall, Alfred. 1923. *Money, Credit and Commerce*. New York: Augustus M. Kelley, 1965.

O'Driscoll, Jr., Gerald P. "A Free-Market Money: Comment on Yeager." *Cato Journal* 3 (Spring 1983): 327–33.

O'Driscoll, Jr., Gerald P. "Money in a Deregulated Financial System." Federal Reserve Bank of Dallas *Economic Review* (May 1985a): 1–12.

O'Driscoll, Jr., Gerald P. "Money: Menger's Evolutionary Theory." Federal Reserve Bank of Dallas Research Paper No. 8508 (1985b); forthcoming, *History of Political Economy* (1986a).

O'Driscoll, Jr., Gerald P. "Deregulation and Monetary Reform." Federal Reserve Bank of Dallas *Economic Review* (July 1986b).

O'Driscoll, Jr., Gerald P., and Rizzo, Mario J. *The Economics of Time and Ignorance*. Oxford and New York: Basil Blackwell, 1985.

Osborne, Dale K. "Ten Approaches to the Definition of Money." Federal Reserve Bank of Dallas *Economic Review* (March 1984): 1–23.

Osborne, Dale K. "What Is Money Today?" Federal Reserve Bank of Dallas *Economic Review* (January 1985a): 1–15.

Osborne, Dale K. "On the Theory of Laissez-Faire Payments Systems." Dallas, 1985b. Photocopy.

Sargent, Thomas J., and Wallace, Neil. "The Real-bills Doctrine versus the Quantity Theory: A Reconsideration." *Journal of Political Economy* 90 (December 1982): 1212–36.

Timberlake, Jr., Richard H. "The Central Banking Role of Clearinghouse Associations." *Journal of Money, Credit and Banking* 16 (February 1984): 1–15.

Wallace, Neil. "A Legal Restrictions Theory of the Demand for 'Money' and the Role of Monetary Policy." Federal Reserve Bank of Minneapolis *Quarterly Review* (Winter 1983): 1–7.

White, Lawrence H. *Free Banking in Britain: Theory, Experience, and Debate, 1800–1845.* Cambridge: Cambridge University Press, 1984a.

White, Lawrence H. "Competitive Payments Systems and the Unit of Account." *American Economic Review* 74 (September 1984b): 699–712.

White, Lawrence H. "Accounting for Non-interest-bearing Currency: A Critique of the 'Legal Restrictions' Theory of Money." New York, 1986. Photocopy.

Wood, John H., and Wood, Norma L. *Financial Markets.* New York: Harcourt Brace Jovanovich, 1985.

Yeager, Leland B. "Essential Properties of the Medium of Exchange." *Kyklos* 21 (1968): 45–69.

16

COMPETITIVE MONEY,
INSIDE AND OUT*
Lawrence H. White

The aim of this essay, unlike so many works on monetary policy, is not to argue that the government monetary authorities ought to behave in a proper manner rather than the improper manner they have so often behaved in. Instead, it argues that the public ought not be forcibly subject to the vagaries of government monetary control. The way in which Federal Reserve officials choose to act is by no means a matter of indifference. It is, on the contrary, a matter of grave concern for anyone concerned about the values of his assets and the health of the economy. Monetary policy matters very much. But precisely because the public is so vulnerable to the errors of monetary policy, it is vital that some means of real protection be available. Attempts to elicit better behavior from the Fed do not go far enough in the way of vindicating the public's interest. Members of a free society should not have to suffer government control over their money at all.

The most fundamental question of monetary policy is whether government has any legitimate role to play in producing, or regulating the private production of, monetary assets. The question is especially crucial for those who, in the tradition of classical or real liberalism, are wary of the encroachment of coercive state power in areas competently handled by voluntary market interaction. As Milton Friedman has put it, "one question that a liberal must answer is whether monetary and banking arrangements cannot be left to the market, subject only to the general rules applying to all other economic activity."[1] Enthusiasm for monetary policy x or monetary policy y presupposes the belief that government involvement is better than free markets in money and banking. Yet the reasoning behind

*Reprinted from *Cato Journal* 3 (Spring 1983): 281–99, with revisions.

The author is Assistant Professor of Economics at New York University.

[1]Milton Friedman, *A Program for Monetary Stability* (New York: Fordham University Press, 1960), p. 4. While characterizing himself as "by no means convinced that the answer is indubitably in the negative," Friedman answers in the negative.

this belief has been little explained by monetary policy enthusiasts, too few of whom have been troubled by the question.

Deregulation of Inside Money

Note the conjunctive phrase used by Friedman, "monetary and banking arrangements." There are two types of money used in our economy, as in other advanced monetary economies the world has known. They are (1) basic cash, in the United States today produced only by the Treasury (coins) and the Federal Reserve System (dollar bills), and (2) bank liabilities such as deposits transferable by check, usually privately produced, whose value derives from their being redeemable for basic cash. The distinction between these two types of money is usefully expressed by calling them "outside" money and "inside" money respectively. The question of market or government provision of money therefore resolves into two sub-questions, each dealing with one of the two types of money. It is possible to support deregulation of inside money without necessarily questioning the government position as sole producer of outside money. It is also possible to favor a system of privately produced outside money, for example, a specie standard, without questioning bank regulation.

Deregulation of banking is properly a microeconomic issue, not an issue of monetary policy. The economic argument for abolishing any of the numerous ill-considered restrictions on banking is that free and open competition would better serve consumer wants. Full deregulation would eliminate the obvious waste created by erecting barriers around which competitors must maneuver. Numerous examples come to mind. Elimination of the interest ceiling on all deposits—now underway—will clearly benefit depositors. Clearing away the entry barriers that prevent non-bank financial firms and even non-financial firms from engaging in "banking" practices would widen the array of financial services and suppliers available to individuals and businesses. Legalization of interstate branch banking would permit the convenience of getting cash or paying by check away from home. The agenda for decontrol is a long one even after interest ceilings are lifted.

To summarize it briefly, the agenda for banking deregulation includes as its major items (1) repeal of lingering restrictions on loan and deposit interest rates and other pricing variables such as minimum balances, (2) elimination of restrictions on the asset portfolios of banks and especially thrift institutions (the difference between banks and thrifts in this regard is entirely artificial and should be eliminated by freeing the asset-holding choices of both), (3) lifting of archaic geographic restrictions, (4) removal of regulatory barriers to entry into all aspects of the banking and financial industries, (5) an end to the peculiar taxes on deposits known as "reserve requirements," (6) privatization of deposit insurance, and (7) phasing out of the Federal Reserve System's roles as holder of bank reserves, including a closing of the discount window at which the Fed loans reserves to commerical banks and privatization of check-clearing services.[2]

One would expect some resistance to decontrol of banking to come from bankers themselves. Like the members of any industry, they enjoy restrictions that dampen the need to compete. Given the instability of private cartels, regulatory controls combined with closed entry are the only way to secure extra-competitive profits. And, in fact, there has been some pressure from banking industry groups to moderate the extent and slow the pace of deregulation.

Resistance to decontrol has also arisen, however, from a more ominous source—the Federal Reserve System—on the grounds that deregulation of inside money poses a threat to the effectiveness of monetary policy. In November 1982, for example, the Deregulation Committee issued regulations governing the "money market" deposit accounts that banks and savings institutions began offering in December. The Committee laudably introduced no reserve requirements. Rather than leave free the minimum balance for an account and the number of transfers per month that may be made from an account, however, the Committee arbitrarily imposed a minimum balance of $2500 and a maximum of six transfers per month to third parties, only three of them by check. Press reports noted that Paul Volcker, Chairman of the Federal Reserve, had favored the transfer limitation and had argued for an even higher minimum balance of $5000, the highest Congress would allow. Volcker's argument: Greater freedom from restrictions would allow the accounts to become more attractive to consumers than ordinary savings and checking accounts. This, he believed, would render more difficult the Fed's policy of controlling statistical measures of the money supply.[3]

Thus we see illiberal and inefficient regulations on banking activity defended as a means toward accomplishing the goal of targeted

[2]Compare Catherine England, "The Case for Banking Deregulation," Heritage Foundation *Backgrounder*, March 26, 1982, p. 2, which mentions only the first three items. Privatization of deposit insurance in advocated by Catherine England and John Palffy, "Replacing the FDIC: Private Insurance for Bank Deposits," Heritage Foundation *Backgrounder*, December 2, 1982.

[3]*New York Times*, November 16, 1982, p. D14; *Wall Street Journal*, November 16, 1982. p. 2.

monetary growth. This is sadly ironic. The monetarist program of targeting monetary aggregates has long been advocated by Friedman not as an end in itself, but as "the only feasible device currently available for converting monetary policy into a pillar of a free society rather than a threat to its foundations."[4] If it is true that targeting broader monetary aggregates such as M1 and M2 requires restrictions on the freedom of banks and financial institutions to serve consumers efficiently, the game is not worth the candle, given the stated values of the game's best-known advocate. It would be more consistent for a free-market monetarist to favor targeting of the stock of government currency liabilities alone. I specify the stock of currency held by banks and the public rather than the aggregate presently called the monetary base (the sum of currency plus bank reserves held as currency-redeemable deposits at the Fed) only because full deregulation of inside money would fully privatize check-clearing and the holding of reserves.

Friedman, in fact, long ago acknowledged that "merit" exists in the proposal, which he attributed to Gary Becker, "to keep currency issue as a government monopoly, but to permit 'free' deposit banking, without any requirement about reserves, or supervision over assets or liabilities, and with a strict *caveat emptor* policy."[5] And today he goes beyond merely acknowledging its merit. In his most recent writings on monetary policy, he suggests replacing the Federal Reserve System either with a fixed money supply growth rule *or* a freezing of the stock of currency with no regulatory restrictions on private bank deposit creation. The latter, he now affirms, represents "the best real cure" for the instability of the current monetary regime.[6] Why then have Friedman (in the past), other free-market monetarists, and *a fortiori* other monetary economists yet been reluctant to endorse free deposit banking? What are the arguments, explicit or implicit, against free competition in the production of inside money?

---

[4]Milton Friedman, "Should There Be an Independent Monetary Authority?" in *In Search of a Monetary Constitution*, ed. Leland B. Yeager (Cambridge, Mass.: Harvard University Press, 1962), p. 243. An identical statement appears in Friedman, *Capitalism and Freedom* (Chicago: University of Chicago Press, 1962), p. 55.

[5]Friedman, *A Program for Monetary Stability*, p. 108 n. 10. Though Friedman gave no citation, Becker's proposal is expounded in Gary S. Becker, "A Proposal for Free Banking," unpublished manuscript (1957).

[6]Milton Friedman, "Monetary Policy for the 1980s," in *To Promote Prosperity*, ed. John H. Moore (Stanford, Calif.: Hoover Institution Press, 1984). The latter option has also been suggested by R. H. Timberlake, Jr., "Monetization Practices and the Political Structure of the Federal Reserve System," Cato Institute *Policy Analysis*, August 12, 1981, pp. 10–12.

In large part the skepticism or hostility of even free-market-oriented economists toward free markets in banking appears to be the result of their accepting at face value the myths that prevail with regard to the historical record of unregulated banking in the last century. The following earlier statement by Friedman is perhaps representative of a widely shared reading of history:

> The very performance of its central function requires money to be generally acceptable and to pass from hand to hand. As a result, individuals may be led to enter into contracts with persons [i.e., to accept the notes of bankers] far removed in space and acquaintance, and a long period may elapse between the issue of a promise and the demand for its fulfillment. In fraud as in other activities, opportunities for profit are not likely to go unexploited. A fiduciary currency ostensibly convertible into the monetary commodity is therefore likely to be overissued from time to time and convertibility is likely to become impossible. Historically, this is what happened under so-called "free banking" in the United States and under similar circumstances in other countries.[7]

In fact, according to the recent work of the economic historians who have seriously investigated the question, losses to noteholders under most state "free banking" systems in the United States were a much more minor problem than once supposed. The evidence "presents a serious challenge to the prevailing view that free banking led to financial chaos."[8] Nor did other nations' free banking systems show an inherent tendency toward over-issue.

The convertibility problems that did exist in a few states were not due to some inherent instability in unregulated banking. On the contrary, those problems may be traced to the state regulations that framed the systems. While the so-called free banking systems did provide for entry into banking without the need to obtain a special charter from the legislature, their leading feature was the require-

[7]Friedman, *A Program for Monetary Stability*, p. 6. I hope it is clear that I have no special animus against Friedman. Quite the contrary: I have singled out his statements for criticism only because our values are similar and, to his credit, his chains of reasoning on this topic are particularly clear and explicit. I also make these criticisms in *Free Banking in Britain: Theory, Experience, and Debate, 1800–1845* (New York: Cambridge University Press, 1984), chap. 5, with special emphasis on the evidence from free banking experience in Scotland. Friedman recently, in an article coauthored with Anna J. Schwartz, has explicitly reconsidered his earlier position on the rationale for government involvement in the monetary and banking system: Milton Friedman and Anna J. Schwartz, "Has Government Any Role in Money?," *Journal of Monetary Economics* 17 (January 1986): 37–62.

[8]Arthur J. Rolnick and Warren E. Weber, "The Free Banking Era: New Evidence on Laissez-Faire Banking," Federal Reserve Bank of Minneapolis Research Department Staff Report 80, May 1982. See also Hugh Rockoff, "The Free Banking Era: A Reexamination," *Journal of Money, Credit and Banking* 6 (May 1974): 141–67.

ment that issuers deposit approved bonds with state officials as collateral against their notes. Because this requirement forced banks to devote a major share of their assets to state bonds, the banks were failure-prone during periods of declining state bond prices. This was the principal source of their notoriously frequent inability to redeem their notes at par.[9] Unregulated banks would naturally diversify their asset portfolios. In addition, perhaps because the banks provided a market for state debt, state legislatures sometimes intervened by passing suspension acts to block the enforcement of redemption obligations against over-extended banks. This encouraged overissue by reducing the legal penalty for it. There also remained in place restrictions against inter-regional branch banking, a development that would have promoted stability and the wide circulation of trustworthy notes. For these reasons "free banking" as applied to these systems is a misnomer; "compulsory bond collateral systems" would be more accurate.

For evidence on the stability or instability of a virtually unregulated banking system it is instructive to turn to Scotland, which had a genuinely free and remarkably stable banking system for more than a century prior to amalgamation with the English system in 1844.[10] There, due to vigorous competition among widely branched banks, the notes of bankers "far removed in space and acquaintance" could not gain currency. A very short period elapsed between the issue of any note and its return to the issuer for fulfillment of its promise to pay. Competition had led all issuers to accept one another's notes at par and to join in a single note-exchange (clearinghouse) system. Notes issued by Bank A in a loan would, after being spent by the borrower, soon come into the possession of individuals who deposited them with Banks B through Z; these banks would return the notes to Bank A through the note-exchange system and demand redemption of them. No individual bank could over-issue without rapidly being disciplined by adverse clearing balances. The case of the Ayr Bank, discussed at length by Adam Smith,[11] bears witness to the efficacy of the note-exchange mechanism.

[9]Arthur J. Rolnick and Warren E. Weber, "Free Banking, Wildcat Banking, and Shinplasters," Federal Reserve Bank of Minneapolis *Quarterly Review* 6 (Fall 1982): 10–19.

[10]See Lawrence H. White, *Free Banking in Britain*, chap. 2; Rondo Cameron, *Banking in the Early States of Industrialization* (New York: Oxford University Press, 1967), chap. 3; S. G. Checkland, *Scottish Banking: A History, 1695–1973* (Glasgow: Collins, 1975).

[11]Adam Smith, *An Inquiry into the Nature and Causes of the Wealth of Nations*, ed. R. H. Campbell, A. S. Skinner, and W. B. Todd (Indianapolis: Liberty Classics, 1981), pp. 313–17.

In the United States the situation of distant bankers overissuing notes with poor homing power, suggested by the quote from Friedman, was experienced in a few states. These issuers were the "wildcat" banks, so called because the bank offices were supposedly located out in the untamed forests among the wildcats. It is clear that today's advanced communications networks eliminate a necessary condition for wildcat banking.[12] Even in the last century, however, wildcat banking was by no means inevitable. It did not occur in Scotland. It was made possible in the United States only by the reluctance of state governments to prosecute fraud where it did occur. It was abetted by the prohibition of interstate branch banking. Bank notes could find their way beyond the areas where they could be redeemed only because redemption areas were circumscribed. Bank notes traded at a discount in cities outside the area of redeemability. Individuals were willing to bear the loss in value from carrying notes from the area of redeemability, where the notes traded at par, to an outside city, where the notes traded at a discount, only because the superior alternative—a bank note redeemable in both locations and therefore valued at par in both locations—was ruled out by the ban on interstate banking.

The pyramiding of reserves, which has been thought to make banking inherently unstable and in particular to have produced the panics of late 19th-century America, was the product of the artificial unit banking system.[13] That a large group of banks came to trust their reserves to a single bank or to a smaller group of banks was, as it was in England, the result of artificially excluding banks from regional and national financial centers. In Scotland each bank held its own reserves; there was no pyramiding. (Scottish banks did have correspondent arrangements with London banks, which may have allowed them to economize somewhat on primary reserves, but this was due to their legal exclusion from opening their own London offices.) No less an authority than Walter Bagehot pointed out that each bank holding its own reserves was the natural system that would emerge in the absence of intervention. Bagehot was unequivocal in saying that one central bank holding reserves for the entire system was a poor idea. It had grown up in England as the perverse consequence of unwise banking legislation.[14]

---

[12]As Friedman, in *A Program for Monetary Stability*, p. 108 n. 10, recognized.

[13]See Vera C. Smith, *The Rationale of Central Banking* (London: P. S. King & Son, 1936), pp. 138–40.

[14]Walter Bagehot, *Lombard Street* (London: Henry S. King & Co., 1873), pp. 66–69, 100.

If the objections to full deregulation of inside money creation are largely based on a misreading of history, as I believe they are, the case in favor of it based on its enhancement of liberty and efficiency is a strong one. There seems to me no inherent reason why monetarists, gold standard advocates, and denationalization of money advocates cannot all join in supporting deregulation of banking.

For monetarists, as already indicated, this would mean shifting to a monetary rule based on the growth of the monetary base or stock of currency rather than a broader monetary aggregate.[15] If some monetarists in the past have favored targeting a broader aggregate, it is because historically they have found its measured velocity to have been slightly more stable than the velocity of the monetary base. In an era of major innovations in the payments system and the variety of near-money instruments—the past few years have already seen two redefinitions of the broader aggregates—the monetary base is a safer bet.

Gold standard advocates should also find deregulation of inside money congenial with their free-market outlook. Some have, it is true, defended 100 percent reserve requirements on banknotes and demand deposits on the grounds that fractional reserve banking is somehow inherently fraudulent.[16] But it is difficult to see why fraud is inherent in the issue of—as opposed to the failure to redeem— ready claims to gold against which less than a 100 percent reserve is held at any moment, provided that the claimholders not be misled about the arrangement. If it is inherently fraudulent for a bank, is it also inherently fraudulent for an insurance company to issue more claims than it could redeem were all to come due at a single moment? It seems more just to say that a claimholder suffers an actionable breach of contract only when the claim issuer actually fails to honor the claim, not when the issuer's ability to honor all its claims (in the event of their arriving simultaneously and unexpectedly) falls below 100 percent. It is at least not clear why such a non-bailment contract between bank and customer is inadmissible. The legal prohibition of fractional-reserve banking would mean an abridgement of freedom of contract and a blockage of opportunities for mutually beneficial exchange. Under a gold coin standard with deregulation of inside

---

[15]Eugene Fama, "Fiduciary Currency and Commodity Standards," unpublished manuscript (January 1982), has adopted this position.

[16]Murray N. Rothbard, "The Case for a 100 Per Cent Gold Dollar," in *In Search of a Monetary Constitution*, ed. Leland B. Yeager (Cambridge: Harvard University Press, 1962), pp. 113–20. Rothbard argues that a demand deposit should be treated in law as a warehouse receipt or bailment. But why should the law prohibit contracts that by mutual agreement do not treat demand deposits as bailments?

money, those individuals who insist on 100 percent bank liquidity could have their wants satisfied by 100 percent reserve institutions. Individuals who prefer the higher interest that a fractional-reserve bank can pay (because it holds some interest-earning assets) would likewise be free to hold contractual claims to gold issued by those institutions. Historical experience with free banking in Scotland indicates that fractional-reserve banks under conditions of free contract can operate with sufficient security to outcompete 100 percent reserve banks totally, though this fact of course does not answer the normative jurisprudential question of whether such freedom of contract should be allowed.

Denationalization of Outside Money

Even more fundamental—and hence more controversial—than deregulation of inside money is the question of denationalization of outside money. We are indebted to F. A. Hayek for raising this question to prominence by publication of his booklet *Denationalization of Money* in 1976, with a second edition in 1978.[17] The advocate of competitive market provision of ouside money is somewhat at a disadvantage in stating his case. In contrast with the advocate of a specific government monetary policy, he cannot with certainty spell out in exhaustive detail the institutional change his program would bring. That is because an essential part of free-market provision is the freedom of institutions to develop and adapt themselves to consumer wants in unforeseeable ways. Market competition is a discovery procedure, as Hayek has remarked.[18] Its results are different than anyone could predict or deliberately bring about, and therein lies its virtue: Its unpredictability is owing to its aptitude for discovering that goods and ways of providing goods not previously known, or at least not previously known to be profitable, are in fact profitable. This is as true of competition in the provision of outside money as in the provision of any good. Only through the competitive process can we discover what sorts of outside money, and what ways of supplying it, are best suited to consumer preferences.

Any scenario of a future free-market monetary system, then, should be considered conjectural in its details. The suppositions the sce-

---

[17]F. A. Hayek, *Denationalisation of Money*, 2d ed. (London: Institute of Economic Affairs, 1978). For an able survey of the literature on this topic see Pamela J. Brown, "Constitution or Competition? Alternate Views on Monetary Reform," *Literature of Liberty* 5 (Autumn 1982): 7–52.

[18]F. A. Hayek, "Competition as a Discovery Procedure," in *New Studies in Philosophy, Politics, Economics and the History of Ideas* (Chicago: University of Chicago Press, 1978), pp. 179–90.

narist makes concerning the dominant forms of outside money are necessarily no more than suppositions, whose purpose is simply to illustrate the idea of privately produced money. (Some forms of outside money are more plausible than others, of course.) This is worth keeping in mind because the advocacy of monetary freedom should not be identified with the advocacy of particular forms of money. There is a danger, for example, that Hayek's conjectures concerning the sort of outside money that might come to dominate under open competition (namely, privately issued inconvertible currencies whose purchasing powers are kept stable in terms of market baskets of wholesale commodities by means of quantity control) will give his work an air of what we may call social-science fiction. Hayek's attempt to forecast "the future unit of value" can only be regarded as an entrepreneurial speculation, not as a prediction derivable from economic theory.[19]

Such speculation should not be allowed to distract attention from Hayek's most valuable message:

> [T]here is no reason whatever why people should not be free to make contracts, including ordinary purchases and sales, in any kind of money they choose, or why they should be obliged to sell against any particular kind of money. There could be no more effective check against the abuse of money by government than if people were free to refuse any money they distrusted and to prefer money in which they had confidence.[20]

Economists have recently explored the properties of three systems under which government would not produce outside money. (1) Hayek and Benjamin Klein have conceived of a multiplicity of privately produced non-commodity outside monies.[21] (2) Fischer Black, Eugene F. Fama, Robert L. Greenfield, and Leland B. Yeager have conceived of a payments system, based on checkable mutual funds, that is devoid of outside money.[22] (3) Elsewhere I have discussed a

---

[19]See F. A. Hayek, "The Future Unit of Value," in *Currency Competition and Monetary Union*, ed. Pascal Salin (The Hague: Martinus Nijhoff, 1984), chap. 1.

[20]F. A. Hayek, "Choice in Currency: A Way to Stop Inflation," in *New Studies*, p. 225. In this essay, written earlier than *Denationalisation of Money*, Hayek was willing (p. 227) to entertain the possibility that gold would prove the most popular currency.

[21]Benjamin Klein, "The Competitive Supply of Money," *Journal of Money, Credit and Banking* 6 (November 1974): 423–53.

[22]Fischer Black, "Banking and Interest Rates in a World Without Money: The Effects of Uncontrolled Banking," *Journal of Bank Research* (Autumn 1970): 9–20; Eugene F. Fama, "Banking in a Theory of Finance," *Journal of Monetary Economics* 6 (January 1980): 39–67; Robert L. Greenfield and Leland B. Yeager, "A Laissez-Faire Approach to Monetary Stability," *Journal of Money, Credit and Banking* 15 (August 1983): 302–15. For criticism of the concept of a competitive payments system devoid of outside money, see Lawrence H. White, "Competitive Payments Systems and the Unit of Account," *American Economic Review* 74 (September 1984): 699–712.

free-banking system based on convertibility into a commodity money, such as coined precious metal, which could be privately produced.[23]

History has seen privately produced commodity money, in particular privately minted gold and silver coins,[24] but so far as I know has not seen competition among privately produced non-commodity outside monies, nor sophisticated payments systems devoid of outside money. For this reason free banking on a specie standard is the most plausible monetary system free of government involvement. (Again, this is not to suggest that markets should not be open to other forms of private money or barter.) It clearly is the system that would have emerged in the absence of the state interventions of past centuries. We today have a system of government-issued fiat currencies only because governments successively monopolized the coinage, monopolized the issue of banknote currency through the creation of central banks, and permanently suspended convertibility for central bank liabilities. No private firm under open competition could have taken the first two of these steps in the absence of "natural monopoly" conditions. Suspension is a breach of contract that only a government or government-sheltered agency can commit with impunity. Economists who defend the government's monopoly provision of outside money presumably defend each of these steps, or think it not advisable to reverse them having once taken them.

The standard approach used by economists to justify government production of a good, or regulation of its private production, is to argue that the good in question is a "public good," or good that generates Pareto-relevant positive externalities. Because the potential producer of a public good cannot sell the external benefits he would generate, the good may be underproduced or not produced at all if left to the profit-driven free market. It is possible to challenge this approach on the scientific ground that its theoretical concepts are lacking or on the ethical ground that the production of an external benefit does not create a right to seize compensation from those benefited.[25] In the case at hand neither challenge is necessary because it is obvious that money—being simply an asset generally accepted in payment—is not a public good. The market did not fail to produce

---

[23]Lawrence H. White, "Free Banking as an Alternative Monetary System," in *Money in Crisis*, ed. Barry N. Siegel (Cambridge, Mass.: Ballinger Publishing Co., 1984), chap. 11. Admittedly the emphasis there was on deregulation of inside money.

[24]On the American experience see Donald H. Kagin, *Private Gold Coins and Patterns of the United States* (New York: Arco Publishing, 1981).

[25]For the first challenge see Tyler Cowen, "The Problem of Public Goods: A Preliminary Investigation," unpublished manuscript (1982); for the second see Robert Nozick, *Anarchy, State, and Utopia* (New York: Basic Books, 1974), p. 95.

money. Money satisfies neither the nonrivalness-in-consumption criterion nor the nonexcludability criterion associated with public goods: The money one individual owns is excluded from ownership by anyone else, and the liquidity services provided by that money cannot simultaneously be enjoyed by anyone else.[26] It is true that government monetary policy can affect the serviceability of money when government controls the production of money, but that does not justify government production of money or show money to be a public good. The public-goods argument for government production of money boils down to the claim that government can produce a money with desired characteristics that private firms cannot produce. There is no evidence that this is the case, although there is plenty of evidence that a government monopoly can stay in business producing a money worse than any private producer could.

It may be argued that uniformity of money is a public good because it reduces informational burdens on transactors, and that government may provide that good by suppressing the variety of monies that prevails under open competition.[27] The argument proves too much, however: It holds equally against proliferation of a variety of products or brands in an industry. It amounts to arguing that too much choice makes life difficult for consumers and ought to be suppressed by government choosing for them. This sort of intervention in fact eliminates the only process available—market competition—for discovering which products and how many brands best serve consumer preferences. Even if the market process will eventually converge on a single type of money, e.g., converge out of a state of barter on a single precious metal as the outside money commodity, the time spent converging is not a wasteful aspect of competition that may efficiently be supplanted by government edict. Government would not be in a position to know what the market process would have

---

[26]See Roland Vaubel, "The Government's Money Monopoly: Externalities or Natural Monopoly?" *Kyklos* 37, no. 1 (1984), esp. pp. 28–45. After a thorough investigation Vaubel concludes (p. 45) that "externality theory fails to provide a convincing justification for the government's monopoly in the production of (base) money."

[27]Carl Menger surprisingly makes this argument in chap. 5 of his article "Geld," reprinted in *The Collected Works of Carl Menger*, ed. F. A. Hayek (London: London School of Economics and Political Science, 1936); unpublished abridged English translation by Albert H. Zlabinger. The argument is also made by Karl Brunner and Allan H. Meltzer, "The Uses of Money: Money in a Theory of an Exchange Economy," *American Economic Review* 41 (December 1971): 801–802. It is cited and criticized by Vaubel (pp. 30–31, n. 12). In particular Brunner and Meltzer assert that the suppression of multiple bank note issuers in Britain by the Act of 1844 "raised economic welfare by reducing costs of acquiring information." Having studied the Act and the circumstances surrounding it, I find this statement incredible.

selected as most suitable. If the market will instead support a number of brands, as under competitive conditions it has in the production of coins and inside money, entry barriers serve no welfare-enhancing purpose.

The question of the optimal number of money producers may be approached in another way. Proponents of government production of money have argued that "the production of a fiduciary currency is, as it were, a technical monopoly," or a "natural monopoly," so that competition is not feasible.[28] If the phrase "fiduciary currency" is intended to cover fractionally backed inside currencies such as specie-redeemable bank notes or dollar-redeemable traveller's checks, then the natural monopoly argument is empirically false. No tendency toward the dominance of a single producer due to unlimited economies of scale was seen in the Scottish free-banking system; nor is such a tendency evident among traveller's check producers today.

There is more room for believing that the production of fiat outside money, if this is all that "fiduciary currency" means, is akin to a natural monopoly. This is because there is an inherent tendency for traders in an economy to converge on a single good (or a very small number of goods) as outside money. Carl Menger long ago explained why: Each individual in pursuit of the easiest way of completing his desired trades finds it advantageous to accept and hold an inventory of the good or goods that other individuals will most readily accept.[29] Where the traders converge on a commodity money, as they naturally will out of a barter setting, no natural monopoly problems arise. Neither the mining nor minting of precious metals gives an indication of being a natural monopoly.

Where government has suppressed commodity money in favor of fiat money the question of natural monopoly does arise. Whether the production of fiat money is in fact a natural monopoly, i.e., whether traders in region would in fact use a single fiat money were they free to use any potentially available, is not *a priori* obvious. Even if the answer were positive there would be no rationale for legal barriers to entry. Nor would it follow inevitably that fiat money production should be nationalized; a private monopoly disciplined by potential competition and competition at the borders might be better. Most importantly, to argue from potential natural monopoly in fiat money production that government should provide fiat money is entirely to beg the question. Why fiat money at all rather than commodity out-

[28]Milton Friedman, *A Program for Monetary Stability*, p. 75; Roland Vaubel, "Free Currency Competition," *Weltwirtschaftliches Archiv* 112 (1977), pp. 437, 458.
[29]Carl Menger, *Principles of Economics* (New York: New York University Press, 1981), chap. 8.

side money? I do not know of a single historical case of fiat money supplanting commodity money through competition rather than compulsion. Where then is the evidence that consumers prefer fiat outside money to commodity outside money?

It might be argued that inconvertibility of money confers social benefits because it reduces costs of producing money, yet these cost savings cannot be realized through market processes because fiat money cannot emerge in piecemeal fashion. It is true that an established monetary standard spontaneously persists as a social convention because no trader by himself finds it advantagous to abandon it. All money-users must be compelled to switch over simultaneously if inconvertible paper is to gain currency. If the public is to choose intentionally between standards it must do so in a setting of constitutional choice. But it cannot be claimed that one standard is Pareto-superior to another unless the other has no partisans in this choice setting. The fact that a switchover must be compulsory robs us of any assurance that the change is for the better as consumers view it. The argument that compulsion is justified because it is necessary to reach a new social convention might be made not only in money but also in language (e.g., a compulsory switchover to Esperanto) or weights and measures (e.g., compulsory metrification). Yet a social engineer's confidence that his blueprint will prove superior to a system evolved spontaneously out of the interaction of many minds must rest in large measure on constructivist hubris. Seldom if ever does a complex social institution operate according to a blueprint.

The belief is common among economists that the replacement of commodity money by paper money constitutes a social savings because paper is cheaper than precious metal. Yet this overlooks the possibility that consumers prefer commodity money to fiat money strongly enough to consider the resource costs worth bearing. Monetary theorists may assume that what consumers care about is simply the quantity of real money balances, or that plus the first and second moments of a probability density function over rates of change in the purchasing power of money. For many analytical purposes these assumptions are useful. But to use such assumptions in comparing alternative outside monies is illegitimate. Economists are not in a position to divine consumers' true preferences in a hypothetical constitution-like choice and thereby to design optimal social institutions for them. In particular it cannot be taken for granted that money users are unwilling to forego some alternative uses of a precious metal (or of the resources necessary to supply the precious metal) in order to use some of it as outside money.[30]

[30]It cannot even be taken for granted that resource costs incidental to the system are

Consumers would conceivably consent to the replacement of a commodity currency by a fiat currency only if they themselves enjoyed the resource savings. A government earnestly desiring to make a Pareto improvement might then offer fiat currency in proportion to a citizen's holdings of specie, but allow him to retain the specie. Historically the introduction of fiat money has not come about in this way. It has instead come about by permanent suspension of redeemability of central bank liabilities, enriching only the government. The hypothesis that fiat money is potentially Pareto-superior, even if true (which is doubtful), would therefore not explain historical transitions to fiat money. Those who agree with Milton Friedman, that government expenditures will rise to more than dissipate any level of income government can extract, would rather doubt that government passes on the savings from fiat money to the citizenry through lower overt taxation. Transition of fiat money gives government opportunities for further self-enrichment at the clear expense of the populace through inflationary finance. It can now commandeer resources from the private sector simply by printing the greenbacks to pay for them. Fear of this possibility would rationally create a preference for hard outside money were a choice between standards offered at a constitutional level.[31] America's Founding Fathers placed a prohibition of fiat currency into the Constitution, for whatever that fact is worth. It cannot be said that the fear of reckless monetary expansion under irredeemable currency is historically groundless.[32]

A final argument made for nationalization of outside money is that it is necessary to the existence of a lender of last resort, that is, a central banking institution standing ready to lend reserves to solvent but illiquid commercial banks. It cannot be argued that illiquid banks would have no recourse in the absence of a central bank: There would exist a system of interbank lending of existing reserves, such as the Federal funds market that operates today. If a temporarily illiquid bank is solvent and worth saving, a profit can be made lending

---

higher under a gold standard than under a fiat standard. See White, *Free Banking in Britain*, pp. 148–49; Roger Garrison, "The Cost of a Gold Standard," in *The Gold Standard*, ed. Llewellyn H. Rockwell, Jr. (Lexington, Mass.: Lexington Books, 1985); and Milton Friedman, "The Resource Cost of an Irredeemable Paper Money," *Journal of Political Economy* 94 (June 1986): 642–47.

[31] As recognized by J. Huston McCulloch, *Money and Inflation: A Monetarist Approach*, 2d ed. (New York: Academic Press, 1982), pp. 75–76. McCulloch makes an interesting case for silver as a better monetary metal than gold.

[32] As noted by Phillip Cagan, "The Report of the Gold Commission (1982)," *Carnegie Rochester Conference Series on Public Policy* 20 (1984): 251. On the U.S. Constitution's intended prohibition of fiat money see Kenneth W. Dam, "The Legal Tender Cases," *Supreme Court Review* (1981), pp. 381–82.

to it, and lenders will be forthcoming. If the bank is insolvent and not worth saving, the real resources tied up in it are best freed to find more productive uses elsewhere through the bank's dissolution. Certainly there are wealth losses associated with the failure of a bank, as with the failure of any business firm, but these are not Pareto-relevant externalities. The failure of one bank should not lower public estimate of the soundness of other banks where banks are free to invest in establishing distinct identities in the public's mind. No runs on the banking system occurred in Scotland under free banking.

It is not even true that a lender of last resort (i.e., an institution able to increase the system's total existing reserves) can exist for a regional banking system only if some central body can create outside money at will. Under an international specie standard, for instance, it is possible for banks of one nation to borrow reserves from banks or other specie-holders of another nation. Only when a banking system is coextensive with the currency area of its outside money can the volume of total outside money reserves be augmented for the banking system as a whole solely through the agency of a lender of last resort able to create outside money at will. The power to create outside money at will is consistent only with fiat money. It is doubtful that an unconstrained power to print cash can be created without being subject to abuse. The lender of last resort function is clearly inconsistent with a strict quantity rule governing the creation of outside money. Monetarists who advocate both a lender-of-last-resort role for the Federal Reserve System and a rule-bound path for bank reserves or outside money (a.k.a. the monetary base) must have in mind a less-than-strict quantity rule.

Milton Friedman, to his credit, has called for a permanent closing of the Fed's discount window.[33] This change would eliminate the Fed's capacity to function as a lender of last resort in the classic sense. It is true that under Friedman's proposal of an M1 or M2 quantity rule the Fed could deliberately vary the stock of outside money in an attempt to offset temporary changes in the real demand to hold outside money. But this seems no different in principle from deliberately varying the stock of M1 or M2 (via the monetary base) in an attempt to offset temporary changes in the real demand to hold one of those aggregates, a policy Friedman would properly criticize.

The injection of new outside money by a central bank acting as lender of last resort, like the injection of outside money in any way

[33]Milton Friedman, *A Program for Monetary Stability*, pp. 44, 100. On the other hand Friedman, "Commodity-Reserve Currency," *Essays in Positive Economics* (Chicago: University of Chicago Press, 1953), p. 218, endorses the holding of an ultimate reserve for a fractional reserve banking system.

other than through a perfectly anticipated proportional addition to every person's holdings of outside money, redistributes wealth involuntarily. Rather than having to induce holders of existing outside money to lend it voluntarily by offering an attractive interest rate, the illiquid bank receives new cash loaned at a below-market rate that tacitly dilutes the purchasing power of existing holdings. That an increased public demand to hold cash may make cash scarcer for banks is a pecuniary externality, not a Pareto-relevant externality that could be invoked to justify subsidization of banks. At bottom, the lender of last resort function undertaken by a fiat-money-issuing central bank is a device for shifting from bank shareholders to the money-holding public the burden of bearing a risk associated with their banking business.

Because the lender of last resort relieves the bank shareholders of some of the risk of illiquidity from bad loans, profit-maximizing banks can be expected to take on loans riskier than they otherwise would have. Western banks would not have made such large loans to governments of less-developed countries—loans that have been much in the news since their riskiness became manifest—had they not believed that an international lender of last resort, namely the International Monetary Fund, would absorb the risk.[34] The question now is whether that belief will be vindicated, the American taxpayer or dollar-holder being forced to pick up the tab for loan losses that should properly fall on bank shareholders.

The Agenda for Denationalization of Outside Money

There is no justification in benefits to the public for government production of outside money. In fact, political control over the quantity of outside money is responsible for the monetary ills of inflation and recession we suffer. What then is to be done? The very least to be done is to open the production of outside money to potential competition from commodity monies, private inconvertible currencies as envisioned by Hayek, and foreign currencies. The legal and regulatory barriers to private production of alternative outside monies are greater than is typically recognized by economists considering the possibility. The following list of barriers present in the United States is probably not exhaustive: (1) private minting of coins has been illegal since 1864; (2) purchases of commodity monies are subject to sales taxes; (3) holdings of non-dollar currencies are subject to capital gains taxation; (4) though gold clauses are legal for indexing

---

[34]But for a contrary view see Charles Goodhart, *The Evolution of Central Banks* (London: London School of Economics and Political Science, 1985), p. 65, n. 2.

dollar obligations, it is doubtful that courts would compel specific performance of an obligation to pay something other than dollars; and perhaps most importantly (5) the unwarranted power of state and federal regulatory bodies to restrict entry into banking can be (and has been) used to suppress the establishment of alternative monetary systems.[35]

Were these restrictions eliminated, transactors would at least be free to use outside monies other than the one produced by the domestic government. None of the arguments above that seek to justify government production of outside money, even if they were valid, would justify a compulsory monopoly for government. There is no rationale for preventing attempts to produce a "public good" privately, or attempts to compete with a "natural monopoly." Should potential or actual competition make the real demand for government-produced outside money more sensitive to its depreciation, the real seignorage yield for any given rate of monetary expansion would fall, reducing government's ability to tax money holders covertly through inflationary finance. Open competition, that is, could erode the monopoly profit government currently enjoys in the production of outside money.[36]

Would it then be enough to allow private producers of outside money to compete with the Federal Reserve? Unfortunately it most likely would not be. It is doubtful that a parallel monetary system could gain much of a foothold even in the absence of legal impediments, because of the natural tendency of money users in a region to converge on a common monetary unit. Each trader finds it most convenient to hold the money that he believes others most likely to accept in the near future, which normally is the money they have been accepting in the immediate past, even if that money is depreciating. Historical bouts with hyperinflation suggest that this momentum can carry an outside money at least through double-digit inflations. I hope that hyperinflation will not be necessary in the United States before competition in outside money can prevail.

---

[35]As evidence of this last barrier in practice, an experiment with privately issued indexed currency and deposits in New Hampshire in 1972–74 was ended under legal pressure from the Securities and Exchange Commission. (Incidentally, the experiment was proving unprofitable.) See "Paying with Constants Instead of Dollars," *Business Week*, May 4, 1974, p. 29. On the other hand, the Secret Service has apparently found nothing illegal in the issue of gold-redeemable certificates by an individual in Maryland. See Irving Wallace et al., "Significa/The Money Maker," *Parade*, February 21, 1982, p. 20.

[36]See David Glasner, "Seignorage, Inflation, and Competition in the Supply of Money," unpublished manuscript (February 1981).

If competition from alternative currencies would not be enough to neutralize the Federal Reserve's ability to do monetary damage, then the opening of competition must be supplemented by some policy for dealing with the supply of fiat dollars. A moderate policy would freeze the monetary base.[37] A more thorough policy would retire the stock of Federal Reserve notes and Treasury token coins via redemption for a potential commodity money. The commodity money could most plausibly be silver or gold. One advantage gold has over silver as a potential money in this connection is that the federal government already has a large stockpile of gold that ought to be disgorged in any event. The advantages of silver are its greater circulability in coinage (a 20-dollar gold piece would at today's prices be a very slight coin) and the greater geopolitical dispersion of silver mines. The point here is not to reestablish a link between government-issued money and a precious metal; it is to phase out government-issued money.[38] Given the market's tendency to evolve and sustain a payments system based on one and only one outside money, conversion to a precious-metal-based monetary system seems our best hope for a competitive supply of outside money.

[37]See Friedman, "Monetary Policy for the 1980s," and Timberlake, "Monetization Practices and the Political Structure of the Federal Reserve System." Timberlake adds that the gold in Fort Knox should be liberated to allow a private gold standard to emerge.

[38]For further elaboration see Lawrence H. White, "Gold, Dollars, and Private Currencies," Cato Institute *Policy Report* 3 (June 1981): 6–11, and White, "Free Banking and the Gold Standard," in *The Gold Standard*, ed. Rockwell.

PART VI

THE FUTURE OF
MONETARY POLICY

17

MONETARY POLICY: TACTICS VERSUS STRATEGY*

Milton Friedman

Introduction

Monetary policy can be discussed on two very different levels: the tactics of policy—the specific actions that the monetary authorities should take; and the strategy or framework of policy—the ideal monetary institutions and arrangements for the conduct of monetary policy that should be adopted.

Tactics are more tempting. They are immediately relevant, promise direct results, and are in most respects easier to discuss than the thorny problem of the basic framework appropriate for monetary policy. Yet long experience persuades me that, given our present institutions, a discussion of tactics is unlikely to be rewarding.

The temptation to concentrate on tactics derives in considerable part from a tendency to personalize policy: to speak of the Eisenhower, Kennedy, or Reagan economic policy and the Martin, Burns, or Volcker monetary policy. Sometimes that approach is correct. The particular person in charge may make a major difference to the course of events. For example, in *Monetary History*, Anna Schwartz and I attributed considerable importance to the early death of Benjamin Strong, first governor of the Federal Reserve Bank of New York, in explaining monetary policy from 1929 to 1933. More frequently perhaps, the personalized approach is misleading. The person ostensibly in charge is like the rooster crowing at dawn. The course of events is decided by deeper and less visible forces that determine both the character of those nominally in charge and the pressures on them.

Monetary developments during the past few decades have, I believe, been determined far more by the institutional structure of the Federal

---

*Excerpted, by permission, from *To Promote Prosperity*, ed. John H. Moore (Stanford, Calif.: Hoover Institution Press, Copyright 1984, Board of Trustees of the Leland Stanford Junior University), chap. 2, with new title.

The author is a Senior Research Fellow at the Hoover Institution and recipient of the 1976 Nobel Memorial Prize in Economics.

Reserve and by external pressures than by the intentions, knowledge, or personal characteristics of the persons who appeared to be in charge. Knowing the name, the background, and the personal qualities of the chairman of the Fed, for example, is of little use in judging what happened to monetary growth during his term of office.[1]

If the present monetary structure were producing satisfactory results, we would be well advised to leave it alone. Tactics would then be the only topic. However, the present monetary structure is not producing satisfactory results. Indeed, in my opinion, no major institution in the United States has so poor a record of performance over so long a period yet so high a public reputation as the Federal Reserve.

To summarize its 69-year record: two major wartime inflations; two major depressions; a banking panic far more severe than was ever experienced before the Federal Reserve System was established; a succession of booms and recessions; a post-World War II roller coaster marked by accelerating inflation and terminating in four years of unusual instability—the whole relieved by relative stability and prosperity during the two decades after the Korean War.

Granted, the Fed alone is not to blame for this dismal record. Yet it is—to put it mildly—hardly an impressive performance compared either to our nation's experience before the Federal Reserve System was established or to the record of some other nations with a different monetary structure. It is time for a change.

The conduct of monetary policy is of major importance: monetary instability breeds economic instability. A monetary structure that fosters steadiness and predictability in the general price level is an essential precondition for healthy noninflationary growth. That is why it is important to consider fundamental changes in our monetary institutions. Such changes may be neither feasible nor urgent now. But unless we consider them now, we shall not be prepared to adopt them when and if the need is urgent.

The Tactics of Monetary Policy

Three issues are involved in the tactics of monetary policy: adopting a variable or variables as intermediate target or targets; choosing the desired path of the target variables; devising procedures for achieving that path as closely as possible.

---

[1]Robert E. Weintraub has suggested that learning the name of the president is of somewhat more value. See his "Congressional Supervision of Monetary Policy," *Journal of Monetary Economics* 4 (April 1978): 341–62.

The Intermediate Targets

The Fed has vacillated between using one or more interest rates or one or more monetary aggregates as its intermediate targets. In the past decade, however, it joined monetary authorities in other countries in stressing monetary growth. Since 1975, it has been required by Congress to specify explicit numerical targets for the growth of monetary aggregates. Although many proposals have recently surfaced for the substitution of other targets—from real interest rates to sensitive commodity prices to the price of gold to nominal GNP— I shall assume that one or more monetary aggregates remains the intermediate target.[2]

In my opinion, the selection of a target or of a target path is not and has not been the problem. If the Fed had consistently achieved the targets it specified to Congress, monetary growth would have been highly stable instead of highly variable, inflation would never have become the menace it did, and the United States would have been spared the worst parts of the punishing recession (or recessions) from 1979 to 1982.

The Fed has specified targets for several aggregates primarily, as I have argued elsewhere, to obfuscate the issue and reduce accountability.[3] In general, the different aggregates move together. The exceptions have essentially all been due to the interest rate restrictions imposed by the Fed under Regulation Q and the associated development of new forms of deposit liabilities. And they would not have arisen if the Fed had achieved its targets for any one of the aggregates.

The use of multiple intermediate targets is undesirable. The Fed has one major instrument of monetary control: control over the quantity of high-powered money. With one instrument, it cannot independently control several aggregates. Its other instruments—primarily the discount rate and reserve requirements—are highly defective as instruments for monetary control and of questionable effectiveness in enabling it to control separately more than one aggregate.[4]

It makes far less difference which aggregate the Fed selects than that it select one and only one. For simplicity of exposition, I shall

---

[2]For a thoughtful evaluation of proposed price rules, see R. E. Hafer, "Monetary Policy and the Price Rule: The Newest Odd Couple," *Federal Reserve Bank of St. Louis Review* 65 (February 1983): 5–13.

[3]See Milton Friedman, "Monetary Policy: Theory and Practice," *Journal of Money, Credit, and Banking* 14 (February 1982): 98–118.

[4]See my *Program for Monetary Stability* (New York: Fordham University Press, 1959), chap. 2.

assume that the target aggregate is M1 as currently designed. Selection of another aggregate would alter the desirable numerical targets but not their temporal pattern.

The Target Path

A long-run growth rate of about 1 to 3 percent per year for M1 would be roughly consistent with zero inflation.[5] That should be our objective. Actual growth in M1 was 8.5 percent from fourth quarter 1981 to fourth quarter 1982. A crucial question is how rapidly to go from that level to the 1 to 3 percent range. In my opinion, it is desirable to proceed gradually, over something like a three- to five-year period, which means that the rate of growth should be reduced by about 1 to 1.5 percentage points a year.

The Fed has consistently stated its targets in terms of a range of growth rates. For example, its initial target for M1 for 1983 was a growth rate of 4 to 8 percent from the fourth quarter of 1982 to the fourth quarter of 1983. That method of stating targets is seriously defective. It provides a widening cone of limits on the absolute money supply as the year proceeds and fosters a shift in base from year to year, thereby frustrating accountability over long periods. This is indeed what happened. In July 1983, Chairman Volcker announced a new target of 5 to 9 percent for the second quarter of 1983 to the second quarter of 1984 but from the second quarter 1983 base, which is 3 percent (6 percent at an annual rate) above the top of the earlier range.

A better way to state the targets is in terms of a central target for the absolute money supply plus or minus a band of, say, 1.5 percent on either side—about the range the Fed has specified for annual growth rates.

Figure 1 exemplifies monetary targets stated in this way for a five-year period. The actual values of M1 available in mid-1983 are also plotted on the chart. The United States is heading either for a renewed

---

[5]Over the past three decades, M1 velocity has risen about 3 percent a year. Given a long-term rate of real growth of about 3 percent per year, continued velocity growth of 3 percent a year would mean that zero M1 growth would be required for zero inflation. However, part of the velocity growth has been a reaction to rising inflation and interest rates, which have made it more costly to hold cash. Successful disinflation has the opposite effect. Since the third quarter of 1981, M1 velocity has declined (by 6 percent to the second quarter of 1983) rather than risen. In addition, technological improvements in cash management cannot continue indefinitely. It therefore seems safer to suppose that M1 velocity will cease rising as rapidly as in the past, which explains the 1 to 3 estimate in the text. It implicitly allows for about a 1 to 2 percent per year velocity growth.

FIGURE 1

PROPOSED MONETARY TARGETS FOR M1,
DEC. 1982–DEC. 1987

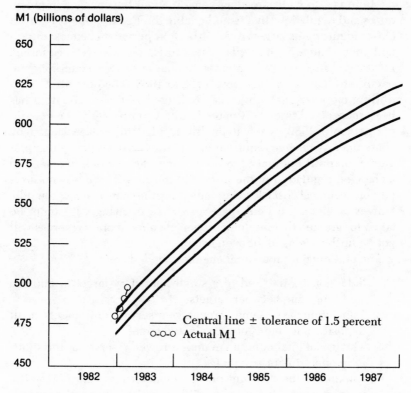

M1 (billions of dollars)

Central line ± tolerance of 1.5 percent
o-o-o Actual M1

NOTE: Initial rate of growth: actual 8.5 percent, 4th quarter 1981 to 4th quarter 1982; terminal rate of growth: 2 percent.

upsurge of inflation or for a sharp monetary—and therefore probably economic—contraction.

Procedures for Hitting the Target

There is widespread agreement both inside and outside the Federal Reserve System that current procedures and reserve regulations make accurate control of monetary growth over short periods difficult or impossible. These procedures and regulations do not explain such long-sustained departures from the targets as the monetary explosions from April 1980 to April 1981 or July 1982 to July 1983 or the monetary retardations from April 1981 to October 1981 or January 1982 to July 1982. However, they do explain the wide volatility in monetary growth from week to week and month to month, which introduces undesirable uncertainty into the economy and financial markets and reduces Fed accountability for not hitting its targets.

There is also widespread agreement about the changes in procedures and regulations that would enable the Fed to come very much closer to hitting its targets over fairly short periods. The most important such change is the replacement of lagged reserve accounting, introduced in 1968, by contemporaneous reserve accounting comparable to that prevailing from 1914 to 1968. The obstacle to controlling monetary growth posed by lagged reserve accounting has been recognized since 1970 at the latest.[6] Unfortunately, the Fed did not act until 1982, when it finally decided to replace lagged by contemporary reserve requirements. However, it has delayed implementation until February 1984—the longest delay in implementing a changed regulation in the history of the Fed. There was no insuperable technical obstacle to implementing the change more promptly. However, given the Fed's past resistance to change, it cannot be taken for granted that implementation of contemporary reserves will not be further delayed, or even occur.

The other major procedural changes needed are:

1. Selection by the Fed of a single monetary target to end the Fed's juggling between targets;
2. Imposition of the same percentage reserve requirements on all deposit components of the selected target;
3. The use of total rather than nonborrowed reserves as the short-term operating instrument;
4. Linking of the discount rate to a market rate and making it a penalty rate (unfortunately, neither this change nor the preceding is feasible for technical reasons under lagged reserve accounting and hence must await the implementation of contemporaneous reserve accounting);
5. Reduction of the churning in which the Fed engages in the course of its so-called defensive open-market operations.[7]

Even without most of these changes, it would be possible for the Fed to put into effect almost instantaneously a policy that would provide a far stabler monetary environment than we have at present, even though it would by no means be ideal. The obstacle is not

---

[6]George Kaufman warned of the problem before lagged reserve accounting was introduced. See my "Monetary Policy," pp. 110–13, for a detailed discussion of lagged reserve requirements.

[7]For a fuller discussion, see my "Monetary Policy."

feasibility but bureaucratic inertia and the preservation of bureau-cratic power and status.

A simple example will illustrate. Let the Fed continue to state targets for M1 growth. Let it estimate the change in its total holdings of U.S. government securities that would be required in the next six months, say, to produce the targeted growth in M1. Divide that amount by 26. Let the Fed purchase the resulting amount every week on the open market, in addition to any amount needed to replace maturing securities, and make no other purchases or sales. Finally, let it announce this schedule of purchases in advance and in full detail and stick to it.

Such a policy would assure control over the monetary aggregates, not from day to day, but over the longer period that the Fed insists is all that matters. It would enable the market to know precisely what the Fed would do and adjust its own actions accordingly. It would end the weekly guessing game that currently follows each Friday's release of figures on the money supply. The financial markets have certainly demonstrated that they have ample flexibility to handle whatever day-to-day or seasonal adjustments might be needed. It is hard to envisage any significant adverse effects from such a policy.

A few numbers will show how much difference such a policy would make to the Fed's open-market activities. In 1982, it added an average of $176 million a week to its total holdings of government securities—an unusually high amount. In the process of acquiring $176 million, it purchased each week an average of $13 *billion* of securities and sold nearly as much. About half of these transactions were on behalf of foreign central banks. But that still leaves roughly $40 of purchases or $80 of transactions for every one dollar added to its portfolio—a degree of churning of a customer's account that would send a private stockbroker to jail, or at least to limbo.

Increased predictability, reduced churning, the loss of inscruta-bility—these are at the same time the major reasons for making so drastic a change and the major obstacle to its achievement. It would simply upset too many comfortable dovecotes.

The Strategy of Monetary Policy

The chief problem in discussing the strategy or framework of mon-etary policy is to set limits. The subject is old, yet immediately pertinent; numerous proposals have been made, and few, however ancient, do not have contemporary proponents. In view of my own belief that the important desiderata of structural reform are to reduce the variability of monetary growth, to limit the discretion of the monetary authorities, and to provide a stable monetary framework, I shall limit myself to proposals directed at those objectives, proceeding from the least to the most radical.

Imposing a Monetary Rule on the Fed

I have long argued that a major improvement in monetary policy could be achieved without any significant change in monetary institutions simply by imposing a monetary rule on the Fed. From an economic point of view, it would be desirable to state the rule in terms of a monetary aggregate such as M1 that has a close and consistent relation to subsequent changes in national income. However, recent years have demonstrated that the Fed has been unable or unwilling to achieve such a target, even when it sets it itself, and that it has been able to plead inability and thereby avoid accountability. Accordingly, I have reluctantly decided that it is preferable to state the rule in terms of a magnitude that has a somewhat less close relation to national income but that unquestionably can be controlled within very narrow limits within very brief time periods, namely, the Fed's own non-interest-bearing obligations, the monetary base.

In *Free to Choose*, my wife, Rose, and I proposed a specific form of rule as a constitutional amendment:

> *Congress shall have the power to authorize non-interest-bearing obligations of the government in the form of currency or book entries, provided that the total dollar amount outstanding increases by no more than 5 percent per year and no less than 3 percent.*
>
> It might be desirable to include a provision that two-thirds of each House of Congress, or some similar qualified majority, can waive the requirement in case of a declaration of war, the suspension to terminate annually unless renewed.[8]

A constitutional amendment would be the most effective way to establish confidence in the stability of the rule. However, it is clearly not the only way to impose the rule. Congress could equally well legislate it, and, indeed, proposals for a legislated monetary rule have been introduced in Congress.

This proposal has the merit that it minimizes the extent of institutional change. However, that is also its chief shortcoming. So long as the current institutional arrangements remain in being, strong pressure will be brought to bear to use them in ways that would avoid or evade the rule. Moreover, as a political matter, a constitutional

---

[8]Milton and Rose Friedman, *Free to Choose* (New York: Harcourt Brace Jovanovich, 1980), p. 308.

amendment is unlikely to attract support sufficient for passage except under circumstances of deep and widespread dissatisfaction with monetary arrangements. Since such circumstances would also permit more far-reaching and fundamental changes, why settle for a half-measure?

I remain persuaded that a monetary rule that leads to a predictable long-run path of a specified monetary aggregate is a highly desirable goal—superior either to discretionary control of the quantity of money by a set of monetary authorities or to a commodity standard. However, I am no longer so optimistic as I once was that it can be effected by either persuading the monetary authorities to follow it or legislating its adoption. Congressional attempts in the past decade to push the Fed in that direction have repeatedly failed. The Fed has rhetorically accepted monetary targets but never a firm monetary rule. Moreover, the Fed has not been willing even to match its performance to a rhetorical acceptance of monetary targets. All this suggests that a change in our monetary institutions is required in order to make such a rule effective.

An International Monetary Rule

Some economists, in particular Ronald McKinnon, have accepted the case for a monetary rule but have argued that if applied on a national basis, it would be rendered largely ineffective by substitution of other market currencies for the one being controlled by the rule. Hence they propose the adoption of a rule by a group of countries with respect to an aggregate of their money supplies, which implies, of course, some agreement on the exchange rates at which the monies will be combined. McKinnon has suggested that Japan, the United States, and Germany should adopt such a rule for a total including the yen, the dollar, and the mark.

This proposal has received considerable attention, particularly with respect to the substantive contention that even under floating exchange rates currency substitution renders control of the U.S. money supply "increasingly inefficient for . . . stabilizing American income and prices."[9] The bulk of the evidence does not support McKinnon's contention.[10] Rather, it suggests that substitution of other currencies

[9]Ronald I. McKinnon, "Currency Substitution and Instability in the World Dollar Standard," *American Economic Review* 72 (June 1982): 332.

[10]Henry N. Goldstein and Stephen E. Haynes, "A Critical Appraisal of McKinnon's World Money Supply Hypothesis" (unpublished paper, March 1983), conclude, "In a number of important respects . . . his interpretation seems strikingly at odds with the empirical evidence." A similar negative conclusion is reached by Thomas D. Willett, "U.S. Monetary Policy and World Liquidity," *American Economic Review* 73 (May 1983): 43–47.

for the dollar is a trivial impediment to the effectiveness of a monetary rule for the dollar alone.

The economic objections to the proposal are dwarfed by the political objections. A verbal agreement is possible, but a credible and enforceable one, next to impossible.[11] But even if it were, the proposal involves giving great and essentially discretionary powers to an international body independent of any political control by citizens of each member-country short of withdrawal from the agreement. As I indicate below, I regard the independence in a democracy of a national central bank as highly objectionable on political grounds. The objection is vastly stronger to an independent world or tri-country central bank.

Separating Regulatory from Monetary Functions

A modest institutional reform that promises considerable benefits is to separate the regulatory from the monetary functions of the Fed. Currently, regulatory functions absorb most of the attention of the Fed. Moreover, they obscure accountability for monetary control by confusing the two very separate and to some extent inconsistent functions.

As has recently been proposed in a study of the Federal Deposit Insurance Corporation (FDIC), the Fed should be stripped of its regulatory functions, which would be combined with the largely overlapping functions of the FDIC, the Federal Savings and Loan Insurance Corporation (FSLIC), and the comptroller of the currency. Such a combined agency should have no monetary powers. It also might well include the operating functions of the Federal Reserve Banks—the monitoring of reserve requirements, issuance of currency, clearing of checks, reporting of data, and so forth.[12]

A separate monetary control agency could be a very small body, charged solely with determining the total quantity of high-powered money through open-market operations. Its function would be clear, highly visible, and subject to effective accountability.

Ending the Independence of the Fed

An approach that need involve relatively little institutional change— although it is far more drastic than the preceding—and that could be implemented by legislation would be to end the independence of the Fed by converting it into a bureau of the Treasury Department.

[11]See George M. von Furstenburg, "Internationally Managed Moneys," *American Economic Review* 73 (May 1983): 54–58.

[12]See Federal Deposit Insurance Corporation, *Deposit Insurance in a Changing Environment* (April 15, 1983), esp. pp. xxi–xxiv and chap. 6.

That would end the present division of responsibilities for monetary and fiscal policy that leads to the spectacle of chairmen of the Fed blaming all the nation's ills on the defects of fiscal policy and secretaries of the Treasury blaming them on the defects of monetary policy—a phenomenon that has prevailed for decades. There would be a single locus of authority that could be held responsible.

The immediate objection that arises is that it would make monetary policy a plaything of politics. My own examination of monetary history indicates that this judgment is correct, but that it is an argument for, not against, eliminating the central bank's independence.

I examined this issue at length in an article published more than two decades ago entitled "Should There Be an Independent Monetary Authority?"[13] I concluded that it is

> highly dubious that the United States, or for that matter any other country, has in practice ever had an independent central bank in [the] fullest sense of the term. . . . To judge by experience, even those central banks that have been nominally independent in the fullest sense of the term have in fact been closely linked to the executive authority.
>
> But of course this does not dispose of the matter. The ideal is seldom fully realized. Suppose we could have an independent central bank in the sense of a coordinate constitutionally established, separate organization. Would it be desirable to do so? I think not, for both political and economic reasons.
>
> The political objections are perhaps more obvious than the economic ones. Is it really tolerable in a democracy to have so much power concentrated in a body free from any kind of direct, effective political control? A "liberal" often characterizes his position as involving belief in the rule of law rather than of men. It is hard to reconcile such a view with the approval of an independent central bank in any meaningful way. True, it is impossible to dispense fully with the rule of men. No law can be specified so precisely as to avoid problems of interpretation or to cover explicitly every possible case. But the kind of limited discretion left by even the best of laws in the hands of those administering them is a far cry indeed from the kind of far-reaching powers that the laws establishing central banks generally place in the hands of a small number of men.
>
> One [economic] defect of an independent central bank . . . is that it almost inevitably involves dispersal of responsibility. . . .
>
> Another defect . . . is the extent to which policy is . . . made highly dependent on personalities. . . .

[13]In Leland B. Yeager, ed., *In Search of a Monetary Constitution* (Cambridge, Mass.: Harvard University Press, 1962), chap. 8; reprinted in M. Friedman, *Dollars and Deficits* (Englewood Cliffs, N.J.: Prentice-Hall, 1968), chap. 6.

> A third technical defect is that an independent central bank will almost inevitably give undue emphasis to the point of view of bankers. . . .
>
> The three defects I have outlined constitute a strong technical argument against an independent central bank. Combined with the political argument, the case against a fully independent central bank is strong indeed.[14]

The experience of the past two decades has led me to alter my views in one respect only—about the importance of personalities. They have on occasion made a great deal of difference, but additional experience and study have impressed me with the continuity of Fed policy, despite the wide differences in the personalities and backgrounds of the persons supposedly in charge.

For the rest, experience has reinforced my views. Anna Schwartz and I pointed out in *Monetary History* that subservience to congressional pressure in 1930 and 1931 would have prevented the disastrous monetary policy followed by the Fed. That is equally true for the past fifteen years. The relevant committees of Congress have generally, though by no means invariably, urged policies on the Fed that would have produced a stabler rate of monetary growth and much less inflation. Excessively rapid and volatile monetary growth from, say, 1971 to 1979 was not the result of political pressure—certainly not from Congress, although in some of these years there clearly was pressure for more rapid growth from the administration. Nonetheless, no political pressures would have prevented the Fed from increasing M1 over this period at, say, an average annual rate of 5 percent—the rate of increase during the prior eight years—instead of 6.7 percent.

Subordinating the Fed to the Treasury is by no means ideal. Yet it would be a great improvement over the existing situation, even with no other changes.

A Gold Standard

Superficially, there appears to be widespread support for a "gold standard." However, as the report of the Gold Commission demonstrated, the apparent consensus disappears when the question is what kind of gold standard.[15] Some who refer to themselves as proponents of a gold standard simply want the Fed to use the price of gold as a guide to increasing or decreasing the growth rate of the money supply without buying or selling gold and without committing itself to keep-

[14]Ibid., pp. 180, 184, 186, 188, 190.
[15]See *Report to the Congress of the Commission on the Role of Gold in the Domestic and International Monetary Systems* (March 1982), vols. 1 and 2.

ing the price of gold within any specified limits. Others want to add a commitment by the Fed to specific numerical limits on the price of gold. Still others want to fix dollar prices at which the Fed—or the Treasury—will buy and sell gold, generally with the proviso that other major countries agree to do the same in terms of their own currencies. Finally, a small minority wants a "real" gold standard in which the Fed and the Treasury would cease issuing any non-interest-bearing obligations other than, perhaps, warehouse certificates for specified physical amounts of gold, and in which gold coins or warehouse certificates, or their equivalent, would be the circulating medium.

For reasons that I have spelled out elsewhere, I regard only the last—a real gold standard—as constituting an improvement rather than a deterioration in our monetary arrangements. And that alternative, which is by no means ideal, has minuscule political support.[16]

Competitive Issue of Money

Increasing interest has been expressed in recent years in proposals to replace governmental issuance of money and control of its quality by private market arrangements. One set of proposals would end the government monopoly on the issuance of currency and permit the competitive issue of currency. Another would eliminate entirely any issuance of money by government and, instead, restrict the role of government to defining a monetary unit.

Choice in Currency and a Tabular Standard. This set of proposals derives largely from a pamphlet by F. A. Hayek entitled *Choice in Currency: A Way to Stop Inflation.*[17] Hayek proposed that all special privileges (such as "legal tender" quality) attached to government-issued currency be removed, and that financial institutions be permitted to issue currency or deposit obligations on whatever terms were mutually acceptable to the issuer and the holder of the liabilities. He envisaged a system in which institutions would in fact issue obligations expressed in terms of purchasing power either of specific commodities, such as gold or silver, or of commodities in general through linkage to a price index. In his opinion, constant-purchasing-power moneys would come to dominate the market and largely replace both obligations denominated in dollars or pounds or other similar units and in specific commodities.

---

[16]See my "Real and Pseudo Gold Standards," *Dollars and Deficits,* chap. 11; and "The Role and Value of Gold," *Reason* 7 (June 1975): 87, 91–94.

[17]Institute of Economic Affairs, Occasional Paper 48 (London, 1976).

The idea of a currency unit linked to a price index is an ancient one—proposed in the 19th century by W. Stanley Jevons and Alfred Marshall, who named it a "tabular" standard—and repeatedly rediscovered.[18] It is part of the theoretically highly attractive idea of widespread indexation. Experience, however, has demonstrated that the theoretical attractiveness of the idea is not matched by practice. Nothing has prevented the widespread use of indexation in one form or another—indeed, the voluntary adoption of the equivalent of a tabular standard—in the United States, Britain, or other capitalist countries. Yet indexation has been extensive only when inflation has been extremely high and variable, as in some South American countries and Israel. Indexing, though frequent, is of minor importance except in labor contracts, and even in that area, it is far from dominant.

I approve of Professor Hayek's proposal to remove restrictions on the issuance of private moneys to compete with government moneys. But I do not share his belief about the outcome. Private moneys now exist—traveler's and cashier's checks, bank deposits, money orders, and various forms of bank drafts and negotiable instruments. But these are almost all claims on a specified number of units of government currency (of dollars or pounds or francs or marks). Currently, they are subject to government regulation and control. But even if such regulations and controls were entirely eliminated, the advantage of a single national currency unit buttressed by long tradition will, I suspect, serve to prevent any other type of private currency unit from seriously challenging the dominant government currency, and this despite the high degree of monetary variability many countries have experienced over recent decades.

The recent explosion in financial futures markets offers a possible new road to the achievement, through private market actions, of the equivalent of a tabular standard. This possibility is highly speculative—little more than a gleam in one economist's eye. It involves the establishment of futures markets in one or more price indexes— strictly parallel to the markets that have developed in stock price indexes. Such markets, if active and covering a considerable range of future dates, would provide a relatively costless means of hedging long-term contracts against risks of changes in the price level. A combination of an orthodox dollar contract plus a properly timed set

[18]For an interesting recent rediscovery, see the article by R. W. R. White, governor of the Reserve Bank of New Zealand, on a proposed purchasing-power-adjusted money of account that he termed the "Real" (*Reserve Bank of New Zealand Bulletin* [October 1979]: 371–74). This article was followed by a series of five articles in successive monthly issues of the *Bulletin* dealing with the possible effects of the Real on various aspects of the economy.

of futures in a price level would be the precise equivalent of a tabular standard, but would have the advantage that any one party to a contract, with the help of speculators and other hedgers in the futures market, could have the benefit of a tabular standard without the agreement of the other party or parties.

Recent changes in banking regulations have opened still another route to a partial tabular standard on a substantial scale. The Federal Home Loan Bank has finally authorized federally chartered savings and loan associations to offer price-level-adjusted mortgage (PLAM) loans. Concurrently, the restrictions on the interest rate that can be paid on deposits by a wide range of financial institutions have been eased and removed entirely for deposits of longer maturities.

This would permit financial institutions simultaneously to lend and borrow on a price-level-adjusted basis: to lend on a PLAM and borrow on a price-level-adjusted deposit (PLAD), both at an interest rate specified in real rather than nominal terms. By matching PLAM loans against PLAD deposits, a bank would be fully hedged against changes in inflation, covering its costs by the difference between the interest rate it charges and pays. Similarly, both borrowers and lenders would be safeguarded against changes in inflation with respect to a particular liability and asset.

As yet, I know of no financial institutions that have proceeded along these lines. I conjecture that no major development will occur unless and until inflation once again accelerates. When and if that occurs, PLAMs and PLADs may well become household words and not simply mysterious acronyms.[19]

Eliminating Government Money. A number of economic theorists who have been re-examining the foundations of monetary systems have recently offered a new set of proposals. The basic idea is that the government simply define a monetary unit—for example, the value of a specified basket of goods—and play no other role in the monetary system. Private institutions would issue claims denominated in the officially defined unit (as, in futures markets, they now issue promises to deliver wheat or gold or silver specified in officially defined units). The role of government would be restricted to enforcing such contracts, preventing fraud, and the like.[20]

---

[19]See J. Huston McCulloch, "PLAMs: Affordable Mortgages from Inflation-Proof Deposits," Federal Home Loan Bank of Cincinnati *Quarterly Review* 3 (1982): 2–6. Also see my *Newsweek* column, "PLAM's and PLAD's," 13 June 1983.

[20]See Robert E. Hall, "*Monetary Trends in the United States and the United Kingdom: A Review from the Perspective of New Developments in Monetary Economics,*" *Journal of Economic Literature* 20 (December 1982): 1552–56, for a succinct and authori-

The set of ideas underlying these proposals is intellectually excit-
ing and will contribute to a fuller understanding of the role and value
of money. But, as yet, they seem too radical, too unsupported by
evidence, to be regarded as a practical proposal for institutional
reform. As Robert Hall, one of the main contributors to these developments, states, "All of these proposals share a basic microeconomic
goal—full deregulation of transaction services and intermediation
[borrowing from some and lending to others]. None of them would
rely on the concept of a money stock or its stability relative to total
income. Whether their macroeconomic performance would equal
that of a simple money growth rule is still a matter of controversy."[21]

Freezing High-Powered Money

The final proposal combines features from most of the preceding.
It is radical and far-reaching, yet simple. The proposal is that, after a
transition period, the quantity of high-powered money—non-interest-bearing obligations of the U.S. government—be frozen at a fixed
amount.[22] These non-interest-bearing obligations now take two forms:
currency and deposits at the Federal Reserve System. The simplest
way to envisage the change is to suppose that Federal Reserve deposit
liabilities were replaced dollar for dollar by currency notes, which
were turned over to the owners of those deposits. Thereafter, the
government's monetary role would be limited to keeping the amount
constant by replacing worn-out currency. In effect, a monetary rule
of zero growth in high-powered money would be adopted. (In practice, it would not be necessary to replace deposits at the Federal
Reserve with currency; they could be retained as book entries, so
long as the total of such book entries plus currency notes was kept
constant.)

As noted above, the Fed currently has two roles: determining the
quantity of money; and regulating banking institutions and providing
such services as collateralized loans, check-clearing, wire transfers,
and the like. Under this proposal its first role would be eliminated.
In this sense, the proposal would end the independence of the Federal Reserve System. Its second role could, if desired, be continued,

---

tative summary of recent ideas. Robert L. Greenfield and Leland B. Yeager, "A Laissez-
Faire Approach to Monetary Stability," *Journal of Money, Credit, and Banking* 15
(August 1983), is an excellent analysis of the theoretical basis of this collection of
proposals.

[21]Hall, "New Developments in Monetary Economics," p. 1555.

[22]In deferrence to tradition, I designate currency and deposits at the Federal Reserve
as "obligations," but they are not in any meaningful sense obligations of the U.S.
government, or, indeed, anyone else. They are simply pure fiat money.

preferably by combining it with the similar roles of the FDIC, the FSLIC, and the comptroller of the currency, as suggested earlier.

This proposal would be consistent with, indeed require, the continued existence of private institutions issuing claims to government currency. These could be regulated as now, with the whole paraphernalia of required reserves, bank examinations, limitations on lending, and the like. However, they could also be freed from all or most such regulations. In particular, the need for reserve requirements to enable the Fed to control the quantity of money would disappear.

Reserve requirements might still be desirable for a different though related reason. The new monetary economists argue that only the existence of such government regulations as reserve requirements and prohibition of the private issuance of currency explains the relatively stable demand for high-powered money. In the absence of such regulations, they contend, non-interest-bearing money would be completely dominated by interest-bearing assets, or, at the very least, the demand for such money would be rendered highly unstable.

I am far from persuaded by this contention. It supposes a closer approach to a frictionless world with minimal transaction costs than seems to me a useful approximation to the actual world.[23] Nonetheless, it is arguable that the elimination of reserve requirements would introduce an unpredictable and erratic element into the demand for high-powered money. For that reason, although personally I would favor the deregulation of financial institutions, thereby incorporating a major element of Hayek's proposed competitive financial system, it would seem prudent to proceed in stages: first, freeze high-powered money; then, after a period, eliminate reserve requirements and other remaining regulations, including the prohibition on the issuance of hand-to-hand currency by private institutions.

Why zero growth? Zero has a special appeal on political grounds that is not shared by any other number. If 3 percent, why not 4 percent? It is hard, as it were, to go to the political barricades to defend 3 rather than 4, or 4 rather than 5. But zero is—as a psychological matter—qualitatively different. It is what has come to be called a Schelling point—a natural point at which people tend to agree, like "splitting the difference" in a dispute over a monetary sum. Moreover, by removing any power to create money it eliminates

---

[23]The empirical issue is the same as that embedded in the extreme form of the rational expectations hypothesis, which asserts the complete inability, even over short periods, of perceived changes in monetary policy to affect real magnitudes.

institutional arrangements lending themselves to discretionary changes in monetary growth.

Would zero growth in high-powered money be consistent with a healthy economy? In the hypothetical long-long-run stationary economy, when the whole economy had become adjusted to the situation, and population, real output, and so on were all stationary, zero growth in high-powered money would imply zero growth in other monetary aggregates and mean stable velocities for the aggregates. In consequence, the price level would be stable. In a somewhat less than stationary state in which output was rising, if financial innovations kept pace, the money multiplier would tend to rise at the same rate as output and again prices would be stable. If financial innovations ceased but total output continued to rise, prices would decline. If output rose at about 3 percent per year, prices would tend to fall at 3 percent per year. So long as that was known and relatively stable, all contracts could be adjusted to it, and it would cause no problems and indeed would have some advantages.[24]

However, any such outcome is many decades away. The more interesting and important question is not the final stationary-state result but the intermediate dynamic process.

Once the policy was in effect, the actual behavior of nominal income and the price level would depend on what happened to a monetary aggregate like M1 relative to high-powered money and what happened to nominal income relative to M1—that is, on the behavior of the money multiplier (the ratio of M1 to high-powered money) and on the income velocity of M1 (the ratio of nominal income to M1).

Given a loosening of the financial structure through continued deregulation, there would be every reason to expect a continued flow of innovations raising the money multiplier. This process has in fact occurred throughout the past several centuries. For example, in the century from 1870 to 1970, the ratio of the quantity of money, as defined by Anna Schwartz and me in *Monetary History*, to high-powered money rose at the average rate of 1 percent per year. In the post-World War II period, the velocity of M1 has risen at about 3 percent per year, and at a relatively steady rate. This trend cannot of course continue indefinitely. Above, in specifying a desirable target for the Fed, I estimated the rise in velocity would slow to about 1 or 2 percent per year. However, a complete end to the rapid trend in velocity is not in sight.

[24]See my "The Optimum Quantity of Money," in *The Optimum Quantity of Money and Other Essays* (Chicago: Aldine, 1969), chap. 1.

There is no way to make precise numerical estimates, but there is every reason to anticipate that for decades after the introduction of a freeze on high-powered money, both the money multiplier and velocity would tend to rise at rates in the range of historical experience. Under these circumstances, a zero rate of growth of high-powered money would imply roughly stable prices, though ultimately, perhaps, slightly declining prices.

What of the transition? Over the three years from 1979 to 1982, high-powered money grew an average of 7 percent a year. It would be desirable to bring that rate to zero gradually. As for M1 growth, about a five-year period seems appropriate—or a transition that reduces the rate of growth of high-powered money by about 1.5 percentage points a year. The only other transitional problem would be to phase out the Fed's powers to create and destroy high-powered money by open-market operations and discounting. Neither transition offers any special problem. The Fed, or its successor agency, could still use part of the existing stock of high-powered money for similar purposes, particularly for lender-of-last-resort purposes, if that function were retained.

The great advantage of this proposal is that it would end the arbitrary power of the Federal Reserve System to determine the quantity of money and would do so without establishing any comparable locus of power and without introducing any major disturbances into other existing economic and financial institutions.

I have found that few things are harder even for knowledgeable nonexperts to accept than the proposition that 12 (or 19) people sitting around a table in Washington, D.C., subject to neither election nor dismissal nor close administrative or political control, have the power to determine the quantity of money—to permit a reduction by one-third during the Great Depression or a near doubling from 1970 to 1980.[25] That power is too important, too pervasive, to be exercised by a few people, however public-spirited, if there is any feasible alternative.

There is no need for such arbitrary power. In the system I have just described, the total quantity of any monetary aggregate would be determined by the market interactions of many financial institutions and millions of holders of monetary assets. It would be limited by the constant quantity of high-powered money available as ultimate

[25]The Open Market Investment Committee, which has the power, consists of the 7 members of the Board of Governors plus 5 of the 12 presidents of Federal Reserve Banks; hence the number 12. However, all 12 presidents attend the meetings of the committee and engage in the discussion of policy, although only 5 vote; hence the number 19.

reserves. The ratios of various aggregates to high-powered money would doubtless change from time to time, but in the absence of rigid government controls—such as those exemplified by Regulation Q, fortunately being phased out—the ratios would change gradually and only as financial innovations or changes in business and industry altered the proportions in which the public chose to hold various monetary assets. No small number of individuals would be in a position to introduce major changes in the ratios or in the rates of growth of various monetary aggregates—to move, for example, from a 3 percent per year rate of growth in M1 for one six-month period (January to July 1982) to a 13 percent rate of growth for the next six months (July 1982 to January 1983).

Conclusion

Major institutional change occurs only at times of crisis. For the rest, the tyranny of the status quo limits changes in institutions to marginal tinkering—we muddle through. It took the Great Depression to produce the FDIC, the most important structural change in our monetary institutions since at least 1914, when the Federal Reserve System began operations, and to shift power over monetary policy from the Federal Reserve Banks, especially that in New York, to the board in Washington. Since then, our monetary institutions have been remarkably stable. It took the severe inflation of the 1970s and accompanying double-digit interest rates—combined with the enforcement of Regulation Q—to produce money market mutual funds and thereby force a considerable measure of deregulation of banking.

Nonetheless, it is worth discussing radical changes, not in the expectation that they will be adopted promptly but for two other reasons. One is to construct an ideal goal, so that incremental changes can be judged by whether they move the institutional structure toward or away from that ideal.

The other reason is very different. It is so that if a crisis requiring or facilitating radical change does arise, alternatives will be available that have been carefully developed and fully explored. An excellent example is provided by international monetary arrangements. For decades, economists had been exploring alternatives to the system of fixed exchange rates, in particular, floating exchange rates among national currencies. The practical men of affairs derided proposals for floating rates as unrealistic, impractical, ivory tower. Yet when crisis came, when the Bretton Woods fixed-rate system had to be scrapped, the theorists' impractical proposal became highly practical and formed the basis for the new system of international monetary arrangements.

Needless to say, I hope that no crisis will occur that will necessitate a drastic change in domestic monetary institutions. The most likely such crisis is continued monetary instability, a return to a roller coaster of inflation about an upward trend, with inflation accelerating to levels of 20, 30, or more percent per year. That would shake the social and political framework of the nation and would produce results none of us would like to witness. Yet, it would be burying one's head in the sand to fail to recognize that such a development is a real possibility. It has occurred elsewhere, and it could occur here. If it does, the best way to cut it short, to minimize the harm it would do, is to be ready not with Band-Aids but with a real cure for the basic illness.

As of now, I believe the best real cure would be the reform outlined in the preceding section: abolish the money-creating powers of the Federal Reserve, freeze the quantity of high-powered money, and deregulate the financial system.

The less radical changes in policy and procedures suggested in the section on tactics seem to me to offer the best chance of avoiding a crisis. They call for the Fed to change its procedures so as to enable it to control more accurately a chosen monetary aggregate; to choose a single monetary aggregate to control; and to specify in advance, and adhere to, a five-year path for the growth of that aggregate that would bring it to a rate consistent with a healthy noninflationary economy. Figure 1 shows an illustrative path.

These tactical changes are feasible technically. However, I am not optimistic that they will be adopted. The obstacle is political. As with any bureaucratic organization, it is not in the self-interest of the Fed to adopt policies that would render it accountable. The Fed has persistently avoided doing so over a long period. None of the tactics that I have proposed is new. The proposed changes would have made just as much sense 5 or 10 years ago—indeed, if adopted then, the inflation and volatility of the past 10 years would never have occurred. They have had the support of a large fraction of monetary experts outside the Fed. The Fed has resisted them for bureaucratic and political, not technical, reasons.[26] And resistance has been in the Fed's interest. By keeping monetary policy an arcane subject that must be entrusted to "experts" and kept out of politics, incapable of being judged by nonexperts, the Fed has been able to maintain the

[26]See George Kaufman, "Monetarism at the Fed," *Journal of Contemporary Studies* 6 (Winter 1983): 27–36.

high public reputation of which I spoke at the outset of this paper, despite its poor record of performance.

One chairman after another, in testimony to Congress, has emphasized the mystery and difficulty of the Fed's task and the need for discretion, judgment, and the balancing of many considerations. Each has stressed how well the Fed has done and proclaimed its dedication to pursuing a noninflationary policy and has attributed any undesirable outcome to forces outside the Fed's control or to deficiencies in other components of government policy—particularly fiscal policy. The Fed's pervasive concern has been and continues to be the avoidance of accountability—a concern with which it is easy to sympathize in view of the purely coincidental relation between the announced intentions of Fed officials and actual outcomes.[27]

Clearly the problem of monetary policy instability is not chiefly a problem of right tactics by Fed decision makers, but inherent in the system itself. The chief problem is one of strategy or selecting the appropriate monetary framework for stable money, not the person who happens to be chairman at any given time. Until the proper monetary framework is adopted, therefore, we should not expect good intentions of Fed officials to secure sound money and stable prices.

---

[27]Excerpts from the congressional testimony of the four most recent chairman of the Fed reveal how their pronouncements diverge from actual policy outcomes. See M. Friedman, "Monetary Policy for the 1980s," in *To Promote Prosperity*, pp. 54–56.

18

TOWARD A FREE-MARKET MONETARY SYSTEM*

Friedrich A. Hayek

When I first proposed in 1975, almost as a sort of bitter joke, that there was no hope of ever again having decent money unless we took from government the monopoly of issuing money, I took it only half seriously. Nevertheless, my initial suggestion for denationalizing money—by replacing government money with private competing currencies—proved extraordinarily fertile.[1] Many people have since taken it up and have devoted a great deal of study and analysis to the possibility of moving toward a free-market monetary system. As a result, I am more convinced than ever that if we ever again are going to have sound money, it will not come from government; it will be issued by private enterprise.

Private enterprise can be expected to provide the public with money it can trust and use because it is profitable to do so, and competition will impose a discipline on private issuers to which the government has never been and cannot be subject. Unlike government, a private issuer must supply the public with a money as good as that of his rivals or go out of business.

The Key to Sound Money

If we are to understand fully why private issuers have an incentive to maintain the value of their currencies, we must free ourselves from

---

*Reprinted, by permission, from *Journal of Libertarian Studies* 3, no. 1 (1979): 1–8; with revisions by the editors. This paper was originally delivered at the Fourth Annual New Orleans Financial and Economic Conference, sponsored by the National Committee for Monetary Reform, November 10, 1977.

The author is Professor Emeritus of the University of Chicago and the University of Freiburg. He is a Fellow of the British Academy and recipient of the 1974 Nobel Memorial Prize in Economics.

[1]Hayek introduced his idea for competing private currencies and the denationalization of money in his lecture at the 1975 Lausanne Conference sponsored by the National Committee for Monetary Reform. He formalized the idea in his 1976 book *Denationalisation of Money*, and further expanded his ideas for monetary reform in 1978 with the second edition of his book. For additional refinements of Hayek's proposal for a free-market monetary system, see Hayek (1984, 1986).

what is a widespread but basically wrong belief. Under the gold standard, or any other metallic standard, the value of money is not really derived from gold. The fact is, the necessity of redeeming the money they issue in gold places on private issuers a discipline that forces them to control the quantity of money in an appropriate manner. I think it is quite as legitimate to say that under a gold standard it is the demand for monetary purposes that determines the value of gold, as the common belief that the value which gold has in other uses determines the value of money. The gold standard is the only method we have yet found to place a discipline on government, and government will behave reasonably only if it is forced to do so.

I am afraid I am convinced that the hope of ever again placing this discipline on government is gone. The public at large has learned to accept, and I am afraid a whole generation of economists has been teaching, that government has the power in the short run to relieve all kinds of economic evils, especially unemployment, by monetary stimulus. Experience has shown, however, that rapid increases in the quantity of money—although they may temporarily reduce unemployment—become in the long run the cause of much greater unemployment. Yet, what politician can possibly care about long-run effects if in the short run he buys support?

My conviction is that the hope of returning to the kind of gold standard that worked fairly well over a long period is absolutely vain. Even if by some international treaty the gold standard were reintroduced, there is not the slightest hope that governments will play the game according to the rules, and the gold standard is not something that can be restored by an act of legislation. The gold standard requires constant observation by government of certain rules, including occasional restriction of the total circulation. But no government nowadays is willing to restrict total circulation and chance a recession when both the public and, I am afraid, all those Keynesian economists who have been trained in the last 30 years will argue that it is more important to increase the quantity of money than to maintain the gold standard.

I have said that it is an erroneous belief that the value of gold or any metallic standard directly determines the value of the money. The gold standard is a mechanism that was intended to, and for a long time did, force governments to control the quantity of the money in an appropriate manner, so as to keep its value equal to that of gold. But there are many historical instances which prove that it is certainly possible, if it is in the self-interest of the issuer, to control the quantity even of a token money in such a manner as to keep its value constant.

The Principle of Stable Money Illustrated

Three interesting historical instances come to mind—instances that were largely responsible for teaching economists the essential point that ultimately it is the appropriate control of the quantity of money, and not its redeemability into something else, that is the key to sound money. Redeemability was necessary only to force governments to control the quantity of money appropriately. This I think will be done more effectively not if some legal rule forces government, but if it is the self-interest of the issuer which makes him do it, because he can keep his business only if he gives the people a stable money.

The first two historical instances I shall mention do not refer directly to the gold standard as we know it. They occurred when large parts of the world were still on a silver standard and when in the second half of the last century silver suddenly began to lose its value. The fall in the value of silver brought about a fall in various national currencies, and on two occasions an interesting step was taken. The first occasion, which produced the experience I believe inspired Austrian monetary theory, happened in my native country in 1879. The Austrian government happened to have an excellent adviser on monetary policy, Austrian Carl Menger, and he told them, "Well, if you want to escape the effect of the depreciation of silver on your currency, stop the free coinage of silver, stop increasing the quantity of silver coin, and you will find that the silver coin will begin to rise above the value of their content in silver." The government followed Menger's advice and the result was exactly as he had predicted. One began to speak about the Austrian "Gulden" (the unit then in circulation) as bank notes printed on silver, because the actual coins in circulation had become a token money containing much less value than corresponded to the Gulden's value. As the price of silver declined, the value of the silver Gulden was controlled entirely by the limitation of the quantity of the coin.

The same experiment was performed 14 years later by British India. It also had had a silver standard and the depreciation of silver brought the rupee down lower and lower till the Indian government decided to stop the free coinage; and again the silver coins began to float higher and higher above their silver value. Now, there was at that time neither in Austria nor in India any expectation that ultimately these coins would be redeemed at a particular rate in either silver or gold. The decision about this was made much later, but the development was the perfect demonstration that even a circulating metallic money may derive its value from an effective control of its quantity and not directly from its metallic content.

My third illustration is even more interesting, although the event was more short-lived, because it refers directly to gold. During World War I the great paper money inflation in all the belligerent countries brought down not only the value of paper money but also the value of gold, because paper money was in a large measure substituted for gold and the demand for gold fell. In consequence, prices in gold rose all over the world and affected even the neutral countries. Sweden was particularly worried because it had remained on the gold standard and was flooded with gold from the rest of the world. Prices in Sweden, therefore, rose along with prices in the rest of the world. At the time Sweden happened to have two very capable economists who repeated the advice Menger had given concerning silver in the 1870s: "Stop the free coinage of gold and the value of your existing gold coins will rise above the value of the gold they contain." The Swedish government did so in 1916 and what happened was again exactly what the economists had predicted: the value of the gold coins began to float above the value of their gold content and Sweden, for the rest of the war, escaped the effects of the gold inflation.

I mention the example of Sweden only to illustrate what among economists who understand their subject is now an undisputed fact, namely, that the gold standard is a partly effective mechanism to make governments do what they ought to do in their control of money, and the only mechanism that has been tolerably effective in the case of a monopolist who can do whatever he likes with money. Otherwise, gold is not really necessary to secure a good currency. I think it is entirely possible for private enterprise to issue a token money, which the public will learn to expect to preserve its value, provided both the issuer and the public understand that the demand for this money will depend on the issuer being forced to keep its value constant; because if he did not do so, the people would at once cease to use his money and shift to some other kind.

Two Kinds of Competition

In the second edition of *Denationalisation of Money* (1978), I arrived at one or two rather interesting new conclusions that were not evident to me earlier. In my 1975 proposal, I was merely thinking of the effect competitive selection of issuers would have, namely, that only those financial institutions controlling the distinctly named money they issued and providing the public with a stable standard of value would survive. I have now come to see that there is a much more complex situation, that there will in fact be two kinds of competition: one leading to the choice of the standard that may come to be generally accepted; the other to the selection of particular institutions that can be trusted in issuing money of the chosen standard.

I believe that if all the legal obstacles preventing the issuance of private money under distinct names were removed, people would once again start using gold. But, after a while, the fact that people are rushing to gold would make it very doubtful whether gold was really a good monetary standard. Holding gold would turn out to be a good investment because the increased demand for gold would increase its value, but that very fact would make it unsuitable as money. Individuals would not want to incur debts in terms of a unit that constantly increases in value, and they would begin to look for another kind of money. Most important, if they were free to choose the money in terms of which they kept their books, made their calculations, incurred debts or lent money, they would prefer a standard that remains stable in purchasing power.

Such a stable standard reduces to a minimum the risk of unforeseen changes in the prices of particular commodities because with a stable standard it is just as likely that any one commodity will rise in price or will fall in price. In addition, with a stable standard of value the mistakes people at large will make in their anticipations of future prices will just cancel each other because there will be as many mistakes in overestimating as in underestimating. If such a money were issued by some reputable institution, the public would probably first choose different definitions of the standard, that is, adopt different kinds of price indices in terms of which the standard is measured. The process of competition, however, would gradually reveal to issuing banks and the public the kind of money that would be most advantageous.

The interesting fact is that the government monopoly of issuing money has not only deprived us of good money but has also deprived us of the only *process* by which we can find out what would be good money. We do not even quite know what exact qualities we want because in the 2000 years in which we have used coins and other money, we have never been allowed to experiment with it; we have never been given a chance to find out what the best kind of money would be.

In my publications and in my lectures I constantly refer to the government monopoly of issuing money. But this situation is legally true only to a very limited extent in most countries. We have indeed given the government, for fairly good reasons, the exclusive right to issue gold coins. And after we had given the government that right, it was equally understandable that we also gave the government control over any money or any paper claims, for coins or money of that definition. That people other than the government are not allowed to issue dollars if the government issues dollars is a perfectly reasonable arrangement, even if it has not turned out to be completely beneficial. And I am not suggesting that other people should be entitled to issue dollars. All the discussion in the past about free banking was really about whether institutions other than government should be allowed to issue dollar notes. That, of course, would not work. But if private institutions began to issue notes under some other names without any fixed rate of exchange with the official money or each other, so far as I know this is in no major country actually prohibited by law. I think the reasons it has not been tried is that we know that if anybody attempted it, the government would find so many ways to put obstacles in the way of the use of such money that it could make it impracticable. So long, for instance, as debts in terms of anything but the official dollar cannot be legally enforced, it is clearly impracticable. Of course it would have been ridiculous to try to issue any other money if people could not make contracts in terms of it. But this particular obstacle has fortunately been removed now in most countries, so the way ought to be free for the issuing of private money.

If I were responsible for the policy of any one of the large U.S. banks, I would begin to offer to the public both loans and current accounts in a unit which I undertook to keep stable in value in terms of a defined index number. I have no doubt, and I believe that most economists agree with me on this particular point, that it is technically possible to control the value of any token money used in competition with other token monies so as to fulfill the promise to keep its value stable. The essential point, which I cannot emphasize strongly enough, is that we would get for the first time a money where the whole business of issuing money could be effected only by the issuer issuing good money. He would know that he would at once lose his extremely profitable business if it became known that his money was threatening to depreciate. He would lose it to a competitor who offered better money. As I said before, I believe this is our only hope at the present time.

A Question of Freedom

I do not see the slightest prospect that democratic government— under which every little group can force the government to serve its particular needs—can ever again give us stable money, even if its money-creation powers were strictly limited by law. At present the prospects are really only a choice between two alternatives: an accelerating open inflation, which is absolutely destructive of a market order, or, more likely and still more destructive, a suppressed inflation using price controls, which will lead to increasing control of the whole economic system. Thus, it is not merely a question of giving us better money under which the market system will function infinitely better than it has ever done before, but of warding off the gradual decline into a totalitarian, planned system. In a country such as the United States, totalitarianism will not come because anybody wants to introduce it; it may come step-by-step in an effort to suppress the effects of ongoing inflation.

I wish I could say that what I propose is a plan for the distant future, that we can wait for a free-market monetary system. There was one very intelligent reviewer of the first edition of my *Denationalisation of Money* (1976) who said, "Well, 300 years ago nobody would have believed that government would ever give up its control over religion, so perhaps in 300 years we can see that government will be prepared to give up its control over money." Unfortunately, we do not have that much time.

We are now facing the likelihood of the most unpleasant political development, largely as a result of an economic policy with which we have already gone very far. My proposal is not, as I would wish, merely a sort of standby arrangement of which I could say we must work it out intellectually to have it ready when the present system completely collapses. It is not merely an emergency plan. I think it is very urgent that it become rapidly understood that there is no justification in history for the existing position of a government monopoly of issuing money. It has never been proposed on the ground that government will give us better money than anybody else could. It has always, since the privilege of issuing money was first explicitly represented as a royal prerogative, been advocated because the power to issue money was essential for the finance of the government—not in order to give us good money, but in order to give to government access to the tap where it can draw the money it needs by manufacturing it. That, of course, is not a method by which we can hope ever to get sound money. To put it into the hands of an institution which is protected against competition, which can force us to accept the money, which is subject to incessant political pressure, such an authority will not ever again give us good money.

Experimenting with Private Monies

I think we must hope that some of the more enterprising and intelligent financiers will soon begin to experiment with private monies. The great obstacle is that the denationalization of money involves such great changes in the whole financial structure that, and I am saying this from the experience of many discussions, no senior banker who understands only the present banking system can really conceive how such a new system would work, and he would not dare to risk and experiment with it. Hence, I think we will have to count on a few younger and more flexible brains to begin and show that competing private currencies are a viable alternative to government monopoly of issuing money.

In fact, free-market money is already being tried in a limited form. As a result of my proposal I have received many letters from small banking houses telling me they are trying to issue gold accounts or silver accounts, and that there is a considerable interest for these. Nevertheless, I believe they will have to go further, for the reasons I have already sketched. In the course of such a revolution of our monetary system, the values of the precious metals, including the value of gold, are going to fluctuate a great deal, mostly upward. Those interested in my proposal from an investor's point of view, therefore, need not fear. But those who are mainly interested in a good monetary system must hope that in the not too distant future another system of control over the monetary circulation, other than the redeemability in gold, will be generally applied. In the transition process, the public will have to learn to select among a variety of monies and to choose those which are good.

If we start on this process soon, we may indeed achieve a situation in which at last capitalism is in a position to provide itself with the money it needs in order to function properly, a thing which it has always been denied. I think if the capitalists had been allowed to provide themselves with the money which they need, the competitive system would have long overcome the major fluctuations in economic activity and the prolonged periods of depression. At the present moment we have of course been led by official monetary policy into a situation where it has produced so much misdirection of resources that one must not hope for a quick escape from our present difficulties, even if we adopt a new monetary system.

References

Hayek, Friedrich A. *Denationalisation of Money*. Hobart Paper Special 70. London: Institute of Economic Affairs, 1976. (2d extended ed., 1978.)

Hayek, Friedrich A. "The Future Unit of Value." In *Currency Competition and Monetary Union*, pp. 29–42. The Hague: Martinus Nijhoff, 1984.

Hayek, Friedrich A. "Market Standards for Money." *Economic Affairs* 6 (April/May 1986): 8–10.

19

THE POLITICAL ECONOMY OF INFLATION*
Fritz Machlup

The Problem of Inflation

With regard to the political economy of inflation, I could easily imagine the following kind of controversy:

> Well, inflation—it's a monetary problem. No, it's a fiscal problem. No, it's a monopoly problem. It's a labor-market problem. It's a sociological problem. It's a distributional problem. It's a psychological problem. It's a game-theoretic problem. It's a system-theoretic problem. It's an ideological problem. It's a moral problem. It's a political problem.

Well, of course, all these are right. And, you can now conclude: *It certainly is a problem.* But even to that some people might object: "It is no longer a problem." And I quote: "Now that the back of inflation has been decisively broken, the stage is set for a long period of steady real growth." So the back of inflation has been broken? I think the back has at most been scratched.

Now, here is a question. What do my noble fellow economists think about the backbreaking of inflation? I refer here to one of the wise forecasters, Otto Eckstein, who is an awfully nice fellow—only his forecasts are not very good. He wrote a book on core inflation and said you must distinguish demand inflation, shock inflation, and core inflation.[1] Now, shock inflation and core inflation are both cost-push inflations, but shock inflation has to do with increases in the prices

---

*Reprinted from *Cato Journal* 3 (Spring 1983): 15–21, with revisions by the editors. This paper is adapted from the author's luncheon talk at the Cato Institute's conference on The Search for Stable Money, January 22, 1983. It was his last formal address before his death on January 30. Footnotes and subheads were added by James A. Dorn. He wishes to thank Peter B. Kenen and Úna Mansfield of Princeton University for their assistance in preparing Professor Machlup's talk for publication.

The author was Professor of Economics at New York University and Professor Emeritus at Princeton University.

[1]U.S. Congress, Joint Economic Committee, *Tax Policy and Core Inflation*, by Otto Eckstein, Joint Economic Committee Print (Washington, D.C.: Government Printing Office, 1980).

FUTURE OF MONETARY POLICY

of farm products and fuels, but nothing to do with the prices of labor and capital.

Eckstein measured these different contributions to the inflationary problem for several periods. He found that during the period 1973 to 1979, core inflation contributed 7.1 percent to the average, annual rate of inflation; shock inflation, 1.8 percent; and demand inflation, minus 0.7 percent. Over the same period, the consumer price index rose by an average of 8.5 percent per year.[2]

Eckstein thought that a reduction in the core inflation rate would be a major achievement. However, he thought that it could not be reduced more than 1 percent by 1985, and perhaps 1.3 percent by 1990.[3]

This is how my colleagues the forecasters perform. I do not make any forecasts and am very proud of that. It takes a certain kind of restraint not to make forecasts, and people will believe you are either too honest or a bad economist if you say "I don't know."

Now, I do not know whether Otto Eckstein's econometric methods for distinguishing the different kinds of inflation make any sense. I rather doubt it. I doubt also whether it would take 10 years to reduce core inflation by 1.3 percent. In 10 years we could still have an inflation rate of 8 or 9 percent. He did not say what would happen in that case.

Stopping Inflation: Gradual or Instantaneous?

This raises the question of choosing between gradually stopping an inflation or instantaneously stopping an inflation. Here I must relate my experience, having been a victim of hyperinflation. When I went to graduate school in economics [in the early 1920s], we had the Austrian inflation going. It was not as severe as in neighboring Germany—we reached a price level only 14,000 times the prewar price level—but we did have to face the question: Gradual or instantaneous?

Now, it was quite clear: There is no gradual stopping of an inflation. It is like gradually getting rid of a smoking habit or gradually getting rid of a drug addiction. If you stop, it is very unpleasant—withdrawal symptoms are painful—and you say "let's stop the stopping process." In other words, you can make up your mind too often. Hence we agreed at that time—and it looks amazing that in 1921 I was already among those who could agree or not agree, but this is the case—that we had to stop inflation *immediately*.

[2]Ibid., p. 2.
[3]Ibid., p. 4.

Incidentally, the same discussion about gradually or instantaneously stopping an inflation, and the same results, occurred in Austria after the Second World War, in 1951. A few years after Austria had a post-war inflation, the decision was again to *stop it immediately.* And in this last case, in 1951, it was like this: In one year the inflation rate was still 30 percent per annum, and in the subsequent year it was zero. Indeed, for several parts of the year there was a negative inflation rate. The results were terribly painful. Unemployment increased by 100 percent, *but only for a year,* and then a nice prosperity developed.[4] So you can see why I am persuaded that a gradual disinflation simply does not work.

Now, this looks like a prediction. It is not. It is a tentative conclusion based on my own personal experience and additional theoretical insights, and I do not swear by it. I may be wrong. Maybe it is possible for some countries to stop inflation gradually, but maybe you have to be Swiss to make it work.

The Politics of Inflation

I want to say why I believe it is so unlikely that we will stop inflation. It is unlikely, especially in our political system, because either you have the inflationists in the administration or you have them in the opposition. If you have them in the opposition, the administration must make concessions and compromises. If it does not, it will be voted out of office and the opposition with its inflationary program will get back in. So I really do not see any solution.

This morning I listened to the honorable congressman from Texas [Ron Paul] and he was very hopeful, very optimistic that we would lick inflation, but, of course, only after the monetary system has completely collapsed. There would then be chaos, and people might be willing to accept a system—probably the gold standard—a system that would no longer permit such an inflation. Well, I really don't know whether I should call that optimism or pessimism.

---

[4]For a more detailed analysis of the inflation and subsequent stabilization that took place in Austria in the early 1950s, see Gottfried Haberler, "Austria's Economic Development After the Two World Wars: A Mirror Picture of the World Economy," in *The Political Economy of Austria,* ed. Sven W. Arndt (Washington, D.C.: American Enterprise Institute, 1982), pp. 68–69.

According to Haberler, the consumer price index increased by 27 percent in 1950 and 18 percent in 1951, but *declined* by 5.4 percent in 1952. This stabilization process was achieved by significant monetary and fiscal restraint, and by a devaluation of the schilling. Although employment decreased by 3 percent in 1952, real economic growth resumed the following year.

It is really a terrible pessimism. But you see, the slogans that we hear chiefly from the opposition—in the Republican or in the Democratic party—are designed to sustain the inflationary tendency of the people. It is not only that the newspapers are so inflationist in their attitudes, but that the costs of stopping an inflation are so clearly visible. For example, it is often said that "unemployment is too high a price to stop inflation." Well, that means we do not want to stop the inflation because there is no way of stopping an inflation without experiencing unemployment.

It is of course a malicious trick to say that we want unemployment so that prices go down. No, the idea is that the only cure we have for stopping inflation has unemployment as one of its by-products. But to say then, "unemployment is too high a price to stop inflation," means we shall not stop inflation, and it is too bad that some people do not have the courage to speak in this fashion.

Frédéric Bastiat once wrote: "The state is the great fictitious entity by which everybody seeks to live at the expense of everyone else."[5] Now, whatever plan you have, it always goes back to some creation of new money. If you want more employment, create money. If you want faster growth, create money. If you want more capital, create money, although it is quite clear that money is not capital. If you want lower interest rates, create money, although usually it does not work that way. If you want to help the poor, create money. If you want to help minorities, create money. If you want more schooling, create money. If you want better health, create money. It is always the same thing, only that everybody thinks someone else will pay for it.

The interesting thing is that the very same people who once acted as if they were nonmonetarists or antimonetarists now stress the use of money more than anyone else. What did the antimonetarists say? "It is not true. Money does not matter. It is other things that matter." But what do they say now? That we have restrained the increase in the money supply too much. So the very same people who say, "we are against the monetarists or against anybody who believes that inflation is a monetary problem," now blame the recession or depression—whatever you want to call it—on the Federal Reserve for having *restrained* the money supply too much. So evidently the antimonetarists seem to believe that money matters a great deal.

[5]Frédéric Bastiat, *Selected Essays on Political Economy*, trans. Seymour Cain, ed. George B. De Huszar (Irvington-on-Hudson, New York: The Foundation for Economic Education, 1964), p. 144.

Inflation, Wage Rigidity, and Unemployment

But I see very complicated problems quite apart from mere ideology. The point is that the inflexibility of our wage system makes the choice between unemployment and inflation practically inevitable. We know that any kind of change in the economic system, whether it be technological progress, shifts in demands, you name it, leads to a change in the wage rates of different groups. Now, if relative wage rates cannot be changed by lowering the wage rate of anybody, it means that you have to have higher wages year after year. But, you cannot have higher wages year after year without having a constant inflation.

The question then is: Do we want permanent unemployment? Do we have to have year after year an increase in the core inflation or whatever you like to call it? Do we want inevitable inflation? It is a dilemma that I cannot solve and that the people eventually will have to solve for themselves.

Another highly important thing—and it is perhaps related to what Eckstein had in mind with his notion of core inflation—is the expectation of a pay raise. The idea of having an annual pay raise is so clear to everybody, so absolutely necessary, but that idea cannot be carried out without permanent inflation. You see, needless to say, there are annual pay raises—merit raises. As people grow in age, experience, and efficiency they can have wage increases. But that everybody—say all the workers in a particular industry—can get an annual raise of 4, 5, 6, 7 percent is simply not in the picture.

Now, what is a possible annual raise? Very little, if the government makes an increasing claim on the national product. If you speak of an increase in labor productivity of 3 percent—which is highly optimistic if you want to sustain it—and if the government takes away, through its increased governmental tasks, 1 or 2 percent from that productivity gain, what is left? Just an annual raise of 1 percent. There is not enough for a 5 percent, 6 percent, or 8 percent raise for anybody. So this is another great difficulty that will force us to rethink these problems.

Since I spoke of wage increases, let me also mention this: In a recent speech before the American Academy of Arts and Sciences, Robert Solow showed that we know so much more than we did so many years ago. There was Pigou who thought that the elasticity of demand for labor was about 4 or 5, and Solow says, "Oh, now we know it is at best .4 or .5." But that misconceives the entire problem. Most of our unemployment problem is *not* the *average* wage rate. *It is the distribution of wage rates.* This can be very easily explained, and perhaps I should give three different examples to show you what I mean by the distribution of wage rates.

Let us begin with wage rates in a heavily unionized sector of the economy—steel or automobiles. Suppose these strong unions make very high wage demands that are subsequently met. If the industries seek to protect themselves from the effects of these wage increases, you will see one enormous problem. What it means is, of course, that the industries will limit the number of jobs available, and force a large number of people to look for work elsewhere.

Let us take a second important example, one that has to do with relative efficiencies. We all know that in terms of the efficiency of people, measure it by whatever you wish (course grades, piecework, or any kind of handwork), the difference between the average and the least efficient is very great. Now, if wage rates are not permitted to show these differences in relative efficiencies, if minimum wages make it necessary to pay to the least efficient only say 20 percent less than is paid to people of average efficiency, you just keep the less efficient workers out. They are *unemployable*.[6] They could be employed only if the wage differential was commensurate to the efficiency differential. But with our present institutions this is out of the question.

There is a third point, and that has to do with the workers in one industry holding up the rest of the economy for ransom. Take the subway workers in New York City, for example. By striking they force the city to give them the wage increase they want. This can happen in any kind of utility where the services seem to be absolutely necessary. In such cases, [union] workers can hold up the rest of the economy and take a large part of the national income for themselves at the expense of their brothers, at the expense of the rest of the labor force.

Now, here is a problem. Inflation serves the purpose of taking away from these workers what they have been able to capture in the bargain. In the wage settlement they acquired a 10 percent wage increase at the expense of others. So by inflating you reduce their real income. This problem is very difficult to solve and if there is no solution—and I do not think of governmental wage controls as a solution—it may make perpetual inflation inevitable.

---

[6]If employers are forced by law to pay low-productivity workers a wage that exceeds the value of their marginal product, these workers will become unemployable. In addition to violating the right of employers to lower their wage offers, the minimum wage legislation attenuates the right of workers to accept employment at a freely chosen wage rate.

Index

Acceleration effect, 283
Acceptability of money, 306, 343
Accountability of Fed, 50, 381
Actual units of account, 309–10
Aggregate demand, 136, 149, 297–98
Aggregate real effects, 167
All-around indexing, 307
Alternative monetary regimes, 149
Ambiguity. *See* Uncertainty
Analysis, monetarist analysis, 163–71
Arbitrary gold supply, 245
Argentina, 97, 106–8
Assets: asset-market interaction, 184–87; barren money, 329, 330–31; money as financial asset, 320–21
Asymmetrical base-drift, 37
Austria, 79, 100, 392
Austria-Hungary (dual monarchy), 100–1, 105, 385
Austrian economics, 68, 79–80
Authority, rules versus authority, 120–23
Axilrod, Stephen H., 222–23, 225

Bagehot, Walter, 345
Balance of payments, Argentina, 107–8
"Bancor," 272
Bank of England, 141, 287
Banks and banking: bank panics, 97, 139, 354; banks and money, 322–23; borrowing function and Fed, 40; competitive money, 340; definition, 246–47; deregulation, 321, 329–29; fractional reserve banking, 265; free banking, 104, 214–17; free-market currencies, 314; Hayek on, 80; monetary controls, 136; monetary rules, 189; portfolios, 323–24; price of credit, 138; private banks, 216–17; private money, 310, 390; unit of account, 388; unregulated

banks, 344. *See also* central banks
Barren money, 329–34
Barter system, 325
Base dollars, 272, 273
"Base drift," 235
Base money, 205, 274
Basket currencies, 301–4, 306, 375
Bastiat, Frédéric, 394
Bearer notes, 333
Bernholz, Peter, 119–23, 125–27
BFH system, 315–17
"Bills only" policy (Fed), 40
Black, Fischer, 321
"Blueback scheme," 133
Bollmann, Erick, 6–8
Bonds, 134: as currency, 320–21; state-chartered banks, 344
Borrowings abroad, 106, 355
Borsodi, Ralph, 302
Brennan, Geoffrey, 86
Bretton Woods Conference, 139, 250, 251–52, 380–81
Brown, Harry Gunnison, 11–12
Brunner, Karl, 21
Buchanan, James M., 86, 148–49
Budget (Federal budget), 42, 209
Bureaucrats. *See* civil service
Business cycles: countercyclical policy, 53–54; FOMC, 49–50; Keynesian view, 189; monetary control, 31–45, 137; money, deregulation, and business, 319–37; money changes, 56; "Number one problem" syndrome, 34–35; peaks of cycles, 212; political manipulation, 154; U.S., 2, 10, 264

Cagan, Phillip, 12
Canada, 74
Capital and risk. *See* Risk
Carter, James E., 192
Cash: cash balances, 308; inside money, 340
Central banks, 23, 80, 189–90: competition 282–85; efficiency,

397

218; foreign central banks, 281; gold flows, 265; Has monetarism failed?, 192–93; illiquid banks and, 353; independence, 371; inflation, 283; monetary stability, 104; money growth, 204, 225–26; reserves, 215; "technological symmetry," 322
Certificates, 226
Checks, free-market currencies, 316–17
Choice: choice in currency, 373–75; compulsion and choice, 352; liquidity and choice, 332; toward a positive theory, 122–23
Churning (Fed), 366
Civil service, 34, 38–39, 156–57, 284, 381
Classification of events, 206
Clower, Robert W., 325
Coin shortages, 142
Commitments to money, 305–6
Commodity currencies, 213–14, 315, 348–49, 352
Commodity standard, 119, 138, 203, 210
Common money and government, 290
Compensated dollars, 261–77
Competition: competing currencies, 281–96; competitive banking, 214–17; competitive issue of money, 339–57, 373–76; private money, 312; two kinds of competition, 386–88; unemployment, 76
Composite bundle of commodities (Greenfield/Yeager), 326
"Compromise" approaches to monetary reform, 150–55
Compulsion and choice, 352
"Compulsory bond collateral systems," 344
Congdon, Tim, 217
Congress, 34, 39, 43–44, 372
Consensus among experts, 50–51, 148
Consistency, Federal Reserve goals, 47
Constant monetary growth, 66–67, 207–8

Constant unit and indexing, 305–9
Constitutional rule on money growth, 83–160, 262
Constraints on government, 129–43
"Constructivism," 253
Consumer Price Index, 302
Consumption externality, 288
Controllability of money, 51, 169, 177–80
Convertibility: compensated dollars, 274; convertibility principle, 136, 139, 142; convertibility theory, 20; gold, 262, 269–75; inconvertibility of money, 219, 352; paper money, 219; price stability, 268
Core inflation, 392, 395
Cost of living: France, 109–10; U.S., 109–10
Credibility: "disinflationary announcements," 174; monetary rules, 17, 126; uncertainty, risk, and real income, 206–9
Credit, 11, 138, 225
"Crude barter," 325
Currencies: case for free entry, 281–96; debauchment of currency, 139; Eurostables, 302–4; interest-bearing assets, 333; international currency competition, 283–84; international monetary rule, 369; monetary reform, 205; non-interest-bearing obligations, 368; reference currency, 291; rule of steady monetary growth, 79; stable money and free-market currencies, 297–317; undervaluation, 96–97, 99
Customary arrangements, 68, 80
Czechoslovakia, 112

Davenport, Herbert Joseph, 11
Decontrol of banking, 340–47
Deficit spending, 74
"Definability" of money, 177–80
Deflation: output growth, 263–64; U.S., 264
"Demand deficiency," 185

About the Editors

James A. Dorn received his Ph.D. in Economics from the University of Virginia. He is Editor of the *Cato Journal* and Associate Professor of Economics at Towson State University. He is also a Research Fellow at the Institute for Humane Studies at George Mason University and a member of the White House Commission on Presidential Scholars.

Anna J. Schwartz received her Ph.D. in Economics from Columbia University. She is a Research Associate of the National Bureau of Economic Research and served as Staff Director of the U.S. Gold Commission (1981–82). She is the author of numerous articles on monetary economics and is coauthor with Milton Friedman of *A Monetary History of the United States, 1867–1960*.